Defining the
Sovereign Community

DEMOCRACY, CITIZENSHIP, AND CONSTITUTIONALISM

Rogers M. Smith, Series Editor

Defining the Sovereign Community

The Czech and Slovak Republics

Nadya Nedelsky

PENN

UNIVERSITY OF PENNSYLVANIA PRESS

PHILADELPHIA

Published by
University of Pennsylvania Press
Philadelphia, Pennsylvania 19104-4112

Printed in the United States of America on acid-free paper
10   9   8   7   6   5   4   3   2   1

Library of Congress Cataloging-in-Publication Data

Nedelsky, Nadya.
    Defining the sovereign community : the Czech and Slovak Republics / Nadya Nedelsky.
        p.   cm. — (Democracy, Citizenship, and Consitutionalism)
    ISBN 978-0-8122-4165-5 (alk. paper)
    Includes bibliographical references and index.
    1. Czech Republic—Politics and government—1993–   2. Slovakia—Politics
and government—1993—   3. Czechoslovakia—Politics and government. I. Title.
JN2220 .N43   2009
943.703—dc22   2008042188

For Martin and Thomas

CONTENTS

Introduction

In the autumn of 1992, Czech and Slovak leaders decided to bring their two nations' near-century of common statehood to an end. They had been negotiating new terms of union since shortly after the Velvet Revolution overthrew the Czechoslovak Communist regime in late 1989 and were frustrated by differences on crucial issues, such as the direction and speed of economic reform. No disagreement, however, was more fundamental than that concerning the source of the new state's sovereignty and the political arrangement that it would produce. Czech leaders argued that sovereignty's proper source is the "free and equal citizen" and that the new state should be a federation with a strong central government representing a "federal people"[1] (i.e., a nation of citizens), while Slovak leaders held that sovereignty issues from the ethnic nation, requiring a confederation of two sovereign states. Even before the two sides formally announced that their differences were irreconcilable, the Slovak republic-level parliament passed a Declaration of National Sovereignty, and once the decision to separate was final (resulting in the Velvet Divorce) the two nations founded new states based on their respective understandings of sovereign community. The Czech Constitution thus employs the civic model, founding the state in name of, "we, the citizens of the Czech Republic in Bohemia, Moravia, and Silesia," while its Slovak counterpart uses the ethnic model, and speaks in the voice of "we, the Slovak nation."

This book asks two central questions. The first is, to what extent are the post-Communist Czech civic and Slovak ethnic understandings of nationhood rooted in political culture? And second, what are their implications for minority political membership and individual rights? My approach to these questions is comparative and historical. The comparison is exceptionally useful not only because the Czechs share decades of political history with the Slovaks, thus holding in common many variables that could be relevant to the development of understandings of nationhood, but also because they founded their independent state on "alternative" definitions of sovereignty, making it possible to examine whether sufficient subsequent practical differences exist between the two cases to support a conceptual distinction between the ethnic and civic models. As Kevin Deegan-Krause argues, the two nations' common history offers what amounts to a "natural experiment" for understanding post-Communist developments.[2] In addition, the two nations played such an important role in each other's development that any analysis of their recent politics that takes history into account requires consideration of the relationship between them. I take an overall historical approach because gauging the extent to which post-Communist understandings of nationhood are culturally rooted (or, alternatively, should be regarded as malleable) requires focused study of particular norms over a substantial time span, with attention both to the extent of their continuities and to the ways they have been shaped by situational factors such as political leadership and considerations of material interest during this extended period.

While scholars have devoted substantial attention to post-communist factors affecting nationalist politics, very little has been devoted to this kind of targeted historical study. Much of the literature dealing with normative understandings of nationhood is either highly theoretical or made up of case studies that are too short for in-depth, long-term, focused study of particular norms. My investigation of the civic and ethnic models' practical implications for individual rights and minority membership is unusual as well. Although the validity of the conceptual distinction has come under scrutiny, most analysis of the relationship between nationalism and il/liberalism tends either to focus on the political-philosophical underpinnings of civic and ethnic models rather than on their actual effects, or to explain elite behavior in strategic terms rather than in relation to political principles. I seek to integrate these concerns, examining the extent to which regime principles affect specific political choices about how to structure both the minority's and the broader citizenry's relationship to the state. In addition, I draw on the evidence produced through investigation of my first question to further explore the second, asking whether political-cultural orientations affect how Czechs and Slovaks interpret and apply regime principles.

This study contributes to two overlapping and recently intensifying debates: on the nature of nations and nationalism and on the validity of the civic/ethnic dichotomy. I outline first the contending perspectives in these debates and their application in the broader post-Communist region and more specific Czech and Slovak contexts, and why the dominant theoretical approaches produce unsatisfactory answers to my questions. I do not claim to debunk the perspectives I survey here—indeed, they offer significant insight into questions of national identity and community. Rather, I intend to complement them by identifying considerations necessary for more balanced and comprehensive analysis of the questions at hand.

Debate 1: The Nature of Understandings of Nationhood

Let me begin by unpacking the "understandings of nationhood" whose nature, development, and implications are central to this study.[3] I mean by this a principled political orientation including both the definition of the community that is the authentic source of state sovereignty and a broad view of the proper nature of the resulting political authority.[4] The second part of this understanding flows from the first: the sovereign community confers authentic authority to the state, and those who take on government roles exercise this authority with the expectation that the governed will willingly comply.[5] Many definitions of sovereignty do not, however, transfer total authority to the state (which would produce a totalitarian regime); rather, citizens retain some authority over their lives in the form of rights. The balance of authority that is struck depends on how the relationship between the individual and the political collective is structured, which varies greatly across communities and depends on the regime's political-philosophical foundations. For example, drawing on Charles Taylor's comparison of regime types, a regime may be based a liberal philosophy that (reflecting the influence of Immanuel Kant) "understands human dignity to consist largely in autonomy, that is, in the ability of every person to determine for himself or herself a view of the good life."[6] This view of legitimate political authority would privilege individual liberty in relation to the collective. Taylor then offers an alternative and conflicting set of foundational principles that organizes political authority so as to pursue and promote a definition of the "good life" that by nature "requires that it be sought in common." It thus privileges certain collective goals, making them "a matter of public policy" that allows political authority to circumscribe individual autonomy in ways unacceptable under the first regime type.[7] I investigate whether there are continuities in understandings of nationhood over time and also whether there is a necessary or close relationship between the first element of the understanding—the definition of sovereignty—and the second—the view and practice of resulting political authority, as it relates particularly to liberal values of individual autonomy and minority membership.

These are, admittedly, very particular sets of norms. The question of the sources and malleability of these *kinds* of norms—those that frame and justify politics in a community that understands itself as a nation—falls within the scope of the broad literature on the nature of nations and nationalism, where debate is ongoing about the extent to which such norms should be seen as organic or constructed, shared or contested, stable or fluid, rooted or subject to manipulation. Two contending perspectives—one focusing on society (often called "primordialist" or "essentialist") and one on elites ("instrumentalist" or "constructivist")—dominate this literature, though they have more recently been challenged by a third (the "ethno-symbolist" or "social-constructivist"), which seeks to bridge the two. I take each in turn.

The Primordialist Approach

The primordialist perspective on nations and nationalism originated with the German Romantic philosophers, who in the eighteenth century began to extol the ethnic nation as the source of human culture and the most natural and fitting form of community. Its position on the norms that govern the community's life and their potential for change is captured by Johann Gottfried von Herder's assertion that "nations modify themselves, according to time, place, and their internal character; each bears in itself the standard of its perfection, totally independent of all comparison with that of others."[8] According to this view, the nation's norms are organic and unique, and the only healthy change is that which is consonant with its essence, allowing the culture to retain its coherence. Malleability is thus strictly limited.

More recent society-based approaches, such as Clifford Geertz's conceptualization of "primordial attachments," are less deterministic, holding that the community's power to bind its members together within a normative framework is neither inherent nor unchanging, but something attributed to it by its members. The attachments to the community, Geertz argues, derive from the "givens" in social life, such as the language, religion, social customs, and other normative structures and sources of identity into which a person is born. While the strength and importance of these attachments varies over time and among individuals and societies, "for virtually every person, in every society, at almost all times, some attachments seem to flow more from a sense of natural—some would say spiritual—affinity than from social interaction."[9] To the extent that these attachments are understood as relevant to political life (as, for example, religion and social customs often are), then the resulting political norms share their "primordial" character. Such attachments may become objects of intense and even fierce loyalty when members are asked to subordinate them in favor of allegiance to another group. Attachments can and do change, but given the depth of their anchoring, they are not highly malleable.

These are just two examples, but Herder and Geertz's theories capture two themes common to this sort of primordialist perspective. The first is a view of the member's relationship to the nation's norms as "natural" and reflexive, and only weakly (if at all) mediated by choice or reflection on either principle or material interests. The second is the suggestion that norms governing community life form a coherent and internally harmonious culture, of which specifically political norms are one interlocking element.

In the post-Communist context, primordialist analysis frequently describes understandings of nationhood and nationalist conflicts as "returning" or "reawakening" after a period of suspension under Communism. Its means of storage during that period, in Jacques Rupnik's apt description, are "summarized by the metaphors of the 'refrigerator' or the 'cauldron.' Communism acted as a freezer, chilling certain problems, aspirations, controversies which one finds intact or (where the refrigerator broke down) in a nauseating condition half a century later. The metaphor of the cauldron suggests that imperial Soviet power kept the 'captive nations' under the lid, with their conflicts and hatreds fully cooked and now released."[10] This view thus holds that post-Communist understandings of nationhood are essentially pre-Communist understandings reanimated, having proved impervious to Communist attempts to uproot them. Depending on their view of nationalism, however, those employing this type of approach differ on whether a sleeping beauty or a monster has arisen. Nationalists themselves often use a primordialist framework to invoke the nation's timeless bonds and its opportunity after the defeat of Communism to realize its natural right to self-determination, long denied it by the previous regime or the state's other ethno-national groups. Critics of such projects, on the other hand, often decry nationalism's tribalism and intractability based on a similar understanding of the nation's roots; for example,

U.S. President Bill Clinton repeatedly condemned the "ancient hatreds" that fueled the Balkan wars.[11]

In the case of the former Czechoslovakia, primordialist accounts have come primarily from Czech and Slovak sources. These analyses tend to portray the Czech and Slovak nations as have opposing orientations: the Czechs are anticlerical and the Slovaks deeply Catholic; the Czechs are democratic and the Slovaks authoritarian; the Czechs are urban and the Slovaks rural; the Czechs are materialistic and the Slovaks spiritual; the Czechs are cosmopolitan liberals and the Slovaks ethnic nationalists; and so on along these lines. According to this view, the political choices their leaders made in the post-Communist period, including their civic and ethnic definitions of the sovereign community, reflected these deep and largely immutable differences in national culture and character, which so complicated the search for a common political vision under a democratic system that the eventual breakup of the Czech-Slovak union was likely, if not inevitable.

Coming so often from Czech and Slovaks themselves, one cannot easily dismiss such characterizations of what distinguishes the nations from one another. There are, however, several problems with relying on them to explain the differences in Czech and Slovak post-Communist understandings of nationhood. First, stark portrayals of national differences in the post-Communist period are misleading, as by all major indicators of socioeconomic development (including education, industrialization, urbanization, and values expressed in opinion polls), the Czechs and Slovaks had become practically indistinguishable.[12] Second, polls also showed that majorities in both nations wanted their political union to continue. Clearly, many of the differences that had once separated the two nations had proved mutable, and those that remained were, in the view of most citizens, bridgeable. And third, the Czechs had never built a state on the civic model before 1993 (all the Czechoslovak states had had a strong ethnic component to their definitions of sovereignty), undermining claims of a long-standing Czech orientation toward the civic principle. It is simply historically inaccurate to portray understandings of nationhood as one element in a largely stable aggregate of societal norms; in other words, the cultures, writ large, *have* changed. Thus, it is problematic to explain the difference in the two nations' understandings of nationhood on the basis of irreconcilably opposing national essences or characters, broadly construed.

The Elite-Centered Approach

A second approach to the study of nations and nationalism challenges the central premises of society-based primordialist approaches, focusing instead on elites. Objecting to the idea that "a group of people 'has' a culture in the way that animals have fur, inherited as genes are inherited,"[13] proponents of this approach view societal norms as fluid, heterogeneous, and the product of deliberate, constant decision-making.[14] Culture may thus be described as "a field of creative interchange and contestation, often around certain shared symbols, propositions or practices, and continuous transformation,"[15] which is growing with the flow of information, goods, and people worldwide made possible by new technologies.[16] Individuals have much greater autonomy in relation to collective norms than the primordialists suggest and *choose* to identify with some and disagree with others. No group or community and its attendant normative framework (political, religious, linguistic, ethnic, occupational, sexual, generational, etc.) has natural primacy in human life; all identities resulting from membership are in flux; and people regularly change priorities and/or shift allegiances when their circumstances change.

In contrast to primordialist approaches, then, this view sees human identities as highly malleable.[17] This malleability prompts focus on how elites shape normative orientations toward nationhood, for two reasons. Like all human communities, nations are best understood as human constructions. They arise out of a particular context—in the view of many scholars, that of modernity—and are consciously built by people who appropriate particular cultural norms and shape them strategically to build the community's framework. In so doing, these nation-builders interpret or even fabricate substantial elements of "national" identity and history in ways conducive to their project. According to this view, nation-builders more often produce broad-based understandings of community than they reflect them; as historian Eric Hobsbawm famously observed, "Nations do not make states and nationalisms but the other way around."[18] To understand the nation as a community, then, one must understand the project, and therefore its planners. And second, because the nation is just one of many communities with which people may identify, and because identities are in flux, nationalist ideologies and related political movements reflect ideas deliberately developed or chosen, organized and put forward by particular individuals, with specific interests, seeking to shape how people orient themselves politically. Thus, again, to understand political movements based on the nation, one must look first not to those who are moved, but to the *movers* and their motivations.

Moving—or shaping—understandings of community is easier during periods of upheaval. This was profoundly true of post-Communism, the aftermath of the collective rejection of an ideological system that had claimed, and attempted to enforce, authority in all aspects of human life. The metaphor often used by elite-centered analysis to describe nationalism's entry into post-Communist politics is that of an ideology filling a "vacuum" or "void" left by Communism's demise. This implies that nationalism is an ideology brought into the political sphere by elites to occupy a place that it had *not* held during the previous period; simply put, Communism moves out, nationalism moves in. According to Milada Vachudová and Tim Snyder, the potential for former Communists to use nationalism to legitimize themselves was particularly high in countries where there had been few dissidents during the Communist era, and therefore few alternative elites in the new political arena: "Ethnic nationalism worked as a kind of political shortcut. Relatively unreconstructed Communist parties (or, in Slovakia, a new patriotic movement led by Vladimír Mečiar) offering rhetoric of 'the nation' rather than a program of reform were able to attract uninformed electorates who felt threatened by the attendant uncertainty of political and economic change."[19] While people tend to respond to nationalist mobilization when they are unsettled and other aspects of their identities unmoored, elites provide the impetus for such politics. Elite motivations and interactions are thus crucial to understanding the nature and development of post-Communist nationalism.

The Czech-Slovak divergence in the post-Communist period prompted a fair amount of elite-focused analysis, which is not surprising given that elites were the negotiators in constitutional talks who eventually decided to dissolve the union without a referendum, overriding the popular preference for continued common statehood. Some of this analysis is narrow and instrumentalist, arguing that economic considerations determined elite positions.[20] The dominating Czech party in the June 1992 elections (Václav Klaus's Civic Democratic Party, ODS) wanted to reform the entire state's economy according to market principles rapidly, while the most successful Slovak party (Vladimir Mečiar's Movement for a Democratic Slovakia, HZDS) was full of former Communists who hoped to pursue a "third way" economic system. This was due partly to ideological and partly to structural differences, as the two nations' economic prospects differed substantially: the Czech lands had become an industrial powerhouse by the early twentieth century, while Slovakia's industry was largely developed under Communism and faced a far more painful transition. Thus, some analysts argued, Slovak elites preferred the maximal political (and hence economic) autonomy of a confederation, while Czech leaders sought central control over the state, via a tight federation, to ensure comprehensive market reform. Because the constitutional framework within which the negotiations took place (held over from the previous regime in the meantime) essentially gave each nation veto power, the country faced a stalemate, and divorce was the most rational option for each side to proceed with its preferred transition type. Other elite-centered analyses focus on the personal political ambitions of Klaus and Mečiar, the leaders who presided over the split and then dominated Czech and Slovak politics respectively for several years thereafter. Still other accounts have been broader, looking beyond the post-Communist period and its defining power/material interests to explore the relevance of Communist-era elite interactions and orientations. Gil Eyal, for example, locates the origins of elite-level differences in the purges that followed the 1968 Prague Spring's disastrous end, which, over time, polarized Czech and Slovak elites and produced "alternative visions of postcommunist society, and of the role of intellectuals within it."[21] Thus, the Czech and Slovak "ideological packages"—including the Slovak insistence on ethnic sovereignty and the Czech focus on building civil society—"were generated by a process that, while continuously guided by considerations of political and electoral strategy, was also strongly determined by the inherited identities, tastes, and modes of reasoning of the key political actors on both sides."[22]

Sufficient evidence exists to conclude that power-political strategizing, economic considerations and ideological orientations shaped by the post-Prague Spring period all contributed to elite differences on the issue of sovereignty's proper source. There is, however, also evidence indicating that these analyses are too narrow in terms of both time frame and their focus on elites to fully explain these differences. Eyal's study makes clear that an exclusive, "presentist" focus on the post-Communist period misses important contributing factors. As he observes, at the outset of the post-Communist period, Czechoslovakia's elites were divided into a "tripolar" configuration made up of the centralist Czechs, their Slovak allies, and the Slovak autonomists—a configuration present in Czechoslovak politics since the First Republic (founded in 1918) that had "proved quite resilient."[23] Still, his own location of the "principle of genesis"[24] of post-Communist perspectives in the Prague Spring's aftermath leaves these potentially relevant continuities with earlier orientations unexplored. And second, narrowly elite-centered analysis itself appears to be misplaced in the Czechoslovak case. While analysts who use this approach usually stress that the Velvet Divorce lacked popular support, they also often neglect to address poll results showing that strong majorities in both nations either *agreed* with their leaders' views on how the new common state should be arranged or went even farther (the majority of the Czechs, for example, favored a unitary state).[25] Thus, though they shared a preference for continued common statehood, the two nations' views of its proper foundations were at least as irreconcilable as those of their representatives—whom, it should be noted, they had elected overwhelmingly. Moreover, Deegan-Krause has found that, although Czech and Slovaks showed similar value orientations in opinion polls, "national claims" were far more relevant to Slovaks' political *choices* than to Czechs', and thus had very different implications for nationalism's influence in the political sphere.[26] Given the consonance of elite and mass perspectives on the issue of sovereignty and evidence of certain long-standing differences in orientation, an analysis that focuses only on elites or the recent past can at best incompletely explain the differences between Czech and Slovak post-Communist understandings of nationhood.

The Ethnosymbolist Approach

This brings me to the third and most recently developed approach to the study of nations and nationalism, often called "ethnosymbolism" or "social-constructivism," which owes much to the work of Anthony Smith. Something of a middle ground between society- and elite-centered approaches, it criticizes some points and supports others in both approaches. Beginning with the former, Smith's critique of primordialism targets its denial of individual autonomy. He argues that people belong to various social groups whose importance shifts over time,[27] and economic, political, and social change puts pressure on community ties. In an era of high mobility, people increasingly choose the community (or communities) to which they belong. Moreover, intermarriage, conquest, and migration undermine the primordialist notion of an organic communal essence. This critique, then, is quite similar to that made by the elite-centered perspective.

While Smith finds serious flaws in the primordialist approaches, he cautions against rejecting them wholesale. Criticisms that do this trivialize "feelings of belonging and obligation, of antiquity and dignity, the sense of a tie which is prior to and more powerful than other ties."[28] Moreover, he argues that many such criticisms do not adequately distinguish between the individual and the collective.[29] Individuals do have autonomy in relation to collective norms, but at the collective level, ethnicity has the power to sustain a "participants' primordialism," a voluntary bond between the community and its members that endures even when they move on to join other communities.[30] The nation, in particular, has this power because it is deeply grounded, and nationalism "derives its force from its historical embeddedness. As an ideology, nationalism can take root only if it strikes a popular chord, and is taken up by, and inspires, particular social groups and strata. . . . Its success, therefore, depends on specific cultural and historical contexts, and this means that the nations it helps to create are in turn derived from pre-existing and highly particularized cultural heritages and ethnic formations."[31] This understanding of the nation's cultural and historical roots is central to ethnosymbolism's challenge to the elite-centered approach. According to Smith, the nation as a community is undergirded by strong cultural patterns of authority, symbols, values, political and social traditions, myths and memories, all of which undergo reinterpretation over generations and through political mobilization, but which also tend to retain many significant lines of continuity. Unscrupulous and unprincipled leaders may spearhead mobilization; however, "the ethnic past sets limits to the manipulations of the elites and provides the ideals for the restored nation and its destiny. In this way, the nation remains embedded in a past that shapes its future as much as any present global trends."[32] The focus of analysis therefore "can be neither the aims and activities of the intellectual, professional and other elites, nor the mass sentiments and memories of the common people, but the often complex relationships between the two."[33] I thus draw on Smith's approach to explore my first question, concerning the sources of post-Communist Czech civic and Slovak ethnic understandings of nationhood, because it offers a framework for exploring such norms' links to *both* political culture *and* factors such as leadership—neither of which, as the above overview of scholarship indicates, can comfortably be excluded from an analysis of these cases. It thus offers a good foundation for assessing the relative effects of situational and political-cultural factors on recent normative orientations.

My Approach

The legitimacy of the concept of political culture is a topic of some debate, and its application in the Czecho-Slovak cases has met with rather sharp criticism. Much of this is based on the notion that political cultural approaches share central premises with primordialism, such as a view of culture as a set of cohesive, unchanging norms that determine political outcomes. At the same time, many of these same analysts do acknowledge that history (especially involving ethnonational conflict or insecurity) is politically relevant in the present, but they do not explain *how it becomes so*, beyond the subject matter relating to the same groups and issues. The relevance may appear in some ways obvious, but when scrutinized, the continuities over time in how people make sense of historical events and apply particular lessons to political life indicate a tradition of judgment about right and wrong, justice and injustice, and the boundaries and purposes of community. It is highly unusual for people repeatedly to analyze afresh their community's history, using continually changing frameworks; history becomes relevant, at least in part, via a culturally grounded normative orientation through which people understand its substance and relationship to current issues. Political culture is thus a concept necessary for studying how the past is related to the present. Moreover, while some conceptualizations of political culture may use strong primordialist assumptions, many, including my own, do not.

I define political culture as a configuration of political values, attitudes, and behaviors widely shared within a society and abiding, in that it has shown strong elements of consistency over a significant period of time.[34] My definition differs from the classic conceptualization developed by Gabriel Almond and Sidney Verba, which stresses the patterns of citizens' internal disposition and orientation toward politics,[35] because (following Robert Tucker) mine also includes behavior. This makes it possible to distinguish between patterns of political-cultural belief and political-cultural behavior when the two are not in harmony, rather than distinguishing between political culture and conduct.[36] Beyond this, I make three further crucial distinctions. First, following H. Gordon Skilling, I distinguish between the "official" political culture, which is based on the regime's formal principles, and the "dominant" culture of the people, which may or may not be in harmony.[37] Second, I allow for the possibility that a society may contain subcultures that are strongly at odds with the dominant culture. And third, if a state has more than one self-defined "people"—as in a multinational or federated state—I expect that each people may have its own dominant culture; thus, in the former Czechoslovakia, there were both dominant Czech and dominant Slovak cultures, each with their own subcultures.

In examining whether post-Communist Czech and Slovak understandings of nationhood have political-cultural roots, I want to emphasize that I am not suggesting that situational factors would be irrelevant to debates and decisions concerning sovereignty and political authority, or that the understandings would have been static over time. As Skilling argues, the study of political culture "is something more than an examination of 'traditions' since it embodies not only the old, but also elements of change, and represents a kind of synthesis between the two."[38] Political-cultural orientations are also not monolithic, and, broadly speaking, they influence rather than determine the choices of elites and masses. Leaders act for all kinds of reasons, and strategic power-political and material considerations will certainly play a role in the programs they put forward. Whether people actually support them, however, depends in part on the program's consonance with their own values, and to the extent the proposed program differs from these, on whether people are willing to reject or substantially amend those values or take up new ones.

This is a question highly relevant to the Czech and Slovak experiences. During the twentieth century the two nations underwent numerous regime changes, sometimes very quickly—moving, for example, from democracy to fascism/ultra-nationalism to Communism in less than ten years (1939–48). For all these regimes to have been legitimate (in the sense of conforming to the citizens' views of acceptable standards and principles of governance), there would have to have been repeated, sharp changes in popular value orientations, which would in turn indicate that these orientations are highly malleable. Alternatively, if not all these regimes were legitimate, and if societal understandings (in particular, those concerning nationhood) show strong continuities over time, this would indicate that they are less susceptible to factors such as political leadership—or, to put it more darkly, to elite manipulation—and may be characterized as elements of political culture.

I thus trace the evolution of Czech and Slovak understandings of nationhood over the course of a century-and-a-half (from the mid-nineteenth-century Czech and Slovak "National Awakenings" until 2008) and six regime types (Habsburg/Austro-Hungarian monarchy, interwar democracy, fascism/ultranationalism, postwar democracy, Communism, and post-Communist democracy). I gauge both the extent of their continuities and their malleability in response to political leadership, considerations of material interest, and the evolving relationship between the two nations. I choose the period of National Awakenings—a term with tremendous primordialist connotations—as a starting point because this was the time when elites (or "awakeners") consciously developed understandings of nationhood in order to mobilize their ethnic communities to understand themselves as "nations." Having laid this foundation as a baseline for further comparison, I trace continuities and discontinuities in Czech and Slovak understandings using a number of sources that reflected and articulated them, including constitutions, laws and policies; government behavior; the writings, platforms, speeches, and behaviors of political elites, including both government and party leaders and politically engaged intellectuals; and the citizens' electoral support of particular parties, polling data, and willingness to obey the laws. Many of these sources are unavailable under authoritarian regimes, making it much more difficult to discern patterns that differ from the official political culture. Still, orientations repressed under authoritarianism may also become visible during times of liberalization or revolt, as well as through dissident writings and activity. Moreover, as Carol Skalnik Leff argues, the way that state leaders respond to such challenges may offer insight into the strength of submerged orientations.[39] And finally, the "reopening" of Czech and Slovak politics in the Velvet Revolution's aftermath has allowed people not only to voice positions on current issues, which may be compared to those expressed during the pre-Communist periods of political openness, but also to reflect upon what views were suppressed in previous decades.

This study thus takes up the question of normative continuity in the context of enormous change. The Czechs and Slovaks lived under the most powerful—and mutually hostile—ideological systems of the twentieth century. Each regime, in addition to being a link in the broader chain of my investigation, therefore offers the opportunity to explore theories of nationhood in the context of very different political, socioeconomic, and historical circumstances. Ultimately, this allows me to offer the substantial evidence necessary to conclude that the Czech and Slovak post-Communist understandings of nationhood should be viewed not as a configuration of highly malleable, and hence situational, political norms, driven to seemingly opposite corners by post-revolutionary political and economic conditions, but as orientations with strong political-cultural roots. It also lays the foundation for addressing my second set of questions, to which I now turn.

Debate 2: Civic and Ethnic Models of Nationhood

My second question, again, concerns the implications of the Czech civic and Slovak ethnic definitions of sovereignty for minority political membership and individual rights, and it engages with a debate over the validity of the conceptual distinction between the civic and ethnic models of nationhood. While long employed in the study of nations and nationalism, this dichotomy has become the subject of controversy in recent years. The original dichotomy owes much to Hans Kohn, who argued that Western and Eastern nationalisms are essentially opposite types: "while Western nationalism was, in its origin, connected with the concepts of individual liberty and rational cosmopolitanism current in the eighteenth century, the later nationalism in Central and Eastern Europe and in Asia tended towards a contrary development."[40] He uses the example of German nationalism to define the Eastern type, observing that it "substituted for the legal and rational concept of 'citizenship' the infinitely vaguer concept of 'folk,'" whose "roots seemed to reach into the dark soil of primitive times and to have grown through thousands of hidden channels of unconscious development, not in the bright light of rational political ends."[41] Kohn's conception of the Western model's positive attributes has been carried forward in some recent analyses of civic nationhood. Michael Ignatieff, for example, observes that the civic model "envisages the nation as a community of equal, rights-bearing citizens, united in patriotic attachment to a shared set of political practices and values."[42] Jürgen Habermas also endorses the civic nation, arguing that the "nation of citizens does not derive its identity from some common ethnic and cultural properties, but rather from the *praxis* of citizens who actively exercise their civil rights."[43] In his view, it is "constitutional principles rooted in a political culture" rather than "an ethical-cultural form of life as a whole" that provides the basis for civic nationhood.[44] He also emphasizes that it is important to distinguish between the political community and sub-political communities, because otherwise the majority culture will become overbearing and violate the rights of other cultures to equality and "mutual recognition."[45]

Will Kymlicka and Anthony Smith, among others, have challenged such conceptualizations of the civic nation. Both note that little historical evidence supports claims that civic nations are based on exclusively rational political ties and are culturally neutral. According to Smith, the barrier to such claims "springs from the internal contradiction at the heart of the national state between a universal conception of citizenship, with its uniform rights and duties, and an inevitably particularlist conception of 'the people,' i.e. the community of which each citizen is a member. Here we have to return to the ethnic basis of so many nations."[46] Kymlicka illustrates the point with the American example, observing that when the United States was founded the majority of the new nation's members had common roots in the English language, literature, and religion.[47] While he acknowledges that the nation's founders emphasized certain political principles ("liberty, equality, democracy"), he argues that it is wrong to "conclude from this that American nationalism is ideological *rather than* cultural. . . . Ideology shaped, but did not replace, the cultural component of national identity."[48]

Given that civic nations are not culturally neutral, Smith and Kymlicka argue, there is no reason to assume that minorities will be granted membership readily. Civic nations often require that ethnic minorities relinquish or privatize important elements of their distinctive identity in order to become citizens,[49] and marginalizing or repressing their cultures in order to assimilate them can lead to conflict or oppression just as easily as traditionally conceived ethnic nationalism—as happened, for example, with the Native Americans in the U.S. and the Kurds in Turkey.[50] In other cases, majorities may reject minorities' voluntary assimilation, as the French did in response to Jewish attempts to assimilate.[51] Taking the criticism a step further, Bernard Yack and Kai Nielsen find the concept of the civic nation so ideologically loaded and empirically unconvincing as to be of little analytical use. According to Yack, it reflects a "mixture of self-congratulation and wishful thinking"[52] and is less an analytical tool than a project to "find and preserve a form of national community that is compatible with liberal political commitments."[53] While sympathizing with this goal, he argues that inherited culture and political principles are so deeply intertwined that a dichotomy based on nations of choice versus nations of inheritance is untenable: "It may be reasonable to contrast nations whose distinctive cultural inheritance centers on political symbols and political stories with nations whose cultural inheritance centers on language and stories about ethnic origins. But it is unreasonable and illegitimate to interpret this contrast as a distinction between the rational attachment to principle and the emotional celebration of inherited culture."[54] Yack thus finds that the civic nation is a "myth." Nielsen also argues that the dichotomy between the civic and the cultural nation is insupportable, concluding that "Talk of civic nationalism had better be dropped from our political vocabulary (including the vocabulary of political theory) if we wish to be clear and coherent in our analyses of the real world."[55]

The concept of the ethnic nation itself has been less controversial. Though the civic/ethnic dichotomy suggests symmetry, the ethnic nation is not a neat oppositional counterpart to the civic nation, which is a specifically political community. The ethnic nation, by contrast, may exist under a variety of circumstances—it may have its "own" state, but may also be divided between states or be one of several nations within the same state—and it has no necessary relationship to political ideology. Thus, debate of the sort that surrounds the civic nation only arises when an ethnic nation makes a particular political claim. Under consideration here is the claim that the ethnic nation (rather than the citizenry) should be the exclusive source of state sovereignty, and this has, in fact, provoked a fair amount of academic and political conflict. While many nationalists see this as a natural right (a view rooted not only in Herderian nationalism but also the Wilsonian principle of self-determination), European and North American scholarly perspectives on this claim mostly fall within a spectrum that ranges from cautious to condemnatory.

Taking a cautious approach, Ghia Nodia argues that there is nothing inherently undemocratic about the idea of ethnonational self-determination realized through sovereignty; indeed, democracy and nationalism are in a sense inseparable, as the nation "is another name for 'We the People.'" Still, it raises problems for liberalism: "Most denunciations of nationalism in the name of democracy are actually denunciations made in the name of *liberalism*. By liberalism, I mean that doctrine which holds individual liberty to be the foremost political value. Nationalism, on the other hand, gives preference to collective claims based on race, culture, or some other communal identity. Liberalism champions a person's right to *choose*, while nationalism gives pride of place to something that does not depend on personal choice" (emphasis original).[56] At the same time, he argues that there is "some *positive* link between liberalism and nationalism," in that national self-determination takes the liberal ideal of individual autonomy to a collective scale. Authoritarian tendencies in new states based on this principle usually stem from problems associated with a transition to democracy that may "sweep the national idea away from its democratic and isothymic ["demanding of equal recognition"[57]] moorings and carry it to the far shores of racism and fascism,"[58] but these have no necessary relationship to nationalism.

Kymlicka takes a cautious stance as well, arguing that, because all states promote a common societal culture, what distinguishes them is not whether the promoted bonds are political or cultural, but how liberal or illiberal the nation-building project is. He identifies nine dimensions for comparison, all of which concern the level of freedom people have in the public space to express and develop identities other than that of the state-promoted societal culture. One of these dimensions is how open the definition of the national society is: the more restrictions on membership (such as ethnic or racial criteria), the more illiberal nation-building is on that particular measure. This has important implications for other dimensions of il/liberalism. States with an "open" definition of the nation promote a much "thinner conception of national identity," and "in order to make it possible for people from different ethnocultural backgrounds to become full and equal members of the nation, and to allow the maximum room for individual dissent, the terms of admission are relatively thin—e.g., learning the language, participating in common public institutions, and perhaps expressing a commitment to the long-term survival of the nation."[59] By contrast, in "non-liberal states," "acquiring a national identity typically requires a much thicker form of cultural integration, involving not only a common language and public institutions, but also elements of religion, ritual, and lifestyle." In turn, partly because the culture promoted by liberal nation-building is thinner, a diversity of social groupings is allowed to flourish, and the nation is valued because it provides the "context" within which individuals are able to define and pursue their own goals and relationships. Illiberal nationalisms, by contrast, often subordinate all chosen or private aspects of life to purposes of "national greatness." Thus, while Kymlicka does not argue that an ethnic definition of sovereign nationhood is the *primary* reason for broader patterns of illiberalism (his scheme is more descriptive than systematically explanatory), it is one in a constellation of factors that contribute to them.

Robert Hayden is more critical, arguing that because it entrenches civic inequality, "ethno-national self-determination is an anti-democratic principle."[60] This principle (which produces a regime type he calls "constitutional nationalism") sets off a chain reaction of practical effects somewhat different from the one Kymlicka describes, as it not only alienates minorities by excluding them from full membership, but also jeopardizes the broader security of civil rights because any resulting challenges from the minority may be considered an attack on the "state-founding nation's" sovereignty and used to justify repressive governance that affects the entire society. Moreover, the view of the nation as a "collective individual" dangerously undermines the citizen's autonomy in relation to the state. This last is a point that Liah Greenfeld explains well, arguing that "collectivistic ideologies are inherently authoritarian, for, when the collectivity is seen in unitary terms, it tends to assume the character of a collective individual possessed of a single will, and someone is bound to be its interpreter. The reification of a community introduces (or preserves) fundamental inequality between those of its few members who are qualified to interpret the collective will and the many who have no such qualifications; the select few dictate to the masses who must obey."[61]

Thus, a point of agreement in these analyses is that there is something about the ethnic nation as a community—its involuntariness, the thickness of its shared identity, its exclusivity, its collectivistic unity—that, when understood as the basis of political sovereignty, may justify the constriction of individual liberty. At the same time, the analysts vary on how threatening this potential is to liberal democracy; Nodia only sees a tension between ethnic sovereignty and liberalism, while Hayden views them as fully incompatible.

This brings me back to the Czech and Slovak cases. At the level of constitutional principle, they appear to epitomize the civic/ethnic dichotomy, a sense reinforced by the oppositional characterizations of the two nations during the post-Communist state-building discussions leading up to their divorce. Moreover, for the first several years after Slovakia founded its independent state, the Mečiar governments (June 1992–March 1994 and October 1994–September 1998) used ethnic nationalism to justify illiberal governance, clearly linking the two. Still, analyses written recently (and thus able to take into account the political changes brought about by the post-Mečiar governments) have offered different accounts of the nature of the relationship between nationalist principle and illiberal practice in Slovakia. Many argue that Mečiar and his allies used nationalism instrumentally to cloak and publicly rationalize their attempts to minimize constraints on their *own* power (rather than, in any meaningful sense, that of the nation). Tim Haughton thus argues that the most important factor undermining democracy under Mečiar's governments "was their illiberalism not their nationalism (the latter being a constituent component of the former). Nevertheless messages wrapped up (at least partially) in nationalist language were useful in legitimating parties' programmes."[62] Nationalism thus supported rather than produced illiberalism, giving it a "national accent."[63]

Others see nationalism as causing illiberalism. Erika Harris, for example, argues that Slovak nation-building damaged democracy by constitutionally and legally privileging the Slovak majority over the Hungarian minority and fomenting "nationalist demagoguery"; she thus concludes that the "main criterion by which democratic progress in Slovakia can be measured is the level of tension between the two groups."[64] Harris further argues that ethnic politics played well with the majority population largely because Slovak nationhood has historically been insecure (a point with which Haughton agrees); at the same time, she holds that national identity is by nature "situational,"[65] and therefore that the Mečiar governments' divisive nationalist principles are not deeply rooted in Slovak culture. Indeed, the subsequent governments' inclusion of Hungarian party representatives signaled a move toward a "multicultural understanding the state" and offers insight into nationalism's nature: "The most important implication is that this change could finally remove nationalism from political life; were that the case, if it would show that nationalism is not inherent to Slovak or any other society. It would also demonstrate that the level of nationalist mobilisation depends on political developments in the state and on national elites, who can instrumentalise, but also reduce or even eliminate nationalism, according to their commitment to democracy."[66]

Still another perspective, offered by Deegan-Krause, focuses less narrowly on elites and argues that post-Communist Slovak society was divided over both the role of the nation and the level of accountability required of good government. In the first years of the new state, opinion polls showed that these divides were not closely aligned (undermining claims that Slovaks are stably oriented toward authoritarian nationalism). With the goal of securing and maximizing their political power, the Mečiar governments used nationalism to draw these divides together, linking the protection of national sovereignty to the concentration of power in a government led by the "father of the nation," Mečiar himself. The government thus relied "on the support of voters who explicitly *do not care* about accountability" (emphasis original).[67] Deegan-Krause further argues that the Mečiar governments chiefly harmed democracy not through antiminority discourse or restrictive language legislation, as the ethnic Hungarians' access to the electoral process was not threatened, but rather by limiting the ability of the political opposition to enforce accountability on the government.[68] He concludes that while subject to an apparent "mutual attraction" and destructive when aligned, nationalism and authoritarianism have no *necessary* relationship, as "the affinity depends on election, understood both as personal choice and as political victory. If would-be authoritarian leaders lack national credentials or if nonauthoritarians pose a meaningful national challenge, the two issue divides simply may not come into alignment. Furthermore, as post-Mečiar Slovakia suggests, once the leader has gone, the connection between unaccountable authority and nationalism may once again fall slack."[69]

Thus, though there are important differences between these analyses of the Slovak case, they agree that the relationship between nationalism and the illiberal use of authority was produced neither by the necessary implications of the regime definition of sovereignty (as, for example, Greenfeld or Hayden might expect) nor primarily by a strongly rooted orientation of the Slovak citizenry, but rather by particular political leaders with specific agendas. In examining whether the combination of the Slovaks' use of the ethnic model and their political-cultural understandings of nationhood has significantly constrained their leaders' choices in a way that produced illiberal governance, then, this study has the potential to challenge the above consensus.

By contrast, the Czech case in many ways conforms to traditional expectations concerning civic nations. As Gil Eyal has shown, the new post-Communist Czech elites were generally driven by more liberal concerns than their Slovak counterparts, as "both dissidents and monetarists sought to create conditions under which individuals will govern themselves."[70] Moreover, Deegan-Krause offers strong evidence that Czechs have been most deeply divided—and influenced in their political choices—not by ethnonational issues but by differences over how reform the economy.[71] The only issue that has prompted a notable nationalist response was the debate over reparations for the Sudeten Germans, a once-substantial minority that the Czechoslovak government expelled in World War II's aftermath; this is, however, "a question of foreign policy and relations with Germany rather than of domestic cultural policy."[72]

This relative lack of nationalist politics in the Czech Republic is unsurprising for two reasons. First, whereas the Velvet Divorce left Slovakia with a substantial Hungarian minority, the Czech Republic came away as one of the most ethnically homogeneous states in the world. Second, the Czechs never felt their identity threatened by Czech-Slovak union in the way the Slovaks did; their population was twice as large, and they had entered the common state in 1918 as by far the more politically experienced and socioeconomically advanced nation, allowing them to assume a dominant position. Over time the Slovaks caught up in many ways, but the Prague central government always exercised more control over the country's affairs than did any powers in Bratislava, and Czechs did not feel negated the way Slovaks did by the international tendency to use "Czech" as shorthand for "Czechoslovak." Defending national identity was simply not a primary concern for most Czechs.

Thus, Czech politics has not been characterized by either nationalism or authoritarianism comparable to that in Slovakia, and its leaders, broadly speaking, are more liberal. There is, however, a significant blot on the Czech Republic's post-Communist human rights record, and this concerns the treatment of the Roma minority, roughly 3 percent of the population. Strong evidence, some of it gathered by the Czech government, substantiates serious allegations of widespread discrimination and the failure to offer recourse to Roma targeted by violent skinheads. Clearly, then, the ethnic Czech population *does* have a troubled relationship with an ethnic minority. But this relationship differs in several important ways from the one between the Slovak majority and the Hungarian minority. Many Roma communities are not only marginalized, but also self-marginalizing, maintaining a culture that eschews integration into the majority society and holds outsiders at a significant distance. They do not tend to make the kinds of demands that politically assertive minorities in Slovakia and other countries have; they have generally not called, for example, for language rights or territorial autonomy (indeed, some Roma leaders have argued that Romani-language schools would only foster further segregation). They are, moreover, members of a large, broadly dispersed diaspora, without a "homeland," long-settled territory, or history of self-definition as a nation (though some Roma leaders are trying to promote such consciousness among European Roma). Finally, unlike the Slovak Hungarians, they are differentiated from ethnic Czechs by both socioeconomic status and by race, at least as it is understood in Czech society, where Roma are often called "black."

The literature thus does not tend to frame the Czech treatment of the Roma in terms of nationalist politics and conflicting rights claims; it does not parallel analysis of Slovakia. Much of the literature on the Czech case has been generated by human rights organizations and European Union accession-oversight bodies, as well as a fair number of Czech analysts, and it is dominated by extensive cataloging of human rights abuses, measures of ethnic Czech attitudes toward the minority, and assessments of both the government's and the Roma community's attempts to address key problems. Scholars have also taken up the question of how the Roma community should be conceptualized by analysts and political leaders, given that they do not fit easily into existing categories used to examine ethnonational relations and related rights claims.[73] In addition, a theme common in this literature is a sense of disappointment with the Czechs, given their well-lauded civic/democratic orientation (one article, for example, is subtitled "Expecting More of Havel's Country"[74]), and some authors have noted that the "civic principle" of ethnic neutrality has at times cloaked exclusionary goals and impeded necessary state action.[75]

The existing literature thus firmly establishes that the Czech Republic has not secured civic equality for the Roma minority. What has not been systematically explored, however, is whether this failure to realize one of the civic model's central principles means that its practical implications *do not differ significantly* from those of the ethnic model, as the stronger critics of the civic/ethnic dichotomy hold. To come to some conclusion about this requires a comparison of the Czech political practice with that of a state based on the ethnic model, like Slovakia.

My Approach

To frame this second part of my investigation, I begin by noting that regime principles (civic or ethnic) do not themselves determine how authority is exercised, but must be interpreted and applied to specific situations by those with political power. Thus, I ask, have Czech and Slovak political leaders used the civic and ethnic definitions of sovereignty as principled justifications for particular laws and policies? If so, have these laws and policies affected minority membership and individual rights differently? How significant are these differences? In addition, to avoid an overly narrow focus on laws invoking civic equality in the Czech case, I ask, are there also laws, official policies, or behaviors that violate the regime's principle of civic equality by discriminating against a minority? I am interested in the extent to which the state's relationship to minority citizens differs from its relationship to the ethnic majority. My standard for judging membership is thus internal to the society (rather than, for example, using international minority rights standards). I consider particularly the nature and impact of the state-promoted societal culture (to use Kymlicka's concept) on minority participation in the political and public spheres. To measure individual rights, I examine whether the laws and policies under consideration serve to constrict or enlarge individual autonomy in relation to the state.

In setting up the comparison this way, part of what I measure is the elasticity of civic and ethnic principles. One purpose is to see how similarly (or differently) they may affect individual rights and minority membership; another is to identify where the constraints or boundaries on elasticity (if there are any) come from. Interpreting the regime principles and applying them in the form of law and policy may be left *entirely* to the discretion of government elites. In constitutional democracies, however, there are (at least) two possible sources of constraints on that discretion. The first comes from formal checks on political power, which could include constitutional oversight by the judiciary, veto power by some member of the executive, the legislature's ability to override vetos and, in some cases, force a cabinet's resignation, and the citizens' ability to vote elites out of office if they consider their interpretation and/or application of principle to be illegitimate. The second source (which may exist regardless of a constitution) comes from resistance, if those empowered to scrutinize the application of principle or carry out laws and policies refuse to do so, and more broadly through citizen noncompliance with laws.

To compare the implications of the Czech civic and Slovak ethnic definitions of sovereignty (and thereby assess the conceptual distinction), I look not only at whether elites have used these principles to justify laws and policies in ways that affect minority membership and individual rights, but also at whether interpretation and application are constrained by formal checks (whether laws/policies been overturned or vetoed, or electoral support for the parties associated with them affected) and/or resistance (whether state officials and the broader citizenries generally comply with the laws/policies). And finally, I draw on the historical evidence to assess whether elite interpretations of regime principles reflect political-cultural patterns, and whether there is any relationship between the level of consonance of these interpretations with political culture and the extent to which other political actors and the broader publics find them legitimate. This offers a potentially critical, historically grounded explanation of the constraining factors on elite interpretation/application of regime principles. More broadly, this brings further insight into both the dynamics between situational and rooted factors and their relative importance in shaping post-Communist Czech and Slovak understandings of nationhood. Ultimately, this helps build a stronger foundation for assessing the means and likelihood of overcoming their more illiberal nationalist elements in the pursuit of individual rights, inclusive minority membership, and European integration.

An Overview of the Book

Chapter 2 explores the mid-nineteenth-century period of Czech and Slovak "National Revival," when "national awakeners" first consciously developed and propagated modern conceptions of Czech, Slovak, and Czechoslovak nationhood. I set the baseline for my study of continuities and discontinuities in understandings of nationhood up through the post-Communist period by exploring the political ideas of five of these awakeners, who were particularly influential. I also situate these men and their projects in the context of the turbulent mid-nineteenth century, examining how specific factors may have affected both how they structured their conceptions of nationhood and how people responded to them. These factors help explain the development in the early to mid-nineteenth century of three patterns of orientation that bear important resemblances to orientations and cleavages in Czech and Slovak politics today.

Chapter 3 explores the waning decades of the Habsburg Empire (1860–

1914), when nation-building efforts among its "subject peoples" intensified. Czech historian Miroslav Hroch has offered an analysis that explains their different fortunes during this period, using an instrumentalist theory that finds the material interests of both nationalist leaders and broader populations to be the central source of nationalism's ideological substance and popular appeal.[76] It clearly differs from an ethnosymbolist approach in the factors he identifies as primary, and I therefore engage with it to assess the importance of materialist factors relative to the influence of the principled conceptions of nationhood developed by the "awakeners." I find that while considerations of material interest and power were certainly important factors in nationalism's content and appeal, in the Czech and Slovak cases, traditions of political and religious thought, particularly as developed and articulated by the awakeners, were critical as well. Developments during this period thus indicate that by the early twentieth century, the awakeners' ideas were increasingly embedded and activated as elements of Czech and Slovak political culture.

Chapter 4 explores the First Czechoslovak Republic (1918–38), focusing on the roots of the Czechoslovak and Slovak nationalist understandings of nationhood (comparing them to those traced in preceding chapters) and on the reasons why they became a source of enduring conflict in the First Republic. Based on evidence from the period, I argue that although material and power-political inequities were again certainly important, a more fundamental source of conflict lay in their very different understandings of the proper source of state sovereignty (one nation versus two) and of legitimate political authority (liberal-democratic versus clerical-nationalist).

Chapter 5 examines the Wartime Slovak State[77] (1939–45), which departed radically from the First Republic in its ultranationalist official ideology and behavior. I ask whether any substantial continuity exists between the Slovak state's ideology and the traditions of Slovak political thought that I have traced so far. I also look at the implications of this ideology for governance during the state's brief existence. Based on this examination, I argue that the state's ideology both drew on and diverged from the traditions of Slovak nationalism. I also note that five years after the state's founding, Slovak democrats and Communists cooperated in an uprising against it, dramatically illustrating the continuing divisions within the Slovak nation.

Chapter 6 examines the short-lived Third Republic (1945–48). Though within three years of the war's end the Communist Party took control of the state, the Third Republic offers a window into the Czech and Slovak orientations after their separate wartime experiences. My question in this chapter, then, is in what ways Czech and Slovak understandings of nationhood emerged from the war changed, what elements of continuity remained, and what accounts for both. To assess this, I focus on the Czech and Slovak parties' positions on how the two nations' relationship to the state should be structured, and at state policy toward national minorities. The evidence points to a mixture of normative continuity and change in both nations: the Slovaks' sense of distinct nationhood had been consolidated, and the Czechs had become more illiberal.

Chapter 7 looks at the Communist state (1948–89) to see whether the Czech and Slovak orientations traced to this point survived, and remained potent, in the face of a powerful and hostile regime. I do this by focusing on periods of reform and periods of repression, when it was possible to gain a sense of submerged or repressed orientations. Based on this investigation, I argue that the Communist regime was not capable of rooting out previously dominant political-cultural orientations, which continued to play an important, and at times pivotal, role in state politics. They were in fact vital enough to challenge the political system so extensively that in 1968, foreign military intervention was required to quell them. They also indicated the continuing existence of very different national priorities during periods of reform, which had a critical impact on the development of national relations as well, as each found the other's priorities as threatening their own. I conclude by arguing that a true ideological "vacuum" or "void" would not be left in Communism's wake.

Chapter 8 explores the role of Czech and Slovak understandings of nationhood in the debate over the future of common statehood after the Velvet Revolution (1989–92). My focus is on how the Czechs and Slovaks differed with regard to the source of state sovereignty and how post-Communist interpretations of the history of Czech-Slovak relations throughout the twentieth century related to the debate over sovereignty. I conclude that although the dominant perspectives on this question were not unaffected by post-Communist leadership and material considerations, these situational factors did not *produce* these contending understandings. It is clear from the discourse over the historical legacies of the Czech-Slovak relationship that the two nations saw themselves as heirs to competing traditions whose principles stood in fundamental conflict with those of the other, and that this shaped and constrained political possibilities on both sides, including that of a future together.

Chapter 9 turns to the second set of concerns: the implications of constitutional definitions of sovereignty for minority membership and individual rights. I examine how successive post-Communist Slovak governments

(1993–2008) invoked ethnic sovereignty to justify specific laws and policies, as well as their effects on the state's ethnic Hungarian minority and the scope of individual freedom more broadly. I also examine the factors that may have enabled or constrained such policy-making, including formal checks on government power, legislation intended to mitigate the effects of other measures, and, more broadly, the political-cultural orientations of elites and the broader public. I find that government zigzagged between more and less liberal interpretations and application of ethnic sovereignty, reflecting the continuing influence of two understandings of nationhood with roots stretching back to the nineteenth century. Ultimately, I conclude that while leadership is very important in determining levels of individual rights and minority membership in Slovakia, the constitutionally enshrined principle of ethnic sovereignty and the political-cultural orientations that hold it as central are also critically important factors constraining leaders' choices and shaping the public's response to them.

Chapter 10 examines the implications of the civic model in the Czech Republic. I look at how laws, policies, and behavior based on the civic principle—as well as those that directly violate it—have affected the membership of the Roma minority. I also explore how members of the ethnic Czech majority, including both political elites and private citizens, have conceived of their relationship and obligations to the Roma and at how these conceptions relate to the civic principle. On this evidence, I argue that the civic principle has been interpreted in a variety of ways, but that the most flagrant violations of the Roma's civic equality stem from resistance to, rather than application of, the civic principle. This resistance, in turn, reflects long-standing popular animosity toward the Roma and norms permissive of discrimination against them, which is enabled (but not caused) by particular interpretations of the civic principle. The Czech case, then, supports the argument made by critics of the traditional civic/ethnic dichotomy that ethno-cultural identity remains politically relevant in civic nations as well as ethnic nations, and may undermine civic equality under either regime type.

In the concluding analysis I argue that approaches that undervalue the political-cultural and historical context of post-Communist understandings of nationhood will likely overemphasize the importance of situational factors and so misunderstand the deeper roots of nationalism's substance and continuing appeal. Although ethnicity remains relevant at the level of political practice in both the Czech and Slovak states, it does matter whether regime principle justifies the stratification of citizenship. Ultimately, I argue that while the traditional civic/ethnic dichotomy overstates the difference between the two models, a distinction, amended to reflect the importance of ethno-cultural identity in civic as well as ethnic communities, remains necessary for understanding the factors that shape relationships between states and majority and minority citizens.

CHAPTER ONE

Awakenings

MANY CENTRAL EUROPEANS view the nineteenth century as a time of national "revival" and "awakening" after hundreds of years of submersion within Empire. During this time, men who came to be known as the "awakeners" and "fathers" of their nations wrote histories, novels, poetry, music, linguistic studies, ethnographies, journal articles and more, seeking to lay the foundation for a broad ethnonational consciousness. Though their ranks include many, I have chosen to begin this study by exploring the political thought of five awakeners whose work was especially and enduringly influential: the "Father of the Czech Nation," František Palacký, the "Father of the Slovak Nation" Ľudovít Štúr, the Slovak poet Jan Kollár, the Slovak scholar Pavel Josef Šafařík, and the Czech journalist Karel Havlíček—all of whom knew and influenced each other. To be sure, their ideas are not the "understandings of nationhood" I defined in the preceding chapter, but rather precursors to these, as Czech and Slovak nationalist thought at this point had strong pan-Slavist elements and had not yet reached a point where national community was directly linked to sovereignty—and in any case the political context forbade any such assertion. Their ideas on the nature and boundaries of the nation (especially the relationship between the Czechs and Slovaks) and the foundations of legitimate authority nevertheless laid crucial groundwork for the development of modern Czech and Slovak understandings.

This level of individual influence on national consciousness could be seen as evidence to support the instrumentalist contention that the modern nation's origins lie largely in a construction project run by elites with their own agendas. The awakeners certainly consciously promoted a particular conception of community and identity, which was only taken up over time by the nation's "membership." This process does refute the primordialist notion that national identities were ancient and organic. At the same time, it is important not to assume that because they were consciously constructed, these understandings of nationhood lacked cultural authenticity. Such anchoring was important to the awakeners, and would turn out to be both crucial to their success and divisive, as certain of the resulting conceptualizations have tensions and conflicts between them that reflected real differences between and within the Czech and Slovak communities. These would prove enduring and underlie the triad of orientations that broadly characterized Czechoslovak politics throughout the twentieth century: Czechs seeking unity with the Slovaks but privileging Czech identity; the more liberal Slovaks who allied themselves with the Czechs in their unification project but also found the Czechs' dominance frustrating; and, as rival to both, somewhat less liberal Slovaks who sought to assert an identity (with resulting rights) entirely distinct from the Czech. These orientations did evolve and change in some ways over time, but they nevertheless preserved quite remarkable continuities, as from this historical period forward Czechs and Slovaks interpreted, reassessed, invoked, and built on the awakeners' ideas. Every Czechoslovak, Czech, and Slovak regime has incorporated into its governing principles at least one of the above triad of orientations' core elements, and every shared state has also violated at least one and faced strong challenge because of it. The durability of the broad political perspectives that developed out of these awakeners' ideas is thus key evidence for my contention that Czech and Slovak understandings of nationhood are not highly situational or manipulatable, but rather became elements of political culture, and as such often serve to *constrain* political leaders' ability to execute or impose policy on related matters. The awakeners' ideas thus form the starting point for this study's exploration of continuities and discontinuities in normative orientations toward nationhood across time and regime change, up through the post-Communist period.

The Mid-Nineteenth-Century Czech and Slovak Environments

The five chosen awakeners were active during the early to mid-nineteenth century, which falls within "Phase B" of Czech historian Miroslav Hroch's periodization of European national movements. This phase built on the narrow philological and literary work done during the period of "scholarly interest" in nationhood ("Phase A"), and under the awakeners' leadership, the interests, aims, and demographic composition of the national movements began to expand. While both the Czech and Slovak movements grew in this way, differences in their environments affected how their leaders structured their conceptions of nationhood and how people responded to them. I thus begin with a brief, broad overview of the contexts in which they worked.

The Czech lands of Bohemia and Moravia lay in the Austrian part of the Habsburg Empire, where mid-eighteenth-century fiscal and agricultural reforms had prompted the rural population to grow rapidly.[1] Emperor Joseph II alleviated the resulting population pressure by abolishing serfdom in 1781 and banning corporal punishment for noncriminal offenses, which made peasant life less fearful.[2] Many moved to towns and cities, and the state supported an industrial revolution in the Czech lands.[3] Reform of the imperial administration further enhanced economic opportunities, as competitive exams joined social origin as an entryway to civil service.[4] It also became bilingual, with lower civil servants speaking Czech as well as German. All these developments spurred socioeconomic diversification, and the Czechs developed both a middle and a working class. Communication between urban and rural areas improved, literacy spread, and an ensuing proliferation of publishing in the Czech language strengthened a sense of common culture. Moreover, although the aristocracy were mostly unsympathetic to nationalism and considered Czech a language of low status, some lent cautious, critically needed financial support and political influence to the middle-class nationalists.[5] Thus, the socioeconomic situation in the early nineteenth century was conducive to the Czech National Movement's development; in Hroch's apt description, "powerful integrating factors stood around its cradle."[6]

The political situation was, however, less friendly. Ethnic Germans continued to dominate Bohemian political and bureaucratic institutions and tried to limit Czech influence.[7] The Austrian government likewise bristled at any suggestion of Slav nationalism, and the government censored political expression.[8] The awakeners thus concentrated on developing Czech language and culture, cultivating a broad consciousness of national identity so that, if the opportunity to assert a Czech political program arose, there would be a base of popular support.

Compared with the Czech lands, the Slovak situation in the Hungarian part of the Empire was unsupportive of the development of a strong national movement. The Slovak population was 90 percent rural[9] and suffered from famine and epidemics.[10] Hungarian industrial development lagged far behind the Austrian lands and was simply too weak to produce the type of radical social change that occurred in the Czech lands. Slovak society thus retained the pre-modern social structure of a large peasantry, entrenched nobility, and insubstantial middle class. A literate and economically independent mass public capable of supporting the Slovak national awakeners did not emerge during this period.

If the socioeconomic situation was unfavorable to national development, the political situation was much worse. In the second half of the eighteenth century, the Magyars (ethnic Hungarians) of Hungary began to develop a nationalist movement. Up to this point, the multi-ethnic nobility comprised the Hungarian nation, or *natio hungarica*. Under the influence of new currents of nationalist thought spreading from German universities, however, a more ethnic conception of nationhood gained hold.[11] This boded ill for Slovak national development. In Hungary, the Slovaks did not have the status of a "nation" with a historical tradition of political and territorial autonomy; "Slovakia" had never existed as an independent political entity. The Slovaks were thus neither recognized in the constitution nor protected as a separate group.[12] Things worsened in 1830, as the tide of "Magyarization" began to swell: in ensuing years, the scope of mandatory use of Magyar broadened until in 1843 it became the exclusive language of government, legislation, official business, and in principle public instruction.[13] Even before the movement toward a monolingual state, knowledge of Magyar had been required for upward mobility, and for Slovaks "the path to personal and social advancement was a one-way street" to Magyarization.[14] In turn, these Slovaks supported the state policy of Magyarizing their fellows.

A further challenge to Slovak national unity came from the cleavage between Catholics and Protestants. The first awakeners during Phase A were members of the Catholic intelligentsia who developed the principles of a Slovak literary language separate from Czech.[15] The Slovak Protestants, by contrast, used biblical Czech as their liturgical language, and although the Czechs had been largely re-Catholicized after their defeat by the Habsburgs in 1620, this linked the Protestant Slovaks linguistically to Czech culture. During the eighteenth century, Protestants began "to define their ethnic group as Czecho-slovak, whereas the Catholics continued to define their identity within the boundaries of Hungary."[16] A further notable difference was that Protestants were much more active in the nationalist cause, for three main reasons. They were not only more highly educated than Catholics (a larger portion of whom were peasants), but also often studied in Germany, which exposed them to the latest developments in nationalist thought.[17] Second, the state barred most Protestants from positions in the central administration, undermining their connection to Hungary. And finally, Lutherans were particularly targeted by Magyarization, increasing their sense of insecurity.[18]

While both the Czech and Slovak awakeners faced daunting challenges, the Slovaks had concern for their very survival as an ethnic community. This shaped the Slovaks' conceptions of nationhood, and it also divided them, as the following discussion will show. In exploring the five awakeners' ideas, I look first at views on the boundaries of nationhood and legitimate authority before 1848, when overt, regime-challenging political speech was restricted, and then turn to their ideas and actions during the 1848 Revolution, when such expression became possible. I begin with the Slovak "Czechoslovaks" Jan Kollár and Pavel Josef Šafařík, as they contributed strongly to both national movements, and Ľudovit Štúr, who both drew on and broke with them. I then turn to the Czechs František Palacký and Karel Havlíček.

Nation-Building Before the 1848 Revolution

Though both were Slovaks, scholars debate whether the Czech or Slovak National Revival has a greater claim to the poet Jan Kollár (1793–1852) and his colleague, scholar Pavel Josef Šafařík (1795–1861). Both attended the University of Jena, a hotbed of German nationalist thought,[19] where Herder's ideas on nationhood, and in particular his descriptions of the Slavs, captivated them.[20] They returned to Slovakia bearing this new understanding of nationhood and developed and spread it effectively, though with different methods and nuances.

Kollár took a dramatic approach, bringing nationalism to the public with "prophetic force and with a poet's vision."[21] Thousands throughout the Slavic world read his writings, the most influential of which was *Slávy dcera* (*The Daughter of Sláva*), an ecstatic epic poem that predicted that the Slavs would overthrow despotism and replace German dominance in East-Central Europe.[22] His definition of nationhood here was broad, holding that "all Slavs are One Blood, One Body, One People."[23] Within this pan-Slavic nation, he identified four "tribes" (or national subunits) with corresponding dialects: Polish, Illyrian, Russian, and Czechoslovak.[24] Kollár called on the tribes to foster national unity through intellectual and literary "reciprocity," but made clear that this did "not consist in the political unification of all Slavs or in any turbulent demagogical undertakings directed against governments or administrations; such undertakings result only in confusion and misfortune."[25] Still, his conception of nationhood did involve a notion of legitimate political authority: "The state," he argued, is "an association of several lands and various peoples under a common head; its role is protection, justice and promotion of culture among the peoples entrusted to it."[26] Following Herder, he argued that the nation, by contrast, is the natural unit of humanity, ordained by God as best for realizing human potential.[27] The nation is morally prior to the state, and "the smaller must be subordinate to the greater, nobler, love of one's country to love of one's nation."[28] Kollár thus portrayed the ethnic community as a rights-bearing entity within the state, and legitimate political authority as that which fosters its bonds. In addition, he identified four areas of life into which the state must not intrude: "a man's religion, a man's language and nationality, a man's (nation's) customs and fourthly, 'old laws' [Pynsent interprets this as customary law]."[29] The state's authority should, therefore, be limited.

Kollár also argued that the nation's members are obliged to nurture it. He noted that this service must issue from a position of intellectual freedom grounded in individual responsibility. He rejected a collectivist understanding of community that would undermine individual autonomy, as the nation is best served by the free exchange of ideas—"no writers' and scholars' aristocratism, no monopoly over literature and ideas . . . : a true national and spiritual free community."[30] Indeed, he argued, "one cannot live without individual consciousness; destroying that is the grave of all morality."[31] Finally, Kollár placed humanity at the top of his ordering of human community, famously cautioning: "Consider the nation only as a vessel of humanity/ and always when you cry 'Slav,' let the echo of your cry be 'human being.' "[32]

Though Kollár's definition of nationhood included all Slavs, he argued that reciprocity was a particularly promising project for the Czechs and Slovaks. He placed them together in the Czechoslovak tribe knowing that they were not a cohesive group, and thus sought to cultivate ties. This project was driven, at least in part, by his grim view of the Slovaks' internal resources to protect and develop their identity: "The life of the Slovaks is without history . . . a numbing emptiness and spirit-destroying wasteland prevail in their past."[33] The Czechs, by contrast, had a history of statehood until the fifteenth century, a well-established literary and scholarly tradition, and a more secure existence in the Empire, showing the potential to become an even stronger presence. Kollár's appraisal of this gulf between the Czech and Slovaks can be described, to use Anthony Smith's phrase, as a recognition of "the uneven diffusion of ethno-history."[34] Ethnohistory is not the objective compilation of historical fact, but rather "represents an amalgam of selective historical truth and idealization, with varying degrees of documented fact and political myth, stressing elements of romance, heroism and the unique, to present a stirring and emotionally intimate portrait of the community's history, constructed by, and seen from the standpoint of, successive generations of community members . . . [it includes] above all a myth of the golden age of warriors, saints and sages, which provides an inner standard for the community, an *exemplum virtutis* for subsequent emulation, and a spur and model for ethnic regeneration."[35] Smith argues that some ethnic groups have difficulty developing their ethnohistory: "Their memories are tenuous, their heroes shadowy, and their traditions, if not entangled with those of other, more powerful neighbors, are patchy and poorly documented."[36] Such, Kollár understood, was the Slovak situation. Moreover, as educated Slovaks abandoned their language, it was left dependent on poor peasants,[37] many of whom were illiterate.

Kollár thus saw union with the ethnolinguistically similar but much better situated Czechs as the Slovaks' best hope. To this end, he proposed the creation of a Czechoslovak literary language and appealed to the Czechs to recognize Slovak influences as the language developed.[38] He also argued that a common language would strengthen the Slovaks by reuniting the Catholics to "the common Czecho-Slovak trunk" that they had abandoned by attempting to develop a Slovak literary language.[39] Kollár thus staunchly opposed any further attempts to develop such a language. Most Czechs intellectuals were, however, uninterested in linguistic compromise or mutuality, and they accused him of undermining Czechoslovak unity by attempting to Slovakize the "common" literary language. Frustrated, he asked: "When the Slovaks have been willing to sacrifice everything to the Czechs with respect to the language, why then could not the Czechs give way at least a little bit to the Slovaks?"[40] In his view, the Czechs' stubborn refusal to compromise put the Slovaks in a position of "self-annihilation and unconditional Czechization."[41] Thus, while Kollár did much to develop an alliance with the Czechs, real tensions developed over the balance of Czech and Slovak influences on the "Czechoslovak" identity. As I noted at the outset, this would become an abiding element of the triadic relationship.

Kollár's friend and fellow awakener Pavel Josef Šafařík approached nation-building similarly, but was the more scholarly of the pair.[42] Two of his works were especially influential: *Geschichte der slawischen Sprache und Literatur nach allen Mundarten* (*History of the Slavic Language and Literature in All Dialects*, 1826), and *Slovanské starožitnosti* (*Slav Antiquities*, 1837), a Slav ethnography that augments the *Geschichte*.[43] In the *Geschichte*, Šafařík followed Kollár's *Slávy dcera* in asserting the idea of Slav nationhood, with a corresponding understanding of the Slav identity: "Amongst the basic characteristics of the Slav nation as a whole are: a religious frame of mind, a love of work, simple, sincere merriness, love of their native language and tolerance."[44] This formulation is almost exactly the same as Kollár's (who based his on Herder's), with a small difference in "the omission of 'towards other nations' after 'tolerance,' which serves to make the Slavs more generally libertarian or liberal."[45] He further developed his view of Slav national identity in *Slovanské starožitnosti*, writing that "in the earliest of times all Slavs were, to be sure, equal before the law and free men," and the "administration of communal matters was in the hands of the nation itself."[46] By emphasizing the democratic and liberal elements in Slav political culture, Šafařík aimed to "make the Slavs representative of the finest aims of Western society."[47]

Though Šafařík's definition of nationhood is very similar to Kollár's, he constituted it differently, separating the nation into two groups of four tribes.[48] The North Western group included the Bohemians (including Moravians) and, separately, the Slovaks. He divided the corresponding dialects into two groups of five, and in the North Western dialects included Czech and Slovak separately.[49] Unlike Kollár, then, Šafařík offered the Slovaks a distinct identity. Still, he posited a special relationship between Czech and Slovak, observing that, "for centuries in regard to literature the Slovaks for very good reason have joined in with the Czechs."[50] While he supported this position, he favored a separate status for the Slovak vernacular. As he told Kollár, "We should look more to ourselves than to the Czechs . . . I don't want to be understood, though, as demanding that the language of our people be introduced directly into books."[51] With Kollár, he believed that the Czechoslovak literary language should incorporate Slovak influences.

Unsurprisingly, the Czechs were no more sympathetic to Šafařík's perspective than to Kollár's, and he too was disappointed. In a letter to Kollár, he wrote: "The style common to Czech writers at present can never become the national style of us Slovaks,"[52] and he worried that the Czechoslovak literature would be inaccessible to the Slovak public.[53] He also wrote to Palacký that it was a "sin" to consider Czech and Slovak as identical languages.[54] Over time, however, Šafařík revised his position. After being dismissed from his job as a gymnasium director in Slovakia for being a Protestant, he took a position with the Czech nationalist organization Matice česká's journal *Časopis*. Thereafter, he became more supportive of closer ties between Slovak and Czech. This probably reflected his intimate connection with the Czech awakeners, his material dependence on them,[55] and his fear that a growing movement for Slovak linguistic separatism among the younger generation of Slovak nationalists would undermine the increasingly beleaguered Slovaks' vital links to the Czechs. This shift is evident in *Slovanské starožitnosti*, where he proposes a new, simpler understanding of the Slav nation's components, combining Bohemians, Moravians, and Slovaks into the "Czechoslovak" tribe.[56] Šafařík also contributed to a volume of essays critical of linguistic separatism, arguing that the Czech language was more developed than its Slovak relative.[57]

In order to build a foundation for national consciousness, then, Kollár and Šafařík undertook a project that involved "historical reappropriation." As Smith argues, "It is essential for any nationalist aspirations to be satisfied, that the chosen community be furnished with an adequate and authentic past. This is why the concept of 'authenticity' is so important . . . since Herder's advocacy of the idea of the original and authentic spirit of a nation, authenticity has become the litmus test for any cultural, and hence political, claims. To say that an *ethnie* lacks an authentic culture and ethno-history is to deny its claim to national recognition."[58] Building upon the cultural and linguistic ties between the Czechs and Slovaks, Kollár and Šafařík met this challenge by defining the Slovaks and Czechs as members of one grand Slav nation who also belonged to the same "tribe" and shared a "dialect" (literary Czech). This made the Slovaks heir to the ethnohistory of not only the Czechs but all Slavs.

While Šafařík and Kollár had great impact on the Slovak nationalism, their ideas also came under serious challenge by its next generation, led by Ľudovít Štúr (1815–56). A scholar of Slavic culture and history, Štúr's most dramatic departure from Šafařík and Kollár came on February 14, 1843, when he and five others decided to abandon Czech in favor of Slovak as the written language (a group of Slovak students later approved their decision).[59] In 1844, they publicly announced that Central Slovak had been chosen as the Slovak literary language,[60] after which Štúr set out to develop the grammatical principles. This decision set off a firestorm of controversy. Kollár, Šafařík, Palacký, and Havlíček, believing in both the principle and the necessity of Czechoslovak unity, reacted with anger, disappointment, and a certain amount of condescension. As Brock argues, "They all regarded the schism as an unfortunate and hopefully brief aberration on the part of a few young hotheads."[61] Kollár in particular reacted bitterly, and with Šafařík's backing gathered contributions criticizing Štúr's stance, which the Matice česká published in the 1846 volume, *Voices Concerning the Need for a Unified Literary Language for Czechs, Moravians, and Slovaks.*[62]

In response, Štúr and the group surrounding him, known as the Young Slovaks, argued that there were compelling reasons to develop a Slovak literary language. To begin, there was the question of the "Czechoslovak" language's accessibility to Slovaks. Because the Czechs refused to significantly Slovakize the Czech literary language, the Young Slovaks doubted that less educated Slovaks would be either willing or able to read publications in Czech.[63] Moreover, they were keenly aware of the Magyar threat to Slovak identity and the cooptation of the Slovak nobility, as well as the Vienna government's unwillingness or inability to help the Slovaks in their battle against Magyarization. They further expected that the power struggles between Vienna and Budapest would likely lead to some sort of dualism in the Empire, and that if so separated, the Czechs would be unable to protect the Slovaks from Hungarian authorities.[64] The Slovak split along confessional lines worked also against the use of Czech, since many Catholics associated it negatively with the Hussite Protestant Reformation.[65] National survival, the Young Slovaks concluded, required a Slovak literary language.

Beyond these considerations, Štúr's move to establish a Slovak literary language was based on his understanding of Slav nationhood. Following Kollár, Štúr posited that the Slav nation was comprised of various Slavic tribes distinguished by dialects, and drawing on Šafařík's early work, he argued that the Slovaks were distinct as a tribe with their own dialect.[66] This "peculiarity and uniqueness of language" led Štúr to argue that tribes are politically, socially, and morally unique communities,[67] as such community develops through a shared tongue. Broadly, he explained: "Every nation is most ardently coupled with its language. The nation is reflected in it as the first product of its theoretical spirit; language, is, then, the surest sign of the essence and individuality of every nation. Just like an individual human being, the nation reveals its deepest inner self through language; it, so to speak, embodies its spirit in language; this external form corresponds exactly with the inner self of the nation at all stages of its development; the spirit of the nation develops in and with the language in the form most appropriate to it: they are interdependent, and so one cannot exist without the other."[68] It would thus be a crime against any community to deprive it of its language, its spiritual lifeblood. He further argued that "Slav life is divided like a linden tree into many branches, the nation is one, but one in diversity . . . *Czech* in our nation is only the name of a part, of one tribe, for which reason the works of another tribe may not be subordinated to it as partial."[69] The Slovaks were thus entitled to recognition. Still, Štúr vigorously denied that he meant to undermine legitimate connections between the two tribes, writing: "some may even think that we want to separate from the Czechs, but God preserve us from all separation."[70]

Štúr's understanding of legitimate authority is also linked to his view of the Slovaks as a distinct community, which he developed in his influential history of Great Moravia, a Slavic state that lasted from around 833 until its defeat by the Magyars in 907. Pynsent describes this history as "consciously a literary work, intended to inspire national pride and devotion, not only to instruct Slovaks in their past; Great Moravia is in essence Slovak."[71] According to Štúr, it was also a democracy: "Who is that, staff in hand, enveloped in a thin, shabby cloak, climbing up onto a lone rock in an empty field, and what is that multitude gazing respectfully at the sturdy figure on the rock? It is their elected ruler, who must remember whence he had come and that he may go if he does not rule his people justly. And the rulers ruled the people justly and the people lauded and honoured their rulers."[72] The first of these was King Mojmir, whose baptism prompted many to willingly convert. His example was also important to subsequent rulers, for as a "caring and wise king, he ruled his people as a good family father his house."[73] Štúr thus used Great Moravia to establish a tradition of Slovak statehood (a controversial claim), providing a historical justification for Slovaks' demands that the state recognize them as a nation. It also provided a model of good government, in which the ruler is elected and accountable to the people, but is also a patriarchal figure.

Štúr's history also included Great Moravia's fall to the Magyars. After their defeat, the Slovaks set to work teaching the Magyars how to farm and build houses. Though the Magyars had a hard time adjusting to such a life, "the Slovaks restrained them from pillage and showed what they had gained from the womb of the land by their toil, telling them that they would do this well if they became accustomed to work, and thus by their example did they give them courage."[74] The Slovaks also converted the Magyars to Christianity. Štúr thus cast the Slovaks as the civilizers of the Magyars, overall, something of a thankless task: "because the Slovaks excelled the Magyars thus and had gained greater riches than they through their industry, envy began to awaken in Magyars who were angry that they were unable to equal the Slovaks in intellect or property. And these envious people began to invent all manner of calumny on the Slovaks and to consider how they could excel the Slovaks; when nothing occurred to them, their hatred grew and increased."[75] Thus, by the early nineteenth century, relations between the peoples had soured significantly.

In defining Slovak national identity, then, Štúr contrasted the civilized Slovaks with their oppressors and cultural inferiors, the "barbarian" Magyars. He also compared Western Europeans unfavorably with Slavs: "In the West we see this preoccupation with the material, personal interest, as if that were the fulfillment of everything, not just an aid or means to life. . . . In contrast to that, we see among the nations of Eastern Europe stimulation to higher concerns, spiritual concerns."[76] He further observed that "among the Slavs, the individual as individual cannot love only for himself, but he serves the true commonality."[77] Pynsent argues that this makes them "natural collectivists."[78] Štúr further developed this view of individualism in a discussion of the differences between Germanic and Slav love: "Among Germanic peoples a family comes into existence when two human beings fall in love; and their goal is self-satisfaction; when these two people attain inner satisfaction, they leave their families and found a new one. This is quite different from the way Slav families are founded: among our peoples the oldest member of the family has the power to betrothe . . . [in comparison to romantic love] Slav love is quite another thing; it is *contentment in the family circle*, in that natural moral bond. Not one person's satisfaction in another person, but in the family."[79] Moreover, he argued that Slovak lyric verse is the most developed among Slavonic verse because Slovak love "is not for individuals, but is inclined toward the family."[80] Underlying Štúr's anti-individualism, then, is both the moral authority of the family as a community and the natural authority of the "oldest member of the family" over the other members. Indeed, the first of the three essential virtues that Štúr demanded of the Slavs was obedience: "Anyone who wishes to be a Slav must learn obedience—like our national heroes."[81] Overall, this portrayal stands in striking contrast to Kollár and Šafařík's emphasis on the essential moral worth of individual freedom and on the harmony between Slavic and Western European values.

Ultimately, Štúr's project shared with his elders the goal of authenticating Slovak identity. His approach, however, offered the Slovaks their own ethno-history, as well as their own linguistic identity. Smith argues, "authenticity and dignity are the hallmarks of every aspect of ethnic culture, not just its ethno-history. Of these the best known and most important is language, since it so clearly marks off those who speak it from those who cannot and because it evokes a sense of immediate expressive intimacy among its speakers."[82] Language thus provided Štúr a strong basis for justifying Slovak distinctiveness. It also marked the contours of a divide between the Slovak awakeners that involved both principled and strategic differences.

These differences also characterize the divide between the Young Slovaks and the Czech awakeners, who allied themselves with Kollár and Šafařík on the issue of a common language (though, clearly, not to their Slovak colleagues' satisfaction) and were also similarly liberal. Most prominent among these Czechs, and Štúr's counterpart in national "fatherhood," is František Palacký (1798–1876). Born in a Moravian village, Palacký attended the Protestant lycée in Bratislava, gaining a familiarity with the Slovak situation uncommon among Czechs at the time.[83] He subsequently moved to Prague, and in 1829 the Diet appointed him Historiographer of the Bohemian Estates. In this role he "contributed more than anyone else to the cultural reawakening of Czech historical and political consciousness."[84]

The state of Czech historiography at this point was depressing: "what remained to the Czechs of their past literature and history, especially of the proud Hussite period, had been thoroughly denationalized by the Jesuit counter-reformers and the Enlightened Despots who followed them."[85] Palacký spurred re-nationalization with his ten-volume life's work, *Dějiny národu českého* (*The History of the Czech Nation*), which sought to combine objective historiography with a nationalist message,[86] developing a philosophy of Czech history and a corresponding conception of national identity. It was, then, quintessential ethnohistory.

The *History* is centrally concerned with the conflicts between Czechs and Germans and between Rome and the Reformation, which Palacký depicted as interrelated.[87] In exploring these, he focused particularly on the history of the Protestant reformer Jan Hus (1369–1415) and the Hussites. He held this as the Czechs' greatest period, arguing that its two central ideological themes were nationality (*národnost*) and the relationship between those in authority and their subjects.[88] At its crux was the question of the source of legitimate authority. The Hussites, he argued, concluded that the Catholic Church did not fit this description. Still, they found that "even the freest society needs authority. The authority of family, parish or state is inadequate; only religion and *národnost* can supply such authority."[89] Palacký illustrated the nation's authority through two further developments during this period: the intensifying conflict between the Czechs and the Germans (with "the Germans representing authority"), and the beginnings of Panslavism, as the Hussites allied themselves with various other Slavs, including the Slovaks, or "Hungarian Slavs."[90] As Palacký interpreted these interactions, the Hussites' questioning of authority not only led to religious reforms but also fundamentally redefined the individual's relationship to the collective. On the one hand, the individual was freed from servitude to illegitimate authority; on the other, he was more strongly bound to both the legitimate authority of the nation's collective conscience and the broader community of fraternal nations. Ultimately, as Barbara Reinfeld argues, though the Hussite Revolution was defeated and Hus burned at the stake as a heretic, Palacký found that "the Hussites and the Czech Brethren, who followed them, had foreshadowed the future Reformation and Enlightenment of the West, and they had initiated the process of freeing the human spirit. In spite of repeated repression, the defense of freedom and the establishment of a more humane society remained the Czechs' historical mission."[91]

While Palacký did much to develop and augment Czech ethnohistory, its foundations were strong, particularly with regard to Hus and the Hussite period. His interpretation of the fifteenth-century Hussite battles as a revolution against German and Catholic authoritarianism resonated with a population that had been forcibly re-Catholicized as recently as the seventeenth century and lived with German dominance on a daily basis. This history anchored his interpretation of the Czech political tradition as privileging individual freedom and rejecting authoritarianism, and also justified a special relationship to the West.

Palacký's work differs from Šafařík's and Kollár's in that it focused on the *Czech* nation, not the broader Slavic world. This is not to say that he was unconcerned by the Czech-Slovak relationship; indeed, during the 1848 Revolution, he sought to strengthen it (I return to this below). Still, his heroes are specifically Czech, and his work is not outward-reaching in the way the Slovak Czechoslovaks' studies and poems were. Moreover, while Protestant Slovaks could conceivably share in his celebration of Hussitism, this was entirely unlikely for Slovak Catholics, roughly two-thirds of the Slovak population. His work's potential to support an inclusive and cohesive Czechoslovak identity was, therefore, questionable, to put it mildly. But, in contrast to Šafařík and Kollár, this was not a central aim of his project.

The final of the five awakeners, the journalist Karel Havlíček (1820–56), belonged with Štúr to the younger generation. As a student in Prague, Enlightenment philosophy fascinated him. In 1840, he entered the Archbishop's Seminary, but became disillusioned with the Catholic Church and turned to "a firm rationalism with strong anti-clerical overtones."[92] He remained in Prague to study independently and became friends with Šafařík. In 1845, he wrote a review of a nationalist romance by Josef Kajetán Tyl, a very popular Czech writer of the time (who also authored the words of the National Anthem), which brought him into the public eye. Titled *Posledni čech* (*The Last Czech*), the novel had won popular and critical acclaim, including an award for excellence from the Matice česká. Havlíček, however, found its nationalism superficial and its writing overblown.[93] He argued that Tyl's sentimental style was typical of Czech nationalist literature and that its idealization of the past reflected an unhealthy German influence.[94] Observing that it would be easier to die for one's country than to read its literature,[95] he called on nationalists to move beyond emotional reveries and to act purposefully, educating the nation.

Havlíček's bold critique of Tyl's novel and the state of Czech nationalist literature in general ignited a debate over its merits, drawing in both the nationalist community and the broader Czech reading public. Palacký in particular was impressed and suggested him as editor for the political journal *Pražské noviny* and its literary supplement. From the start, Havlíček sought to educate the nation by not only reporting on newsworthy political issues, but also by explaining various concepts of liberal democracy, such as popular sovereignty, constitutionalism, equality, the rule of law, and the rights and duties of individuals and nations. A good example is a series of articles titled "*Co je obec?*" ("What Is a Community?"). Here, he argued that the origins of community lie in the voluntary association of individuals who, having found themselves unable to survive in the state of nature independently, joined together to gain security through the creation of a common good.[96] "In such a situation," he wrote, "each man knew the laws, his own duties and rights."[97] He continued:

> On the other hand, when people live in a community without participating in its affairs, they do not usually know its government and they are not citizens in the true sense. The end result we know full well. People become interested exclusively in their own property; they live for themselves alone, and they cheat the state at every opportunity because they consider it their enemy. Such people have no notion of a civic spirit. When this is lacking no one will undertake anything for the common good, the good of anyone other than himself, and when employed as a public servant a man will do the minimum that he thinks the state requires of him. . . .But in a community where citizens rule themselves, the people know the laws and customs of the town, they know their duty, and there a civic spirit reigns. Here people are willing to sacrifice of their time and talent for the community at large, because they know that the benefits of any enterprise will be shared by all.[98]

Havlíček's understanding of the properly ordered community clearly reflects the influence of Western liberal political theory. In contrast to the more Romantic nationalists, and particularly to Kollár and Štúr, who portrayed the nation as God-given and sacred, Havlíček's account of the origins of community emphasizes the rational individual self-interest. Like the other awakeners, he opposed selfish individualism and supported sacrifice for the common good, but unlike them, he based this obligation less on the moral priority of the nation or pride in its glorious past and future than on its necessity for realizing a rational civic culture. His understanding of good government was thus based on his view of universal qualities in human nature rather than on a belief that the Slavs are naturally democratic or on Palacký's vision of the Czech religio-historical mission.

Another point of disagreement between Havlíček and his fellow nationalists concerned the boundaries of the nation. His travels in Russia and Poland convinced him to oppose the idea of a Slav nation, given the cultural and political differences he found among Slavs, as well as their frequent history as each other's enemies.[99] He thus declared, "With great national pride I say, 'I am a Czech,' but never, 'I am a Slav!'"[100] He did, however, share his peers' view of the Czech-Slovak relationship and joined the crusade against Štúr's linguistic separatism, fearing that the Czechs would not realize the extent and importance of the separation in time to prevent an irreparable split: "Then we will look around ourselves in pain; our numbers will seem to us scanty before our powerful and inimical neighbors, and we will yearningly stretch out our arms to Slovakia; but perhaps it will be too late if we neglect [to take action at] this decisive time."[101] Thus, he considered the political and cultural cooperation of the Czechs and Slovaks strategically necessary, given their position in the Empire. Overall, his vision was more practical and less mythic than his colleagues', and when the Revolutionary Period of 1848 began and the freedom of the press was declared, he, along with the other awakeners, leapt into political action.

The Revolutionary Period of 1848

In March 1848, events in Vienna and Budapest brought down the Metternich government and set into motion a political revolution that swept through the Empire. Palacký observed that the Vienna government had brought the crisis upon itself: "For many years it misunderstood or refused to understand the only possible moral basis for its existence: the principle of equal rights and privileges for all the nationalities and creeds united under its rule."[102] Despite the Empire's past mistakes, Palacký believed that reform was possible and necessary, and proposed a federation of equal nations under the rubric of "Austro-Slavism." He worked to build support for this plan at a June Congress of all the Empire's Slavs (Šafařík gave a rousing opening address there that many considered a high point of the event).[103] Palacký's central argument for Austro-Slavism was that alone, none of the Empire's Slavic groups were strong enough to force concessions, but together, they could overcome Magyar and German dominance. He encountered resistance, however, from Štúr's camp because he proposed the political union of the Czechs and Slovaks within the federation. This stance, combined with the growing Slovak support for linguistic separatism, frustrated Palacký and his allies; focusing on similarities in their status as repressed minorities within the Empire, Palacký argued that "what was needed. . . was unity and a common front of opposition, not particularism and independent solutions."[104]

For his part, Havlíček moved quickly to start a new, independent newspaper called *Národní noviny*, whose purpose was to "defend democracy. We define this as full equality of nations and individuals within each nation."[105] The paper became very popular, especially with the middle class. He also joined Palacký in advocating specific reforms within an Austro-Slav framework, advocating "everything positive that the American 'model' could offer—especially since, in his view, democracy of the American type was the best safeguard against the danger of revolution and socialism."[106] He was, however, less conservative than Palacký and called for a unicameral house elected through universal male suffrage, proportional representation, and the abolition of all class distinctions (though of middle class background himself, Palacký favored retaining some noble privileges and larger representation for cities, where the intelligentsia lived).[107] In response, the broader public, including not only intellectuals, but also the middle and working classes and the peasantry, supported the assertion of the democratic, nationalist Czech political program. During the Revolution, then, Czech nationalism became a mass movement.

That fall, both Palacký and Šafařík were delegates to the Kroměříž Diet (in Moravia, where the Vienna Reichstag was moved temporarily),[108] which sought to draft a new, liberal constitution. Proposals (largely shaped by Palacký) included a definition of sovereignty as proceeding entirely "from the people," not "from the Monarch."[109] Despite resistance from Slovak leaders, it was also proposed that an administrative unit combine Bohemia, Moravia,

Silesia and Slovakia (the Moravians and Silesian delegates protested this as well).[110] The proposed constitutional changes would thus have quite radically redefined both the source of political authority and its exercise.

For the Slovak nationalists, the "Spring of Peoples" brought even more dramatic events. As the Revolution began, the Magyar nobility, under the leadership of Lajos Kossuth, declared that it intended "to create an entirely Magyar state."[111] Štúr and the Young Slovaks reacted by organizing resistance. In April 1848, they drafted the "The Demands of the Slovak Nation," which included "recognition and guarantee of national identity; the transformation of Hungary into a state composed of equal nations, each with its own parliament and equal representation in the Hungarian Diet; and the use of Slovak in all Slovak county offices," as well as universal, equal suffrage and the complete abolition of serfdom.[112] In response, the Hungarian government issued arrest warrants for Štúr and his close colleagues.

Things developed rapidly thereafter. On September 16, Štúr and these colleagues founded the Slovak National Council, which Kirschbaum calls "the first modern Slovak political institution."[113] Three days later, the Council declared that Slovakia had separated from Hungary and called the Slovak nation to rise up. A series of military clashes between Hungarian and Slovak nationalist forces followed, but many Slovaks—particularly Catholics—remained indifferent, and peasants largely joined the Hungarian forces instead of following the Slovak leaders.[114] This reflected the lack of a broad national consciousness, whose spread before the Revolution had been impeded by ethnic repression and the lack of socioeconomic modernization in the Slovak areas. Indeed, though they were targeted as beneficiaries, Štúr's democratic and egalitarian Slovak held little appeal to the peasants. As Hroch argues: "It was in particular patriarchal relations and the patriarchal mode of thought which gave to the peasants a system of values in which there was only a place for national demands in so far as they had the character, in appearance or in reality, of a defense of patriarchal relations. The patriarchal colouring of peasant patriotism naturally conserved within itself strong features of a feudal patriotism to which the ideas of civil equality and social progress were alien, and in which there continued to exist relics of racial xenophobia."[115] Štúr's definition of Slovak national identity did reflect some elements of such peasant patriarchal values, particularly with regard to his definition of legitimate authority and the relationship of the individual to the collective. Still, it failed to fuel a mass movement during or shortly after the Revolution, and though the nationalists fought with some success, they were ultimately defeated.

The broader "Spring of Peoples" was likewise quashed. In March 1849, the emperor dissolved the Kroměříž Diet,[116] and repressive, absolutist rule ensued for the entire decade of the 1850s. Most nationalists refocused their efforts on cultural development. Havlíček, however, continued publishing. Arguing that both liberal constitutionalism and national rights remained the Czechs' chief goals, he wrote, "we do not want nationality without freedom, nor liberty without nationality, since the two cannot really be separated."[117] These writings "became part of the so-called 'freedom literature' that was circulated by the common people throughout the country."[118] Soon, however, authorities exiled him to Brixen in the Tyrol, where he contracted tuberculosis and died in 1856 at the age of thirty-five. Five thousand people joined in the funeral procession. He thus became a national hero, symbolizing the struggle for freedom against illegitimate authority.

Years later, Palacký wrote that while the Revolutions of 1848 were animated by the same spirit in the East and West, France "had no problem of nationality to be solved. What was at stake there were political and civil liberties. And in this realm, liberalism was victorious. But in those empires composed of various peoples, the question of national liberty was paramount."[119] In assessing the priorities of reform, then, he placed the nation over the individual, in contrast to Havlíček's view of their equal entitlement. Ultimately, Vienna's stubborn refusal to grant equal rights to the empire's nationalities led Palacký to conclude that the empire would not exist much longer. He also held fast to the belief that the Czech nation would survive its fall, expressed in his famous statement: "We were here before there ever was an Austria, and we shall be after she has passed."[120]

Conclusion

These five awakeners set out to develop principled conceptions of the ethnonational community that would be taken up by, and sustain, its members. Their projects had much in common: all were democrats, viewing both the individual and the ethnonational community (defined as nation or tribe) as rights-bearing entities. The careful political-philosophical and historical foundations they laid to justify these rights would, indeed, become central to future Czech and Slovak understandings of nationhood, as following chapters will show. To the extent that the Czechs' and Slovaks' political futures would be bound up together, they also laid groundwork for principled conflict. Štúr's anti-individualism stood in tension with the others' emphasis on individual freedom and generally Western orientation, and his view of the distinctiveness of Slovak identity was difficult (perhaps impossible) to reconcile with the "Czechoslovak" idea. Furthermore, the Czechs' refusal to draw on Slovak influences in building this purported joint identity frustrated even their staunchest Slovak allies. Palacký's emphasis on the centrality of the anti-Catholic Hussite period in Czech history—especially for defining the nature of legitimate authority—was also certainly unacceptable as a pillar of identity for Catholic Slovaks, though during the mid-nineteenth century they remained largely politically unengaged, and so the issue was not yet pressing. Within the Czech camp, as well, there was disagreement over the relative priority of individual rights and collective national rights, but because they ultimately won recognition of neither, they did not need to fully confront this problem during this period.

By the end of the "Spring of Peoples," then, there were clearly discernable tensions between the awakeners' perspectives. This was largely a disagreement among intellectuals; both the Slovak Czechoslovaks and the Young Slovaks had yet to move the masses, and regime repression blocked political action from any side. The potential for both their ideas and the accompanying disagreements to become *lastingly* relevant to the broader Czech and Slovak publics—in other words, to become part of political culture—depended on the reopening of political space for nationalist agitation and on the reasons *why* Czechs and Slovaks were, in fact, mobilized by them. I turn to these concerns in the following chapter.

CHAPTER TWO

Nation-Building in the Empire's Waning Years

THOUGH THE SPRING of Peoples ended unhappily for the Czech and Slovak awakeners, as the nineteenth century progressed their movements gained ground. The Czechs flourished and the Slovaks struggled, but by the outbreak of World War I national consciousness had taken solid (if, in the Slovak case, uneven) root in both nations. In this chapter, I investigate three key aspects of this development, looking at the continuities between these increasingly diffused and politically activated views of nationhood and those of the awakeners developed in the preceding period (and chapter), the ways these views evolved under the influence of new leaders and circumstances, and the reasons why during this time very substantial numbers of people adopted the identities proffered by nationalist leaders and became mobilized in the national community's support.

Normative orientations toward nationhood tend to be resilient over time in part because they reflect culturally embedded self-understandings that people also often accept in a principled way, in that they have a reasoned (and not just reflexive) view of the norms as legitimate. Broadly speaking, shifting power-political and economic interests are not the *primary* factors defining the content and appeal of understandings of nationhood (though on an individual basis, this may well be the case). To show this, my analysis of this period engages with a materialist account of the development and diffusion of national consciousness by the highly regarded Czech Marxist scholar Miroslav Hroch. This is illuminating not only because Hroch's analysis is targeted to the cases at hand and richly historically informed, but also because it does an excellent job of identifying the factors whose *relative* importance I seek to challenge.

I compare the influence of Hroch's material interests with the influence both of the principles developed by the awakeners, as interpreted by succeeding generations of national political leaders, *and* of the traditional Catholic norms used by Slovak clerical-nationalists to draw the Slovak peasants into the national movement for the first time in the latter part of the nineteenth century. I find that while Hroch's factors often constituted important considerations in the formulation of political positions, national leaders drew very substantially on *already existing* traditions of national-political and religious thought to ground and justify their demands for democratization and national rights and to mobilize the broader populations in their support. Their articulation and interpretation of these values and principles served to broaden the base for, further define, and anchor the triad of orientations whose early development was traced in the preceding chapter, and which would go on to shape Czech and Slovak politics for more than a century to come. Thus, neither material considerations nor political competition specific to this period *produced* the normative frameworks for these demands in the way that Hroch (and, more broadly, the instrumentalist school, which broadly shares his central premises) suggests. I begin, then, with an introduction to Hroch's theory.

Hroch's theory

Hroch defines the nation as a social group based on relationships between individuals who share a common consciousness of national identity and membership. Such groups only develop under certain conditions;[1] not every ethnic group in Europe developed into a modern nation. In analyzing the factors that allowed some movements to reach the stage of mass mobilization, Hroch argues that "the determination of class and group interests is an important guide to the motives behind the individual attitudes of people who belong to this or that class or group."[2] Nationalism's capacity to mobilize and its central ideas can thus be explained by studying the movement's relationships to particular classes and groups, which must, in turn, be studied in their broader political, economic, and social context.

Hroch argues that in nineteenth-century Central and Eastern Europe there were four key ingredients for national movements to gain a mass following. First, both the bourgeoisie and the peasantry had to join.[3] Second, social mobility was necessary to allow an elite capable of national leadership to develop. Third, communication links were needed to spread nationalist ideas. And finally, there had to be "the conflict of material interests," and, in particular, "nationally relevant conflicts of interest," meaning that they occur between classes and groups that are *also* divided by linguistic, and sometimes religious, differences.[4] Such reinforcing "conflicts of interest were articulated not (or not only) at the social and political level appropriate to them but at the level of national categories and demands."[5] Hroch's examples include conflicts between large-scale producers of a dominant nation and small-scale producers of a subject nation, barriers to upward social mobility for those who refuse to assimilate to the dominant identity, and the conflict between the principle of civic equality and Estate privileges guarded by the dominant nation. In Hroch's view, nationalism's articulation and defense of such material interests, rather than its relationship to such "super-structural attributes" as history, culture, and language,[6] is the core of its appeal.

Hroch further argues that Eastern European nationalism's political content developed in three stages: substitution, participation, and secession.[7] The first stage, substitution, occurred when regimes repressed political activity, prompting nationalists to focus on constructing linguistic and cultural demands and a national mythology. The second stage, participation, followed the introduction of constitutional government and involved demands to participate in legislative, judicial, and executive institutions at both the local and state level. In areas where the subject nationality constituted the majority, but was under-represented in political bodies, the nationalists responded "by demanding a reform of electoral laws: democracy entered into their political programmes."[8] With the push for such reform, the balance of power within the nationalist movement would shift from the previously dominant conservatives to more democratic leaders. Hroch notes that "this trend was especially strong in those national movements where the only way towards participation for the non-dominant ethnic group was to give political rights to lower social classes—that is, to support the concept of democracy."[9] Finally, during the secession stage, the national movement attempted to gain political autonomy. In most cases, actual independence was not a goal until external factors, such as World War I, weakened the political system.

Because successful nationalist movements had to draw in the bourgeoisie *and* the peasantry, the nationalist program needed not only to be democratic, but also to convincingly represent and defend the key material interests of both. This was a challenge. The middle class, as a product of social and economic change, was likely to support demands for national self-determination, civic equality, social mobility, and political rights. The peasantry, with its patriarchal value system, frequently found such projects alienating. Over time, however, the peasants' perspective drew closer to that of the middle class, as their emancipation combined with increased social communication and mobility to broaden their cultural and economic horizons. In particular, Hroch argues that the peasants required "a definite level of education, enough to allow them to grasp the connection between national ideology and their own material interests. A special place among these educational requirements was occupied by the necessity for secularization of the peasants' conception of society, their liberation from the domination of a religious ideology."[10]

In sum, Hroch finds that the nationalist orientation toward democracy results from strategic considerations in the struggle for participation in a constitutional system—in other words, from power-political considerations, and that nationalism appeals to the masses because it articulates and defends, in national terms, their material interests. I now explore whether these expectations are borne out in the Czech and Slovak cases, looking also at the role played by the "super-structural" factors I hold to be primary.

The Czech Lands

In 1860, the Habsburg emperor issued the "October Diploma," introducing limited constitutional rule that allowed nationalities to establish political parties. Under the leadership of Palacký and his son-in-law František Rieger, the Czechs founded the Czech National Party. It demanded equal civil rights for all "races," freedom of the press, and "national freedom," meaning that "our people be treated with the honor and consideration due to it as a historic nation," meaning one with a history of prior independent statehood.[11] At its inception, the party was a middle- and upper-middle-class organization, representing the traditional wellspring of Czech nationalism. In January 1861, however, Palacký and Rieger forged an alliance with the Bohemian great landowners, based on a common vision of historically based Bohemian state-rights.

The new Czech National Party faced a hostile environment in the Austrian political system. Seton-Watson describes the parliament as "a pretentious sham"[12] with an "artificial German majority,"[13] and in 1863 the Czechs withdrew from it in protest of increased centralization and government refusal to acknowledge Bohemian state rights. The abstention lasted sixteen years, during which the Czechs had very limited political influence.

Though National Party discipline was fairly strong during the 1860s, contention over several aspects of its program gradually increased within its ranks. First, the party's alliance with the great landowners was controversial.[14] Second, some argued that national autonomy should derive not from a grant from the crown, but from the nation's natural right to cultural development and political autonomy. They also argued that state rights declarations should include demands for extended manhood suffrage and civil liberties.[15] Finally, some challenged the wisdom of passive resistance. These disagreements reflected socioeconomic differences: upper-middle-class scholars, lawyers, landowners, and businessmen tended to take a more conservative position, while the middle-class farmers, small-town businessmen, and journalists were more liberal and activist.[16]

In September 1874, party discipline finally collapsed and a number of more liberal Czechs reentered the Bohemian Diet. That December, this wing broke away and founded a new party called the Young Czechs. The National Party was thereafter usually called the Old Czechs, although the members of the two parties did not differ widely in age.[17] In their program, the Young Czechs pledged themselves to educate the nation, to actively participate in politics, to pursue state rights, national equality, and universal suffrage, and to increase popular participation in national and political affairs.[18] Identifying these principles with Havlíček's political philosophy, the party claimed status as his heir. Bruce Garver argues that this identification served three key purposes. First, Havlíček provided the party with a symbol "comparable in stature to the Old Czech mentor, František Palacký."[19] Second, Havlíček was a role model for the many journalists in the party who regularly confronted heavy-handed government interference. And third, more than any other awakener, Havlíček stood for the principles of universal manhood suffrage, the separation of church and state, and the protection of civil liberties, the three issues which most distinguished the Young Czechs from the Old Czechs.[20] We see here, then, an explicit and principled continuity between a key awakener and an important segment of the next generation of Czech political leaders, as well as a political division that flowed directly from political-philosophical differences between two awakeners (the more liberal Havlíček and the more conservative Palacký).

In breaking away from the National Party, the Young Czechs opened the door to a national multiparty system, a development that reflected the increasing diversity and modernity of Czech society. In 1869, the Czechs had gained control of their own school system, and by 1882 they had their own Czech-language branch of Charles University in Prague. Literacy rates, social mobility, and democratic national consciousness (strongly imbued in the schools) all continued to increase. These, combined with urbanization, population growth, and industrialization, produced a modern class structure, and those working in agriculture became better known as farmers than as peasants. Civil society flourished as the Czechs founded a vast network of cultural, professional, and political associations. Many of these had a nationalist bent, for example, the Sokols, a gymnastic society inspired by Havlíček's vision in which physical exercises were supplemented by "intellectual drill in the ethics of citizenship."[21] The opulent National Theatre in Prague was also a source of great pride, as it was built during the period with popular funds. Thus, by the later nineteenth century Czech society could offer substantial support to groups and associations representing its various interests.

In turn, the political spectrum continued to diversify, and the year 1890 marked a major shift in the balance of national power. The impetus was the Vienna Compromise, an agreement the Old Czechs made with the Bohemian Germans, offering them significant concessions.[22] When its terms became public, it prompted widespread anger and a sweeping Young Czech electoral victory in 1891. Riding on the wave of nationalist fervor, they pushed for franchise expansion and other progressive reforms. Partial success came in 1896, when the franchise was extended to 3.5 million new voters.[23] This victory came at a price, however, as the Young Czechs thereafter lost ground to the Social Democratic and Agrarian Parties.

It is worth noting here the appearance of another party whose influence was limited, but whose leader, Tomáš Garrigue Masaryk, would go on to become the "father" of Czechoslovakia. He founded the Czech People's (Realist) Party in 1900 (it was reorganized as the Czech Progressive Party in 1906, restating the Realist principles in its program). A professor of philosophy at Charles University, Masaryk's own political thought strongly influenced the party's orientation. As a student, he had studied the work of Herder and its interpretation by Kollár, Šafařík, Palacký, and Havlíček (as well as further key awakeners Dobrovský, Jungmann and the philosopher Augustin Smetana). Masaryk wrote that "In Palacký's historical works I found a reasoned philosophical justification for the Palacký political program along with his conception of the Czech question and his appreciation of the Czech Reformation and humanitarian ideal."[24] Following this key awakener, Masaryk saw the Hussite period as decisive for the Czech national mission, and defined its key achievement as the location of legitimate religious authority in the individual conscience (drawing on the Christian Bible) rather than in the Catholic Church. He further saw the Hussites' ideals as animating the Czech National Awakening, observing that "men like Kollár, Palacký, Šafařík are direct descendants of the Bohemian Brethren [Hussites]"[25]; indeed, "the so-called rebirth of our people was thus a historical process of re-Protestantization, a continuation of the ideas of our Reformation."[26] It was, in this sense, a reaction against Catholicism, which made people "subject to authority. The people are used to being led and they want to be led, and they do not know how to lead themselves."[27] Masaryk was also profoundly influenced by Havlíček's liberal political philosophy, and observed, "I kept finding he had written nearly everything I wanted to say about politics."[28] This is apparent in Masaryk's rejection of collectivism and his argument that "the body politic becomes legitimate when it is established, not by a collective or general will, but by the individual will of individual people, to each of whom it leaves that sacred sphere of right without which obedience is unfree."[29] Finally, Masaryk, whose father was Slovak and mother Czech, drew on the awakeners' view of the close relationship between the two. Thus, Masaryk's political philosophy incorporated the awakeners' ideas about nationhood in a principled and considered way.

Reflecting Masaryk's political thought, then, the Realist and then Progressive programs called for the strengthening of civil liberties and civic equality (including women's suffrage), as well as the natural (rather than historical) rights of the nation. The 1900 program included the Slovaks as part of "our nation," and though it did not call for unification, it did "demand full nationality protection for the Slovaks and for all non-Magyar nations."[30] It also identified clericalism as its "main philosophical enemy"[31]—a core view of Masaryk's that would have significant implications when the Czechs and predominantly Catholic Slovaks set up their common state.

Masaryk (with the help of the Social Democrats) was elected to Parliament in 1907 and 1911, but the Realist/Progressive parties were not especially popular. In particular, many in the Catholic clergy were hostile to him, and one leaflet accused him of being "a candidate for the Jews who wished to fling religion out of the schools. Once a German, he now pretends to be a Czech. He sided with Hilsner the Jew and brought disgrace on the whole Czech nation."[32] This last accusation referred to Masaryk's 1899 defense of a poor Jewish man accused of murdering a Czech girl, based on the libelous superstition that Jews need the blood of a Christian to make the Passover bread. After Hilsner was convicted and sentenced to death, Masaryk published a pamphlet that pointed out serious mistakes in the prosecution's forensic analysis. Though this drew the ire of many nationalists, Hilsner was granted a new trial and the prosecution was prohibited from arguing the blood libel as the motive. Masaryk's involvement in the case raised his profile internationally,[33] and in ensuing years he worked to cultivate relationships both with influential political leaders abroad and with the Czech immigrant community in the United States.[34] Few other Czech politicians did this, and it laid crucial groundwork for his leadership of post–World War I Czechoslovakia.

During the Empire's waning years, however, Masaryk was one among many political leaders competing on an increasingly diversified playing field. The movement toward more specialized representation of interests did not, however, preclude cooperation among Czech parties. In 1905, the Social Democrats began agitating for universal male suffrage. The movement grew rapidly, drawing the Czech nationalist and Social Democratic parties together, as each sought to draw on the other's strengths and support bases. This was a particularly important step for the Social Democrats, as for some time there had been conflict between the leadership's upper levels, which emphasized internationalist socialist ideals, and the local leaders, who actively and successfully encouraged nationalist activity among the workers. By this point, however, the socialists knew that their best chances for success lay in appealing to nationalist sentiments and invoking the interests of the entire nation.[35] As a result of this cooperation, the Czech middle class, students, and workers demonstrated together, and victory came in December 1906, when universal male suffrage for the lower house of Parliament was adopted in the Austrian half of the monarchy.

Over the last fifty years of the Habsburg Empire, then, Czech nationalism became more inclusive, egalitarian, and participatory. As Leff argues, it is "possible to speak of a 'democratization' of nationalism in the national revivals of the nineteenth century, at least insofar as the 'people' rather than a narrow elite was increasingly perceived as the proper repository of national sovereignty."[36] The path of this development conforms in important ways with Hroch's expectations, and there is no reason to argue that material interests were unimportant, as the trend toward democratization benefited both the power-political interests of the more liberal nationalists (at least initially, before the rise of class-based parties) and the economic interests of their middle and lower class supporters.

At the same time, the nationalist political programs of the later nineteenth century were clearly strongly influenced by the frameworks of principle that the awakeners developed *before* the introduction of constitutional rule. Palacký, an awakener himself, personally shaped the Old Czech orientation, and the Young Czechs directly invoked Havlíček's political ideals. Moreover, the ideological differences between conservatives and liberals on questions of civic equality (especially the privileges of the nobility, the structuring of representation, and the proper extent of the franchise) can already be seen in disagreement on theses issues between Havlíček and Palacký in 1848. These orientations could not, then, have been entirely and straightforwardly *produced by* political party competition. Thus, a focus such as Hroch's on the "the coordinates of power-competition,"[37] leading to the conclusion that political conflict leads to ideological content, offers at best an incomplete picture, as it leaves aside the influence of a political-philosophical tradition that preceded this competition. Moreover, even after the Czech political spectrum had diversified to the point that specifically class- and economic-based parties dominated, these parties felt the need to appeal to nationalist principles to sustain mass support. If material interests were in fact primary, this would seem an unnecessary complication of an otherwise winning message. At the very least, it indicates that nationalist principles had, in themselves, gained legitimacy among the broader population and were relevant to political choices.

All this is by no means to suggest that the Czech nationalists' democratic principles were unrelated to power politics and material interests; quite the opposite. Democracy is about structuring power, and it counts the negotiation of competing material interests among its concerns. It is, rather, to argue that the fact that material and power-political interests of many elites and the broader populations were served well by democracy and civil equality is not evidence that the former were *driving* the latter. Many Czechs likely supported democracy both because it benefited them and because they considered it just and proper; material interest and principle could be mutually reinforcing. And finally, given the concerted effort to politically socialize children according to broadly supported democratic and nationalist norms, it seems clear that they had become part of the broader Czech political culture by the time the Empire fell.

The Slovak Experience

Like the Czechs, Slovak nationalists used the 1860 October Diploma as an entryway into politics. A crucial first step was a meeting in the town of Turčiansky

Svätý Martin, where they produced the Memorandum of the Slovak Nation. Drawing on the awakeners' thought, its authors wrote: "We consider nations as moral personalities of mankind; through nations, even though they may vary in form, mankind advances to its own destiny, that is, to perfection."[38] They further declared that "the recognition of national individuality is the first requirement of national equality, the cornerstone of the constitutional structure, which can be built solidly and permanently only on a natural, Divine Providence-given basis for the welfare and benefit of our entire country."[39] On this philosophical foundation, the Memorandum demanded for the Slovak nation "equal rights with the Magyars, the recognition of their national individuality by law, the formation of a North Hungarian Slovak District, Slovak as the official language of administration of this district, a Slovak Academy of Law and a chair of Slavonic studies in Pest, and the repeal of all Hungarian laws that infringed on the principles of the equality of the nationalities."[40]

The Slovaks submitted the Memorandum to the President of the Parliament, but nothing ultimately came of it. Undeterred, they continued their efforts to gain national rights and recognition. They succeeded in some respects, particularly in the field of education: in 1862 three Slovak *gymnazia* were opened (one Catholic and two Lutheran). The next year, with a 1,000 gold florin donation from the emperor, the cultural society Matica slovenská was opened in Turčiansky Svätý Martin, making the town the national movement's center. In 1868, they founded the Slovak National Party, but the same year brought the Austro-Hungarian Ausgleich (Compromise), as the increasingly weak emperor accepted a Hungarian proposal for a Dual Empire, with two autonomous states connected by a common crown, army, foreign office, and exchequer.[41] Having lost recourse to Vienna, the Slovaks were thereafter at the mercy of the Hungarian state, and within a few years their situation deteriorated dramatically. In 1874, the government closed the Slovak *gymnazia*, and the next year it dissolved the nationalists' beloved Matica slovenská, "its endowments, buildings and collections being confiscated without the slightest attempt at justification."[42] A Serb deputy sent an interpellation to the Hungarian premier requesting the return of the funds to the Slovak nation, to which he ominously replied, "There is no Slovak nation."[43]

In the face of these setbacks, Slovak leaders reevaluated their strategy. The first Slovak National Party leader, Viliam Pauliny-Tóth, died in 1877, and the Lutheran poet Svetozár Hurban Vajanský, son of one of Štúr's closest associates, emerged as the new generation's leader. Vajanský was strongly influenced by Štúr's ideas, particularly those expressed in his last work before his death, when he began to advocate political passivity and Slavic union under the Russian Czar.[44] He also followed Štúr in contrasting God-fearing Slavdom with the materialistic West, arguing that liberalism was both the enemy of national rights (at least in the Hungarian practice) and, through its separation of political and religious authority, a source of moral corruption. The anti-modern nationalists surrounding Vajanský became known as the "Martin Group," as they met in Turčiansky Svätý Martin and organized various festivities there celebrating a romantic view of Slovak peasant culture. Interestingly, the peasants themselves were not drawn to these. As Hroch observes, in the majority of the cases he studied, "the patriots [nationalists] identified themselves more enthusiastically with the peasantry and its life-style than the peasantry did with those very patriots and their national programme."[45] Skilling likewise observes that these intellectuals "had no close relations with the people."[46]

Through the 1880s, then, Slovak nationalism remained an elite affair. Not only did the Martin Group's message fail to resonate, but the means of social communication also remained relatively weak, reflecting Hungary's continuing lag behind the Austrian half of the Empire in social and economic development. Large-scale industrialization did not begin until around 1870, emigration levels were high,[47] and the Slovak population actually declined in percentage terms between 1880 and 1910.[48] Literacy rates were low (35% in 1880, 50% in 1900[49]) and in 1910, nearly three-quarters of Slovaks still worked in agriculture. Few were represented in the professions, and of 6,285 civil servants in the Slovak area, only 164 were Slovaks.[50]

If Hroch is correct that both peasantry and middle class need to be successfully mobilized for a nationalist movement to succeed, then something new needed to happen. And, indeed, after 1890, both groups were mobilized, though quite separately, and not by the Martin intellectuals. The peasants were mobilized by the Catholic clergy, who became widely politically active in 1894. The catalyst was the legal reform of church-state relations, which introduced compulsory civil marriage, divorce, and the official recognition of Judaism's equal status with other religions.[51] This drew strong opposition from the Catholic Church and prompted the founding of the clericalist Hungarian People's Party. Parish priests agitated among the peasantry, calling on them to "swear on the Crucifix that they would vote for the People's Party."[52] Mobilization against the reforms was quite successful, especially among Slovaks.

Though the Church Laws were not repealed, the political activation of the lower clergy and their parishioners was important to the Slovak nationalists a few years later, when they looked for mass base of electoral support.[53]

Many priests then joined the nationalist cause, according to David Paul, for two main reasons. First, they opposed Magyarization (which was driven by the increasingly popular political ideal of ethnically homogeneous political community) and especially the Magyar clergy's role in strongly pressuring minorities to assimilate to the majority language and culture.[54] And second, priests saw in their parishioners "a natural political constituency" that drew on long-established relationships: "Within the flock, strict patriarchal authority over the family mirrored the authority of the priest over the village. . . From these deeply ingrained microsocial patterns evolved parallel strains in the Slovak nationalist movement."[55]

The mobilization of the small but growing Slovak middle class came at about the same time, but its substance was very different. As the Hungarian economy became more centralized and competitive, the pressures on non-Magyar capitalists to assimilate had increased. The largely Protestant Slovak middle class resisted, and instead developed relationships with Slovak peasants, farmers, and other members of the middle class with whom they did business.[56] Two overlapping liberal political movements particularly appealed to them: one called the "Hlasists," and the other led by politician and journalist Milan Hodža.

The Hlasists grew out of collaboration between Slovak students and Masaryk. Together, they put out a Slovak journal called *Hlas* (*Voice*), whose program reflected Masaryk's views on Czech-Slovak relations and the state of Slovak politics. Written by the Slovak medical school graduate Vavro Šrobár, who would become a leader in the First Czechoslovak Republic, the program promoted democratic reform and rejected the Martin Group's ideas, arguing that "Pan-Russianism and Slavic cosmopolitanism must be replaced by the idea of Slavic Reciprocity in the cultural sense of Kollár and Šafařík."[57] In both the journal and their public projects, the Hlasists devoted themselves to realizing Masaryk's vision by improving the nation's economic situation, literacy, educational system, and health conditions. They focused particularly on educating the Slovak peasant, "especially to free him from the influence of the clergy."[58] Though they remained a fairly small group, their Czechoslovak ideology was influential among politically aware Slovaks,[59] laying crucial groundwork for Czech-Slovak cooperation during World War I.[60]

One of *Hlas*'s founders and contributors was Milan Hodža, who became a political force of his own. With the Hlasists, he rejected the Martin Group's passivity and dreamy nationalism, arguing that national advancement depended on broad political participation and economic development. He thus advocated universal manhood suffrage and cooperation with the more modern Czechs. In 1903 he began publishing a newspaper called *Slovenský týždenník*, which contributed to the Slovaks' political education. He was elected to the Hungarian Parliament in 1905 and 1906, but by 1908 had grown disillusioned with the system. He then turned his efforts to promoting cooperative farming to foster national political cohesion.[61] In this, he drew on Czech assistance, strengthening their connection. He would, moreover, go on to become a key leader in the first Czechoslovak state, and as such, would become an important source of continuity between this period and the following.

During the last decade of the nineteenth century, then, Slovak nationalism finally made substantial inroads with both the middle class and the peasantry. Both were represented under the umbrella of the Slovak National Party. Although increasingly well organized, however, the Slovaks enjoyed very limited electoral success, as laws restricted the franchise and their candidates and voters were harassed and intimidated.

Another important turning point came in 1907, with events in Černová, the home village of a Catholic priest named Andrej Hlinka. The year before, after campaigning for Vavro Šrobár, Hlinka had been charged with incitement, tried, and sentenced to two years imprisonment. While he was in jail, a new church that had been funded largely by his collections was to be consecrated. The authorities would not release him to perform the ceremony, sending a Magyar-speaking priest instead. On October 21, a crowd of peasants demonstrated peacefully against the priest. Authorities opened fire on them, killing twelve men and three women and wounding around sixty. The next year, Seton-Watson reports, "fifty-nine of those who had dared to survive 'the massacre of Černová' . . . were tried on charges of 'violence against the authorities,' and received sentences totaling thirty-six years."[62] The incident and its aftermath rallied the movement and made Hlinka a national symbol. Like Hodža, he would go on to become an extremely important leader in the First Czechoslovak Republic—though for the majority of the time, in *opposition* to its government.

In the ensuing years, the bonds that had brought Slovak nationalists together under the Slovak National Party umbrella came undone. The Catholics found the Hodža-Hlasist Protestant, anticlerical orientation unattractive, and moved toward the Right.[63] Hlinka became increasingly powerful in this group and in 1913 became president of the new Slovak People's Party. In line with the dominant Slovak clerical orientation during the association with the Hungarian People's Party, it invoked an anti-Semitic orientation that attacked

Jews (who were largely assimilated, powerful in industry and commerce, and among the young generation, often Left-oriented) as "Magyarizers, capitalists, radicals, and (as the traditional tavern owner) promoters of alcoholism."[64] Ultimately, as Paul observes, "the last half-decade prior to the world war might be seen as an interregnum during which the most important forces among the Slovak nationalists polarized into the Hodža-Hlasist tendency (middle-class, pro-Czech, liberal-democratic), and the clerical-populist Hlinka group (peasant-based, skeptical of the Czech alliance, and highly authoritarian)."[65]

Compared with the Czech case, Slovak development during this period presents more problems for Hroch's instrumentalist theory. In some ways, it does conform to his expectations: the Martin Group was unsuccessful in mobilizing the Slovaks with a program that did not speak to their material interests, and the Hodža/Hlasist programs did appeal to those of the middle class. The differences between peasant and middle-class nationalists, however, are not adequately explained by his theory. At its core, it holds that the articulation of group- or class-based interests as "nationally relevant" works to expand people's sense of community to encompass the nation, rather than just those whose material interests are largely the same as one's own (such as fellow members of a social class). Essentially, people come to see their own material interests as bound up with the nation's, and this makes nationalism unifying. Hroch further argues that the ability to understand interests this way requires a kind of reasoned, autonomous thinking of which uneducated peasants strongly under the clergy's sway are incapable. Thus, they need to be educated and secularized before they can become true nationalists.

In the Slovak case, the peasants were not secularized when the clergy mobilized them over the issue of the Church Laws. Quite the opposite: the issue that first drew them into democratic participation concerned the relationship between religious and political power, and they stood in defense of the Church against secularism. Given the apparent legitimacy of clerical political authority in their eyes, then, it is problematic to assume that the peasants' subsequent nationalist mobilization by the clergy was based on an appraisal of the relationship between their material interests and that of the broader nation, rather than on the grounds of principle (in the sense of agreeing with the clergy) or culture (following from long-standing obedience to the clergy or the view that nationalism defended their living culture).

The relationship between this strand of Slovak nationalism and that of the middle class is instructive as well. Around the turn of the century, the two did join forces under the National Party, and campaigned for one another (such as

Hlinka for the liberal Šrobár—who would eventually become bitter political enemies during the First Republic). This suggests a cohesive, overarching view of the national interest, especially as it related to the threat of Magyarization. Within very few years, however, they moved apart because of fundamental political-philosophical differences, such as the *nature of legitimate political authority*. The disagreement here was very sharp, pitting politically active clergy against middle class nationalists who were strongly influenced by Masaryk, one of the most anti-clerical politicians in the Czech lands. It appears that the Slovaks were, in important ways, less unified than the Czechs, who were significantly more socioeconomically diversified and had more political parties. Differences over principle may, then, be more polarizing than class or material differences (though of course in the Slovak case the two were often reinforcing).

The polarization of Slovak nationalism also offers some insight into the relationship between nationalist ideology and preexisting culture. The socio-cultural divide between the Protestant minority and the Catholic majority both predated the national movement and was reflected in its subsequent cleavages, supporting the idea that the successful "construction" of national identity depends on some consonance between an ethnic population's understandings of both legitimate authority and the relationship of the individual to the collective. The divide would also prove enduring, as future chapters will show.

All that said, an alternative, instrumentalist explanation of the divide between the middle class and clerical nationalists could hold that the peasants, though clearly mobilized around a nationalist message, simply were not yet socially, economically, and culturally modern enough to be rational political actors the way the middle class was. If so, then socioeconomic and cultural modernization would gradually bring their orientation into line with the middle-class orientation. This was, in fact, what both the middle class nationalists and, eventually, the First Czechoslovak Republic's leaders expected, and it was the guiding assumption of many of their policies. How profoundly mistaken this was is a central concern of the next chapter.

Conclusion

On the eve of Czechoslovak statehood, principled orientations toward nationhood were organized into a triad. This was related to, but not simply a straightforward outgrowth of, the triad of awakeners' orientations in the early to mid-nineteenth century (Czech Czechoslovaks, Slovak Czechoslovaks, and Young Slovaks). By the early twentieth century, the Czechs had a broadly diffused national consciousness that included among its core principles the legitimacy of democracy, civil liberties, popular sovereignty and ethnonational rights; its roots in the awakeners' thought are clear. The Slovak nationalists agreed on the legitimacy of an expanded franchise and national rights (and as a corollary, the illegitimacy of Magyarization), but were deeply divided on questions of the Slovaks' relationship to both the Czechs and the West and on the source of legitimate political authority. The middle-class orientation built on the awakeners' ideas, especially those of the Czechoslovak Slovaks, as well as Masaryk's interpretation of their work. The clerical-nationalist orientation was, by contrast, new to the Slovak political sphere. Still, it had important similarities with Štúr's ideas. Though he was a Protestant and no advocate of Catholic Church political authority, his emphasis on a Slovak cultural-linguistic identity distinct from the Czech and in tension with Western liberalism laid important groundwork for the clerical-nationalist movement. There are, then, important lines of continuity between all three parts of the triad and the orientations of the preceding period.

Thus, when the Habsburg Empire crumbled at the end of World War I, the Czechs and Slovaks had behind them several generations' development of nationalist thought, which was becoming well-established as political tradition. The politics of national identity were about to change dramatically, however, as the two nations turned from confronting their imperial dominators to facing one another in a common state.

CHAPTER THREE

The First Republic: Czechoslovakism and Its Discontents

In October 1918, the Czechoslovak Republic was founded in the name of the sovereign "Czechoslovak" nation. At the same time, the state's leaders understood that the Czechs and Slovaks did not in fact constitute a cohesive community. Viewing the differences as primarily the result of the different levels of sociocultural modernization, they began a nation-building project based on an approach called "Czechoslovakism," which centered, in Masaryk's words, on "a comprehensive policy of culture and education."[1] As Štefan Osuský, one of the First Republic's Slovak founders, explained, "the aim of such a state is not to create unity of blood and speech, but unity of political outlook."[2]

This nation-building project failed. Throughout the state's existence, orientations toward nationhood remained deeply divided: the Czechs and their Slovak allies supported a Czechoslovak identity, while a Slovak movement, led by clerical-nationalists, strongly asserted Slovak nationhood and corresponding rights, including recognition of its distinct sovereignty within the state. Representing the latter position, Hlinka's Slovak People's Party (HSPP) challenged the legitimacy of Czechoslovak nation-building with the support of a substantial proportion of Slovak voters. Many Slovaks beyond the party's support base also rejected the Czechoslovak identity and favored increased Slovak autonomy. This conflict ultimately contributed to the breakup of the Republic, instigated by Nazi Germany in 1939, which led to the founding of a separate Slovak state.

In this chapter, I explore two concerns related to this conflict, which build upon one another. The first is the extent to which the understandings of nationhood that clashed here reflect continuities with those developed and activated in preceding periods. This offers another link in this study's historical chain tracing the roots of post-Communist understandings of nationhood. My second concern is the extent to which conflicts over these principles contributed to the failure of the nation-building project, relative to material (economic and power-political) and state security interests. On the latter count, the state's substantial ethnic German minority, which developed strong ties to Nazi Germany, had the potential to launch a significant challenge to the Czechoslovak state, and eventually did. Thus, ethnically based autonomy, such as the clerical-nationalists demanded, was a dangerous proposition in the view of many state leaders. Nationally relevant conflicts of material interests were also certainly present, as there were both substantial power-political and economic inequities between the Czechoslovaks' and the clerical-nationalists' support bases. The question, then, is not whether security and material interests were relevant to the conflict over national identity and sovereignty, but whether they *produced* it.

I argue that they did not, in part because—as I find in answering my first question—the contending views of nationhood in many ways preceded the state's founding. Crucial further evidence on my second question can be drawn from the dynamics and substance of that clash as it played out over the course of the First Republic. I explore this by looking at how each side's leaders applied their core principles to concrete goals and purposes, including defining the regime's constitutional foundations and the direction of state policy, as well as how they characterized the opposing side's position. Contrary to the suggestion of the Czechoslovak leaders quoted above, the difference between the perspectives on nationhood was *not* that one was based on ethnically neutral political values and the other, on conservative ethnic nationalism. Rather, these were rival sets of political values that were *both* integrated with key elements of ethnic identity. Many of the regime's political values and symbols were specific to the historical and intellectual traditions and experiences of the dominant "Czechoslovak" community that were not only different from, but *directly at odds with* the clerical-nationalist understanding of nationhood. The implications of the regime's principles went beyond the realm of economic policy and political access, affecting how core aspects of community identity were officially defined and expressed, including language use in the public realm and the history and values taught to children in the schools, both crucial elements of cultural reproduction.

My analysis of the substance and stakes of this conflict contributes to my broader investigation of understandings of nationhood in several ways. First, because this was the first time that Czech and Slovak principles determined the direction of state-building, it is possible to see their actual effects on citizens' lives, not only with regard to material interests, but also in how they allowed state leaders to privilege certain identities, with attendant values and principles, and to seek to undermine others, even though (or perhaps because) they were central to certain communities within the citizenry. That they had these kinds of implications offers insight into why these norms mattered to people, which helps explain their durability. It also lends further weight to the argument that while material and security interests contributed to the high salience of national identity issues, they did not produce them. And finally, it offers an important illustration of the ways that the distinctions between civic and ethnic values can break down, or at least become quite muddy, when brought to bear on the politics of specific communities. This last was a lesson that Slovaks learned well during the First Republic, and which they raised vehemently in the post-Communist period when the Czechs claimed to favor a "civic" approach to state-building. I begin, then, with the Republic's turbulent founding, when justifying the first joint Czech-Slovak state to the international community required a definition of their relationship.

The Birth of Czechoslovakia

In December 1914, with World War I underway, Masaryk went into exile in France. With great flair, he used the 500th anniversary of Jan Hus's burning at the stake to make a speech in Geneva calling for an end to Austria-Hungary and the founding of a Czechoslovak state.[3] Toward this end, he established the Czechoslovak Foreign Committee, an organization of mostly Czech and a few Slovak exiles. Under the guidance of Masaryk, Eduard Beneš, and Milan Štefánik (a distinguished Slovak airman who died in a plane crash in 1918), the Czechoslovak movement maneuvered brilliantly, drawing on increasing international support for national self-determination by positing the ethnonational unity of the Czechs and Slovaks. Broadly speaking, two concerns motivated this claim. First, Masaryk had long viewed the Czechs and Slovaks as branches of a single nation. And second, he and the other leaders were concerned about "ethnic arithmetic"[4]: several nationalities were to be included in the new state, and Germans, not Slovaks, would be the second largest group after the Czechs. A Czechoslovak nation would, however, constitute a healthy majority.

Though the exiles' leadership was vital, Slovaks also worked from home for independence from Hungary, though during the war coordination was difficult. In 1918, in the midst of the chaos surrounding the Empire's impending collapse, they produced a number of resolutions on their nation's political future. On May 1, the Slovak Social Democratic Party held a rally that resulted in the in Liptovský Svätý Mikuláš Resolution, which demanded "an unconditional recognition of the right to self-determination" for "the Hungarian branch of the Czechoslovak family."[5] Not to be outdone, on May 24 the Slovak National Party called a meeting, where Hlinka declared: "The thousand-year marriage with the Magyars has not worked. A divorce is necessary."[6] They produced a resolution stating: "The Slovak National Party favors the unconditional and complete right of self-determination for the Slovak Nation and on this ground claims the right of participation of the Slovak Nation in the establishment of an independent state consisting of Slovakia, Bohemia, Moravia and Silesia."[7] The action both signaled Slovak support for the ongoing Czecho-Slovak project and emphasized the Slovak nation's natural right to make decisions concerning its future statehood.[8]

Less than a week later, on May 30, another historic document was signed in Pittsburgh, Pennsylvania. It reads:

> The representatives of the Slovak and Czech organizations in the United States, the Slovak League, the Czech National Alliance and the Federation of Czech Catholics deliberating in the presence of the Chairman of the Czechoslovak National Council, Professor Masaryk, on the Czechoslovak question and on our previous declaration of program, have passed the following resolution:
>
> We approve of the political program which aims at the union of the Czechs and Slovaks in an independent State composed of the Czech Lands and Slovakia.
>
> Slovakia shall have her own administrative system, her own diet and her own courts.
>
> The Slovak language shall be the official language in the schools, in the public offices and in public affairs generally.
>
> The Czechoslovak State shall be a republic, and its constitution a democratic one.
>
> The organization of the collaboration between Czechs and Slovaks

in the United States shall, according to the need and the changing situation, be intensified and regulated by mutual consent.

Detailed provisions relating to the organization of the Czechoslovak State shall be left to the liberated Czechs and Slovaks and their duly accredited representatives.[9]

A clear recognition of national distinctiveness and a promise of resulting autonomy, Slovak leaders in Hungary did not know the Pittsburgh Agreement existed.

On October 29, 1918, Slovak leaders from various parties met to draft a further resolution. That night, Milan Hodža arrived to inform them that the Czech National Committee had taken authority of the Historic Lands from Austria the previous day. The leaders thus quickly produced a revised resolution, which stated in part:

> 1. The Slovak Nation is part of the Czecho-Slovak Nation, united in language and in the history of its culture, in all the cultural struggles which the Czech Nation has fought and which have made it known throughout the world, the Slovak branch has also participated.
>
> 2. For this Czecho-Slovak Nation we demand an unlimited right of self-determination on the basis of complete independence.[10]

James Felak notes that "these words would come back to haunt Hlinka and other Slovak nationalists who signed it. Masaryk, by the same token, would be haunted by the Pittsburgh Agreement."[11] These documents, Leff observes, reflect the hurried and uncertain action that led to the new state: "The cloak of ambiguity shrouding the liberation struggle produced a misleading aura of consensus, permitting each subgroup to interpret the vocabulary of that struggle without definitive contradiction. In the short run, it is easy to see how this circumstance enhanced collaboration. It is equally easy to predict an eventual showdown in which contradictory understandings of the nature of Czechoslovak unity would surface and clash. When the time came to sustain a state on the basis of these divergent understandings, the bill for prior obscurity fell due."[12]

This happened fairly quickly. In December 1918, Vavro Šrobár became Minister with Full Power for Slovakia, a title that reflected his immense authority.[13] Accompanied by Czech legionnaires (Hungary did not cede the entire territory until March 1919) and a stream of Czech professionals and workmen,

Šrobár set about incorporating Slovakia into the state. The influx of Czechs was necessary, as the Slovaks lacked the consolidated political leadership, administrative personnel (most officials left Slovakia for Hungary), and skilled workforce (such as teachers and engineers) to produce a new infrastructure.

One group of Slovaks who hoped to contribute to state-building were the Catholic clergy. In November 1918, Hlinka founded a one-hundred-member Council of Priests, which made several demands, including a Catholic school system and an end to civil marriage.[14] It also offered a list of twenty-nine priests to participate in the Revolutionary National Assembly, the provisional Czechoslovak parliament.[15] The Council took its proposals to Šrobár, but he was not interested in working with the clergy. Though raised Catholic, he grew up with Czech-language prayer books and hymns; his cultural and linguistic orientation was more similar to that of Slovak Protestants than that of most Slovak Catholics.[16] In addition, as a Charles University student, Šrobár had worked closely with Masaryk and the Hlasists. In appointing administrators and Slovak representatives to the Assembly, then, he turned mostly to Slovak Lutherans and progressives. This rankled many Catholics, who did not appreciate being considered "unreliable elements in their native land."[17] Hlinka's response was to re-found the Slovak People's Party on December 19, 1918.

Although the conflict between Šrobár and Hlinka included an element of personal rivalry, the Prague government shared Šrobár's opposition to a political role for the Slovak clergy. Masaryk, long an outspoken anticlericalist, described the Slovaks as "apt to be fanatically Catholic and priestridden" and deeply distrusted Hlinka.[18] Many in the broader Czech population were anticlerical as well, which was reflected in incidents just days after the state's founding. On November 3, demonstrators in Prague tore down a statue of the Virgin Mary. A fact often left out of written accounts is that the statue was first erected in 1650 by Habsburg-backed Jesuits at the site of the Battle of White Mountain, where Protestant-led Bohemia had lost its independence to the Catholic Habsburgs in 1620. Whether the statue was erected as a victor's celebration of the battle's outcome[19] or as a gesture of gratitude for Prague's delivery from a Swedish attack in 1648 is a matter of dispute.[20] It is clear, however, that many Czechs saw the statue as a symbol of religion as a tool of oppression. The mob would have proceeded to dislodge the statue of St. Jan Nepomucký from the Charles Bridge and drop it over the edge if authorities had not stopped them. Pynsent explains that St. Jan represented "the superiority of spiritual rules over secular." In the seventeenth century, to repair the Czechs' reputation as Hussite heretics and prove their successful return to "civilized" European Catholicism, the clergy began to push for his sainthood.[21] In the heady first days of the new Republic, then, the Czech mob wished to return St. Jan to the Vltava River, where he had been martyred.

While rich in symbolism that invoked principles central to the nineteenth-century Czech national movement (especially its understanding of legitimate authority), these demonstrations horrified Catholic Slovaks. Moreover, the Czechs did not limit their anticlericalism to Prague, but brought it with them on their mission to Slovakia. They confiscated many of the parochial schools and pulled crucifixes from classroom walls. Though the Slovak population was 77 percent Catholic, only 5 percent of the newly appointed school inspectors shared this denomination. According to Seton-Watson, during the Republic's critically important first two years, government authorities "did little or nothing to restrain anti-clerical tendencies among their subordinates, and actually encouraged the agitation against Father Hlinka."[22] By all accounts, the Czech-led attempts to separate church and state showed a callous disregard for many Slovaks' religious sensibilities.

Catholic Slovaks' goodwill toward the Czechoslovak authorities thus eroded rapidly, and the HSPP began to "brand every innovation, political or social, with the name of Hussitism"[23]—thereby appropriating a key symbol of Czech nationhood and turning it against them. According to Francis Hrusovsky, because of conflict over the "religious question," "between the Slovak and Czech nations a crevice of distrust began to form. This fissure deepened when the Czechs in Slovakia acted as though they were in a backward country. Many of them had the idea—even when there was no basis for it—that their role was to bring culture and progress to Slovakia. This condescending attitude offended the Slovaks, who in turn began to ridicule Czech 'progressiveness.' "[24]

The next pivotal event in Czech-Slovak relations came in the summer of 1919, when the HSPP found out about the Pittsburgh Agreement. Armed with this discovery, Hlinka wrote to the prime minister protesting the situation in Slovakia and informing him that he would be forced to go to Paris to demand a hearing at the peace conference. Receiving no reply, he left for Paris, and on arrival circulated a document titled the "Memorandum of the Slovaks to the Peace Conference of 1919." In the document, beneath the title, was written:

Slovakia to the Slovaks:
We are neither Czechs nor Czechoslovaks;
we are just simply Slovaks.

It is in the name of justice and lasting
peace that we demand the autonomy of Slovakia.[25]

The text of the Pittsburgh Agreement follows a short introduction. The memorandum then claims that the Slovak nation had been betrayed, as the "those who seized the political power" were "working to create not only a Czecho-Slovak State, but also a single Czecho-Slovak nation, which is an ethnographical monstrosity. . . . Instead of obtaining Slovak autonomy, we have fallen under Czech domination."[26] In a section titled "The Slovaks Under the Czech Yoke," the memorandum charges the state with economic exploitation, linguistic oppression, and religious intolerance. This last allegation focuses on the complaint that "the heresy of Hus, unknown in Slovakia until now, is strongly propagated by the Czechs in our unfortunate country."[27] The document ends with an overview of Slovak demands, premised on the argument that

> Slovakia, forming nearly half of the Czech and Slovak Republic, cannot be well administered by the central government of Prague, not only because Prague is quite far from Slovakia and not easily accessible, but also because the special character of the Slovak country demands a government other than that of the Czechs. Further, the Czechs and Slovaks are "brothers" who have never seen one another and rubbed shoulders with one another. The mentality and character of the two nations are entirely distinct. The Czechs are an industrial nation, the Slovaks are agriculturalists. The Czechs are in great part Hussites, the Slovaks Catholic. The Czechs have lived with the Germans, the Slovaks with the Magyars. The Czechs are more materialistic, the Slovaks idealistic. There is not a Czecho-Slovak nation, but there is a Czech nation and a Slovak nation. We are not Czechs, nor Czechoslovaks, but Slovaks, and we wish to remain Slovaks forever.[28]

The document calls for a plebiscite, protected by the Entente's forces, to "disclose the real feelings of the Slovak nation." It then declares that the Slovak fate is entrusted "into the hands of the Peace Conference. The right to existence was accorded us by the Creator; we hope that the glorious Peace Conference will guarantee it against the injustice of men." No plebiscite followed, however, and when Hlinka returned home he was arrested for interfering with the peace process.

Though ignored by its intended audience, the memorandum laid a principled groundwork for the autonomy struggle to come. It clearly challenges the legitimacy of the claim that a Czechoslovak nation existed, pointing to the profound cultural, historical, religious, and economic differences between the Czechs and Slovaks. If they constituted not one nation, but two, then it followed from the Republic's own founding logic that the Slovaks should express their own national sovereignty via political autonomy. We see here, then, the articulation of a rival set of foundational political principles that shares a basic premise with the regime's ideology—the right to national self-determination, which long enjoyed legitimacy in the view of both national movements—but actually precludes Czechoslovak national unity.

The Constitutional Definition of the Sovereign Nation

The Czechoslovak Constitution was ratified on February 29, 1920. The body that drafted and passed it was the Revolutionary National Assembly, which was appointed rather than elected. It was composed of Czechs in proportion to the distribution of party seats in the Parliament in 1911 and, again, of Slovaks chosen by Šrobár, who had given more than half the seats to Protestants, clearly reflecting the Czech recognition of, and support for, one side in a long-standing cleavage in Slovak politics. Unsurprisingly, the Constitution reflected the Czechoslovak understanding of nationhood. Its preamble begins: "We, the Czechoslovak nation, in desiring to strengthen the complete unity of the nation, to introduce a just order in the Republic, to promote the peaceful development of our Czechoslovak homeland, to secure the general welfare of all its citizens and the blessings of liberty for future generations, have passed in our National Assembly on 29 February 1920 the Constitution of the Czechoslovak Republic, the text of which follows."[29] The ethnic Czechoslovak nation thereby assumed the exclusive status of "state-forming nation" (státotvorný národ). The state's minorities were barred from participating in writing the Constitution and voting on its ratification. Though it did incorporate the principle of the civil and political equality of the individual, Masaryk was clear that the new Republic was to be a Czechoslovak nation-state that was tolerant toward its minorities, rather than a state with several, equal nations or nationalities.[30] The sovereign community was decidedly *not* a civic nation.

The new regime was centralized (seated in Prague), Felak argues, for several reasons. First, it followed logically from the idea of a single Czechoslovak nation. Second, the state's leaders feared that granting Slovaks autonomy would open the door to demands by Germans and Hungarians for equal treatment. Third, fear remained that Hungary might move to take Slovakia back. Leaders thus saw centralism as a "national security dictate."[31] And finally, most Czechs and some Slovaks considered Slovakia unready to govern itself, expecting that it would be dominated by "reactionary, clerical elements."[32] Clearly, then, it was not only ideological differences, but also internal and international security considerations, that led Czechoslovak leaders to reject Slovak demands for autonomy and assert the existence of common nationhood; the two concerns were reinforcing. That these leaders expected that such nationhood would soon be achieved is, however, clear, as the discussion below shows.

Ultimately, when the vote came, the HSPP Assembly representatives themselves approved the Constitution, "in the interest of state unity".[33] Attached, however, was a proclamation that in so voting, "they are in no way giving up their demand for the autonomy of Slovakia [to be achieved] through a legislative assembly. And they wish that this will be guaranteed for the future."[34]

Challenges to Czechoslovak Nation-Building

While the state's leaders certainly took note of the clerical-nationalist challenge to the regime, they also believed it would be short-lived, expecting that political socialization, especially via education, would eliminate it. In 1921, Masaryk told a French reporter, "There is no Slovak nation. That is the invention of Magyar propaganda. The Czechs and Slovaks are brothers. . . . Only cultural level separates them—the Czechs are more developed than the Slovaks, for the Magyars held them in systematic unawareness. We are founding Slovak schools. It is necessary to await the results; in one generation there will be no difference between the two branches of our national family."[35] Until the education of the next generation of Slovaks was complete, however, it was impossible to consider Slovak autonomy. As Šrobár told the Parliament in 1926, "Our Slovaks have not yet come from Slovak schools and as long as the last Slovak does not come from a Slovak school, there will not be true Slovak thought here. The first voter in Slovakia to come from a Slovak school will vote in 1933."[36]

Though supportive of such values as democracy and equality, the curriculum of the new school system was, however, not particularly "Slovak," at least in the sense of focusing strongly on that distinct culture and history. Czech students were required to have less knowledge of the Slovak language than the other way around,[37] and some of the many Czech teachers in Slovakia spoke only Czech. Textbook authors did try to cover Slovak history, but the thousand years of separation made a common history difficult to produce.[38] Selecting national heroes was especially problematic. Štúr was rejected, as the state's leaders disapproved of his role in separating the Czech and Slovak national movements. Vajanský's role was diminished, because of his opposition to Masaryk, despite being one of the Slovaks' most esteemed poets.[39] These choices reflect consideration of the political ideas that historical figures represented and recognition of the strong tensions between the national traditions, as well as a desire to reject elements of the Slovak tradition hostile to Czechoslovakism (and thereby to rupture certain continuities in that perspective). The curriculum also reflected the Czech tendency, in evidence since the mid-nineteenth century, to strongly privilege the "Czech" in Czechoslovak.

Another crucial aspect of Czechoslovak education was its movement toward secularization, which the Prague government saw as crucial to raising the cultural level of the Slovaks. Thus, for example, Darwinism was taught, and Catholic teachers were "quietly banned" from dealing with medieval history in courses on religion.[40] The architect of the Slovak educational system (himself a Slovak) Antonín Štefánek noted the difficulty in shifting values, observing that it produced "the clash of two very different outlooks upon life. The old school rested on a moral framework provided by the Church, whereas in the new school lay principles of pedagogy are gaining ground . . . free from one-sided denominational tendencies."[41] Ultimately, he argued, this new direction would produce more tolerant, egalitarian, democratic citizens.

In the HSPP view, however, this shift was entirely illegitimate. Party leaders stated in their 1929 Program, "there can be no Slovak nation without Christian morality" and called parochial schools "the foundation of the continuing ethical development of the nation."[42] Hlinka also made this case in an essay titled "The Influence of Religion and Catholicism on States and Individuals." He began by discussing Slovak oppression in Hungary, noting that the "Slovaks had virtually no intellectuals, no hierarchy, not a single secondary school and no history of their own," prompting them to turn to the Church for comfort and strength.[43] He then addressed the relationship between religion and society more broadly, arguing that without Christianity, the community has no moral foundation and will tend toward barbarism, but with it, "religion exerts a taming influence on character, because it renders possible the preservation of the moral law . . . Religious observances have the greatest influence on the formation of States and the conditions prevailing in them, while religious observances in school and home exercise a very beneficial effect upon young and old."[44] They inculcate key values, including equality ("religion removes differences between individuals") and tolerance ("religion has brought understanding between people").[45] The religious individual thus becomes the building block for a moral and legitimate state: "When religion raises the value of man according to his deeds, it raises the authority of the State, the law and society."[46] Moreover, while this individual should enjoy liberty, it must be reigned in by "the supremacy of the divine and human law. . . . Hence not unbridled liberty, but authority, law and Christ's liberty are the pillars of Society and the State."[47] He then returns to the importance of religion to the Slovaks, declaring, "Our Catholicism taught us openness and national pride. . . . With the help of religion we overcome the most powerful enemies. Our 325,856 electors were guided by the idea of religion and autonomy."[48] He thus concluded, "it is in the best interest of States to foster religion and support those who proclaim it, because the basis of States is morality. And the basis of this is religion."[49]

Hlinka's political philosophy, and more broadly, the HSPP ideological platform, thus clearly held Catholicism as an essential aspect of what it meant to *be* Slovak. This was partly descriptive, in that it identified a key characteristic of the majority of the nation's members (and hence marked something of a national boundary between Slovaks and the Czechs). It was also important in a more active sense, as the ideology defined good citizenship (including political orientation and behavior) and the nature of the common good according to Catholic precepts and values, which it held as defining elements of the Slovak national culture. It also justified an important political role for the clergy who, as authorized interpreters of divine law, are well suited to keeping human law aligned with it. The HSPP ideology thus not only set up a close relationship between religious and political authority, but also fused the religious, national, and civic components of Slovak identity—a process begun in the nineteenth century.

The weight the HSPP placed on a Catholic education system can be appreciated in this long-standing political-philosophical context. In the HSPP view, this schooling provided the necessary foundation for Slovaks to understand the nature of legitimate authority, to develop and exercise civic virtue, and to foster the nation's bonds. That Štefánek (and other Czechoslovaks) saw such schooling as *impeding* progress toward these same goals shows just how profoundly differently they defined them.

Adding to Slovak frustration, although the Czechoslovaks were generally hostile to Catholic political authority, the new state's symbols not only were largely Czech, but also left out key Slovak heroes and included significant Protestant religious elements.[50] For example, the anniversary of Hus's martyrdom became a state holiday, prompting the papal nuncio to leave Prague for two years in protest. Štúr, however, received no day of remembrance.[51] Kollár and Šafařík were among the few heroes to bridge the gap between Czech and Slovak figures.[52] The state's choices of symbols thus clearly had alienating potential: "Jan Hus was not a Slovak hero nor Bila hora [the battle of White Mountain] a Slovak tragedy; Saint Stephen [patron saint of Hungary] meant more to most Slovaks than Saint Václav [patron saint of the Czechs]."[53] Even the state's postage stamps, Derek Sayer argues, raised the question, "For whom, exactly, were Hradčany [the district around the Prague Castle] and the Hussites' chalice meaningful symbols of identity?"[54] Indeed, these symbols not only are primarily relevant to the Czechs, but also have clear political meaning that repudiates the Slovak clerical-nationalist understanding of nationhood by celebrating both the sovereignty of the "Czechoslovak" nation and Hussitism, whose central tenets (particularly as interpreted by the "father of the Czech nation") proclaimed the illegitimacy of Catholic religious and political authority. It is thus easy to understand why these caused tensions, and the potential for such had been brewing since the development of mid-nineteenth-century Czech ethnohistory. Perhaps more surprising is the view that these could possibly be integrating symbols under the circumstances.

Ultimately, despite serious complications, the new education system did lead to the rapid growth of a more educated Slovak class. El Mallakh argues that the Czechs could be seen as "too successful": the pool of Slovaks qualified to teach rapidly increased, but many Czechs teaching in Slovakia were unwilling to give up their jobs, especially with the onset of the Great Depression.[55] This was just one repercussion of the influx of Czechs into the Slovak economy. Initially, Slovak leaders understood that they needed Czech help in founding the new regime. Within a relatively short time, however, relations began to deteriorate. Many Czechs spoke Czech on the job and continued to hold even menial jobs in Slovakia after there were enough Slovaks to fill them.[56] The HSPP articulated its position on this issue in its Trnvanský Manifesto of November 1925, point 4 of which states: "The Prague bureaucracy does not understand the Slovak soul, and therefore the laws are passed so restrictively that the sons of the Slovak nation are robbed of their bread. We therefore demand the dismissal of all non-Slovaks who make their living as state employees in Slovakia, the immediate discontinuation of dismissals of Slovak state employees, and the immediate revision of industry and craftsmen under the slogan 'Slovakia to the Slovaks.'"[57]

The question of industry raises still another source of strain between the Czechs and Slovaks. When Czechoslovakia was founded, Slovak economic development lagged far behind the Czech.[58] The Czechoslovak government thus quickly instituted land reform, but the process was controversial: German large landholders protested, and some Slovaks alleged that the distribution favored supporters of the Czechoslovak centralist parties and Czech "colonists"— allegations that El Mallakh finds at least partially valid. [59] Moreover, while Czech manufacturing expanded rapidly after 1923, Slovak industry was weakened when Hungarian-owned enterprises moved to Hungary, and then when non-competitive industries were forced to close.[60] The Great Depression made things worse, as already low living standards in Slovakia fell.[61] The government, however, did not draw up an industrialization program for Slovakia until April 1937, when, unfortunately, there was no longer time to fulfill it.[62] Important conflicts of material interest did, therefore, clearly exist.

All that said, the Slovaks did benefit materially from union with the Czechs. The Czechoslovak state invested in the construction of new schools, telecommunication projects, public building complexes, health services, cultural facilities, spas and tourist industry infrastructure, roads, railway lines, harbors, and airports in Slovakia.[63] Education led to upward mobility, as Slovaks entered careers in finance, medicine, and the service sectors.[64] Thousands of peasants gained land, farming methods were modernized, the cooperative movement expanded, and agricultural production increased. [65] Still, Paul argues that "while in fairness it must be remembered that few Europeans at this time really understood the problems of less developed regions, there is ample reason to believe that Slovak criticisms of the First Republic's economic policies were justified."[66] Moreover, directly contradicting state leaders' expectations, the increasingly socioeconomically developed, educated Slovaks also became increasingly receptive to anti-Czech arguments, which benefited the HSPP.[67] Thus, "the much-anticipated generation of Slovak-educated students proved more radically nationalist than their elders, who had more vivid memories of the Magyar alternative."[68]

Despite this strong support base, however, the HSPP was disadvantaged by the First Republic's proportional representation political system. It was highly fragmented, based largely on the dual cleavages of class (among Czech and German parties) and ethnicity (among Slovak and Magyar parties). At least five parties were necessary to form a working majority. In fact, of all the parties competing in the arena, only five exercised significant governmental power throughout the First Republic: the Agrarian Party, the Social Democrats, the National Socialists, the Czechoslovak Populist Party, and the National Democrats. Leff observes that "this narrowed configuration, the reduction of fifty potential governmental actors to five dominant ones, undoubtedly helped to reduce the scope of conflict over contentious issues to manageable proportions."[69] Stability, however, came at a price: "alternation between the 'ins' and the 'outs' simply did not occur; the pendulum did not swing."[70] This broadly affected Slovak representation, as a substantial number of Slovaks did not vote according to class-based concerns. Of the "Big Five" (or *pětka*) parties, only the Social Democrats and the Agrarians ever won more than 10 percent of the Slovak vote.[71] Still, enough Slovaks voted for the Czechoslovak parties that governments could manage "without the disruptive nationalist parties."[72] For most of the First Republic, then, the HSPP was in the opposition, and no party but the Communists (after 1924) joined it in supporting Slovak national autonomy (though as Prime Minister from 1935–8, Milan Hodža did propose decentralizing reform, which ultimately failed to pass). In turn, this allowed the HSPP to blame all Slovakia's problems on the Prague government without being responsible for their solution.[73]

Despite its marginalization, the HSPP was by far the strongest party in Slovakia, polling 34.3 percent in 1925, 28.3 percent in 1929, and 30.1 percent in 1935 (percentages of the total population in Slovakia, not just ethnic Slovaks; given that minorities did not tend to vote for the HSPP, the Slovak percentage of support for the party is likely higher). Furthermore, El Mallakh points out that this may not reflect the level of support for Slovak autonomy, as "to be an open supporter of HSPP was to put aside or lessen the possibility of material benefits which could accrue from a political affiliation—it was a vote of dedication and opposition." Indeed, it appears that many more favored increased autonomy.[74] Still, the nationalists were never able to gain an absolute majority of the Slovak vote (though a majority of Slovaks did consistently vote for opposition parties). Although it is likely that the material benefits accruing from support of the statewide Czechoslovak parties partly accounted for Slovak support of them, there is no reason to assume this entirely explains why they did not vote for the HSPP.

One thing, however, is certain: by the end of the Republic's first decade, the Czechoslovaks' assumptions about the malleability of Slovak identity had proven unfounded. Unable to count on a rising generation of Czechoslovaks in Slovakia to cement national unity, they were forced to confront the nationalist grievances against the state, and to make an explicit case for Czechoslovak unity. This was a task that fell particularly to the regime's Slovak supporters.

The Slovak Defense of Czechoslovak Unity

The Czechoslovak Slovaks were not a monolithic group. They belonged to different parties and held various policy positions, including on how to structure the Czech-Slovak relationship, with some favoring increased Slovak autonomy. Some, like Hodža, also stated clearly that they did not want Slovak language and culture to simply be overwritten by Czech. Nevertheless, they agreed that Czechoslovak unity was a political, moral, economic, and social good. As the nationalist challenge intensified, they moved to defend the Republic, basing their support for common Czechoslovak state- and nationhood on two main pillars.[75] First, they argued that common statehood was in Slovakia's best interest because it was a dramatic improvement over Hungarian rule. They pointed out that the Czechoslovak state-building process had brought the Slovaks political, religious, and cultural freedom, set up an educational system that used the Slovak language, reorganized the judicial system, improved public works, reformed the economy, modernized banking and finance, provided an economic safety net through social legislation and redistributive justice through land reform, and, finally, allowed administrative reform that included a measure of autonomy for Slovakia. Although economic inequities continued to exist, and there were real problems with how administrative reform was initially implemented, the situation was continuing to improve. Moreover, interests could be articulated in a democratic political arena, and therefore any further conflicts could be resolved fairly and equitably. Given all these benefits, Slovaks had a stake in preserving the Republic, and it was in their self-interest to see that it remained stable and legitimate. The regime's Slovak defenders stressed that all these achievements were the product of union with the Czechs, without whom none of this would have been possible. They thus made a fairly straightforward appeal to material interests.

The second line of argument concerns the idea of common Czechoslovak nationhood. According to the Slovak centrists, theirs was a people without a distinctive history. Štefan Osuský, one of the Slovak founders of the Republic and the Czechoslovak Minister in France, took this argument the farthest, essentially arguing that the Slovaks had neither a philosophical nor an ideological tradition.[76] Other leaders gave the Slovaks more credit, arguing that through their history of cultural contact with the Czechs, they shared in the Czech, or Czechoslovak, tradition. Hodža even suggested that the Slovaks had non-Czech sources for their democratic tradition that predated the Hussite period.[77] They further argued that the Czech and Slovak national awakeners had solidified the moral and cultural bond between the two branches of the nation through their nineteenth-century cooperation, and that their national movements had cherished common principles—especially equality, tolerance, and democracy.

Still, they argued, after centuries of neglect and persecution under the Hungarian regime, the Slovaks were culturally, socially, politically, economically, and some even argued religiously disadvantaged, if not immature. Ivan Dérer, the Social Democratic leader who served as Minister of Education, Unification, and Justice, made this analogy: "The child which awakes out of a long and sound sleep rubs its eyes and does not yet realize that it is no longer asleep, it would like to roll over for another sleep and is angry when its parent rouses it up to greet the bright and happy yet work-filled day. Such is still the state of many Slovaks. That is the very substance of the autonomist and separatist movement. It is a passing condition."[78]

To fulfill their potential to become equal partners in the Czechoslovak nation, then, the Slovaks had to be educated according to a system that held equality, tolerance and democracy as its central values. These, the regime's defenders argued, were rooted in both the Czech and Slovak cultures (particularly, according to Štefánek, as articulated by Kollár, Palacký, Šafařík, Havlíček and Masaryk)[79] and in the Western humanist tradition—again, the appeal to a long-rooted tradition of political thought was overt. At the same time, the Czechoslovak project was described as a matter of consciously constructing community: Šrobár describes it as "seeking to form cultural values [*tvorit' kulturné hodnoty*] for ourselves and mankind."[80] This was difficult, but the Czechoslovaks expressed great optimism, despite early setbacks. Osuský, for example, predicted that the Slovaks' backward superstitions were "bound to melt under the rays of pure intelligence and human affection."[81] Thus, their appeal centered on a combination of material interests and shared values, which were partly grounded in Slovak tradition and partly expected to develop with modern education. Their optimism would not, however, be rewarded (and, indeed, Osuský himself would turn strongly against the project by World War II).

The Slovak Nationalist Movement in the 1930s: End Game

In the late 1920s, the HSPP briefly—and relatively unsuccessfully—joined the government. Its accomplishments were minimal and its popularity suffered. In the early 1930s, it went back into opposition and staged a number of high profile events. One centered on the Matica slovenská, whose leadership had been taken over by Czechoslovak-oriented Slovaks. Nationalists responded to the Matica's publication of a revised *Rules of Slovak Orthography* that drew strongly on Czech by staging a high-profile coup.[82] Felak argues that the "putsch at the Matica was partly a result of Ludak [HSPP] intrigues. However, a large number of Slovaks who were not [H]SPP supporters were dissatisfied by what they perceived as heavy-handed czechization of Slovak culture. They joined with Hlinka and his followers to wrest the Matica out of Czechoslovak hands. In interwar Slovakia politics and culture were closely intertwined. An orthography that brought the Slovak language closer to Czech was an affirmation of Czechoslovakism and centralism. One that stressed Slovak linguistic distinctiveness went hand in hand with autonomy for Slovakia, which explains why the stakes in the battle for control of the Matica were high."[83] This conflict thus highlights both language's political meaning as a demarcation of sovereign community and the widespread unhappiness among Slovaks with the Czechoslovak nation-building project. It also has clear roots going back to the nineteenth-century struggle between the Czechoslovaks and the Young Slovaks over the relationship between the two communities, which centered particularly on language, and is reminiscent of tensions between Czech and Slovak Czechoslovaks over Czech dominance in the development of a "common" literary language.

A second key nationalist event was the June 1932 Congress of the Young Slovak Generation, which quickly deteriorated into a tempestuous pro-autonomy demonstration that included shouting down Czechoslovak-oriented speakers and participants. The large number of young Slovak nationalists was striking, reinforcing awareness that the schools had not had the integrative effect the state's leaders had expected.[84]

During this period, the HSPP also became increasingly radical. In December 1932, when the HSPP and the Slovak National Party met in Trenčín to produce a list of demands, Hlinka said in his keynote address: 'We are behaving only logically and being true to the nation when we proclaim continually and at every opportunity that we will not renounce our right of national sovereignty even at the price of the Czechoslovak Republic."[85] The meeting's final resolution also expressed this, and from then on, questions were increasingly raised about the HSPP's loyalty to the state.[86]

The HSPP charted a more moderate course during 1935 and '36, even voting for Beneš when Masaryk resigned and negotiating to enter the government coalition again, albeit unsuccessfully. Still, the 1935 elections, which provided a sweep for Konrad Henlein's pro-Nazi Sudeten German Party in western and northern Bohemia, also showed continued evidence of voter discontent in Slovakia, with 61 percent of the vote going to parties in the opposition. As Henlein's party grew more powerful, the HSPP moved to take advantage of its political influence. In early 1938, the HSPP decided to create a united autonomist front with the Hungarians and the Germans. About one hundred HSPP members signed a letter of protest, the last line of which was "We strongly support the Czechoslovak Republic as our homeland, not an alliance with Hungarians or Germans."[87] They then resigned from the party. The agreement constituting the "autonomy bloc" became public, however, and there was no turning back.

During the spring of 1938, the autonomists focused their attention on elections in Slovakia's municipalities and rural districts, and the campaign indicated that the party's illiberalism was continuing to grow. The HSPP leaflets were anti-Czech, anti-Semitic, and full of allegations of anti-Catholic oppression, and some reflected the radicalism, and increasingly the Nazi sympathies, of some party members, especially among the youth.[88] This orientation cannot, however, be simply ascribed to the neighboring state's influence. In particular, as previous chapters have shown, anti-Semitism was nothing new in Slovak clerical nationalism. As it had during the waning years of the Hungarian regime, under the First Republic, the HSPP party organs and other Catholic periodicals attacked Jews on many counts. The allegations ranged according to the authors' and publications' perspective: in some, Jews were depicted as rapacious capitalists eager to cheat Slovaks, often also as the source of Bolshevism, and in more extreme versions as sexual deviants, ritual murderers, sub-humans.[89] Overall, and over the years, the tone was hostile: as examples, in 1919, the weekly *Nitra*, edited by Monsignor Jozef Tiso, who would become the leader of the wartime Slovak state, declared Jews to be responsible for "all the misery in the world."[90] An official newspaper of the same county described them as "the main enemy of the Slovak people,"[91] and Andrej Škrábik, who became bishop of Banská Bystrica, one of Slovakia's main cities, in 1926 called them "anti-Christs."[92] It was the most virulent and violent of anti-Semitic perspectives that the HSPP radicals took up as their cause in the mid- to late 1930s.

As intraparty divisions between radicals and moderates deepened, Hlinka's health deteriorated. He was nevertheless able to attend another major event that spring: the 20th anniversary celebration of the Pittsburgh Agreement. A delegation of American Slovaks attended the festivities, bringing with them the original document. On the first night of the two-day celebration, a thousand HSPP supporters marched through Bratislava shouting such slogans as "The Slovak language in Slovakia!" and "Slovakia to the Slovaks, Palestine to the Jews!"[93]

Soon after, the Slovak Agrarians held "Farmer's Day" in Bratislava. The guests included Prime Minister Hodža, Dérer, the provincial governor, representatives of all the coalition parties, and members of the American Slovak League, among others.[94] Speaking to an audience estimated at 100,000, Hodža gave a rousing speech, in which he declared, "Slovak ambition is that in this Republic, no Slovak shall be considered inferior to the rest. His motto is: 'Equal among Equals' . . . the Czechoslovak Republic is the foundation and the base of Slovak independence."[95] This "emotion laden address ended with the crowd joining in a solemn vow to permit no one or nothing from threatening, weakening, or undermining the Czechoslovak state and unity."[96] Clearly, the HSPP was not the only powerful voice in Slovakia at the time, and Czechoslovak leaders were increasingly willing to offer some recognition of Slovak distinctiveness.

Despite state leaders' attempts to deepen national goodwill, a combination of hostile international and domestic factors now deeply imperiled the state. Hlinka died on August 16. Factionalism within the party flared, and intrigues with the Sudeten Germans and the Third Reich deepened.[97] Events unfolded quickly during the rest of the year. On September 29, the United Kingdom, France, and Italy signed the Munich Agreement with Nazi Germany, giving it Czechoslovakia's Sudetenland. On October 5, President Beneš resigned, and the next day Slovaks met at Žilina and declared autonomy. In November, the now-dominant HSPP worked out a constitutional reform bill to institutionalize this autonomy. The Autonomy Act hyphenated the state's name, and its preamble began: "In view of the fact that the Czecho-Slovak Republic came into existence *by agreement of the sovereign will of two peoples of equal status*, and that full autonomy was secured to the Slovak people by the Pittsburgh Agreement as well as in other agreements and proclamations both in the country and elsewhere . . ." (my emphasis).[98]

By March 1939, however, international pressures overtook domestic developments. Hitler summoned the Slovak leader, Msg. Tiso, to Berlin and gave him the choice of independence or remaining with the Czechs, whatever might befall them. Tiso sent word of the ultimatum to the Slovak Parliament, which on March 14 voted for independence. Two days later, Tiso sent a telegram to Hitler stating, "In strong belief in you, the Führer and Reich Chancellor of the Greater German Reich, the Slovak State puts itself under your protection. The Slovak State asks you to assume this protection. Tiso." The answer came: "I acknowledge receipt of your urgent telegram and assume protection of the Slovak State. Adolf Hitler."[99] Thus, the curtain came down on the Republic.

Conclusion

The Czechoslovak nation-building project clearly encountered a rival interpretation of the state's proper foundations. The clerical nationalists did express agreement with certain of the regime's principles: first and foremost, the right of ethnic nations to self-determination via political sovereignty, and, beyond this, tolerance and equality. They had, however, a very different view of the proper sources of such values than the Czechoslovaks, who drew strongly on Czech history and traditions of political thought, on the Slovak-Czechoslovak movement of the nineteenth century, and on the Western humanist tradition. The clerical-nationalists, by contrast, did not have much specifically Slovak history or high culture to draw on, but did have language, religion, and the traditional peasant culture, a combination drawn together by nationalist leaders in the late nineteenth and early twentieth centuries. Unsurprisingly, the Czechoslovak and clerical-nationalist sources produced very different understandings of legitimate authority. The Czechoslovak orientation stressed the authority of the individual conscience, justifying substantial individual autonomy, which in turn was supported by an education based on free inquiry. The clerical nationalist orientation was much more oriented toward religious authority, and accordingly much less open to independent thought leading to the reinterpretation of communal values grounded in dogma, or to the construction of new norms. These two views are quite similar to Charles Taylor's two regime types discussed in the introduction, one of which values individual autonomy, and the other, a collective good that must be sought in common. Thus, the two understandings of nationhood share the principle of who should be sovereign—the ethnic nation—but have incompatible views both on how many ethnic nations founded the state (one versus two) and of the resulting authority (liberal-democratic and individualistic versus clerical-nationalist and collectivist). In founding itself on the principle of ethno-national self-determination, then, the Czechoslovak regime contained seeds of the challenge to its own legitimacy, as it justified the claim that each ethnic nation must follow its *own* notion of legitimate authority.

The centrality of ethnicity to the Czechoslovak nation-building project and the depth of its political-philosophical conflict with clerical nationalism are further illuminated by the state's Czech-centered symbols and heroes. In particular, Hus, a defining figure in Czech ethno-history, is famous precisely for repudiating Catholic authority, and paying for it with his life. The re-gime's celebration of his legacy and incorporation of Hussite symbols into the foundations of Czechoslovak national identity understandably prompted opposition from Slovak Catholics, many of whom saw political and religious authority as mutually reinforcing. This conflict clearly reflects the political—and divisive—meaning of certain ethnic symbols. Likewise, the Slovak focus on language and religion was deeply political, as both are pillars of Slovak national identity: Catholicism, as interpreted by leaders like Hlinka, offered a political philosophy, and language, a basis of identity that stood in for ethno-history in defining the nation's boundaries.

The lines of the political-philosophical conflict were, then, quite stark. Moreover, the contending, principled orientations were consonant with, and rooted in, political-cultural traditions. In the Czech lands, a national con-sciousness that grew out of the awakeners' nation-building project was well and widely established by the founding of the First Republic, and at least a portion of the (relatively small) Slovak middle class was nationally conscious as well.[100] Their orientations were substantially in harmony with the regime ideology, which clearly also drew strongly on the ideas, myths, and symbols central to the Czech National Revival and the Czechoslovak-oriented Slovak National Movement. Things are less clear with regard to the broader, more rural Slovak population: as Leff notes, the first Czechoslovak census in 1921 indicates that national consciousness was not yet broadly diffuse in the Slovak lands. By 1925, however, the HSPP had gained a wide, stable base, and "by the 1930s the leaders and the led almost certainly shared a mutually reinforc-ing set of convictions about the distinctiveness of being Slovak."[101] Thus, na-tional consciousness spread quite quickly due to the consonance of the Hlinka Party's message with long-standing religious and cultural orientations among Catholic Slovaks. Even if, at the Republic's founding, they did not see them-selves first and foremost as members of a Slovak nation, the HSPP characterization of this nation and its interests drew strongly on *existing* value orientations, even as it helped to shape them through the articulation of this message. Indeed, the First Republic's leaders recognized this consonance, and fearing that the clerical nationalist message would resonate with substantial swaths of the Slovak population, sought to limit the political authority of clericals and precluded autonomy for Slovaks until they underwent substantial normative change. They expected that this could be accomplished fairly straightforwardly through sociocultural modernization, clearly viewing identity as malleable and, ideally, the result of individual, rational reflection on modern ideas—hence the centrality of education. It also seems clear that the Czechoslovak project itself reinforced the validity of the HSPP's message concerning the distinctiveness of Slovak identity, as the Czechoslovaks highlighted this with their assertive anticlericalism and approach to the majority of Slovaks as backward and underdeveloped. Indeed, in a sense, the Czechoslovaks defined the new nation *in opposition to* the dominant orientation of Slovaks. This was nothing personal, so to speak, but resulted from the intellectual traditions that influenced them: Protestantism and humanism are both carefully developed reactions against Catholicism. They thus at once considered Slovaks co-nationals and "the other"—a problematic nation-building strategy. Ultimately, then, the evidence indicates that the Czechoslovak and clerical-nationalist principles were, in fact, substantially in harmony with existing patterns of Czech and Slovak political culture.

This brings me, finally, to the question of material interests. There was certainly no shortage of conflicts over these interests in the First Republic. The inequities of land reform, the Czech domination of scarce jobs in Slovakia, the disadvantaged position of Slovak industry in relation to Czech industry, and the exclusion of nationalist parties from government all qualify as issues that could be interpreted in national terms. There is no doubt that these produced Slovak grievances against the state that, for some, enhanced the attractiveness of Slovak nationalist rhetoric. At the same time, the Republic brought important improvements in education and state infrastructure, and support for the Czechoslovak parties had important benefits of patronage. Moreover, both the Czechoslovak and Slovak clericals appealed to the Slovaks in inclusive national terms, and both claimed to represent their material interests. Whose claim was more plausible depended, certainly, on each individual's situation; the point is that the Slovak nationalist party was not the only place where Slovaks could go if material interests were their primary consideration. Indeed, the Czechoslovak class-based and economically oriented parties had important

Slovak leaders and many Slovak beneficiaries, and it is likely that some Slovaks who did not fully subscribe to the "Czechoslovak" identity nevertheless supported these parties precisely for economic and power-political reasons. The HSPP was, however, the only place to go to find a defense of Slovak identity, and support for it actually came at a price with regard to material interests, at least for some. Indeed, in mounting this defense (which drew on the "embattled opposition nationalism" developed during under Hungarian rule[102]), the HSPP sacrificed its own access to power. As Leff and Mikula argue, this was principally because the clerical-nationalist challenge reflected a "stateness problem," which may occur when "there is unresolved conflict over the appropriate institutional guarantees of identity within that state. In the absence of consensus on the constitutional rules of the game, the 'stateness' question remains open."[103] Importantly, the two sides understood the implications of addressing this differently: "For many Slovaks, the stateness question involved how democratic recognition of Slovak identity should be institutionally expressed; for Czechs the stateness question was a security issue . . . a party could be perceived as antisystem—in impact if not in intent—if it challenged the unitary character of the state. Such antisystem parties could not participate in governance without renouncing their programs . . . this exclusion shaped party alignments, government formation, and policy agendas. The interwar republic long survived this internal deadlock because of superior Czech numbers and assets, and a political incentive structure that allowed them to set the agenda."[104] Thus, parties that made economic or class-based issues their priority, and wanted political access, could not challenge the Czechoslovak centrist position on the "stateness question." This helps explain the path taken by the Slovak Agrarians (a popular party in largely rural Slovakia), who under Hungarian rule had participated in the Slovak nationalist discourse. In 1922, having "found that it was no longer possible to speak the languages of nationalism and agrarianism simultaneously," they left the former behind and merged with the statewide Agrarian Party, though they remained a "conflicted component" of it.[105]

Given that the Czechoslovaks and clerical-nationalist Slovaks were divided by both principle and reinforcing political culture, and further, that a substantial penalty accrued from demanding institutional recognition of Slovak identity, it is likely that material interests were *not* the primary factor driving the conflict over the two contending understandings of nationhood, but rather a contributing factor. As Joseph Kirschbaum, who was a student involved in the nationalist cause during the First Republic, wrote, "while there were many serious reasons" for the "disappointment and grievances" of the Slovak autonomists over the years, "the seed of discord is to be found in the Czech tendency to create one single Czechoslovak people in the ethnic sense, with one language and one culture, ruled in a centralized Czech state."[106]

This chapter of Czech and Slovak history thus closes as the previous two did, with a triadic set of understandings of nationhood not primarily (and certainly not exclusively) driven by material interests. By 1939, these understandings were both widespread and had several generations of intellectual development and normative continuity behind them. They were, in other words, now deeply rooted elements of political culture. They also had two decades of specific confrontation between them, which helped alienate many Slovaks from the First Republic. This alienation, in turn, bolstered enthusiasm among some Slovaks for the wartime independent state, a regime that would ultimately deepen divisions among Slovaks. I turn now to this fascinating, and highly controversial, period of Slovak history.

CHAPTER FOUR

The Second Republic and the Wartime Slovak State

BECAUSE THE FIRST Republic's leaders rejected the HSPP's autonomy demands, the clerical-nationalists did not have a chance to govern Slovakia according to their own ideology. Indeed, since their first political mobilization in the late nineteenth century, they had never exercised significant governmental decision-making authority. This changed with the post-Munich Autonomy Agreement in 1938, and then much more profoundly with the founding of the Slovak state in 1939,[1] which has been variously described as authoritarian, totalitarian, and fascist. It was also divisive: five years after its founding, the Slovak National Uprising violently challenged the state's legitimacy, dramatically illustrating the lack of political consensus among Slovaks. In this chapter, I examine these regimes (focusing on the Slovak state), asking three questions. First, what were the regime's central ideological precepts? Second, how did these affect governance? And third, to what extent was this ideology consistent with the norms of Slovak clerical-nationalism traced in the preceding chapters?

The first two questions relate to my broader investigation of how principles of nationhood may affect political practice. These principles must, of course, be interpreted and applied by political leaders, who will be subject to many pressures and constraints, including those of the political system, those stemming from their own orientations and strategic considerations, and, in some cases (including, most decidedly, this one) those imposed by outside powers with strong influence over domestic policies. I am interested, then, in whether there is in fact a close relationship between regime principle and governance—whether leaders invoked these principles and whether their policies are logical or reasonable applications thereof. This is a particularly important question because the state was not only highly illiberal, but its policy toward the state's Jewish population—which its leaders defined as falling outside the boundaries of Slovak nationhood—was not only exclusionary but ultimately genocidal. In the broader interest of understanding the relationship between notions of nationhood and ethnically based persecution, then, the extent to which the state's policies toward this minority were supported and/or justified by its ideology is especially worth investigating.

My third question, concerning the relationship between the Slovak state ideology and understandings of nationhood in preceding periods, relates to my larger task of identifying normative continuities and discontinuities over time. It also gains additional consequence in the context of the second question, because if the state's ideology was supportive or conducive to the extreme persecution of minorities, it is worth determining the extent to which this resulted from norms new and specific to the wartime state, and the extent to which longer-standing ideological elements contributed. If evidence points to any role for the latter (and I argue that it does), then this potentiality must be noted, and if the norms survive this period (as will be investigated in succeeding chapters), then their activation in policy-making must be strictly scrutinized. This caution's relevance is, indeed, highlighted by the composition of the Slovak government at this writing (mid-2008), as the governing coalition includes a party (the Slovak National Party) that is an outspoken supporter of Tiso and his wartime state.

The Second Republic: October 1938–March 1939

As the preceding chapter noted, the Žilina Agreement granted autonomy to Slovakia within the reconstituted Czecho-Slovak state (the Second Republic). Under the Agreement, Monsignor Jozef Tiso became Slovakia's prime minister. Tiso had joined the HSPP in 1918 and quickly became one of its leading lights. He was elected to Parliament in 1925 and accepted the post of minister of public health during the HSPP's brief period in the government. In 1934, the party assigned him the "task of clarifying its ideological and political programme,"[2] and he became the HSPP's "leading ideologist."[3] He was also politically capable, and after Hlinka's death, emerged as the strongest candidate to take over the party's leadership.

One of the party leaders' first acts after the Autonomy Agreement—which placed them in a dominant position—was to rid the political arena of competing parties. They also excluded such major Slovak Czechoslovaks as Hodža, Šrobár, and Dérer from political leadership. The HSPP thus effectively sidelined its rivals, adding the title "Party of National Unity" to its name for good measure. Tiso hailed its creation in the Party journal *Slovák*, writing: "The Slovak nation has become united in the spirit of Bernolák and Štúr, in the spirit of Moyses and Kuzmány, and in the spirit of Hlinka and Rázus. Class distinctions have ceased and we now have only the united Slovak nation."[4] The Party of National Unity thus remedied the economic and political divisions that had characterized Slovak life under the First Republic.

While the HSPP effectively dominated the Slovak political system, its leadership was fractured. Tiso and his clerical-nationalist faction were clearly in charge, but two wings of the party were also becoming strong enough to potentially produce a power struggle. Vojtech Tuka headed one wing, returning to the political scene infirm and almost blind after years in prison for treason.[5] Despite his physical condition, Tuka remained sharp and quickly became the leader of the Hlinka Guard radical wing, based around the growing storm trooper organization and characterized by a rabidly anti-Semitic and pro-Nazi ideology. The other important wing was the Nástup group, an elite organization of nationalistic, Catholic, and authoritarian students and university graduates. The Academic Hlinka Guard was a Nástup organization, and Tiso was so impressed with its commander, Joseph Kirschbaum, that he made him secretary-general of the HSPP (he was removed at German insistence in 1940).

Despite its internal disunity, the Party acted ruthlessly to entrench its position in Slovak society. It dismissed the town and district councils and mayors and replaced them with government commissars,[6] disbanded cultural, youth, and athletic associations and gave their property to the Hlinka Guard,[7] and curtailed press freedom as government representatives censored all non-Party publications. While these policies affected the entire citizenry, the government singled out Czechs and Jews for particularly severe treatment. A government decree on December 23, 1938, transferred roughly 9,000 Czech employees out of Slovakia. Hlinka Guards physically deported some Czechs, dumping them over the border with Moravia. On a number of occasions, Jews were likewise forced over the border with Hungary. Usually, the Hungarians responded by pushing them back into Slovakia, where their property had already been confiscated.[8]

Given the frequent claim in Slovak nationalist histories of the state that Nazi Germany imposed its anti-Semitic excesses, it is important to note how the Jews were treated during the autonomy period *before* Czechoslovakia's division. As previous chapters showed, the HSPP had a generally anti-Semitic orientation from the time of its founding onward. With autonomy, however, this orientation could begin to shape policy. On October 6, 1938, the HSPP declared in its Žilina Manifesto that "we shall persevere at the side of all nations fighting against Jewish Marxism, its ideology, revolution, and violence."[9] Later that month, HSPP representative Ferdinand Ďurčanský informed German Field-Marshall Hermann Göring in Berlin that "the Jewish question will be settled in the same way as in Germany."[10] The autonomous Slovak Government Propaganda Office launched a wave of anti-Semitic pronouncements, and Jews were harassed in their businesses and on the street. In a January 1939 *Slovák* article titled "To the Jews as Many Rights as Belong to Them," Tiso argued that the Jews were disproportionately influential in Slovakia's economy and called for the situation to be remedied.[11] The next month, a government decree stripped citizenship from Jews who had settled in Slovakia from Germany, Hungary, and Poland during the First World War.[12] The Secretary of the U.S. Legation to Prague, George Kennan, described the development of official Slovak anti-Semitism in a dispatch to the U.S. Department of State, observing,

There is no point in reciting here the various statements of Slovak leaders with respect to the Jewish question. There have been many statements of this sort and their tenor has all been more or less the same: that the influence of Jews in the political and economic life of Slovakia would have to be eliminated, and that the Slovak government would not shy at extreme measures in pursuing this purpose. These views were confirmed . . . by the Slovak Prime Minister, Dr. Tiso, in a personal conversation. The Prime Minister stated that the Slovak government intended to take measures toward the solution of the Jewish question independently of Prague and that these measures would probably go farther in scope than any that might be taken by the Prague regime. He also stated the intention of his government to avoid irresponsible excesses and physical cruelty, but I suspect that this statement was made largely for the sake of effect and that the policy of the Slovak government in this point will be governed primarily by considerations of expediency.[13]

Kennan concluded that "it is evident that the Slovak leaders will encoun-
ter little opposition from the Church in the promulgation of an anti-Semitic
policy."[14] This dispatch was dated February 17, 1939, a month before Czecho-
Slovakia's dissolution.

Strong evidence thus clearly backs Slovak historian Ivan Kamenec's argument that the "anti-Semitic politics of the Slovak government arose not only
from existing Nazi pressure, but also from its own sources and motives."[15]
More broadly, from the beginning of the autonomy period, the HSPP regime
had very strong authoritarian tendencies. As with the regime's anti-Semitism,
these cannot be blamed simply on outside influences. The HSPP's arrogation
of political power grew out of its own view of its paramount status in the Slovak political spectrum. According to Kamenec, the "HSPP always regarded
itself as the one authentic representative of the Slovak nation, which in itself
held the possibility of its transforming into an authoritarian, totalitarian state
party."[16] Thus, the party's monopolization of political power, its curtailment
of the freedoms of speech and association, and its inhumane treatment of Jews
and, to a lesser degree, Czechs, show that the regime was fundamentally anti-
pluralist, anti-Semitic, and anti-democratic before it became a satellite of the
Third Reich—which happened on March 14, 1939.

The Slovak State's Ideology and Governance

Once independence was declared, the HSPP quickly set about defining the
state's founding principles. Tuka and the Hlinka Guard hoped to Nazify Slovak
politics and culture, but Hlinka and the clericals, backed by the Nástupists,
rejected this. Hlinka argued in *Slovák*: "Here we stand with our ideology, with
which we have for centuries long struggled in the past, so that we might keep
going and organizing under the great motto: For God and Nation. Therefore,
no deviation from our old ideology, because we would then deviate from the
root. The building of the Government and State shall go along with the same
party, based on the very same program that has led us in the past so that by
our political and structural activity we might lead the nation along the lines
that would safeguard its future. We need not bring into the nation values and
ideals of foreign origin, but we must develop our old spirit."[17] Likewise, the
journal *Nástup* declared: "It is our good fortune that the basic principles of
our ideology, which had led our Party in the struggle, need not be altered even
now after victory. After completing the organizational structure of the Party, it

will be necessary only to give a new form to this ideology and apply it to every sector of our state and national life."[18]

The relationship between church and state was a cornerstone in this state-building project. According to Tiso, who became President of the Slovak Republic, because nations are God's creations, they have an inherent right to freedom, which in turn can only be fully realized in their own state. There, the particular nation and the universal Church are joined. Very similar in orientation to Hlinka, Tiso had written in his 1930 exposition of the "Ideology of the Slovak People's Party," "Religion surely provides the norms for human activity—and politics is such an activity that therefore may not be removed from the province of religion. And on the other side, religion is an element of the nation's culture, and therefore politics must take an interest in this element."[19] He continued by appealing to the philosopher Pierre-Joseph Proudhon, who, he argued, "very clearly captured the connection of politics with religion when he declared: 'Every political question is at its core philosophical; and every philosophical question is actually a religious question.'"[20] Religion is thus prior to politics, and a just government will conform to its dictates: "Only through the acknowledgment of religion's sovereignty may it provide politics and the state with the deep support that is expected of it, i.e., the *binding sanction of authority* in conscience, from which the power of the law flows" (emphasis original).[21]

The preamble of the Constitution of the Slovak Republic, passed July 31, 1939, reflects the clerical-nationalist understanding of the relationship between political and religious authority. Its first sentence reads: "The Slovak nation, under the protection of Almighty God, survived throughout the ages on the territory destined for its national development and there, with the help of God, Who is the Source of all Power and Law, established its independent Slovak state."[22] As Jelinek observes, the preamble is notable "in its denial of the sovereignty of the people, a sacred principle in liberal constitutions."[23] The source of the state's authority is God alone.

Having established the state on these principles, its leaders demanded spiritual allegiance from the citizenry. They required soldiers, many officials, teachers, and students to participate in religious services and organized religious exercises both in parliament and in the professions. Soon the regime's representatives began to speak of "the necessity of 'forming a new man, a new citizen, an ideal Slovakia' which has to have as its purpose the collective honor, duty, responsibility, strict discipline, and blameless Christian life. Understandably, the substance of all of the above-mentioned virtues had to be determined by the state and, therein, the state party."[24] By attempting to control the spiritual lives of the citizens with the goal of producing both a new Slovak man and an ideal Slovakia, then, the regime's leaders clearly rejected the liberal ideal of individual autonomy in favor of a utopian vision of a Christian nation.

The regime's antiliberalism also led it to reject democratic pluralism in structuring the relationship between the nation and its state. According to Tiso, the nation is "a community of people who are of a single origin, single physical type, single character, single language, single set of customs, and single culture of equal goals, and they constitute an organic whole on a coherent territory."[25] Based on this vision of a homogeneous nation, both Tiso and Štefan Polakovič, the state's chief ideologist, rejected liberal democracy as an appropriate form of government, arguing that "liberalism and democracy entailed a split of national unity into political parties, associations and interest groups, setting them one against another. Thus liberalism weakened the nation, denationalized it, and placed it at the mercy of various external and internal enemies."[26] Describing liberalism's ill effects, Polakovič observed that "besides political, economic and social 'freedom,' which in reality enslaves mankind, liberalism also proclaimed freedom of licentious thought" which led to the "loose morality [that] in turn affected the healthy roots of the nation."[27] Liberalism had produced political decay throughout Europe, as "liberal-democratic states began to shrivel like trees that are inwardly corroded by worms."[28] Communism as well had failed. Thus, Polakovič concluded, "Europe needed movements that would regard the national community as a spiritually incontestable unit that is the result of an act of Divine Providence in the development of mankind."[29]

The nation's essential unity could be restored, according to Secretary-General Kirschbaum, if the regime destroyed political pluralism by consistently employing "a single political conception of foreign and internal politics." He continued, "Because a voluntary inclination toward this single path cannot be expected due to the diversity of opinions and the artificial fostering of many paths, the requirement of authoritative direction follows logically."[30] The "authoritative state" capable of providing this direction would involve a "governmental hierarchy of responsible individuals with the power to decide and with the obligation to carry the responsibility for their actions."[31] This ruling elite's power would be limited by one's particular status within the hierarchy and a sense of "responsibility."

Based on this view of "authoritative" government as the key to national unity, Tiso and Polakovič concluded that the state should tightly organize and regulate the society's life. The ideal of political unity would be realized through the Party. In a radio address, Tiso explained the proper relationship between the Party, state and nation: "The nation's instrument for effectively staffing and directing the State institutions for its own benefit has been, and remains, the party. In this mission the party is the supreme guardian of the nation's interests. When necessary it must also be the public prosecutor and the final judge."[32] Thus, the Party is a necessary aspect of national political life. Indeed, Tiso went so far as to argue that "it is a biological fact in the life of a nation; it is here, and as long as the nation exists, the Party will exist also."[33]

The Slovak Republic's Constitution enshrined the principle of the one-party state, declaring in Article 58 that "the Slovak people participate in political life through the medium of Hlinka's Slovak People's Party (the Party of National Unity)."[34] The Party had an authoritarian structure and could delegate power without popular consent. Moreover, in 1942, the Parliament passed the Law on Hlinka's Slovak People's Party, which established the fascist "leader principle." As Aladár Kočiš argued during the parliamentary debate over the law, the "Vodca," or leader, would then have "the supreme right to speak for and make decisions on behalf of the Party and thereby also on behalf of the nation."[35] According to James Mace Ward, this last touch was strategic, designed to help him "defeat the radicals."[36]

A constitutional article did allow for the representation of national minorities, declaring that "the ethnic groups participate in political life through a medium of their own political party, provided that such a party can be considered as a representative of the political will of the entire ethnic group."[37] This right was, however, only extended to those groups officially recognized by the state, a status limited to the Germans and the Magyars. Thus, the political representation of the citizenry was based on collective, ethnic criteria. The state's party system did not provide for the representation of multiple viewpoints within an ethnic group or for the idea of a shared "political will" that would overarch ethnicity. Given the nature of the political system, however, it is clear that the party elite would determine such will.

The regime's ideal of national unity was extensive. With the goal of erasing the social and economic divisions within the nation, the state's leaders attempted to create a corporatist system in Slovakia called "Christian solidarism." The initial attempts were based on an interpretation of the Catholic encyclicals *Rerum novarum* (1890) and *Quadragesimo anno* (1931). The plan "was not, however, satisfactory to Nazi Germany, which did not see in it adequate respect for its will, and it ran into resistance from the local German minority, which feared that individual corporate groups would have a majority of Slovak members."[38] Thus, the state only established a limited system of guilds through which workers lost their right to strike or bargain.

Corporatism was only one element of the HSPP drive to direct broader associational life in the Slovak state. As Kamenec argues, "the HSPP wanted to quickly and completely control the whole of public life. It realized this on the one hand by banning the activities of all non-Ľudak [non-HSPP] organizations and associations (except religious ones), and on the other hand, by establishing its own monopolistic organizations."[39] Certain aspects of this plan (such as compulsory service in the paramilitary Hlinka Guards) encountered popular resistance, however, and despite its best efforts, the HSPP "never did gain complete control over the nation."[40]

While the Slovak state leaders focused largely on the collective nation, they also delineated the rights and duties of the individual. According to Polakovič's clerical-nationalist ideology, individuals "exercise natural rights to life, to bodily integrity, to the necessary means for life, to grow freely in God, to associate and to own private property. Basically, they have equal views and equal will. Freedom of thought is to be admitted in a nation only when it is in harmony with conscience and religious convictions, and promotes constructive thoughts."[41] Polakovič termed this limited view of individual rights "Christian totalitarianism."[42]

The state's leaders further asserted that the nation's rights were prior to those of the individual. As Tiso explained, "The whole survives and lives from the sacrifice of the individual, without this the whole would not survive, but without the health and normal functioning of the whole, the individual could not assert himself."[43] He noted that the HSPP slogan "for God and nation" reflected this principle. Even the "rights and freedoms of every individual to work and lead a dignified life" could not be upheld "if the freedom of the individual would endanger the whole."[44] He concluded that the new "Christian socialism must prove that the individual interest may only be continually protected in the promotion of the interest of the whole."[45]

Through the Party elites' unified leadership, then, nationalism, patriotism, and party loyalty would come to reinforce one another. Polakovič argued, "the Party, the state and the nation today are an entity. The Party and the state serve the nation. Whoever loves the nation, belongs to the Party and is delighted with the state."[46] According to this reasoning, those who opposed the HSPP or its regime were enemies of both the state and the nation. Polakovič thus declared that "he who does not rejoice in the Slovak state is a traitor to the nation, is a Judas who is not fit to set foot on the soil, and it is therefore in the nation's interest for this moral burden to be silenced."[47] In the view of the party leaders, the state's authority was supreme, ordained by God, and not subject to challenge by its citizenry.

While the idea of blood-ties played a small role in the Slovak nationalist tradition, the Slovak state's ideologists made a point of emphasizing a biological element in their definition of nationhood. Jelinek observes that "expressions such as 'race,' 'ethnicism,' and 'biological source' were frequently used in essays of politicians and scholars."[48] Indeed, Polakovič is unambiguous in his declaration that "the Slovak nation developed originally from a single biological source and did not unite with the blood of other nations."[49] This extremely primordial conception of nationhood made the nation's boundaries impenetrable, physically differentiating the ethnic Slovak nation from the national minorities living in "its" territory.

While the Magyars, Poles, Ukrainians, and Russians were excluded to varying degrees from full political membership in the Slovak state, their situation was nowhere near as dire as that of the Slovak Jews, who faced escalating persecution. Anti-Semitic state policy was partially shaped by the ongoing power struggle within the government between the more moderate clerical-nationalists, led by President Tiso, and the Nazi-oriented radical wing, led by the less powerful Prime Minister Vojtech Tuka. In general, the radicals pushed for harsher legislation than the moderates. Kamenec observes that "in the propaganda of both camps, however, a hostile, venomous anti-Semitic campaign predominated, which differed from one another only in the extent of the vulgarity and primitivism."[50]

The strength of the two strains' influence on state policy depended importantly on decisions made by Nazi German leaders. As Ward argues, the Slovak state's treatment of its Jewish population can be divided into two periods. During the first, the clerical-nationalists held sway, and the government used a mainly confessional (rather than racial) definition of Jewish status as it sought to diminish "disproportionate" Jewish influence in the country's economic and cultural affairs. Soon after the state's founding, the government published a decree that had been in preparation since the autonomy period, titled "Concerning the Definition of the Term 'Jew' and the Restriction of the Number of Jews in Certain Free Professions." It established a limit of 4 percent Jewish participation in the legal profession, prohibited Jewish lawyers from representing non-Jewish clients except in exceptional circumstances, and banned Jews from being notaries public or editors of non-Jewish publications.[51] This was followed by a series of decrees that excluded Jews from employment in public offices, banned them from running pharmacies and limited their employment in them, set a limit on the number of Jews allowed to practice medicine, regulated their military service, limited the ability of Jewish lawyers to collect payment for their services, and ordered that Jewish-owned farm land be confiscated.[52] In December 1939, the interior minister sent out an instruction that "labeled Jews not only as enemies of the Slovak state, but also of the Slovak nation."[53] Finally, on May 29, 1940, a statutory decree ordered both Jews and Roma to perform labor for the state instead of military service.

The second period of anti-Semitic policy followed the Salzburg Conference in July 1940, at which Hitler sided with Slovak radicals against the clericals and "personally reshuffled the Slovak cabinet," placing radicals in several key positions and permanently undermining the Nástup group.[54] Thus bolstered, the radicals moved to bring Slovakia into line with Nazi policy and produced the "Jewish Codex," promulgated on September 9, 1941. Modeled after the Nuremberg Laws, the "Codex" actually surpassed the German legislation in severity. For his part, Tiso clearly recognized the utility of more aggressive anti-Semitic legislation in the intra-regime power struggle and oversaw the "Aryanization" of Jewish businesses, a process that confiscated Jewish property and distributed it to non-Jewish Slovaks.

In February 1942, the Slovak government began the final phase of its "solution" to the "Jewish question." Toward this end, Prime Minister Tuka negotiated with German leaders, who offered to accept 20,000 Jews for labor in the east. Without the consent of Parliament (a body of admittedly little power in relation to the executive), the government agreed to begin deportations. As Jelinek argues, that the Slovaks paid 500 marks "to the Nazi authorities for every Jew they agreed 'to care for' is evidence of Slovak eagerness to have the local Jewry deported."[55] The Parliament subsequently passed the Law of Deportation of the Jews, paving the way for the transfer of roughly 60,000 (of 89,000) Slovak Jews to concentration camps and legalizing the Slovak state's participation in the Holocaust. The deportations lasted from March 25 to October 20, 1942, and most of those sent off were murdered.

These extreme actions against the Jews, which were the radicals' only real policy success, stirred controversy in Slovakia. While anti-Semitism was common, the state's policies increasingly contravened Catholic doctrine, prompting strong criticism from some (though others did not respond this way; Ward notes that the "relative proportion between these two reactions is still open to debate"[56]). In particular, important elements in the Catholic Church, both domestically and at the Vatican, opposed legislation that defined Jews racially rather than confessionally, as it then applied to converts and some lifelong Christians.[57] Catholic bishops pushed especially strongly for the protection of these church members and their exemption from anti-Semitic legislation, which they partially secured.[58] With support from the Vatican (which took a leading role on the issue), they also criticized the deportations publicly, arguing that Jews "are also people and therefore should be treated humanely."[59] In spring 1943, when the government threatened to resume deportations, the bishops responded with a condemning pastoral letter, to be read aloud in every parish at Mass.

Tiso is reported to have obeyed the bishops' order himself in his Bánovec nad Bebravou parish.[60] He had also explicitly defended the state's anti-Semitic policy in a speech at Holíč in August 1942, stating: "[People ask] whether it is Christian, what we do? Is it human? Is it not robbery? But I ask: is it Christian, if the Slovak nation wants to get rid of its eternal enemy—the Jew? Is it Christian? Love of self is the command of God, and this love of self commands me to remove from myself everything that damages me, or that threatens my life. And that to the Slovaks the Jewish element threatened life, I think, about this it is not necessary to convince anyone. . . . we determined . . . that 5% of the Jews had 38% of the national income! It would have looked even worse, if we had not pulled ourselves together in time, if we had not purged them from us. And we did so according to divine command: Slovak, cast off your parasite."[61]

According to Ward, Tiso attempted to find a strategically advantageous place in the conflict over the state's anti-Semitic policies. On the one hand, he sought Germany's approval and support in his struggle with the radicals, and knew that the deportations would be helpful on this count. On the other, he understood that, in violating Catholic doctrine, core aspects of the state's anti-Semitic/genocidal policies "threatened the legitimacy of both the president and the state."[62] Tiso's attempt to negotiate a position between these two concerns is evident particularly in the way he granted presidential exemptions allowed by the anti-Semitic legislation, for which individuals could apply. The main category whose applications for exemption from deportation he approved were baptized Christian "Jews" (comprising 75 percent of the exemptions); he also exempted some spouses in mixed marriages and their children. More broadly, the recipients tended to be well educated, in jobs valuable to the state, and wealthy (the fee for exemption slid according to income and assets).[63] An investigation preceded Tiso's decision, and local officials were asked to look into such factors as "whether the applicant is morally behaved and politically reliable and whether it is possible to consider members of his family living with him as reliable from a national and political viewpoint; . . . what kind of family relations he has; what language he speaks at home; to which nationality does he declare himself; and in what spirit does he raise his children, and to what kind of school does he send them."[64] Ward thus concludes that "it would appear that Tiso in part conceived of the presidential exemption as an honor to be earned—generally through assimilation—and not as a means to prevent an unjust deportation of the Jews. For his part, Tiso claimed in his [postwar] trial that he sought the presidential exemption in order to protect the 'people who deserve it.'"[65] These, to Tiso, were few; he placed the vast majority of Jews entirely outside the realm of moral concern, allowing the deportations to continue for months after the Vatican informed him of the Jews' fate.[66] In any case, as Michael Marrus argues, "the character of the deportations themselves ought to have been warning enough. No provision was made for work parties, as with labor conscription; the convoys eventually included women, children, the very young, and the infirm. The victims were jammed into cattle cars, and nothing was ever heard of them after their departure. There seems little doubt: even if some stories were dismissed as exaggerations, or ignored as propaganda, or simply disbelieved, the defense of ignorance cannot be seriously maintained. Many of the details were unknown, but of mass murder there was no serious question."[67]

The Decline and Fall of the Slovak State

The war was never popular with the broader Slovak population. The Axis defeat at Stalingrad and retreat from the Caucasus in early 1943, which nearly annihilated a Slovak division, destabilized the regime. Party leaders attempted to back away from militarily supporting Germany, and religious leaders began to back away from the regime.[68] Already nervous, Slovakia's leaders were shocked when, in July 1943, Mussolini was deposed and, in September, Italian leaders reached an armistice agreement with the Allies. As the Axis powers faltered, the regime's stronghold began to unravel. Understanding that its position was becoming precarious, on September 11, 1943, the regime issued a circular defining certain persons as "unreliable" to state security and therefore eligible for preemptive confinement. The circular focused on Communists and members of the former Czechoslovak parties—two important Slovak political subcultures that had been largely (and forcibly) submerged in the new state.

In singling out these two groups the regime recognized its enemies well. In December 1943, they joined forces by forming an underground Slovak National Council (SNC). The SNC's founding Agreement declared the Slovak state illegitimate and authorized itself to represent the nation until the state was overthrown and elections could be held.[69] It also enumerated the SNC's guiding principles, the first of which stated: "It is our wish that the Slovak and Czech Nations, as the most closely related Slav nations, shape their destinies in the Czechoslovak Republic, in a common State of the Czechs and Slovaks built upon the principle of national equality." Its goals further included "close cooperation with all Slav countries and nations, especially the USSR," "firm but democratic" government, and the separation of church and state. The document ended by resolving that "the definite solution of these problems—in particular the relation between the Slovak and Czech nations as assured by the Constitution—is to be decided by the freely elected representatives of the Slovak Nation."[70] It thus reasserted the ideal of Czech and Slovak union—long held especially dear by the Czechoslovaks—and integrated it with both an Eastern orientation—valued by the Communists—and a more assertive Slovak position in the state, a long-standing Communist perspective which had also gained ground with some Slovak Czechoslovaks during the First Republic, and then with most of them over the course of the wartime state.

Once founded, the SNC began planning an uprising against the regime. It launched prematurely on August 29, 1944, after Moscow unilaterally parachuted guerillas into Slovakia. Although the SNC asked them to delay military action until the underground was ready for the uprising, the guerrillas refused to coordinate efforts. Their activities prompted Germany to invade Slovakia, with Bratislava's encouragement. In response, the SNC called the nation to arms, declaring: "Today the Slovak Nation openly and solemnly joins hands with the Allied nations, which by their struggle and great sacrifices will ensure a free, democratic life to all nations throughout the world—and to our small nation as well. We wish to contribute everything in our power toward the speedy conclusion of this fight for liberty."[71] They also demanded a new Czechoslovak Republic.

Although the Slovak National Uprising did have popular support, its premature start left it short of ammunition, weapons, air support, heavy machinery, and other necessary supplies.[72] Making matters worse, the Moscow-directed guerrillas were "insatiable" in "their demands for weapons, ammunition, and above all for food, clothing and money." Whereas the Soviet Union recognized the Uprising, it was stingy with supplies, and those weapons it did send went mostly to its guerrillas rather than the Slovak army, which was central to the revolt (and, interestingly, had a strong proportion of Protestants in its officer corps and was more anti-fascist than many other government institutions[73]). The Western Allies also provided some assistance, but limited their involvement because they considered Slovakia part of the Soviet sphere of influence. The lack of adequate Soviet assistance to the Slovak fighters led a Czechoslovak diplomat, Dr. Hubert Ripka, to conclude that "the Soviets disliked the Slovak efforts to liberate themselves by their own might. . . .The Soviets would have liked to see Slovakia exclusively grateful to its Eastern liberation."[74] Thus, despite the valiant efforts of Slovak democrats and Communists, the Germans crushed the Slovak National Uprising after two months.

The Slovak regime purchased its survival, however, by surrendering a substantial amount of power over internal politics to Germany. At this point, deportations of the Jews restarted, and another 13,500 were sent to the camps (around 10,000 of whom were murdered).[75] Still, the regime's days were numbered. As the Soviet army moved in, many of the regime's representatives retreated along with the Germans. In April 1945, the Red Army arrived and the Slovak state came to an end. Tiso sought asylum in an Austrian monastery and eventually surrendered to the U.S. army.

The Roots and Implications of the State Ideology

I turn now to the questions of the extent to which the Slovak state's ideology shaped governance, and how grounded it was in longer-standing traditions of Slovak political thought. To begin, given the gulf between Kollár and Šafářík's Czechoslovak orientation and the Slovak state's particularist, anti-Czech nationalism, it may seem that there is no substantial link between the state and this early part of the Slovak intellectual tradition. However, important elements of the Slovak state ideology have their source in Kollár and Šafářík's ideas. First, and fairly basically, the concept of cultural and linguistic nationhood is central to any Slovak nationalist assertion of independent ethnic identity. Second, Kollár argued that "it is not only a natural instinct and a natural right, but also a duty of reason for every nation, that it should seek to maintain its existence in a just manner, to develop its innate forces according to its position among mankind, to give public expression to its manner of life."[76] The

Slovak state ideology embraced this understanding of the natural rights and responsibilities of nationhood. Third, Kollár argued that nations are unique entities, one of the Slovak state ideology's central tenets. Fourth, although it was not dominant, there was a biological element to Kollár's definition of nationhood, which provided a precedent in the Slovak tradition for the Slovak state leaders' later assertion of this idea. Fifth, and finally, Šafářík's scholarly defense early in his career of a distinct Slovak identity laid the groundwork for a fuller assertion of this identity by later generations, including the Slovak state's founders.

While Kollár and Šafářík's contributions to the Slovak nationalist tradition provided some of the state ideology's fundamental elements, its leaders' understanding of the relationship between the individual, the nation, and the state differed radically from that of these awakeners. The awakeners valued freedom of thought and expression, which was alien to the Slovak state ideology. Further, Kollár argued that while God created the nation, humans created the state, which is not a defining element of the nation.

While the state's leaders did not identify themselves with Kollár and Šafářík, they did claim to be Štúr's heirs. Here, with the nation's "father," we do find some important similarities, particularly in his antiliberalism, celebration of patriarchal authority, and collectivism, all important elements of the Slovak state ideology. He was also the first Slovak nationalist to demand political autonomy for Slovakia, and thereby to claim at least a limited Slovak right to political self-determination. The state's political philosophy departed, however, from Štúr's democratic understanding of legitimate political authority.

During the time of his leadership of the nationalist Martin Group, Vajanský also condemned Western liberalism, and, further, attacked the separation of political and religious authority as a source of decadence. Clearly, though, the most direct ideological influence on the Slovak state's leaders came from the late nineteenth and early twentieth-century clerical nationalists, and among them, from Hlinka. Drawing on the Slovak nationalist tradition, Hlinka defined the nation according to cultural-linguistic criteria and invoked natural law to demand the self-determination necessary for the development of its own unique, collective personality. In many ways, then, Hlinka's understanding of nationhood reflects a Štúrian influence. This definition of the nation would become the core of the Slovak state's ideology and is a key element of continuity from Hlinka to Tiso. Hlinka diverges from Štúr, however, in his definition of the political principles necessary to undergird the relationship between the state and the nation. In Hlinka's view, legitimate political authority must conform to divine law, as interpreted by the Catholic Church's earthly representatives. This understanding of authority allows for a particularly comprehensive state role in the lives of the citizens. In addition, the reliance on incontestable religious dogma to define the goals and purposes of at least some elements of state policy limits the development and expression of alternative conceptions of the public good. Thus, the relationship that Hlinka envisioned between church and state has strong potential to produce patterns of governance that are antipluralist and, depending on the extent to which the church involves itself in shaping the state's policies, authoritarian or even totalitarian. As Slovak state leaders used Hlinka's view of the relationship between church and state as a foundation for their plan to build a new, Catholic Slovakia and a new Slovak man, Hlinka's clericalism provides a second critical link between his tradition and the Slovak state.

While the Slovak Republic's patterns of governance were shaped by elements of the Slovak clerical-nationalist tradition, it is important not to exaggerate Hlinka's influence. Under his leadership, the party tended to be anti-Semitic but not genocidal. Further, the HSPP competed in multiparty elections with the goal of achieving recognition of Slovak identity and a significant level of political autonomy. Hlinka did not seek to overthrow the democratic Czechoslovak state and replace it with a theocratic Slovak nation-state. Consistent with Slovak nationalist traditions, he held that the nation was morally prior to the state, and if it was possible to secure the nation's welfare through autonomy, that would be sufficient. If the state could not preserve the nation's integrity and sustain its development, then the nation would not owe the state its ultimate allegiance. Hlinka's ideology did not, therefore, equate national sovereignty with statehood.

By contrast, Tiso and the leaders of the Slovak Republic developed a view of the state that bound it inextricably to the nation. This did not occur until the nation gained its "own" state; despite the HSPP's political dominance during the autonomy period, its willingness to abandon post-Munich Czecho-Slovakia when the opportunity arose (albeit under coercive circumstances) indicates that the party did not strongly identify with that state. The nation's relationship to the state was, however, radically reoriented by the Slovak declaration of independence. According to the HSPP's ideology, the new Slovak political community represented the culmination of national development. Consistent with Hlinka's clerical-nationalist tradition, the state's leaders defined the concepts of "self-determination," "freedom," and "independence" collectively, but diverged from the tradition in asserting that the acquisition and preservation of these national rights was fulfilled through statehood itself. A new element was thus introduced into Slovak nationalism as the state was elevated to the status of the embodiment of the collective nation. This understanding of the basis of political legitimacy mirrored the collectivist ideology of Slovak nationalism in the tradition of Hlinka: just as membership in the nation is essentially primordial and nonvoluntary, so the individual's relationship to the nation's state is organic rather than a reflection of rational consent.

The Slovak state's ideology also drew on certain broader contemporary currents of Catholic political thought. The state's leaders were particularly influenced by the short-lived Austrian "Christian Corporative State," led by Kurt Schnussigg from 1934 to 1938. Slovak leaders drew heavily on the ideas of two of the Austrian state's architects, Mgr. Ignaz Seipel, leader of the Austrian Christian-Social Party, and Othmar Spann, a professor of sociology at Vienna University.[77] Their political vision had two political-theological pillars. The first was "Christian solidarism," which claimed a basis in the dictates of papal encyclicals. One of its founders describes its aims: "We are convinced that the Liberal capitalistic and Socialistic doctrines damaged the natural communities of family and people, and that an essential factor in the social question is the return to a genuine community. . . . The time of unrestrained, atomistic individualism is now definitely at an end. . . . There must be new forms of economy and a regulation of social life that will correspond to human needs, if we are to realize the necessary increase in productive capacity and obtain an abundance of goods."[78] In the Austrian state, under the influence of Seipel and Spann, Christian solidarism took the form of a parliament in which seven vocational corporations replaced political parties.

The Spann/Seipel vision's second pillar was a neo-Romantic theory of the state. This was based largely on Spann's conservative neo-Thomist *designatio* understanding of the origins political authority,[79] which held that "the people in a state are only indirectly the bearers of political power and all they can do is to designate (*designatio*) or elect the immediate bearer of political power to whom this power is then transferred 'by the grace of God.'"[80] This stands in contrast to an alternative neo-Thomist understanding of the source of authority, according to which "the people in a state are themselves the bearers of state power which they transfer directly (delegatio) to the organs of the state in the name of the natural rights of the people, whereby they do not by any means dispose of these rights permanently by their contractual act of delegation, but on the contrary remain the perpetual and original possessors of political power."[81] Of the two interpretations, it was the first that held sway in Austria.[82]

Spann placed this within a neo-Romantic framework and constructed a vision of political community that would be "a 'true' society, an organic state based not so much on social justice as on the stability that only an acceptance of hierarchy and strong differentiation of status and roles could ensure."[83] As John Haag argues, Spann's "universalistic state would be an uncompromisingly anti-democratic order ruled by a highly trained and motivated elite of 'natural' leaders whose high level of spirituality would ensure that the German *Geist* would never again be endangered by the corrosive forces of individualism and materialism."[84] The result would be a "polity based on synthesis and social cohesion rather than on conflict."[85]

These doctrines could be smoothly incorporated into more traditional Slovak clerical-nationalism because they shared two fundamental premises: first, that the nation is an organic community that should, by its very nature, live in unity, and, second, that religious and political authority should be mutually reinforcing. From these foundational ideas, it was a logical step to argue that the best way to protect or restore unity in a diversified nation is for a unified "authoritative" elite to govern it with God-given legitimacy. Combined with Tiso's new definition of the relationship between the nation and its state, this political philosophy justified the government's sacrifice of individual autonomy and political diversity in the name of national unity and the construction of a "new Slovak man." As the party "embodying" both nation and state, the HSPP leadership claimed the role of exclusive interpreter of the common good and, following the Austrian example, attempted to structure institutions so that the party could regulate all aspects of national life from the top down. Moreover, as the state was grounded in Catholic dogma, it embodied both the particular—the unique nation—and the universal—the principles of the Catholic Church. The state was thus sanctioned by divine sovereignty, and derived from this a kind of ultimate and unchallengeable legitimacy. An attack on the state became an attack both on the nation and on God's will.

According to the regime's principles, then, individual citizens lack the moral standing to claim a sphere of speech and action beyond the scope of government control. The citizens are not the source of state sovereignty, and any kind of independence from the party's leadership would disrupt national unity and threaten the state's purpose. The regime's leaders considered national freedom, realized through independent statehood and unified rule, to be prior to any claim to individual freedom by the nation's members. Thus, this case bears out Greenfeld's expectations about the authority structures that collectivistic nationalist ideologies produce, for as "the collectivity is seen in unitary terms, it tends to assume the character of a collective individual possessed of a single will, and someone is bound to be its interpreter"; thus, "a select few dictate to the masses who must obey."[86] Clearly, then, the regime's illiberal, antipluralist, authoritarian governance flowed directly from its core ideological principles.

This brings me to the relationship between traditions of Slovak political thought and the regime's anti-Semitic laws and policies. Three conclusions can be drawn straightforwardly. First, the Slovak radicals consciously and determinedly modeled their ideology after German National Socialism, and their impact on policy was disproportionate to their numbers because of the state's subservient position to this powerful genocidal state. Thus, the viciously anti-Semitic Codex and the deportation of the Jews bear the strong imprint of an interfering foreign power supported by a Slovak subculture. This is not to say that there were not strains of Slovak anti-Semitism that fed into this orientation, or that the radicals did not inflect the orientation with specifically Slovak perspective. Note, for example, the religious language used in a Hlinka Guard leaflet: "The wool is pulled over our eyes by the stupid phrase that the Jew is also a man. Jews are representatives and agents of the devil. The devil, when he wanted to resemble people, created the Jew. The Jew was not created by God, but by the devil, and therefore the Jew is not a man, but only looks like a man. He who in any manner supports or protects Jews—he will not escape God's punishment."[87] The radicals thus sought to ground their rhetoric in cultural mores intelligible within Slovak religious culture.

Second, I conclude that the clericals' persecutory but less extreme measures against the Jews were substantially in line with the type of anti-Semitism that had been evident in clerical-nationalist politics since their activation in the late nineteenth century. Indeed, even the clergy statement protesting the deportations noted that the state did have the right "through legal measures to limit damaging Jewish influence."[88] And third and finally, the Catholic opposition to the racial definition of Jewishness, the deportations, and other brutal measures was based on Church dogma that was also squarely part of the clerical-nationalist tradition. This of course stands in tension with the anti-Semitic elements of the same tradition; nonetheless, both have important status therein.

A thornier question is the relationship between clerical-nationalism and the state's participation in genocide, as the above conclusions might seem to distance the two. On this question, recent scholarship on genocide is illuminating. One key finding is that a population's willingness to accept or participate in the destruction of another group depends on a number of priming factors. Particularly important is "moral disengagement" from the target group. As James Waller argues, this "is not simply a matter of moral indifference or invisibility. Rather, it is an active, but gradual, process of detachment by which some individuals or groups are placed outside the boundary within which moral values, rules, and considerations of fairness apply."[89] One key means to this end is what Alexander Hinton calls the "crystallization of difference," a rigid categorization of identities that divides the target group from others in the society. He argues that "this is a hallmark of genocide: each person is assessed not on the basis of his or her individual characteristics, but in terms of his or her membership in an abstract category that is essentialized, stigmatized, and targeted for elimination." The stigmatization, in turn, is often pursued through ideology, which "is frequently characterized by metaphors of contamination depicting 'them' as permeating the boundaries that have been envisioned and crystallized by the genocidal regime—as an invasion that infects 'us.'"[90] Waller argues that such powerfully constructed messages (which constitute "linguistic dehumanization"[91]) can make mass killing or genocide "personally and socially acceptable" to people "by portraying it as serving socially worthy or moral purposes" and "essential to their own self-defense—to protect the cherished values of their community, fight ruthless oppression, preserve peace and stability, save humanity from subjugation, or honor their national commitment."[92] Hinton further argues that ideological justification is not enough to prompt genocide; the targeted group must also be differentiated from others through structural transformations. Thus, genocidal regimes "usually initiate a series of institutional, legal, social, and political changes that transform the conditions under which the targeted victim group live and, ultimately, perish. The structural changes that underlie this organization of difference create mechanisms, disciplines, and social spaces for distinguishing, dividing, confining, and regulating the target group."[93]

On all these counts, the clerical-nationalists contributed vitally, and in doing so, drew on national traditions. Their understanding of human community itself was essentialized: nations are unique and individual members derive their primary identity from, and are subordinate to, the organic whole. In particular, the Jews, as a community, were essentialized as inimical to the Slovak nation, and the clerical-nationalist ideology demanded that both Slovak individuals and minority communities be "silenced" or "sacrificed" if construed by the state's leaders to be a threat to the nation. The ideology thus laid crucial groundwork for moral justification of strong—even extreme—measures against the Jews as self-defense. Furthermore, state policies that first discriminated against Jews and then systematically deprived them of their property and standing in the community structurally differentiated them from the rest of society in a profoundly demeaning way. While these essentialized notions of community and persecutory policies did not *force* ethnic Slovaks to morally disengage from the Jewish population (and some did not), they surely facilitated such disengagement among many and thus helped pave the road to Slovak participation in genocide.

Conclusion

The Slovak state's ideology both drew on and diverged from the traditions of Slovak nationalism. The clericalism that merged church and state and the collectivist nationalism that merged party and nation derived from the Slovak clerical-nationalist tradition. By the time of the state's founding, these had likely become part of the Slovak nationalist political culture, having long characterized the HSPP's well-received politics (among more than a third of the Slovak population). The elevation of the state to an integral aspect of national existence—the merging of nation and state—was, however, unprecedented in Slovak nationalism. These ideological principles, in combination with imported currents of Austrian Catholic political thought (which, importantly, held that political authority flowed to its leaders from God, as sovereignty's source), straightforwardly justified the state's patterns of governance.

In arguing that the state's leaders acted on principle, I do not mean to suggest that crass power-political motivations were unimportant among the Party leaders. In an environment, both domestic and international, that was terribly brutal, it would be surprising if they did not play a strong role. Likewise, it is very hard to gauge the population's support for the regime, though there was broad, energetic compliance with some aspects (such as Aryanization) and resistance to others, especially where the government tried to radically expand its control over the citizens. To the extent that people did support it, material interests probably played an important role. Still, the state's politics were built on a framework that included key principles that the HSPP and its substantial support base had long put forward as legitimate. Once again, then, there is no reason to assume material interests were primary, as opposed to contributing, factors.

Ultimately, though it owed its existence to Hitler's favor, the wartime

Slovak state produced a sense of national self-sufficiency that profoundly affected the development of both Slovak nationalism and future Czech-Slovak relations. For the first time, the Slovaks were able to undertake state-building without Czech guidance and supervision. The resulting sense of efficacy strengthened Slovak nationalism, making the state "a watershed in the consolidation of Slovak national self-affirmation."[94]At the same time, the Uprising shows that a significant segment of the nation found the regime and its ideology intolerable. This further indicates the continuing existence of a deep cleavage on the issue of legitimate authority. The Slovak National Council also united democrats and Communists in its demands for the reconstruction of Czechoslovakia based on the principle of "equal with equal," indicating the continuing vitality of the idea of Czech-Slovak statehood. The next chapter takes up the question of how this multi-faceted legacy affected the reconstruction of the common state.

CHAPTER FIVE

The Third Republic:
"Putting an End to All Old Disputes"

WITHIN THREE YEARS of the war's end, the Communist Party took over Czechoslovakia's political system and precluded the free expression of political views for four decades. The Third Czechoslovak Republic, which functioned as a precarious democracy, thus offers a brief window into Czech and Slovak orientations after their separate experiences of the war years. This reconstituted common state faced enormous challenges, including finding mutually acceptable principles for the Czech-Slovak relationship and dealing with those in the society—and there were many—who had aligned themselves with what turned out to be the war's losing side. On the international front, the Soviet Union supported one Communist takeover after another throughout the region, making non-Communists very nervous. It is in this context, then, that I examine the new state's understanding of nationhood and compare it with those of preceding regimes. Its definition of sovereignty reflects continuities, in that it used the ethnic model, and a very crucial difference, in that it recognized distinct Slovak national sovereignty. I then explore three key facets of how the resulting governmental authority was exercised. First, I look at its implications for the division of power between Czechs and Slovaks, arguing that Czech dominance of the state's politics, which increased over time, reflected both a continuity with earlier periods and a violation of the state's own founding principle of national equality. Second, I look at the treatment of minorities—especially the Sudeten Germans and Hungarians, but also surviving Slovak Jews—and find that in comparison with the First Republic, it was extremely illiberal. Finally, in the context of the first two questions, I look broadly at the security of civil rights, which became increasingly precarious as the Communists (who had substantial electoral support in the Czech lands) moved to take power in the state.

This investigation offers important evidence concerning the conditions under which norms that had so far proven fairly stable over a significant period of time can change, or their interpretation become much more elastic. As many theorists of political culture argue, norms may be radically altered during crisis or intense upheaval, and World War II would certainly qualify as such a period. In particular, this period in Czechoslovak history highlights the crucial role that anger and a sense of betrayal (which ran in several directions) can play in prompting a shift toward a more illiberal orientation. We also see how the politics of retribution can in turn lead to a new sense of betrayal on the targeted side (this time, the Slovaks, many of whom had already felt betrayed by the First Republic). As future chapters will show, this cycle would encourage the two nations' members to not only view their own norms as different from those of the other, but actually in fundamental *opposition*. Thus, negative interpretations of the interactions and relationships between different communities' norms can come to constitute an element of political culture themselves, and the politics of the Third Republic played an important role in this regard. I begin, then, with the founding of this new republic, the last democratic Czechoslovak state until after the Velvet Revolution.

Union on New Terms

Self-confident from its wartime experiences, the Slovak National Council (SNC) came to the state-building negotiations in the spring of 1945 demanding a federation based on the principle of national equality, with independent national legislatures and a central government and parliament. The non-Communist Czech parties opposed this plan, and under pressure from Communist leader Klement Gottwald the SNC shelved it. Instead, it agreed to a Communist proposal that recognized the SNC as the Slovak executive organ and set up a Board of Commissioners charged with the daily tasks of governing Slovakia. By agreeing to these terms, the SNC "cleared the way for the so-called 'asymmetric structure,' which established the Slovak national constitutional inferiority in the Republic for some twenty-three years."[1] These structures were asymmetric in that the Czech lands had no parallel institutions, but were instead governed directly by central state organs in Prague. This compromise satisfied no one; the Czechs thought that it treated Slovaks specially, while the Slovaks found their autonomy insufficient.

Despite reservations on both sides, the decision was codified as part of the Košice Agreement on April 5, 1945. The section dealing with Slovakia stated: "Putting an end to all old disputes, and proceeding from the recognition of the Slovaks as a nationally independent nation, the government will from its first steps continually strive to realize the principle of 'equal with equal' in the Czecho-Slovak relationship so that the real brotherhood between the two nations would be put into force."[2] While Gottwald's description of the Košice Agreement as the "Magna Charta of the Slovak nation" was certainly an overstatement, it was the first time a Czechoslovak state had voluntarily formally and institutionally recognized the Slovaks as a distinct, sovereign nation (meaning, again, that authentic state authority issues from that nation)—a striking discontinuity with previous definitions of nationhood (except that of the brief Second Republic, which came into existence under coercive circumstances).

When the Košice Agreement was reached, the SNC issued a declaration reaffirming its "decision to live with the Czech nation in a united and indivisible Czechoslovak Republic." The declaration also condemned the wartime Slovak state as a period of "infernal enslavement, physical destruction and systematic ruination of the whole Slovak nation. . . . With the proclamation of the Slovak decision [above] we forever dispelled the hopes of the enemies of our common affairs and the doubts of our friends concerning the will of the Slovak nation."[3]

Such doubts did linger, however, and soon became apparent as state-building proceeded under the authority of the National Front. This coalition included all the parties in the Czech lands and Slovakia except the Hlinka Slovak People's Party and the Czech wartime collaborationist parties (the Agrarians, National Democrats, and Small Tradesmen), who were barred from participating in politics. The remaining Czech and Slovak players were divided by two cross-cutting cleavages: one national, between Czechs and Slovaks, and the other ideological, between Communists and non-Communists.

On the non-Communist side, no statewide parties remained. The Czech non-Communists were represented by three of the five former *pětka* members—the National Socialists, the Catholic Czechoslovak Populist Party, and the Social Democrats. The Slovak non-Communists were represented by the newly founded Democratic Party, whose leadership was largely Protestant but included Catholics. It did attempt to attract all segments of the population, and to gain broader Catholic support it signed an agreement with Church representatives in March 1946, allowing the party to claim that it represented the Catholics. Though this move significantly buttressed popular support for the Democrats, the party also drew in former members of the HSPP, and *Čas*, the party organ, became increasingly anti-Semitic. Despite the HSPP's dissolution, then, elements of its orientation continued to find a political voice.

Cooperation between the Czech and Slovak non-Communist parties was poor, for two main reasons. The first was the generational turnover in political leadership between the First and Third Republics. In the Czech lands, most interwar leaders were aging, dead, or discredited; only five of the more than ninety First Republic ministers held political office between 1945 and 1948.[4] The younger generation of leaders had participated in the London-based exile government under Beneš, but this did not prepare them for the difficult tasks of state-building in the Third Republic. These largely untried leaders stood in stark contrast to the new Slovak generation, who were "nationally self-confident, resistance-bred leaders, whose war achievements included little experience in cooperation with the Czechs."[5] Those interwar Slovak leaders who remained were either elderly (Šrobár) or unsympathetic to Beneš's government (Dérer).[6] Importantly, during World War II, exiled Slovak leaders once loyal to the Czechoslovak idea judged it as a profound failure; both Hodža and Osuský argued that it had led to "state catastrophe" and urged Beneš to consider federation or confederation as the model for the future—and met a hostile response.[7] Thus, by 1945, Czechoslovakism had lost its intellectual respectability among Slovaks, and "Prague had effectively lost its most tested Slovak collaborators."[8] This then was a discontinuity with earlier periods that was seriously unsettling for state politics.

The second, overlapping factor that impeded cooperation was that, broadly speaking, Czech and Slovak political leaders distrusted one another. Like their predecessors, the Czech leaders found the Slovaks' self-assertion frustrating, and the Democratic Party's inclusion of people with links to the wartime regime only heightened Czech suspicion. Leff reports that a "Czech participant in these uneasy relations argues retrospectively that the Slovak leadership 'appeared to the population of Bohemia and Moravia as a renewed form of the Slovak state, of sinister memory,' and admits that none of the non-Communist parties 'were disposed to recognize the Czecho-Slovak dualism which had in fact existed since liberation.'"[9] A 1946 Gallup survey reflected the dominant Czech orientation toward the Slovaks, showing that only 36 percent of Czechs approved of Slovakia's position in the new state and that two-thirds continued to regard Czechs and Slovaks as branches of one nation.[10]

This continuity in the Czech perspective was clearly in strong tension with one now dominant among Slovaks, many of whom responded with disappointment and anger. A 1946 letter to the editor of the Czech periodical *Dnešek* written by a Slovak reader and signed "LOB" articulates a common view: "I think that all of the Czechs who have visited Slovakia in the last years have had it made clear to them that the expression 'Czechoslovak' nation always means separation, an end to the debate. That is why I believe it would be good to finally make it understood that the Slovaks feel themselves to be an independent nation and that this cannot be reduced to another word. The old generation of Slovaks once emphasized the so-called 'Czechoslovak' nation, but the young Slovak generation scorns this. Yes, in the blunt meaning of the word, scorns. Those on the Czech side who do not accept this fact as unequivocal, definite and unchanging, that it does not need, indeed, may not be the subject of further debate, with those we will be by now far from an understanding."[11] In the postwar period, then, the patterns of interaction between the Czechs, the Czechoslovak Slovaks, and the clerical-nationalist Slovaks that had characterized the First Republic's politics shifted with the reorientation of more liberal-democratic Slovaks away from the Czechoslovak identity, leaving "a vacuum where systematic contact had existed before."[12]

A triangular pattern did exist, however, on the Communist side of the ideological cleavage. The three camps were composed of the Czechoslovak Communist Party, based in Prague and headed by Gottwald, and the two wings of the Slovak Communist Party. One wing represented the Communist elements of the "Uprising generation" and was led by Gustáv Husák and Ladislav Novomeský; the other was made up of the "Moscovites," who had either spent the entire war in Moscow or come from there in 1944 to assist in the resistance efforts. Many of these leaders had been arrested shortly after their arrival in the Slovak state, and after an unsuccessful attempt to free them during the Uprising had been sent to the Mauthausen concentration camp. Some died in transport to the camp or while interned there, and many were bitter toward the Uprising generation for (in their view) botching the liberation attempt.[13]

As state-building got underway, a power struggle between these two Slovak camps developed. The Moscovites felt threatened by the Uprising generation, who had gained prestige by their wartime activities, and whose cooperation with democratic Slovaks, begun during the Uprising, continued as they worked together against the reinstitution of Czech dominance in the new state.[14] This angered the Czech Communists, who allied themselves with the Moscovite Slovaks. At a party conference in July 1945, with the balance of power against them, the Uprising generation were pushed out of the party leadership and demoted to lower positions. From this point on, the alliance between the Czech Communists and the Slovak Moscovites—which in practice constituted the subordination of the Slovak to the Czech Communists—worked to the detriment of Slovak nationalism, leaving only the Democratic Party to represent its aims. At the same time, the Communists' at least partial bridging of the national divide gave them an advantage over their non-Communist rivals, as became clear during the continuing negotiations over the Czech-Slovak relationship.

Restructuring the Czech-Slovak Relationship: Negotiations and Machinations

While the Košice Agreement established the foundational principles for the Czech-Slovak relationship, the details were still to be determined. The initial step in this process was the First Prague Agreement, concluded in June 1945. It defined areas of common governance to be temporarily handled by presidential decrees that would require the approval of both the central government and the SNC; a few months later, it was amended to allow decisions on these common areas to be made by a simple majority in the provisional National Assembly, but still required that a majority of Slovak representatives approve decisions concerning Slovakia's status.

The new arrangement did not, however, produce smooth Czech-Slovak relations. The central government accused the SNC, particularly the Board of Commissioners, of both failing to enforce the central government's laws and decrees and developing their own legal norms. Moreover, the debate over postwar industrialization of Slovakia led to a struggle between Slovak Democrats, on the one hand, the Czech non-Communists and Czech Communists (the Slovak Communists deferred to their Czech comrades), on the other, over central versus Slovak control over the process. Through these conflicts, Czechs on both sides of the ideological divide became increasingly convinced that Slovakia's leadership was nationalist, reactionary, potentially separatist, and "a danger to the democratic order of the state."[15] The Communist and non-

Communist Czech parties therefore cooperated to erode Bratislava's autonomy and enhance the central government's powers, a goal partially accomplished through the Second Prague Agreement, which increased the president's statewide prerogatives. The Democratic Party held firm in negotiations over Slovak representation in the statewide Provisional National Assembly, however, and although the lack of cooperation from the Slovak Communists weakened its position, it was able to retain veto power on questions of Slovakia's status.

The Slovak Democratic Party's position and influence were enhanced by the general elections on May 26, 1946. Winning 62 percent of the vote, it roundly defeated its Slovak Communist rivals and confirmed Communism's relative lack of appeal to Slovaks. Although during the First Republic the Communists polled as strongly in Slovakia as in the Czech lands, this was due importantly to support from the Hungarian and German minorities, who were disenfranchised after World War II. The roots of Communism's weakness among ethnic Slovaks lay in their predominantly Catholic, conservative orientation, in the agricultural population's resistance to land reform,[16] and in the Communists' role in recent events. As David Paul argues, "the 'liberation' of Slovakia was greeted with great ambivalence, in comparison with the jubilation with which the Czechs received the end of the war. Many Slovaks had been associated with the [Jozef] Tiso regime, and many others had felt some pride in Slovak 'independence.'"[17] Furthermore, the Soviet Army acted extremely violently in Slovakia, raping and looting, and the Slovak Communists' association with these troops undermined their appeal.[18] With weak popular support, the Slovak Communists became less interested in autonomy.[19]

In contrast to the Slovak Communists' poor electoral showing, the Czechoslovak (Czech) Communist Party enjoyed a more substantial surge compared to prewar support levels, earning 41 percent of the Czech vote and becoming the nation's most powerful and best-organized party—in itself, a notable discontinuity with the past, when it was never included in a First Republic coalition (its best electoral results were in 1925, when it got 12.6 percent of the vote in Bohemia, 11.1 percent in Moravia, and 13.9 percent in Slovakia[20]). Having gained strong governmental influence through the elections, the Czechoslovak Communist Party leaders, alongside the Slovak Communists, quickly set about undermining the Slovak Democrats. They were joined in this effort by the non-Communist Czech parties, who—"blinded by the antipathy toward Slovak nationalism—let themselves be used to their own disadvantage."[21] Using a variety of means, including exclusion from the government coalition and blackmail of certain Democratic leaders, the Communists intimidated the Democratic Party into agreeing to the Third Prague Agreement of June 21, 1946, which thoroughly undermined Slovak institutional autonomy. The Agreement extended ministerial authority over Slovakia, subordinated the Board of Commissioners to the Prague government, gave Prague control over the entire state budget, and required that the central government approve legislation passed by the SNC.[22] Thus, only a month after their resounding defeat at the Slovak polls, the Communists managed to seriously undermine the Democrats'—and more broadly, Slovakia's—power.

Having weakened their Slovak competition, the Communists moved to further hamper potential cooperation between the Czech and Slovak non-Communists. According to Jelinek, their strategy included encouraging displays of nationalistic excess in Slovakia in order to alarm the Czechs and, ultimately, destabilize the Republic: "Extra-parliamentary activity, anti-Czech, anti-Czechoslovakia, anti-Communist, and anti-Jewish demonstrations and riots were grist to the Communist mill. It may well be that some of the outrages were Communist initiated. Nationalist and pro-Fascist elements assisted unconsciously in the Communist surge."[23]

The following year brought both further deterioration in the relationship between the non-Communist parties and between the Czechs and Slovaks more broadly. In particular, the wartime Slovak state's President Jozef Tiso's trial raised tensions precipitously. It followed closely the trial of five Czech high officials of the Protectorate of Bohemia and Moravia who had all received relatively light sentences; despite the government's recommendation in two cases, none were condemned to death, likely because there was little support among the Czech public for stricter punishment.[24] This prompted many Slovaks to expect a similar outcome for Tiso. Still, significant efforts were made to ensure this. Before the trial began, a group of Slovak bishops wrote to President Beneš, noting that "the solution of his personal question will have extensive influence on the thinking and behavior of part of the Slovak nation toward the renewal of the Czechoslovak Republic and its representatives." They therefore argued that it would "very much serve the peace of the nation if the case of Dr. Jozef Tiso were handled in a considerate way and not with ruthless harshness."[25] Popular sentiment was also expressed loudly: on walls throughout Slovakia, supporters wrote, "Long live Dr. Tiso"; pamphlets were distributed calling for his "liberation" and the re-founding of the Slovak state; and a May 1946 soccer match between Bohemia/Moravia and Slovakia in Bratislava was preceded by crowds singing the Slovak state anthem and calling for Tiso's release.[26] In this increasingly agitated climate, the chairman of the

Democratic Party and leader of the Slovak National Uprising, Jozef Lettrich, asked Beneš for a presidential reprieve for Tiso if he were sentenced to death, arguing alongside Catholic leaders that his execution would have three very negative consequences: "(1) it would harm Czech-Slovak relations at a fragile time in their development, and perhaps lead to an outbreak of violence; (2) it would increase tension between Catholics and Protestants in Slovakia, and (3) it would create a martyr for the cause of Slovak nationhood."[27]

The trial began on December 2, 1946. The charges fell into four main categories: the breakup of Czechoslovakia, the fascist state and its support of Nazi Germany, the putting down of the Uprising, and crimes against humanity. Bradley Abrams argues that these charges raise two noteworthy points. First, they heavily emphasized crimes against Czechoslovakia and Czechs; indeed, "even in the list of Tiso's crimes against humanity, thievery from Czechs constituted the first two charges, followed only then by charges related to the deportation of the Slovak Jews." And second, the charges stressed the Slovak state's opposition, expressed through both military and propaganda efforts, to the Comintern and the USSR. Abrams observes, "it seems evident from even the reading of the charges that there was no small measure of Czech national pride at stake in the case and at least part of this was based on the Communist and more 'progressive' Czech political representation's desire to show its faithfulness to its great ally, the Soviet Union."[28]

After seventy-one days, the prosecutor called for the death penalty and the judges began what would be a month-long deliberation about the verdict. This day—March 19, 1947—was also Tiso's nameday, and there were public demonstrations in his support. Thereafter, church and Democratic Party leaders renewed their efforts to gain presidential clemency, and the Slovak bishops wrote Beneš a letter noting that executing Tiso "would shake Slovakia to its foundations, and we do not know when it would be possible to overcome the breach caused by it."[29] Ultimately, these and further, increasingly desperate appeals by the Democratic Party fell on deaf ears. Tiso was convicted and sentenced to death, and clemency was not granted. Czech leaders saw Tiso as a traitor, and many were intent on proving loyalty to the Soviet Union and undermining both Slovak clericalism and what they saw as its ally, the Democratic Party.[30] On April 18, 1947, an unrepentant Tiso went to the gallows.

No violence ensued, but according to Abrams, this outcome deeply demoralized the Democratic Party and widened the gulf between it and its Czech non-Communist counterparts. Moreover, "among a certain proportion of Slovaks the Czechs and the Communists were considered responsible for the judicial murder of the primary symbol of Slovak national consciousness and the sharp curtailment of Slovak self-administration."[31] Ultimately, this "gravely damaged" the "course toward reaching a mutually acceptable form for Czech-Slovak relations".[32]

The international scene was becoming more turbulent as well, as the Communists took over Hungary, Bulgaria, Poland, and Romania. Though Czechoslovakia still functioned as a precarious democracy at this point, in July 1947 Moscow was able to force it to refuse an invitation to join the Marshall Plan. The threatening developments abroad deepened the non-Communists' sense of insecurity, which was compounded by the domestic Communists' use of intimidating tactics.

As the atmosphere of uncertainty and upheaval thickened, the Communists escalated their attacks on the Slovak Democrats. The situation reached a crisis point when an alleged Slovak anti-state conspiracy, led by HSPP exiles in the West but including current Slovak political leaders and deputies, was "uncovered" (and later proven to have been fabricated).[33] Some of the accused conspirators were members of the Democratic Party, and the Communists publicly pressured the Democrats to renounce their implicated members. In addition, the Communists used the Association of Slovak Partisans, a Communist-controlled armed group consisting of both radical Communists and fascists with a history of anti-Semitic violence, to further intimidate Slovak leaders. At this point, the Democrats no longer had the strength to resist the Communist onslaught, and the party gave up its majority on the Board of Commissioners and much of its influence. This phase of the Communist offensive was led by the "Uprising generation," in cooperation with the Slovak Communist leadership. As Jelinek observes, "it is ironical that they succeeded thanks to continuous undermining of the nationalistic policies of the Democratic Party. The shrewd Communist tactics (and the ruthless use of force) deprived the Democrats of the trust and support of non-Communist Czechs and left them alone to defend themselves."[34]

The crisis in Slovakia was something of a "rehearsal" for the coup in February 1948,[35] through which the Communists took over the entire state. The coup was precipitated when twelve non-Communist central government ministers resigned in protest after the Communist Minister of Defense unilaterally promoted his men into the highest positions in the police forces. The ministers expected that President Beneš would refuse their resignations and force the Communists into line. However, strong-arm pressure from Prime

Minister Gottwald and the societal forces he controlled, which included media and violent street forces, as well as police power, effectively forced Beneš to
replace the non-Communist ministers with Communists. Clearly, the Communists did not feel constrained by any notion of "civil rights." A similar
course of events followed in Bratislava, where the non-Communist members
of the Board of Commissioners were dismissed. The curtain then dropped on
the third Czechoslovak state.

Clearly, the conflict between Czech and Slovak perspectives on how to
structure the exercise of the two nations' sovereign authority helped destabilize
the First Republic. I turn now to a second facet of the Third Republic leaders'
interpretation of ethnic sovereignty, on which they were in much more agreement, and for which the state is infamous: the treatment of ethno-national
minorities.

Enforcing the Boundaries of Nationhood: The Status of Minorities in the Third Republic

The Košice Agreement that promised a "brotherly" relationship between the
Czechs and Slovaks also made clear that the state's relationship to two of its
minorities would radically change. Chapter 8 states: "The terrible experiences
of the Czechs and Slovaks with the German and Hungarian minorities, large
segments of whom became the compliant tools of aggressive outside political forces against the Republic, and among these the Czechoslovak Germans
who particularly openly lent support to the internecine campaign against the
Czech and Slovak nations, compel the restored Czechoslovakia to profound
and permanent action."[36] A month after Košice, Beneš took such action by
announcing, "the overwhelming majority of the Germans and Hungarians
will have to leave our land. This is our final decision."[37] A series of presidential
decrees followed, excluding non-Slavs from participation in economic life,
defining Germans and Hungarians as politically unreliable, closing German
and Hungarian schools, and establishing a "Settlement Bureau" charged with
"returning" lands to Slav ownership. These groups were, then, stripped of fundamental civil rights.

Efforts by state leaders to ethnically cleanse the Republic began in earnest
in May 1945. In particular, Czech efforts to rid the state of ethnic Germans
were aggressive and largely uncoordinated, reflecting very high tensions between the two groups in the aftermath of the Protectorate's brutal final period.

As the summer of 1945 progressed, pogroms erupted, as happened in the aftermath of a munitions warehouse explosion in the town of Ústí nad Labem in July, which killed twenty-eight and injured more (including both Czechs and Germans). Locals blamed a German saboteur group called the "Werewolves" and proceeded to go on a rampage against the German population, killing at least two hundred (some claim the numbers were much higher). These included women and children who were thrown from a bridge into the Elbe River and shot at "until they no longer resurfaced."[38] Thereafter, government officials used the massacre to justify intensified efforts to deport the Germans; as Minister of Foreign Trade Hubert Ripka declared on the radio, "one should understand the feelings of our people who are constantly attacked by Werewolf organizations and whose property is still being destroyed. . . . Many of our people still do not feel safe until they know the Germans will go away."[39]

The following month, at the Potsdam Conference, the Big Three powers approved the mass deportation of ethnic Germans from Czechoslovakia. Thereafter, the "wild" deportations, which had already directly or indirectly led 700,000 to 800,000 Germans to leave the country, were replaced by a much more organized "transfer" (*odsun*).[40] The accompanying government and broader journalistic rhetoric, however, remained vitriolic and inflammatory. A key theme was the Germans' collective guilt, the justification for the expulsion. Sometimes it was asserted broadly, as when a headline declared, "The entire German people are responsible for Lidice,"[41] a Czech town whose population was subjected to devastating SS retribution after the Czech partisan assassination of Protectorate leader Reinhard Heydrich in 1942.[42] At other times, collective guilt was linked to that of criminal defendants. For example, before the 1946 trial of Karl Hermann Frank, Nazi state-secretary and from 1942 to 1945 state-minister of the Protectorate (the highest authority in the land, "known for his advocacy of repression and terror"), the state published a 191-page pamphlet containing his testimony under interrogation.[43] In the introduction, the editor argued that, in addition to the Germans' long history of disloyalty to Czechoslovakia, the testimony helped justify the expulsions: "the trial of K. H. Frank, notwithstanding his personal responsibility, cannot be considered a trial of an individual criminal, but a trial of the collective criminality of the German minority in Czechoslovakia."[44] Similarly, following the 1947 conviction of fifteen interwar representatives of Konrad Henlein's Sudeten German Party for treason before 1939 (resulting in six death sentences), a Czech newspaper wrote, "The just punishment, which the Czech people imposed on the Swastika-ed deputies and senators, is the symbolic conclusion to the final parting of the democratic Czech population from the German parasites."[45] Some Czech Catholic Church officials also offered support, as when canon of Vyšehrad Monsignor Bohumil Stašek stated that "once in a thousand years the time has come to settle accounts with the Germans, who are evil and to whom the commandment to love thy neighbor therefore does not apply."[46]

Life was difficult for the ethnic Germans waiting to be deported. They were segregated from the rest of society through restrictions on when they could shop in stores or go to taverns and restaurants and by prohibitions against their walking on sidewalks, sitting on park benches, using trains, and going to movie theaters.[47] Czechoslovak citizens were legally barred from "social relations" with ethnic Germans, and could be punished with jail time.[48] Some Germans awaited expulsion in labor and detention camps, where conditions were very harsh. The majority of those interned were German women and girls, and many were sexually abused and routinely called "Nazi whores" and "pigs."[49] The deportees' property was seized, and the journey out of the country was made very difficult by disease, hunger, exposure, frequent suicides, and sometimes abuse by the authorities. Figures on the resulting deaths vary extremely, but a 1996 Czech-German historical commission estimates that they numbered between 19,000 and 30,000.[50]

While the Allied powers approved the expulsion of the Sudeten Germans (thought not always the methods), the Americans blocked the removal of the Hungarians to Hungary. Nevertheless, the day the Potsdam decisions were published, Presidential decree 33/1945 put a key element of the Košice Agreement into effect by depriving both Germans and Hungarians (roughly 97 percent of Hungarians were affected, as "anti-fascists" were excluded) of their civil rights and ending their access to retirement payments, public health services, and welfare.[51] Thus, while unable to physically deport the Hungarians, Czechoslovak authorities essentially placed them outside the state's responsibility.

Though Potsdam precluded an expedited solution to the "problem" of the Hungarian minority, the Slovaks took the lead in finding other ways of purging the state. They used three main strategies. First, they proposed a voluntary population exchange with Hungary, which, after tense negotiations, resulted in an agreement with Budapest in February 1946. The Czechoslovak leaders hoped that 200,000 Hungarians would leave in exchange for ethnic Slovaks in Hungary, but were ultimately only able to resettle, or in some cases expel, 68,407 Hungarians. A second method was the "Re-Slovakization" campaign.

Launched in 1946, it was based on the idea that many Hungarians were actually Magyarized Slovaks. It offered these ethnic lost children full citizenship rights in exchange for the promise to return to Slovak identity. Roughly 325,000 Hungarians availed themselves of this opportunity to reconcile themselves with the new regime. Despite this impressive number, the Slovak authorities were soon frustrated by the unwillingness of the new "Slovaks" to adopt Slovak language or culture. The third method was the forcible deportation of Hungarians from areas where they were concentrated in southern Slovakia into the Bohemian lands vacated by the expelled Germans. Government leaders justified this measure as necessary for providing labor for reconstruction. Lasting 99 days, from November 1946 until February 1947, the program transferred 44,129 Hungarians from Slovakia to the Czech lands and confiscated their property. The goal appears to have been to disperse the Hungarian minority, but it met with sufficient international condemnation, particularly from the United States, for the state to abandon further transfers.

Though the most dramatic aspects of Czechoslovak minority policies centered on efforts to rid the country of Germans and Hungarians, the government also sought to prevent the redevelopment of a distinct Jewish community in the aftermath of the Holocaust. Even before the state's re-founding, Václav Kopecký, a close associate of Gottwald, announced that "liquidation of anti-Semitism cannot be allowed to cause harm to the national and Slav character of the future Czechoslovak Republic."[52] Consistent with the Czech People's Party declaration that the "Republic is a nation-state, we do not recognize national minorities,"[53] state leaders refused to continue the First Republic's recognition of Jewish nationality. Instead, they requested that Jews either assimilate or emigrate. Jews returning from concentration camps also faced significant obstacles to resuming their lives. Some state leaders resisted returning Aryanized property, from which many Slovaks had profited. Though eventally restitution laws were passed, Husák reflected the continuing anti-Semitism of many leaders in his 1945 statement that "we have no interest in returning the property to these rich men, who never had any understanding of the case of the Slovak people, who put their private interests above the interests of the nation."[54] Anti-Hungarian fervor also provided enhanced opportunities for anti-Semitic measures. During the population exchange with Hungary, using "the pretext that they were Magyars, Bratislava authorities tried to eject to Hungary South Slovakian Jews who had just returned from Nazi concentration camps."[55] Anti-Hungarianism and anti-Semitism thus became mutually reinforcing. Indeed, Kálman Janics suggests that Mach, Tiso's Minister of the

Interior, may have escaped the death penalty during his war crimes trial by explaining that he approved the deportation of Jews to the death camps because he considered them to be "90 percent Hungarians."[56]

Conclusion

The Third Republic's politics reflected a complex combination of continuities and discontinuities with earlier periods. In the Slovak case, one clear discontinuity was the broad acceptance, across the political spectrum, of the Slovak nation as a distinct and sovereign entity. Though the wartime state had prompted Slovaks to take up arms against one another, the period actually undermined the division among Slovaks over the nation's boundaries. This new orientation was particularly straightforwardly communicated by the new generation of Slovak political leaders, as the older generation was no longer significantly politically active during the Third Republic. A clear consensus on sovereignty now existed among Slovak leaders.

The question of how Slovaks understood the nature of the political authority flowing from sovereignty is much harder to answer. The democrats and Communists had clearly rejected the Slovak state and its ideology, through the Uprising and then in declarations such as the one that accompanied the Košice Agreement. They also called for the construction of a specifically democratic state. Still, the Democratic Party's acceptance of former HSPP affiliates, its willingness to allow anti-Semitic nationalists to take over its journal, *Čas*, and its reluctance to return Aryanized property to surviving Jews, or even to allow their resettlement in many cases, complicates the democrats' earlier rejection of clerical-nationalism. More broadly, continuing illiberal nationalist demonstrations (even if some were provoked by the Communists) and widespread popular anger at the judgment against Tiso demonstrated the persistence of certain illiberal orientations dominant under the Slovak state. That said, because the Slovaks' political power was so rapidly circumscribed during the Third Republic, a process which placed the Democratic Party under siege, it is ultimately hard to judge their view of legitimate authority.

The Czech view of sovereignty was much less straightforward than the Slovak. Czechs formally accepted the principle of "equal with equal" sovereign nations, but then vigorously undermined it. In terms of popular attitudes, many Czechs continued to see Slovaks as co-nationals. On the elite level, the behavior of Communists and non-Communists alike is illuminating, as they clearly associated the idea of Slovak national sovereignty with a repressive, illiberal, clerical-nationalist view of the resulting power. Among Czech democrats, this orientation was so strong that it blinded leaders to the Communists' manipulation of the issue. This view in itself reflects continuities with the Czech orientation during the First Republic, though it was certainly reinforced by the Slovak state's politics. Ultimately, given the conflict between stated principle and behavior, the Czech position on the boundaries of the sovereign ethnic nation remained unclear during this period.

Much less ambiguous was the marked increase in Czech illiberalism, which represented a stark discontinuity from the First Republic's commitment to individual rights and liberties. This was evident in the strong Czech support for the Communist Party, which was not only ideologically collectivist, but also intent on increasingly—and at times violently—undermining the security of civil rights in its quest for total state control. Increased illiberalism was likewise evident in the assignation of collective guilt to the Hungarian and German minorities, and especially the brutal expulsion of the latter. While it is important not to overstretch the comparison (there are clear differences between the situations), the Czech treatment of the Sudeten Germans has some parallels with the Slovak clerical-nationalist treatment of the Jews discussed in the preceding chapter. Czech leaders essentialized the ethnic German population as treacherous others collectively guilty of the Nazis' terrible crimes, using strikingly similar dehumanizing language (such as calling them "parasites"), and thereby offering powerful moral justification for expelling a group that the Czechs had lived with for centuries. Moreover, the state structurally differentiated the ethnic Germans from the rest of society by rescinding their civil rights and citizenship, legally enforcing their social segregation, interning some in degrading conditions, and dispossessing them of their property. Certainly, powerful Czech animosity against the Sudeten Germans preceded the Third Republic's rhetoric and policies, but these also facilitated the moral disengagement necessary for a campaign of ethnic cleansing that inflicted terrible suffering on three million men, women, and children.

Key components of the Czech political tradition supported this repressive minority policy. Other, more liberal-democratic elements were diminished and often violated, as both the importance of ethnic boundaries of nationhood and anti-German sentiment were elevated and used to justify extremely illiberal exercise of sovereign authority. As Skilling argues, the Czechs' experiences in the preceding decade contributed to this repudiation of previously prized principles and led to a reorientation in a particular direction: "the Munich surrender, the Nazi occupation, the Slovak separation, and the experiences of war brought about a profound shift in values, including a substantial discrediting of the First Republic and its traditions, and some disillusionment with capitalism and 'bourgeois' democracy, and, at the same time, a rise in the stock of socialism, of Soviet Russia and the Communist party of Czechoslovakia."[57] Ultimately, World War II and the following period did have a powerful impact on both Czech and Slovak understandings of nationhood, offering insight into the conditions under which such norms may become malleable. The Slovak wartime experience, while divisive, served nevertheless to consolidate a sense of distinct nationhood throughout Slovak society. The Czechs, by contrast, entered the postwar period profoundly shaken in relation to their own traditions. For many Slovaks, the wartime period was affirming; for the Czechs it was the opposite. The war and its aftermath in the Third Republic thus drove the two nations' understandings of nationhood—already in some conflict during the First Republic—further apart, and they entered their fourth common state at a point when the sense of betrayal overshadowed a sense of shared purpose.

CHAPTER SIX

The Communist Period: New Vows

Just as the wartime Slovak State was deeply hostile to the First Republic's ideology (recall Polakovič's image of liberal states as "inwardly corroded by worms"), the Czechoslovak Communist regime was profoundly opposed to both clerical-nationalism and liberal democracy, to the point of justifying violence in the struggle against them. If the Communists were successful in their efforts to eradicate these ideological orientations among Czechs and Slovaks, then it is problematic to speak of *continuities* between post-Communist understandings of nationhood and earlier periods, as the traditions would not have been alive, in any meaningful sense, for several decades. In this chapter, I examine the Communist period to see whether the Czech and Slovak orientations I traced to this point survived and remained in any sense potent. I do this by focusing on periods of reform and periods of targeted repression, which offer windows into submerged orientations not otherwise evident in an extremely anti-pluralist regime. For the former, I look to the political discourse during the relatively open period leading up to and during the Prague Spring, as it provides insight into the Czech and Slovak perspectives on the reforms necessary to legitimize the Czechoslovak regime. For the latter, though the evidence is more indirect, I look at how the Communist leadership attempted to repress particular viewpoints through the trials of the "bourgeois nationalists" in the 1950s, and at the relationship between the regime and both the Czechs and Slovaks during the post-Prague Spring "Normalization" period (1969–89).[1]

It is worth emphasizing at the outset that when set in broader historical context, the most striking thing about the Communist period is its *dis*continuity with earlier periods, with regard not only to the official political culture, but also to the broader public's compliance with it most of the time. Keeping this in mind, the challenges to the regime, which grew after the Stalinist period of repression and revolutionary zeal abated, became so strong that the Soviet Union quashed them with military force in 1968. I argue that these were based on values and principles that were central to the political-cultural orientations I have traced, and as such, also reflected long-standing differences between the dominant Czech and Slovak priorities. The two nations' relationships to the post-invasion regime—which, importantly, recognized Slovak sovereignty via federation—were likewise shaped by different views of legitimate authority, supporting religious but very little secular political dissidence in Slovakia, and liberal-democratic human rights-based dissidence in the Czech Republic.

Thus, key elements of traditional normative understandings of nationhood reemerged in the post-Stalinist period to become the subject of active engagement in crucial struggles over how to define the nature and purposes of political community under a regime *dedicated to their destruction*. This is further proof of these norms' remarkable hardiness, and provides the final link in the historical chain from the nineteenth century to the end of the Communist period, which would not end in ideological vacuum. The often contentious interaction between the Czech and Slovak orientations during this period, as well as different elites' relationships to political power during the regime's final twenty years, would also have important legacies in the post-Communist period. Ultimately, then, this sets the stage for my examination of these norms' implications for the final, unsuccessful renegotiation of the Czech-Slovak relationship after the Velvet Revolution.

The Communist Understanding of Nationhood

The preamble of the 1948 "Ninth-of-May Constitution," which founded the Communist state, begins, "We, the Czechoslovak people."[2] This stands in contrast to the 1920 Constitution, which, of course, invoked the Czechoslovak nation. As the 1948 preamble continues, however, it specifies that it is the "Czechs and Slovaks, two fraternal nations" who are establishing the state in conformity with the "progressive and humanist traditions of their history." The language becomes more civic again at the outset of the Constitution's main body, where Article I (2) declares, "The people is the sole source of all power in the state." Directly below, Article II (1) states, "The Czechoslovak Republic is the united state of two equal Slavic nations, the Czechs and the Slovaks." There is, then, some ambiguity in the language, which is sometimes highly inclusive and suggests that the entire population is the source of state sovereignty, but also gives special status to the two founding nations.

In 1960, state leaders promulgated a new constitution to represent the country's graduation from the status of "people's democracy" to "socialist republic."[3] Here, the preamble founds the state in the name of "We, the working people of Czechoslovakia." In Article 1(2), it states very similarly to its predecessor that the "Czechoslovak Socialist Republic is the united state of two equal fraternal nations, the Czechs and Slovaks." It then states in Article 2(1): "All power in the Czechoslovak Socialist Republic belongs to the working people." The 1960 Constitution is thus more class-based and offers a narrower definition of the sovereign body than its predecessor, while at the same time reasserting the two nations' ownership of the state.

Though these invocations of popular sovereignty (especially the 1948 version) resemble the First Republic's definition, the Communist regime's view of the ensuing political authority departed radically from the earlier Czechoslovak state. The 1948 Constitution does not discuss the role of the Communist Party, but its leaders made its dominant status clear. As Deputy František Tymeš (interestingly, himself a former Social Democrat) explained in a June 1948 meeting of the National Assembly, in this new era the state would "authorize" political parties "only if they become instruments of the revolution, if they serve the reconstruction of society. The old type of party from the time of liberalism is dead. . . . For the smooth construction of a socialist state we need a united nation, and the core of this unity is the unified socialist party, the Communist Party of Czechoslovakia."[4] The 1960 Constitution subsequently enshrined the Party's position, stating in Article 4, "The leading force in society and in the state is the vanguard of the working class, the Communist Party of Czechoslovakia."

According to the regime ideology, then, the Party's preeminent status is tied to its relationship to the workers. As the Party Statutes declared, the "working class is the main social force, whose historical mission and most natural interest is the Communist organization of society."[5] The Party held that such organization was both extremely desirable—producing a conflict-free utopia, sustained by a new type of human being—and inevitable, according to the scientific laws of dialectical materialism. Based on its understanding of these universally valid laws, and as the representative of the class central to this progress, the Party claimed to offer infallible leadership of the society's all-encompassing transformation. This entitled it to enormous, exclusive, and unchallengeable political authority. Importantly, this was not circumscribed by the rule of law, as socialist legality held law to bind citizens, but not the state; in essence, "power automatically legalized every Party action."[6] Likewise, citizens' rights did not limit this power. As Vladimir Kusin explains, in the Soviet understanding of rights, which the Czechoslovak regime followed, "collective and social rights are superior to individual and political rights, and such rights as are recognized are superior to freedoms. The 'right to work' occupies a pivotal position in the Soviet interpretation; without it the other rights allegedly have little sense. But 'right to work' is not associated with 'freedom to choose one's work,' just as 'right to education,' commendable as it is, does not entail 'freedom to choose education.' Above all, man as an individual cannot claim a right or a freedom either from the theory of natural law or from supra-national conventions to which his government, not he, is a party. Hence all rights and liberties are conditional on official consent and derive from the state."[7] Thus, although the Constitutions derive sovereignty from the people (or at least the working people), the individual citizen retains *none* of the resulting authority inalienably; it is transferred in its entirety to the state, with the Party at the helm, and what rights may be granted are rescindable. This understanding is, then, profoundly illiberal. It was also notably atheistic, rejecting the legitimacy of any religious authority.

Given that the Party claimed a scientific understanding of human relations, it was undaunted by Slovak nationalism. As Slovak sociologist Ján Pašiak explained, the previous Czechoslovak regime leaders had failed to solve the problems nationalism raised because their "theoretical starting point for the resolution of the national question was that national relations were purely political, cultural or religious. . . . The failures were a result of their unscientific idealistic explanations, and these solutions did not reach the roots of the national problem."[8] According to Marxist analysis, these roots, as those of all modern social conflicts, lie in the economic tensions brought on by class conflict in capitalist society. As the economic foundations of national tensions disappeared, so would nationalism. The Communist leaders thus concluded that the solution to the problem of Slovak nationalism was to industrialize and economically reorganize Slovakia.[9] The resulting material equalization between the Czechs and Slovaks would produce a shared culture over time. Such "optimistic expectations came to be codified in the watchword *sbližování* (Czech) or *zblíženie* (Slovak): 'drawing closer.' "[10] Eventually, this would lead to an overarching, patriotic, socialist identity that would form the basis for political community. As Leff notes, this bears quite a striking resemblance to the First Republic's leaders' expectations concerning the effects of education and socio-cultural development.[11] The Communists undeniably saw identity as extremely malleable: they planned, after all, to produce a "new socialist man."

One complication to the Communist nation-building project was that the Third Republic had formally acknowledged and institutionally represented distinct Slovak nationhood.[12] National autonomy stood, however, in tension with the dictates of the "democratic centralism" necessary for control over the entire society's development. Thus, the 1948 Constitution formally recognized Slovakia's autonomy but situated the real power in the central institutions in Prague. Two months later, a meeting of the Presidium of the Czechoslovak Communist Party announced, "the working class and the toiling masses of Czechoslovakia have to have one political leadership in the form of a united Communist Party."[13] As a result, the Slovak Communist Party merged with the Czechoslovak Party and became subordinate to the Central Committee in Prague, though it was allowed to keep the title Communist Party of Slovakia (CPS). The new state thus retained the outward asymmetric structure of the Third Republic while instituting a highly centralized system.

Though Communist ideology assured the eventual disappearance of nationalism, within a few months of the regime's founding, its leaders took up a more aggressive strategy. During the September session of the CPS Central Committee, Viliam Široký, one of the Uprising generation's known enemies, leveled the charge of "bourgeois nationalism" at his rivals. Nothing happened immediately, but in March 1950 the issue resurfaced as Foreign Minister Vladimir Clementis was accused before the Central Committee of bourgeois nationalism, past hostility to the Soviet Union, and an "intellectualist" approach to Communism.[14] In April, several other members of the Uprising generation, including Gustav Husák and Ladislav Novomeský, were added to the list of suspected enemies of the state. At the Ninth Congress of the Slovak Party in May they were accused of bourgeois nationalism, doing damage to the Slovak National Uprising, alliance with Slovak capitalists against the Czech nation, and both anti-Soviet and anti-Hungarian attitudes. They lost their posts. In early 1951, the charges were elevated to allege a separatist conspiracy, and they were arrested. Their opponents buttressed their accusations by tying "bourgeois nationalism" to clerical nationalism, and more specifically, Karol Bacílek informed the Central Committee, to the "former officials of the republic and the fascist Slovak state."[15] As Leff observes, "clerico-fascism had gone underground, they warned, but it was surviving with the help of the Husáks and the Novomeskýs. This deliberate linkage of the disgraced Slovak Communists with the previous Slovak traitors is one of the most clear-cut manifestations of the cycle of recrimination that has marked Czech and Slovak relations since 1918."[16]

As frequently happens during such purges, the revolution soon began to devour its own. A much broader conspiracy, involving those at the pinnacle of power in Prague, was "uncovered," and Rudolf Slánský, the First Secretary of the Party and a leader among the accusers, soon joined the accused. Clementis was the only one of the alleged "bourgeois nationalists" that faced judgment with Slánský, and like his co-defendants, he duly confessed his guilt. The show trials did not end with the death sentences of eleven of the fourteen defendants, including Clementis, and continued even after both Stalin and Gottwald died in 1953. It was not until April 1954 that Husák and the rest of the accused "bourgeois nationalists" were finally tried. One reason for the delay was that they were uncooperative defendants and would have ruined the careful staging that characterized the trials at the height of the terror.[17] All were found guilty, and Husák was sentenced to life imprisonment. The others were given sentences ranging from ten to twenty-two years and forfeited their property.

Though show trials were rampant throughout Communist Europe during this period, reflecting Moscow's dictates, it is striking that the trials in Czechoslovakia, historically the most liberal-democratic of the states that became Soviet satellites, were particularly brutal and continued long after the coercive element of Stalin's oversight was gone. Skilling thus argues that, in a very real sense, the Communists were successful in their attempt to enforce their values on the Czechs and Slovaks: the "events of the fifties, in particular the terror and the trials, were as much a part of Czechoslovak history as was the First Republic and ought not to be ignored in analysis of the political culture of the two nations."[18] Clearly, then, any notion of continuity with earlier periods must be viewed in the context of vast and violent compliance with the regime ideology. Moreover, the trials would have lasting consequences for Czech-Slovak relations, as the accusations against the Slovak Communists—a response to the Slovaks' "betrayal" of the Czechs in 1938–39—"fed the flames of what Slovaks came to see as a retaliatory betrayal."[19]

Challenges to the Regime in the 1960s

As Stalinism was particularly intense and long-lived in Czechoslovakia, de-Stalinization also came later than in most East Bloc countries. It was not until six years after Soviet leader Nikita Khrushchev's 1956 secret speech to the Twentieth Party Congress, in which he opened the door to criticizing Stalinism, that the process finally got under way in Czechoslovakia. In December 1962, the Twelfth Congress of the Czechoslovak Communist Party disclosed crimes committed by the Stalinist leadership and set up a commission to examine the trials of 1949–1954. In April 1963, this commission produced the "Kolder Report," which detailed the bogus nature of a number of the trials and resulted in the rehabilitation of the Czech Communists. However, the surviving Slovak "bourgeois nationalists," who had been released from prison in 1960, remained officially guilty. The Party leaders' unwillingness to disavow the charge of "bourgeois nationalism" caused an unprecedented outcry from Slovak writers and journalists during the spring and summer of 1963, and public criticism of both Stalinism and the current government grew in Slovakia. In December, revelations about the trials led to the ouster of many of the Slovak members of the Gottwald old guard, including Czechoslovak Prime Minister Viliam Široký and the CPS First Secretary Karol Bacílek, who was replaced by Alexander Dubček.

The central government's grudging accommodation of Slovak demands during 1963–64 encouraged a remarkable resurgence of Slovak nationalism. The regime had also provided essential groundwork for this development: by persecuting Husák as a "bourgeois nationalist," it had unwittingly provided the Slovak intellectual community with a leader who had the moral authority to drive forward the resurrection of Slovak history and identity. In 1964, the twentieth anniversary of the Slovak National Uprising, Husák published a new history of those events. Though authorities limited its publication, it helped spur a reappraisal of this period of Slovak history by such influential scholars as Samo Falťan. A second focus of scholarly reassessment concerned Štúr's legacy. The official view reflected Marx and Engel's condemnation of Štúr's alliance with the Habsburgs against the Hungarians in the 1848 Revolution. During celebrations of Štúr's birthday in 1965, Slovak historians rejected this version and instead heralded Štúr's leadership in the face of Hungarian tyranny. This "strong reassertion of the national viewpoint evoked anti-Hungarian feelings and, by association, anti-Czech feelings as well. As part of the historical parallel the suggestion was unavoidable that the Czechs pursued discriminatory policies."[20]

The reclamation of the Slovak past from the distortions of "official history" thus increasingly spurred Slovaks to critically assess their nation's status in the Communist state. In particular, they criticized the 1960 Constitution, which had severely limited Slovak autonomy. Husák took the lead in demanding that the central government fulfill the promises of national equality and autonomy going back to the Košice Agreement. He argued that the true Marxist-Leninst approach centered on "the right of every nation to self-determination and the democratic right of every nation to occupy a position of equality with all other nations."[21] As Robert Dean points out, "Husák's plea demonstrated the extent to which Slovak intellectuals had adopted the metaphor of 'democratization' in conceptualizing their views on the national problem."[22] On this basis, demands for a constitutional solution increased, at times including references to the HSPP's autonomy program.[23] The possibility of federalization thus entered the debate.

De-Stalinization also prompted Czech scholars to begin to move away from existing orthodoxies and reinterpret history, philosophy, economics, politics, and law. Broadly speaking, a consensus emerged among critical scholars (including historians Milan Hubl and Vilém Prečan, philosophers Karel Kosík and Ivan Sviták, and legal scholars Zdeněk Mlynář and Zdeněk Jičinský, among others) that fundamental aspects of the system were irreconcilable with democratic and humanist principles and would have to be reformed. In essence, these scholars concluded that a state based on falsified history could not support the search for truth; a state based on ideological dictatorship could not foster critical thought; a state based on the denial of the intrinsic worth and natural rights of the individual could not function as a democracy; and a state based on the equation of law with power could not sustain civil liberties. In coming to these conclusions, they sought to remain within the Marxist-Leninist tradition, reinterpreting rather than rejecting it.

The brewing conflict between the regime and the intellectuals escalated at the Fourth Congress of the Union of Writers in June 1967. Many writers had for several years struggled with the regime over the extent of their freedom, with both sides engaging in a certain amount of compromise. During the sessions, a debate over political issues ignited between liberal writers and those more loyal to the regime, and things quickly became "explosive."[24] The writers who launched the challenge were mostly Czech—the earlier Slovak Writers' Congress had been uneventful, and the Slovaks attending the Prague Congress mostly remained uninvolved.[25] Western media reported that much of the Bratislava delegation left on the second day.[26]

The speeches by three of the participants—Ludvík Vaculík, Milan Kundera, and Karel Kosík—give a sense of the nature of the liberal writers' criticism of the regime. In what proved a highly incendiary address, Vaculík criticized the absence of any checks on political power, arguing that as a "result" "the citizen had lost his self-respect, and also his status as a citizen." Not only was such unchecked power unjust, it had proved incompetent: "in twenty years not one human problem has been solved in our country."[27] In looking for remedies, he pointed to pre-Communist traditions, noting that the First Republic was "a state which, in spite of all its imperfections, achieved a high level of democracy in its day."[28] Kundera, as well, appealed to national traditions, arguing that the First Republic had produced a "cultural flowering which is without a doubt the greatest in Czech history." Stalinism, however, had worked to "isolate" Czech culture "from the rest of the world, to destroy its many rich internal traditions and to lower it to the level of fruitless propaganda," alienated from the influences "that were so close to the hearts of the Czech Humanists and Revivalists."[29] This is, then, a view of Czech tradition that emphasizes its symbiotic relationship to other cultures. He thus declared that "any suppression of views, especially any violent suppression of incorrect views, tends eventually to militate against the truth, because truth can only be arrived at by free and equal dialogue. Any infringement of freedom of thought and speech, however discreet the means and however subtle the name for such censorship, is a scandal in the twentieth century and inhibits and shackles the flourishing of our literature."[30] Finally, in his speech, Kosík recounted a letter Jan Hus wrote in prison describing how a theologian had counseled him to submit fully to the Council of Constance (which had sentenced him to death for heresy) to the point of agreeing with them if they declared that he had only one eye, though of course he had two. The theologian assured him that he could escape punishment this way. Hus answered, "And if the whole world told me the same, I, possessing reason, would not be able to acknowledge it without my conscience being repelled."[31] Thus, Kosík observed, "the Czech intellectual of the fifteenth century defended the unity of reason and conscience and refused the offer of the Council as the wrong alternative, for a man who agrees with the Council that he has only one eye although he knows full well that he has two gains nothing and loses everything, for to lose reason and conscience means to lose the basis of his humanity."[32] The allegorical criticism of the relationship between the party-state and the citizen is clear. Though conservative writers, and some who found confrontation unwise, vigorously opposed these speeches, the result of the Writers' Congress was a strong challenge to the regime, calling for a fundamental reinterpretation of legitimate political authority.

By itself, it is unlikely that the writers' challenge would have prompted a major reform movement, but it came in the context of a failing economy, increasing calls among the intelligentsia for political change, and widespread youth and student unrest. These combined factors led to the ouster of rigid Czechoslovak Party first secretary, Antonín Novotný, and his replacement in January 1968 with Alexander Dubček. The first major resulting reform came on March 5, 1968, when the Presidium abolished censorship and proposed changes in the press law, marking the onset of the Prague Spring.[33] Events thereafter moved quickly. In Slovakia, the Plenum took the dramatic step of unanimously approving a detailed plan for the federalization of the state, which included the proposal that statewide bodies be constituted on the principle of national equality to prevent the Slovaks from being outvoted by the Czechs through majority rule. This gained immediate approval from Slovak intellectuals and the broader public: a poll conducted that month showed that 94.3 percent of Slovaks saw the need to reorganize the Czech-Slovak relationship, and of these, 73 percent favored a federal arrangement.[34]

The next major step toward statewide political reform was the adoption of the Action Program of the Communist Party of Czechoslovakia on April 5. This document offered an overview of the reform necessary to produce "a new political system in our lives, a new model of *socialist democracy*" (emphasis original).[35] It called for a new Czechoslovak Constitution to be drafted, widely discussed, and submitted to the National Assembly after the next Party Congress. It also held that the Party had a right to its leading role but must not abuse the accompanying power and privileges. To make it more responsive to the broader population, it would be required to build a partnership—albeit, an unequal one—with the National Front (the Third Republic umbrella party substantively obsolete since 1948). However, the "crucial question as to how elections would be conducted in this peculiar system of non-competitive partnership was not discussed."[36]

Though the Action Program made clear that the Party was unprepared to give up its leading role, the liberalization of speech and association produced a groundswell of independent thought and activity. Included in this "return to politics" were many who had been silenced under Communism and who now set up new organizations without official approval. They quickly pushed the discourse beyond the ideological limitations of even reform-minded Party members, questioning Communist orthodoxies.

One of the non-Communist leaders in the debate over the direction of reform was the young playwright Václav Havel. In early April, he published an influential piece in *Literární listy* titled "On the Subject of Opposition," in which he argued that the officially permissible forms of political opposition "give the impression of a desire 'to have your cake and eat it too.'"[37] The Party hoped to retain an unchallenged position while claiming the legitimacy of a democratic government via free speech, the internal democratization of the Party, the institutionalization of interest-articulation groups, and the reanimation of the "mummified remnants of pre-February [1948] political forces" in the National Front. Havel argued that none of these could bring sufficient counter-force upon government to effectively limit and control it. As competition for power is a fundamental prerequisite for democracy, he continued, a new entity should be formed, "which could be based on a traditional democratic and humanistic spirit and, therefrom, form a kind of *democratic party.*" This would "restore fundamental human individuality to its place at the center of attention much more rapidly" than could the Communist Party, and thereby "re-establish the individual as *the yardstick for society and for the system*" (emphases original).[38]

The writers who had made waves at the Writers' Union Congress also joined the debate. Vaculík's contribution again proved particularly dramatic. At the request of several academics and scientists, he wrote an essay titled "2,000 Words to Workers, Farmers, Scientists, Artists, and Everyone." The "2,000 Words" ended with the signatures of more than sixty people, including famous scholars and artists and ordinary farmers and workers. In it, Vaculík argued that the Communist Party had traded in the people's trust for power, and that the "main guilt and greatest deception perpetrated by these rulers was that they presented their arbitrary rule as the will of the workers."[39] Given the vast damage inflicted on society, "no gratitude is due to the Communist party, although it should probably be acknowledged that it is honestly striving to use this last opportunity to save its own and the nation's honor."[40] Vaculík also addressed the national issue: "We consider the federation a method of solving the nationality question; aside from this, it is only one of the important measures aimed at democratizing conditions. This measure alone cannot by itself ensure better living conditions for the Slovaks. The problem of the regime— in the Czech regions and in Slovakia individually—is not solved by this. The rule of the party-state bureaucracy may still survive—in Slovakia even more so, because it has 'won greater freedom.'"[41] Despite his sharp criticisms of the regime, Vaculík pledged the population's support for the government—"with weapons, if necessary"—as long as it continued to work toward reform. He concluded by observing that "the spring has now ended and will never return. By winter we will know everything."[42]

The "2,000 Words" was published in *Literární listy*, which by now had a circulation of 300,000, and produced a society-wide political crisis. Appearing in late June, it came at a point when the "war of nerves" within the Party had become extremely tense.[43] The Prague Spring's fate was uncertain; liberals feared that conservatives would move to put a brake on reform, and in the background, the Soviet press made ominous noises. Warsaw Pact military maneuvers were scheduled in Czechoslovakia at the end of the month.

The controversy over the "2,000 Words"—which was not a more radical document than many others—highlighted the increasing distance between those who wanted to defend the system, those who wanted to reform it gradually, and those who wanted a new kind of system. The difference between the latter two groups was a natural development of the liberalization process. While in the preceding years, the reformist Communist intellectuals had developed a limited framework within which to criticize Stalinism and its excesses, the openness of the Prague Spring made possible a more fundamental and coherent critique of the Communist system and the articulation of alternatives. The core of the resulting "radical" vision of politics was the moral standing of the individual, and it held that the rights to the free exercise of reason and conscience may not be overridden by the Party or state. As Kosík argued, conscience is "the backbone and strength, the inviolable and inalienable property of man."[44] Together, reason and conscience provide the rational and moral compass for human life, and are therefore integral to human flourishing and the just ordering of society. This view of these faculties thus repudiates the claim by any ideology that the individual must cede them because all truth is already known. Rather, citizens must be able to exercise them in all spheres of life, and no group can claim the individual's allegiance without his or her consent.

The regime's critics based their arguments on both abstract philosophical reasoning and lived experience, arguing that uncontested Communist power had not only denied people their fundamental rights and freedoms but also failed to produce a tendency among leaders to support the greater, collective good. Instead, it had corrupted them, leading them to distance themselves from society and to exploit the powerless. This had sapped the moral strength of the leadership and the people by undermining a sense of responsibility and accountability among both. To guard against its abuse as well as to ensure its legitimacy, they argued, power must be checked through such methods as the competition of parties and their alternation in office, the division of the branches of government, and a free press.

This democratic critique of the Communist system thus drew on a combination of traditional Czech political principles, which had been dominant in the pre-Communist political culture, and on active, considered responses to the first twenty years of Communist rule. The understanding of the authority retained by the individual in political society clearly has philosophical roots in the thought of Havlíček, Palacký, and Masaryk, among others, and both reform Communists and more liberal democrats invoked these leaders as powerful national-political symbols in the discourse over reform. That many (though not all) of the reformers had been Communists themselves highlights the interaction between principled reasoning and political culture, as their political ideas were by no means "organic" or unconsidered cultural attitudes. Still, as Skilling observed, "it seemed almost a miracle that the ideas and traditions characteristic of the First Republic and its late nineteenth-century antecedents could be regenerated after the 'fifties, and after three decades of almost total eclipse since Munich."[45]

The Slovak Question: Federalization Versus Democratization

Though it concerned the same Communist system, the debate over reform in Slovakia differed from that in the Czech lands. This was partly due to the differences between the Czechoslovak Party under Dubček and the Slovak Party under Vasil Biľak. While the Slovak Party pledged its support for Dubček, its leadership had undergone far fewer changes after January 1968 than in the Czech lands, and the Bratislava leaders were more conservative than those in Prague. Slovak Party leaders justified this lack of cadre change by arguing that the Slovaks had already conducted the necessary purges in the early sixties, when the Stalinist centralists were ousted.

Thus, when restrictions on speech, travel, and association were loosened statewide, the Slovak leadership became increasingly wary. Husák, who in April became the Deputy Premier of the new Czechoslovak Government, warned against excessive democratization, writing that "the freedom to criticize is being overstressed; far more urgent is the need to unite people in a positive programme, to solve immediately daily problems."[46] The Slovak leadership emphasized that Slovakia's reform focus was not to be liberalization, but rather the institutionalization of national rights through federalization. "Federation First"—meaning before democratization—became their refrain.

Not all Slovaks agreed with this prioritization, however. Although the idea of federalization won general approval, some prominent Slovak intellectuals publicly disagreed with the Slovak Party stance and argued forcefully for broad-scale democratization. This division prompted a part of the editorial board of the Slovak journal *Kultúrny život* to resign in protest of its excessive support of democratization. Arguing that the journal was no longer representative of the Slovak Writers Union's elected officials, this group founded its own journal, *Nové slovo*. In its first issue, Husák wrote: "And once again we are in the situation that we have all the questions out on table, solved so many times, declared as solved. We approach them in many ways . . . There are also different views which exploit criticisms of past mistakes and deformations, inflame passions, unleash unrestrained pressures, transport the society to the brink of atomization and anarchistic decay, where they capitalize on all sorts of old, surmounted and defeated things. The radical member of the bourgeoisie appears in the pose of a rescuer and reformer. It is a regular crowd of messiahs and prophets, young and old, who from behind grand slogans follow their own group and individual aims. They deepen the differences, increase the tension and thereby, the inevitable political struggle."[47] According to Husák, the only legitimate democratic reform was that which would ensure "sovereignty and equal position within the state" for the Slovaks.[48]

In an April article in *Kultúrny život* titled "Federalization and Democratization," the Slovak philosopher Július Strinka responded to the Federation First position. He began by declaring his support for federalization, stating that "this idea is unquestionably one of the most valuable fruits of the present democratization process, whose realization would be an immense accomplishment not only from the standpoint of the Slovak nation, but also from the standpoint of the democratic structure of the whole republic." He cautioned, however, that "it is precisely in the interest of the actual victory of the federal idea that we take a self-critical look at ourselves, that we realistically assess our preparedness" to guarantee that federalism will lead to "prosperity and progressive, democratic development." Indeed, "it would be a fatal mistake if we separated federalization from democratization, if we saw in it something for its own sake, the attainment of which would alone and in itself solve our nation's problems and secure its unfettered development." In particular, it was essential to prevent undemocratic leaders from continuing to direct Slovak political development: "It would be very dangerous to be dazzled by the vision of federation and thereby not to see that not only for the successful start to federation, but also eventually for federation to indeed become a reality, it is critically important that in Slovakia there be a much more intensive and energetic expansion of the democratization process, the process of reorganization and exchange of cadres from the standpoint of their moral-political trustworthiness, from the standpoint of their real, human, moral and intellectual values."[49] He thus concluded, "federalization without democratization would deprive us of strength."[50]

This view agreed with the Czech reformist position on federation. According to an anonymously written 1979 article in the dissident journal *Listy*, among most Czech reformers,

Federalism was understood as an integral component of the democratization process, in which the central point was the creation and functioning of the democratic political structures of society, in which the democratic rights and freedoms of individual citizens and groups would be ensured. This suggested, however, that federalism for and in itself, without overall democratization of the political structures of Czechoslovak society, would not remove the causes of the contradictions in the Czech-Slovak relationship, and that the real problem was not solely and only institutional reform of the state, but that it had a deeper foundation in the present political system of Czechoslovak society, which precluded the democratic expression of the will of not only the Slovak, but also the Czech nation. It also suggested that the new arrangement must respect universal democratic principles, supported by the equality of citizens without regard to whether they live in the Czech lands or Slovakia, and that the social totality of political relations in Czechoslovakia cannot be reduced to its national components or aspects and that this situation must be respected during the process of founding of state will on the federal level.[51]

Based on their shared vision of reform, then, the democratic Slovak intellectuals allied themselves with the Czech reformers calling for "democracy first."[52]

Opinion polls taken during the reform period indicate that this prioritization was a minority position among Slovaks. In these, Slovaks held national equality as their first priority and democratization second, while the Czechs placed democratization first, and relegated national equality to a strikingly low seventh place.[53] Other polling on reform reflected national differences as well. While 90 percent of Czechs approved of the National Assembly's abolition of censorship, Slovak support was somewhat less overwhelming, with 74 percent agreeing.[54] This is not, however, to suggest that the Slovaks were not in favor of democratization. While little information exists to indicate the orientation of Slovak party functionaries, one late June poll of 465 members and candidates of district committees in Central Slovakia "indicated a substantially progressive viewpoint, with a large majority favoring democratization."[55] A poll of delegates to the 14th Party Congress also showed "relative similarity" in Czech and Slovak functionaries' view of reform (though it should be noted that the Slovaks were not designated by nationality, but by the region they represented, and hence the "Slovak" figures included between 12–13 percent other nationalities).[56] Some moderate differences emerged as well: in answer to questions about the risks of reform, 40.2 percent of Slovaks and 52.7 percent of Czechs answered "rather no" or "decidedly no" to the question, "Do you believe that it is quite dangerous for the party to give up its power position," and only 28.2 percent Slovaks, compared to 73.3 percent of Czechs, answered "rather no" or "decidedly no" to a question focusing on whether they were concerned about the danger to the Party of making "it possible for other parties and organizations to share in decision-making."[57]

Over time, national tensions rose as Slovaks became increasingly frustrated over the seeming Czech indifference to federalization. Even the "2000 Words" downplayed its importance. As Slovak patience wore thin, some intellectuals suggested extreme solutions. Although separatism was not the policy of the Slovak Party, it was widely discussed in the press, as was its historical antecedent; as Dean observes, "perhaps the most extraordinary aspect of this was the sympathetic reappraisal given to the Slovak fascist state of 1939–1945."[58]

Another point of conflict concerned the Slovak demand for parity of representation in the federal institutions and protection for the Slovaks against being outvoted. As J. Brabec summarized the Slovak position, "among nations, only one arithmetic is valid: one nation, one vote."[59] The Czechs rejected this, arguing that democracy is based on the principle of "one man, one vote." Leff observes, "These rival conceptualizations are not only different, but ultimately contradictory. The essence of democratic safeguards under the Slovak formula would necessarily be repudiation of the Czech identification of democracy with majority rule. The converse is also true; acceptance of Czech premises would liquidate the Slovak democratic theory, and, it was feared, perpetuate de facto centralization. To Czech negotiators, therefore, the Slovak formulation was not only somewhat apart from the democratization process; it was in some respects at odds with it from the outset."[60] As with the Czech reform orientation, then, the dominant Slovak view showed strong continuities with earlier patterns of Slovak thought, and in particular with the HSPP ideology in its collectivist understanding of natural rights in which the nation, rather than the individual, was the central rights-bearing entity. An important discontinuity, however, was the general lack of a clerical element. More broadly, during the Prague Spring, we see a now-familiar triad of orientations, with the more liberal-democratic Czechs, a minority of Slovaks with a similar orientation allied with them, and more illiberal Slovaks stressing national rights, once again locked in conflict over the source, nature, and structuring of legitimate authority.

Before an agreement on federation could be finalized, the entire reform process came to a violent end. On August 21, 1968, Warsaw Pact tanks invaded Czechoslovakia and crushed the Prague Spring. The only major reforms carried forward thereafter were the federalization of the state and the promulgation of a nationalities law. The federation agreement was produced and signed by October 28, in time for the celebrations of the fifty-year anniversary of joint Czech-Slovak statehood. According to the new constitutional law's preamble, the state was federalized "recognizing the inalienable right to self-determination even to the point of separation and respecting the sovereignty of every nation and its right to develop freely the manner and form of its national and governmental life."[61]

Despite a number of unwelcome limitations on their autonomy, the Slovaks registered real gains from federation, including much more control over the economy. It also led to considerable bitterness on the Czech side, as "for Czechs and for those Slovaks who had regarded democratization as the primary goal, and had considered federalization without this almost meaningless, this was a confirmation of their worst fears."[62] Many also thought that the Slovaks gained power in federal matters disproportionate to the numbers. Slovak philosopher Miroslav Kusý observes, "the difference between the post-August developments in the Czech lands and in Slovakia are in a certain sense analogous to the difference between the post-Munich developments in the [Czech] Protectorate and in the Slovak State."[63] Indeed, many Czechs saw the new state structure as the Slovaks once again wresting away a victory from Czech defeat;[64] as Kusý put it, the "paradox and tragic moment in August 1968 lies therefore in that federation was the Slovak trailer hooked to the Soviet tanks, and was 'presented' as a bill for democratic socialism with a human face."[65]

Different Responses to the "Normalized" Regime: Dissidence in the Czech and Slovak Republics

The Czechs

Not long after the Soviet invasion, the reconstituted hard-line regime, led by now-First Secretary of the Czechoslovak Party Gustáv Husák, began "Normalization," intended to retrench power and suppress and prevent opposition. Though it was a statewide policy, the government instituted it differently in the newly federated Czech and Slovak Republics, and the two nations responded differently as well. To begin, state leaders held Slovakia "up to the Czechs as a loyalist region that succumbed less severely to the reactionary virus."[66] The highest level of leadership was swiftly purged, and those who managed to keep their positions or take up the vacancies were conservative and, in many cases, Slovak.[67] The exact fate of the Party's lower ranks is a more contested issue, as government and opposition figures on the extent of the purges and firings differ widely. Drawing on both Communist-era reports and a 1993 survey of Czechs and Slovaks concerning the effects of Normalization on their own lives, Eyal offers careful numerical estimates, noting that the available data only support provisional conclusions. Based on his calculations, Eyal finds that the opposition claims concerning the extent and implications of the purges appear to be exaggerated, perhaps because their view "was likely to be tainted by the social circles in which they moved [which were certainly strongly affected], and also by their own ideological interest to present their plight as common to society."[68] He concludes that the government estimate that 326,000 Party members—about 2.2 percent of the broader population—were expelled is likely accurate, and that of these, roughly 30 percent lost their jobs.[69]

The above figures are society-wide. When figures are broken down according to republic, it is clear that the "Czech purge was far more severe than the Slovak one"; Eyal estimates that 24 percent of Czech Party members were expelled, compared to roughly 12.5 percent of Slovak members.[70] In addition, in the 1993 survey, more Czechs (5.7 percent) than Slovaks (3.3 percent) reported losing their job, prompting Eyal to note that "the ratio of about 3.5 Czechs to each Slovak was probably quite striking for contemporary witnesses."[71] Normalization was more severe in the Czech lands in other ways as well. More "cultural officials" were appointed to control developments in the Czech lands than in Slovakia, and the push to have people sign "loyalty questionnaires" was more vigorous.[72] This had important implications, as those members of the intellectual and artistic community who refused to formally affirm the legitimacy of the Soviet invasion were not only forbidden from publishing, but also had their previous works removed from library shelves. To make conditions worse, the Czech lands stagnated economically during the state's last twenty years, partially as a result of the transfer of funds to promote Slovak development.[73]

In the face of this repression, some Czech intellectuals, writers, and ex-reformers began to resist the regime. They gained powerful ammunition in 1975, when Czechoslovakia signed the Helsinki Accords, which included robust human rights commitments. In October 1976, the government published the texts of two United Nations human rights treaties, the International Covenant on Civil and Political Rights (ICCPR) and the International Covenant on Economic, Social and Cultural Rights (ICESCR), which Czechoslovakia had signed in late 1968 and ratified in 1976. This came shortly after the state's persecution and trial of a rock band, the Plastic People of the Universe, which had galvanized the intellectual community to stand up for the freedom of expression.[74]

In December 1976, a group of people from a variety of backgrounds and political orientations drafted the Declaration of Charter 77, named to recognize the Year of the Political Prisoners, 1977. The Charter began by noting the human rights agreements to which Czechoslovakia was a party, arguing that from the date of their ratification, "our citizens have the right, and our state the duty, to abide by them."[75] The Charter then proceeded to enumerate both the rights to which the citizens were entitled and the ways in which the state systematically violated them. These included the rights to freedom of expression, the freedom from fear, the right to education, the right to information, the freedom of the press, the freedom of religion, the freedom of association, the right to take part in public affairs, the right to equal protection under the law, the right to establish trade unions, the right to privacy, the right to defense in court, the right of prisoners to humane treatment, and the right to leave the country. According to the Charter, the responsibility for protection of these rights fell to both the state and the citizenry, and it was toward the fulfillment of this obligation that the Charter had been created.

Though Charter 77 set itself up entirely within the bounds of Czechoslovak law, it struck at the very heart of the regime. Government leaders responded that the treaties cited by the Charter did not limit the scope of state authority, given the Communist understanding of rights as a grant of the state. It was not, however, lost on state leaders that, in Skilling's words, "if the regime were to carry out what was demanded—the full recognition of human rights—it would undermine the very foundations of its authoritarian rule, and by placing law above power, commit suicide."[76] State leaders thus began a campaign against the Charter that was "furious and vicious."[77] The Chartists were relentlessly harassed, some were imprisoned, and one leading member, the philosopher Ján Patočka, died a few days after grueling interrogation by the secret police.

The Chartists nevertheless persisted in publishing, offering both Charter-authorized documents and political *samizdat* (underground publishing) associated with the dissident movement more broadly. In this literature, the dissidents developed their own in interpretation of how values such as humanism, democracy, equality, and civic responsibility could become relevant to, and active in, a society under Communist rule. This approach differed from the Prague Spring orientation in that it turned from trying to reform the system from within its own framework to challenging it through the development of civil society. According to Polish political analyst Aleksander Smolar, this concept of civil society expressed a "twofold opposition." The first was to the Communist authority. The second was to the ethnic nation, whose "potency" in the region "is well known: ethnicity had long furnished the most salient way of dividing 'us' from 'them,' and Marxist class analysis could not rival it for popularity or profundity of influence. . . . By promoting civil society rather than ethnic community, they were not only proposing a wholly different way of defining 'us' and 'them,' but also suggesting a different way of looking at both past and the future."[78] Smolar further offers an excellent overview of the concept of civil society as advanced by Central European and Soviet dissidents:

> The "society-first" program, though formulated in scores of articles, can be summed up in a few sentences. Its first postulate, expressed memorably by Solzhenitsyn and Havel, was *living in truth*. This was a genuine moral imperative, and also a way of denying the legitimacy of a public realm that rested on the forced acceptance of an official definition of reality. The second postulate was the value of *self-organization*. Associations formed and acts of solidarity carried out beyond the purview of the party-state were valued in themselves, and as contributors to the reconstruction of authentic social ties. The third postulate was *respect for law*. Hungarian dissident János Kis wrote of the importance of "the con-

spicuous exercise of rights." The constitutions and laws of the "people's republics" became instruments of the struggle, as did such provisions of international law as the Helsinki Accords.[79]

In articulating their demands, then, the dissidents continued to draw on the rich and extensive human rights framework provided by the treaties that regime leaders themselves had signed. These were sharp, principled weapons. In particular, the ICCPR's rights are based on a notion of the scope of individual autonomy that is entirely at odds with the Communist Party's view of its own authority. As Chartist Jan Tesař observed, "by accepting binding documents of civil rights on the assumption that it would deceive the world public" the regime "has in fact legalized the means by which its own citizens can overcome it."[80] Havel similarly observed that "demanding that the laws be upheld is . . . an act of living within the truth that threatens the whole mendacious structure at its point of maximum mendacity."[81]

Clearly, then, the Charter's founding document offered a universalistic challenge to the regime, focusing on international and constitutional law; the terms of its critique were not anchored in a specifically Czech national or historical context. Still, in some of their further writings (both official and unofficial), the Chartists linked these international human rights principles to the Czech intellectual tradition, culture, and history,[82] invoking such figures as Hus, Havlíček, Palacký, and Masaryk.[83] By choosing to defy the regime's illegitimate demands, they argued, the individual could participate in the development of a civil society with deep roots in his or her own history, which would eventually overcome a repressive state at odds with this tradition.

Despite its best efforts, Charter 77 never brought a substantial portion of the citizenry into its fold, and this "lack of general commitment was almost a greater obstacle to the Charter's work than the repressive measures of a hostile regime."[84] Thus, the Chartists remained a small group, who nevertheless played an immensely important role. As Skilling argues, "Without the Charter, one could say, the links of the Czech nation with its traditions might well already have been completely severed, and their rebirth in the future rendered problematic. In a limited way Charter 77 has served as a kind of lifeline of intellectual, cultural and political continuity."[85]

The Czechs' broad compliance with the Normalization regime thus clearly complicates any claim that the dominant orientation of the population was liberal-democratic, in line with the patterns traced in earlier periods. The Czechs' behavior under Stalinism only compounds this: "For almost a generation Stalinist leaders did succeed in suppressing the previously dominant political culture (at least the real culture of overt behavior) and in introducing a largely alien, and previously subordinate, pattern of politics. The attempt to transform the ideal political culture—the values and beliefs of the people, by massive indoctrination and terror, proved more difficult, but achieved some degree of success, at least in weakening the hold of older ways on people's minds and in discouraging them from acting on these beliefs, and in eliciting from many a positive response toward newer but more alien values."[86]

There are two broad possibilities for explaining this Czech behavior. One would be that the Communist regime had succeeded in transforming the people's orientation (and thereby, the political culture), convincing them of the legitimacy of its foundational principles. A second possibility would be that the regime had convinced people that it would be in their interests (economic, power-political, and/or more basic self-preservation, in the sense of avoiding punishment or other negative repercussions) to comply with it. In this second scenario, people might then comply even though they disagreed with the regime principles, or they might comply because they did find *any* principles to be important. The Prague Spring indicates that explanations of compliance holding either that the Stalinist regime eradicated previous orientations or that Czechs were mostly unprincipled are incorrect; indeed, military intervention was required to quell the groundswell of support for more liberal, democratic ideas. But only few, it would seem, remained committed to principle after the Soviet invasion, at least to the point of acting on them in a way that challenged the regime.

In his Normalization-era writings, Havel carefully considered the question of the reasons for this compliance. In his 1975 essay "Dear Dr. Husák," he wrote, "In a way, we are all being publicly bribed. If you accept this or that official position at work—not, of course, as a means of serving your colleagues, but of serving the management—you will be rewarded with such-and-such privileges. If you join the Youth League, you will be given the right and access to such-and-such forms of entertainment. If, as a creative artist, you take part in such-and-such official functions, you will be rewarded with such-and-such creative opportunities. Think what you like in private; as long as you agree in public, refrain from making difficulties, suppress your interest in truth, and silence your conscience, the doors will be wide open to you."[87] Thus, the regime offered material incentives to override conscience; behavior that responds to these may well not, however, be based on agreement with the regime's ideology. There is also a more passive compliance that Havel illustrates in his 1978 essay "The Power of the Powerless," through his example of the manager of a grocery store who hangs a sign with the slogan, "Workers of the world, unite!" in the window. The exhortation is not the grocer's own. Havel observes, "That poster was delivered to our greengrocer from the enterprise headquarters along with the onions and the carrots. He put them all in his window simply because it has been done that way for years, because everyone does it, and because that is the way it has to be. If he were to refuse, there could be trouble. . . . He does it because these things must be done if one is to get along in life."[88] Thus, the "interests" that motivate compliance need not involve great ambition or greed. Still, Havel sees such behavior as conflicting with the greengrocer's "suppressed identity and dignity." In his view, most people, even those who gave little thought to politics, were not only complying with the system, or furthering their own interests, but also "living within the lie," bespeaking a deep, general tension between people and their behavior.

Eyal also argues that, among Czech elites, technocrats were particularly alienated from the regime. They were based in the state bank and the economics institutes of the Czechoslovak Academy of Sciences, and were not dissidents, but were also neither co-opted, nor reform Communists. They were demoted after 1968 and, with careers stalled, found common interest in monetarist economics. Eyal describes them as being in internal exile, "neither rejecting power, nor contesting it, nor quite serving it. . . . Internal exile meant a retreat into the private sphere, and rejection of ideological and political involvement."[89] In these cases, as with those Havel points to, compliance with the regime did not necessarily indicate support. During this period there was, however, no way to truly gauge the broader public's internal normative orientation; this would have to wait until politics were once again free.

The Slovaks

While the Charter played a prominent role in the Czech lands, its impact in Slovakia was negligible. Only eight of the original 239 signatories were Slovak, and few more signed it over the years. One reason for this was that the Czechs did not consult with the Slovaks in Slovakia (the Slovak signatories lived in Prague) before issuing the Charter. In addition, the government placed as many barriers between the Czech dissidents and actual or potential Slovak counterparts as possible.[90]

Much of the dissident activity that did occur in Slovakia centered on demands for religious freedom, and popular participation toward this goal was far broader than political dissidence in the Czech lands, especially during the regime's last decade (a fact often overlooked in comparisons of the two nations' relationship to the Communist regime[91]). Its main support base was the Catholic "secret church," an underground religious organization that operated in Slovakia from 1943 until 1989. It survived despite severe repression: having recognized the Slovak Church as a very serious opponent (especially in the battle over Tiso's fate during the Third Republic), the Communists moved ruthlessly to undermine it once they took power.[92] By late 1952, the state had "succeeded in decapitating the church hierarchy and the religious institutions that sustained it."[93] Under this terrible situation, with the Vatican's blessing, secret bishops performed ordinations that sustained the underground church. As the regime relaxed somewhat in the 1960s, religious leaders worked to rebuild Catholic community connections. Normalization brought renewed repression, and though it was far less intense than under Stalinism, many priests who had been trained during the more liberal period found participating in the official church alienating and difficult. By 1975, Hoellinger reports, "hundreds lost their pastoral licenses,"[94] and many moved into the secret church.

Normalization thus proved something of a boon to the underground church, which diversified its efforts to reach out to and serve Catholics—and some non-Catholics—throughout the country. It did this in three main ways. First, it published religious *samizdat*, starting 20 new periodicals during the 1980s (compared to four *samizdat* publications put out by the Slovak political opposition).[95] The religious *samizdat* dealt with many areas of Catholic life, including the yearly schedule of pilgrimages, which became the second focus of the underground during the 1980s. These gained tremendous momentum after a 1985 pilgrimage to Velehrad, a village in Moravia, to celebrate the 1,100[th] anniversary of the death of St. Methodius, who with St. Cyril had brought Christianity to the Slavs. The event began with an unofficial gathering of 5,000 young people who, during the night before the official celebrations, chanted slogans such as, "let the Pope come" and "we want cloisters." The following day, a crowd of 100,000–250,000 pilgrims took up similar chants during the state-sponsored events, interrupting the minister of culture's speech with calls for religious freedom.[96] From 1986 to 1989, participation in such pilgrimages skyrocketed, with some locations receiving tens of thousands, and others, hundreds of thousands of pilgrims.[97]

A final core element of underground church activism was the circulation of petitions. This was tied to the previous two, in that *samizdat* published the petitions and they were sometimes read at pilgrimage events. The petitions focused particularly on calls for religious freedom, and one, introduced by a Moravian Catholic in late 1987, "became the largest and most significant petition campaign in Czechoslovakia."[98] It stated its core theme at the outset: "Our fundamental demand is a separation of the Church from the state, which would also have the result that the state will not interfere in the organization and activities of the Church."[99] Ultimately, an estimated 600,000 Czechoslovak citizens signed the petition, 300,000 to 400,000 of them Slovaks.[100]

Though the themes were religious, there are clear political elements in this activism. One of its key purposes was to demand that the regime recognize the right to a sphere of religious life outside the state's authority, which was a profound challenge to Communist ideology. Moreover, the publishing, gathering, and petitioning actively asserted the rights to freedom of expression, conscience, and association that the regime denied. In addition, in March 1988, one of the secret church's key organizers, František Mikloško, and Ján Čarnogurský, a well-known political dissident and lawyer with close ties to both the secret church and Charter 77, sought to organize an independent demonstration in the center of Bratislava (the first such since 1968). They included in the gathering's purposes not only demands for religious freedom, but also for "complete adherence to the civil law in Czechoslovakia,"[101] which Hoellinger notes was "designed to appeal to those interested simply in greater civil rights within the country," and to draw together religious and civic activism.[102] Čarnogurský wrote the required letter stating the demonstration's goals to the local authorities, but because of his prominence as a political dissident, only Mikloško signed it; the secret church, "hoping to avoid additional police persecution, maintained a strict policy of not mixing its activities with that of the political opposition."[103] (The authorities did ban the demonstration, and violently broke up the 2,000 protestors who nevertheless came to the square at the appointed time.)

The distinction made within Slovak dissident circles between religious and political opposition is worth noting, as the former was clearly much more powerful in Slovakia than the latter. This reflects a stark difference between the Czech and Slovak responses to the regime. On the one hand, as noted above, there was *much* stronger popular participation Slovak religious activism (including activities directly critical of the regime) than there was Czech participation in Charter 77. On the other, secular political opposition was significantly stronger in the Czech lands, and Slovaks had no national parallel to Charter 77. In the late 1970s, roughly 95 percent of government suppression of political dissidents occurred in the Czech lands, and over half of the remaining 4 to 5 percent of anti-dissident action that took place in Slovakia was directed at only two dissidents.[104] Over time, the proportion of anti-dissident action occurring in Slovakia rose slowly, but remained at fairly low levels. From September 1981 to December 1982, 9 percent of the government repression was in Slovakia, and from 1984 to 1986, the figure climbed to 13 percent, still well below the statewide proportion of Slovaks to Czechs.[105] It is also worth noting the environmentalist activism in Slovakia. Overall, however, as Czech Chartist and post-Communist Prime Minister of the Czech Republic Petr Pithart has observed, in Slovakia "there actually was no dissident movement, just a few dissidents"; these, he notes, came to be known as "little islands of positive deviation."[106] Given the low levels of arrests and prosecution based on secular dissidence in Slovakia, then, it appears that "the ethnic Slovak at judicial risk for his nonreligious views" was "not conspicuously active in the body politic."[107]

A crucial factor both isolating the Slovaks political dissidents from one another and preventing a greater secular dissident movement was fear, which spread in many directions: fear of inferior employment, fear of being interrogated and followed, and fear for children and family members.[108] In addition, Karol Zlobina, writing in the dissident publication *Listy* in 1978, describes a "still undefined and therefore more dulling fear, not only concerning subsistence, but also existential matters."[109] While the Czechs suffered from such fear as well, the greater purges in the Czech Republic left the Czech intellectuals in a far worse position than many Slovaks. Pithart argues that for many Czech dissidents "there was almost nothing left to lose, and only then did they opt for the life of a dissident."[110] By contrast, most Slovak intellectuals were not destitute, and some could publish, giving them "more to lose, and more to hope for."[111]

Indeed, while the negative factors of fear and isolation were certainly important, a more positive view of the regime among many Slovaks appears to have been a factor preventing secular dissidence. As anonymous authors wrote in *Listy*, given the Slovak priorities during the Prague Spring, the invasion's "consequences" were less "onerous and catastrophic in a political and moral sense" than they were in the Czech Republic.[112] Slovaks had been fighting for control over Slovakia for a very long time, and there was thus a sense of satisfaction with the new federal structure, despite much real power remaining centralized. The influential position of the Slovaks in the federal state helped foster Slovak economic development during the 1970s, which in turn brought

important social change. Combined with the effects of economic modernization that had been going on since the 1950s, the continued industrialization
led to rapidly increasing urbanization and the "gradual disappearance of traditional Slovak villages."[113]

While economic development produced socioeconomic change, the new
political structures also reinforced elements of the pre-Communist Slovak
political culture. Kenneth Jowitt's analysis of Communist Romania is instructive in this regard: "It is significant that the tendency to dichotomize
elite and non-elite membership during the dictatorship of the proletariat has
reinforced the political culture that existed prior to the rule of the Communist party, a political culture in which the elite sector was distinct in character
and prerogative, not simply in role."[114] Similarly, traditional power relations
between the elite and the broader population were reflected in the Slovak
half of the federation. According to Kusý, "just after its inception there was
an enormous growth in corruption, the arrogance of the powerful elite, em-
bezzlement, and so on."[115] This did not, however, produce a concurrent rise in
public dissatisfaction with the government. As Pithart observes, "this system
of nepotism and corruption became the substitute for the clear system of
relations which had once been typical in the just recently defunct rural community. In Slovakia, power continued to be something tangible and human
rather than an impersonal institution: people now had an absolutely positive
relationship with the various Party bosses, secretaries and chairmen, just like
the relationship which had once existed between the peasants and the aristo-
crats in the old village."[116]

Moreover, the federated state was based on an understanding of nationhood that was in many ways consonant with the long-standing goals and principles of Slovak nationalism. The constitutional law that federated the state
declares in its first five, "fundamental provisions" that:

> 1. The Czechoslovak Socialist Republic is the federal state of two
> equal fraternal nations, the Czech and the Slovak.
> 2. The foundation of the Czechoslovak Socialist Republic is the
> voluntary bond between the equal national states of the Czech and
> Slovak nations, established on the right to self-determination of each
> of them.
> 3. The Czechoslovak federation is the expression of the will of two
> independent sovereign nations, the Czech and the Slovak, to live in a
> common federated state.

4. The Czechoslovak Socialist Republic is constituted by the Czech Socialist Republic and the Slovak Socialist Republic. Both republics have equal position in the Czechoslovak Socialist Republic.

5. Both republics mutually respect each other's sovereignty and the sovereignty of the Czechoslovak Socialist Republic; likewise the Czechoslovak Socialist Republic respects the sovereignty of the national states.[117]

This recognition of ethno-national sovereignty was the fruit of a hard-won battle, underway, in one form or another, since 1918. The structure of the ensuing power had strong continuities with the pre-Communist tradition as well, as both HSPP and Communist leaders emphasized the ideal of a united nation led by an elite who exercised very substantial authority, little of which was left to the individual, whose status was lower than that of the collective. This was partly due to the "infallible" nature of the governing ideologies—one linked to religious authority, the other to Marxism-Leninism.[118] Equally important, both regimes understood freedom and self-determination collectively, justifying such ordering of authority. In particular, the understanding of collective ethnonational self-determination was an explicit cornerstone of the wartime Slovak state's ideology, and support for this principle reemerged in the 1960s protests against the Communist regime. As Kusý argues, the "awakening of national consciousness during the sixties meant that Slovaks experienced the oppression of the Novotný regime above all as national oppression."[119] Thus, for many Slovaks, it was not the lack of individual autonomy and consent, but rather *national* autonomy and consent to governance that principally undermined the Communist state's legitimacy during the pre-federal period. This shaped their demands during 1968; as Anonymous authors in *Listy* argued, "federalism as the political recognition and constitutional declaration and safeguarding of the equal rights of the Slovak nation was frequently understood as in itself the core, the essence of democratization; the problem of universal political democracy remained on the side."[120] The institutional recognition of national sovereignty thus increased the post-invasion regime's legitimacy. As Kusý observed in 1985, "the nation is saturated with the achievement of national freedom at present, even to the point that it does not worry about the problems of its human and civil rights."[121] The freedom celebrated was collective freedom.

During the last twenty years of Communist rule in Slovakia, then, we see a substantial convergence of material interests, principle, and political culture. This regime orientation was, in fact, quite successful in securing support, particularly with regard to Slovakia's technocrats, nationalist intellectuals, and enterprise managers. According to Eyal, each of these groups saw its relation to the regime as furthering national progress.[122] Importantly, these included many of the democrats who had struggled with the federalists during the Prague Spring. Under the less repressive Normalization regime in Slovakia, they "searched for a way of remaining within the official sphere, so as to try to promote gradual, cautious, piecemeal reform. As with dissidence or internal exile, this was also a moral and existential choice. . . . The object of this response was not moral individual conduct, but the 'nation,' for the sake of which compromises had to be made."[123] Based on investigation of the numerous Normalization-era projects Slovak elites undertook, as well as interviews with them in the post-Communist period and other sources, Eyal offer key insights into how three main groups saw their purposes: among technocrats, the dominant orientation was reform Communism, with the central goals of more rational economic planning and authentic national autonomy; nationalist intellectuals were co-opted into the project of developing and enhancing Slovak national identity, primarily through historical interpretation; and managers of state enterprises, enterprise lawyers, and deputy ministers were co-opted as well, as their jobs had loyalty to the regime as a prerequisite. According to Eyal, none of these groups could be considered internally exiled.[124]

Overall, then, this period was less oppressive in the Slovak part of the federation. Pithart observed, "in Slovakia everything functioned noticeably better than in the Czech Lands; there was less fear and less hate in Slovakia."[125] The greater harmony between the regime and its Slovak citizens was reflected in public opinion polls taken in the 1970s and 1980s, which "show that the population of Slovakia judged postwar economic and social developments much more favourably than the Czechs, and that until the end of 1989 the Slovaks were more optimistic about the future prospects of the country."[126] It is also worth noting here that a survey conducted in May and June 1991 continued to show strong differences in the Czech and Slovak evaluations of the Communist regime. Respondents were asked to rate the regime on a scale from minus-100 to positive-100, with minus-100 being "the worst." The results found fully 30 percent of Czechs rating the regime at a full minus-100, and 16 percent of Slovaks doing the same. Combined with the rest of the respondents who rated the regime below zero, the negative Czech rating stood at 75 percent, compared to 56 percent in Slovakia.[127] While these numbers could also reflect different experiences in the early post-Communist period, they buttress the conclusion that, in relative terms, during its last twenty years, the regime was more legitimate in Slovakia than in the Czech lands.

This is by no means to argue that the regime was *highly* legitimate in Slovakia. In particular, the strength of Catholic activism under Normalization clearly expressed widespread rejection of the Communist position on religious rights. It also reflects the remarkable resilience of the religious component of Slovak national identity, to which the Communist regime was deeply hostile, and which it had ruthlessly tried to destroy—unsuccessfully.

Conclusion

Gauging Czech and Slovak understandings of nationhood during the Communist period is difficult. Clearly, the official Communist understanding of sovereignty and political authority was the controlling one, and most people conformed their behavior to it. At the same time, the Communist nation-building project, like the First Republic project before it, failed. The state did succeed in equalizing the Czechs and Slovaks in socioeconomic terms; by the late 1980s, they were at essentially the same level. However, as Walker Connor argues, "if ethnonational competition is fundamentally economic in causation, then *substantial* changes over time in the economic relationship should come to be reflected in the ethnonational relationship."[128] Such convergence did not, however, undermine national differences. Indeed, during the state's final, federated twenty years, the two nations lived side by side, but separately. There was little migration across national boundaries, and the Czech and Slovak educational systems grew increasingly apart, as children learned "different histories, with different golden ages, and different heroes and villains. This would have inevitably been true in 1918, but what is interesting is that the passage of time has perpetuated the original separation of existence."[129] Clearly, then, none of the state's strategies for dealing with the "national problem"—not only economic development, but also show trials of "bourgeois nationalists," terror, ideological indoctrination in the schools, liberalization, repression, centralized rule, and then federalized rule—had worked to draw the Czechs and Slovaks together under a common socialist national identity.

It is moreover clear that the differences between the Czech and Slovak understandings of nationhood that became active in the 1960s, and which reflected strong continuities with earlier periods, were important factors in preventing the development of such a common identity. In particular, the

Slovaks resisted the Communist definition of sovereignty in the 1948 and 1960 Constitutions, as they insufficiently recognized and institutionalized Slovak ethno-national sovereignty. Many Czechs and more liberal Slovaks, by contrast, primarily resisted the state's illiberal definition of political authority. The Communist regime had been in power fewer than 15 years when these orientations of older provenance began to put enormous pressure on it. These orientations also came into very serious conflict with *each other* during the Prague Spring. Political leaders on either side then not only articulated this conflict on an abstract, political-philosophical level, but also placed it in the context of the two nations' experiences with one another. Each could point to serious injustices stemming from the historical victories of the other side's guiding principles: the Slovaks, to the repeated denigration (in the First Republic, under Stalinism, and in 1960) of Slovak national sovereignty by the Czech centralists and their allies, who, in turn, could point to extremely illiberal governance by the clerical nationalists. In other words, each side had violated the other's highest principles. And, indeed, this sense of grievance was recharged on the Czech side after the Soviet invasion, under the federalized Normalization regime, when the Czechs were once again subjected to highly illiberal rule, while the Slovaks enjoyed greater collective sovereignty.

Though they showed strong continuities with earlier periods, these understandings of nationhood were thus not simple, primordial manifestations of continuing, essentially static orientations. They were reassessed and reinforced by repeated challenges from contending frameworks. Through these interactions, they also changed in important ways from earlier periods, with the Slovaks' substantially losing their clerical (though not religious) element and the Czechs putting much less emphasis on ethnicity. It is also clear that the relationships between the regime and its citizens (or subjects, if we follow Vaculík's criticism), and also between the more liberal Czech/Slovak alliance and illiberal Slovak nationalists, were not simply based on principle. Economic, power-political, and self-preserving interests were important factors shaping behavior—and among these interests I would include the desire of Havel's greengrocer simply to stay out of trouble, to live "a relatively tranquil life 'in harmony with society,' as they say."[130]

Ultimately, given the resilience of elements of traditional Czech and Slovak political cultures, and, further, the defining role that formerly submerged elites (especially dissidents and technocrats) would play during the post-Communist transition process, no true ideological "vacuum" or "void" would be left in Communism's wake. Still, the question of the Czechs' and Slovaks' dominant, internal normative orientations during the regime's final two decades can only be surmised, given the level of government coercion. Their true expression could only occur under conditions of freedom—which finally came with the Velvet Revolution.

CHAPTER SEVEN

From Velvet Revolution to Velvet Divorce

THE VELVET REVOLUTION followed the Berlin Wall's toppling by a little over a week. It began with a student demonstration in Prague on November 17, 1989, in remembrance of a Czech student killed by the Nazis fifty years before. Having held a ceremony at Vyšehrad Cemetery that included some political speeches, the demonstrators decided to head to the center of Prague. On the way, their numbers grew exponentially, and when they reached National Avenue en route to the central square, riot police met them with brutal force. Timothy Garton Ash writes: "This was the spark that set Czechoslovakia alight." Ash arrived in Prague six days later, "when the pace of change was already breath-taking." There, he recalled, "I met Václav Havel in the back-room of his favoured basement pub. I said: 'In Poland it took ten years, in Hungary ten months, in East Germany ten weeks: perhaps in Czechoslovakia it will take ten days!' Grasping my hands, and fixing me with his winning smile, Havel immediately summoned over a video-camera team from the samizdat *Videojournál*, who just happened to be waiting in the corner. I was politely compelled to repeat my quip to camera, over a glass of beer, and then Havel gave his reaction: 'It would be fabulous, if it could be so . . .' Revolution, he said, is too exhausting."[1]

And, indeed, ten days after the first demonstration, on November 27, a millions-strong general strike deeply undermined the Husák regime, which had stood rigid in the face of revolutionary developments throughout Communist Europe. The government agreed to roundtable talks with the newly constituted opposition movements, represented on the Czech side by the Civic

Forum, and on the Slovak by the Public Against Violence. On December 10 (United Nations Human Rights Day), the Communist government resigned, and Havel replaced Husák as president.

The state that began so romantically ended in a "Velvet Divorce" three years later. Repeated attempts to negotiate a new constitution foundered on the question of how to structure the relationship between the federal and republic level (Czech and Slovak) governments. Much analysis has been devoted to the reasons why no common vision could be reached. Some primordialist explanations point to vast, immutable cultural differences between the two nations, which were politically "reawakened" and revitalized under democratic circumstances. Others focus on institutional factors, such as the veto structure that immensely complicated constitutional change. Still other analyses focus on the role of material interests specific to the post-Communist situation, especially as they related to economic insecurity, political instability, and ideological vacuum. Of these materialist explanations, many highlight the political strategizing of elites eager to gain (or regain) power, as well as the Slovaks' clear disadvantage in comparison with the Czechs in a transition to a market-based economy.

All these factors—cultural, institutional, power-political, and economic— were certainly relevant and important. Ultimately, they also all fall short in explaining the deadlock between Czechs and Slovaks over the issue of sovereignty. A narrow focus on either post-Communist material interests or institutional constraints leaves aside the very striking consistency with which Czechs and Slovaks have employed particular normative frameworks to judge the legitimacy of different political systems, and a broad focus on cultural difference gives the misleading impression that nationwide norms were fixed and unchanging. I thus explore here two facets of the final negotiations over the future of Czechoslovakia: the contending definitions of sovereignty put forward by the Czech and Slovak constitutional negotiators, and how voices in the wider political discourse interpreted the lessons of the previous Czechoslovak (and Slovak) regimes and related them the question of the two nations' future together. I compare both the proposed constitutional principles and the judgments about the common past with the understandings of nationhood traced to this point in order to assess their malleability and functioning in the post-revolutionary period.

I find that the constitutional negotiations reflect both continuities and discontinuities with earlier periods. The Czech insistence on use of the civic principle to define sovereignty was unprecedented, but was also consistent

both with important elements of dissident thought and the more liberal elements of the longer national tradition. On the Slovak side, demands for an
ethnic definition of sovereignty were entirely in line with the Slovak tradition.
An important discontinuity was that there was no strong liberal Slovak faction
that shared the Czech vision of state-building and reform. In the larger societal
debate, I also find strong emphasis on historical continuities in national orientations, very often raised to show how one nation's (usually, not the author's)
principles were repeatedly employed to undermine those most important to
the other nation.

This evidence shows that the understandings of nationhood whose evolution I traced played a crucial role in shaping post-Communist visions of
democratic political community, and that they were *not* produced by factors
specific to post-Communist situation. That said, given the resilience of such
norms, the discontinuities on both sides raise questions about the extent to
which societal consensus actually existed about the validity of the civic principle in the Czech Republic and, on the Slovak side, the nature of the political
authority flowing from ethnic sovereignty, long a source of contention, and a
reason for previous alliances of some Slovaks with the Czechs. These are crucial considerations in my subsequent investigation of the implications of the
civic and ethnic models in the independent Czech and Slovak states, because
the absence of consensus (or political-cultural grounding) complicates the application of principle. I begin here, however, with the last struggle to find
consensus between the Czechs and Slovaks.

Constitutional Negotiations:
Who Should Be the Sovereign Community?

Broad coalitions of Czech and Slovak elites cooperated under the umbrellas of
the Civic Forum and the Public Against Violence for the interim period between December 1989 and the June 1990 elections. During this period, signs of
trouble for future state-building already emerged when the Federal Assembly
sought to change the state's name from the Czechoslovak Socialist Republic to
one that reflected its new orientation. Conflict quickly developed over what
to do with the word "Czechoslovak," as the Slovaks argued that it implied that
the state represented an ethnic "Czechoslovak" nation and that many Western observers used "Czech" as shorthand when describing the state's leaders
and issues, relegating the Slovaks to the background. They suggested that the

name be changed to "Czecho-Slovakia." The Czechs reacted very negatively to this proposal, which evoked the post-Munich federation. Havel attempted (somewhat awkwardly) to bridge the divide by arguing that the Czechs should be more sensitive to the Slovak position: "All of us know that this 'hyphen,' which seems ridiculous, superfluous and ugly to all Czechs, is more than just a hyphen. It in fact symbolizes decades, perhaps even centuries of Slovak history."[2] After a period of highly contentious debate (and some international ridicule), the Federal Assembly finally settled on the name "Czech and Slovak Federative Republic."

In the lead-up to the elections that came soon thereafter, the competing parties focused their campaigns at the republic level, which meant that there "was no overarching party with a statewide base to represent the interests of the whole country in the negotiation process."[3] The clear victor on the Czech side, with 53 percent of the votes, was the Civic Forum. Dominated by former dissidents and monetarist technocrats who had been internally exiled during the Communist period, it also counted social democrats in its ranks. On the Slovak side, the Public Against Violence, which included some dissidents (but, unsurprisingly, far fewer than the Civic Forum) and a large number of Slovak technocrats, won 33 percent of the vote. This necessitated its coalition with the Christian Democratic Movement, led by the former dissident Ján Čarnogurský, which won 19 percent, while the Communists (14 percent) and the ultranationalist Slovak National Party (11 percent) went into the opposition.

The elections also produced a mandate for a new federal constitution, to be drawn up during the two-year term of the Federal Assembly. All agreed that the goal should be an "authentic federation" that would locate real power in the two republics. Nevertheless, it quickly became clear that Czech and Slovak leaders had very different perspectives on its proper foundations. From June 1990 until spring 1992, repeated summit meetings failed to produce an agreement. Though the details of the proposals varied over time, at the core of the conflict was a fundamental difference in the Czech and Slovak view of the source of state sovereignty. The Slovaks wanted to build the federation "from below" (*zdola*), based on a treaty between the two republics.[4] As the Public Against Violence campaign program stated, "We support the view that *original sovereignty is the sovereignty of everyone from both national republics—while sovereignty of the federation is derived, delegated*" (emphasis original).[5] It further declared, "Both national republics must resolve their matters themselves, while leaving foreign policy, defence, financial policy and in a transitional period even some other unavoidable, clearly defined functions to the federation. The goal of our federative model is strong republics, and competent republic governments and parliaments."[6] Moreover, it argued that the new state would have to represent Slovakia as a distinct national entity that would be recognized as such abroad. These demands caused some consternation on the Czech side. Petr Pithart, prime minister of the Czech Republic, relayed how the Deputy Chairman of the Slovak National Council, Ivan Čarnogurský (Ján's brother), had explained the Slovak vision: "He was asked, first of all, whether he favored a common or an independent state. He said he favored a common state. When asked about his conceptions of this state and how he perceives it, he said that a common state is a state comprising two independent states."[7] Essentially, then, this was a vision of a confederation, one of whose members would be a specifically *Slovak* state. As Václav Žák observed, even the Public Against Violence, the "most pro-federalist" party in Slovakia, "did not see the federal republic as *its* state. This thesis became the acid test of the entire negotiation process."[8]

The Czechs, by contrast, wanted a federation constructed "from above" (*shora*). They argued that a treaty between the two republics would violate the existing federal Constitution by bypassing the necessary votes in the Federal Assembly. Havel also argued that "neither the Czech Republic nor Slovakia has the status of a sovereign state, which is required by international law to sign such a document."[9] Eventually, the Czechs agreed to the expression of consent to any new agreement by both National Councils at the republic level. Despite this concession, they continued to envision the new state structure as a federation rather than a confederation. Holding that "without a strong Federation there can be no strong republics,"[10] Havel argued that it was necessary "to build anew all the organs of our Federation . . . to seek their new role, to delimit their contents . . . and respect them in a similar way as citizens of California or Texas respect the powers of all the Federal institutions of the U.S.A."[11] Thus, while rejecting the idea of an ethnic "Czechoslovak" nation, Havel spoke of a "federal people" who would be the federal government's constituency.[12] This reflected the strong influence among Czech leaders of the notion of civil society, the political-philosophical concept developed by the dissidents, whose definition of the primary rights-bearing entity as the "free and equal citizen," rather than the pre-political ethnic nation, also appealed to the liberal monetarists.

From the outset, then, the question of the future relationship between the federal and republic governments was connected "with the question of whether the common state should prefer national or civil principles."[13] Leff aptly describes the conflict:

Perhaps the most striking aspect of the national tensions in Czech-Slovak disputes over the constitutional allocation of power is that these conflicts call into question the Western idea of democracy, which has been based on a theoretical foundation of individual rights and majority rule. The Slovak challenge was to the idea of majority rule. Slovak leaders assumed as a basic article of democratic faith that a system in which the Czech majority could determine policy was no democracy. There was a fundamental problem hidden here. As Sir Ivor Jennings said forty years ago, "The people cannot decide until someone first decides who are the people." Czechs tended to define 'the people' as all the citizens of the state, whereas Slovaks insisted on the existence of two peoples, each of which had the right to decide the fate of its own territory. The quarrel about federation was really a quarrel about what democracy should look like in a multinational state.[14]

As noted above, the problem of finding a workable compromise was further complicated by the Federal Assembly's process for constitutional change. It had two Chambers: one of "People" and one of "Nations." The safeguards against the outvoting of Slovaks instituted during the post-invasion federalization required that a new constitution or constitutional amendment receive a three-fifths approval from all deputies in both chambers, voting separately. This effectively gave both nations veto power over any constitutional change. Combined with the gulf between the Czech and Slovak perspectives, this was a recipe for deadlock. Indeed, by February 1992, all parties were convinced that the negotiations were so unproductive that they should be put on hold until after the June elections.

While the political process that ultimately led to the Velvet Divorce is often criticized for being elite-driven and unrepresentative of the popular preference for continued common statehood, most Czechs and Slovaks held perspectives similar to those of their leaders. In November 1991 and March 1992, the Czech view was 39 and 34 percent (respectively) in favor of a unitary state, 30 and 27 percent in favor of a federation, 4 and 6 percent in favor of a confederation, and 5 and 11 percent in favor of independence (22 percent answered "don't know" or "other" in both polls). Among respondents in Slovakia, 20 and 13 percent supported a unitary state, 26 and 24 percent a federation, 27 and 32 percent a confederation, and 14 and 17 percent independence. These leanings suggest that of those who favored a federation, Czechs envisioned it as close, while the Slovaks wanted it to be looser.[15] Moreover, Leff points out that the

Hungarian minority concentrated in Slovakia preferred a more centralized state, which "suggests that Slovaks were even more supportive of a decentralized solution than the overall poll results in Slovakia would indicate."[16]

The Broader Societal Debate: Interpreting the "Common" Past's Meaning for the Future

There were, then, crucial differences between the Czech and Slovak perspectives on the foundations of political community. As Valerie Bunce argues, "what is at stake in [post-Communist] eastern Europe is nothing less than the creation of the very building blocks of the social order. What is open for negotiation is not just the character of the regime but also the very nature of the state itself, not just citizenship but also identity . . . not just modification of the state's foreign policies, but also a profound redefinition of the role of the state in the international system."[17] Decisions on such questions clearly require reflection on the past as well as the future. The Velvet Revolution was short, and change came, as Ash observed, with "breath-taking" speed. While it was clear that the Revolution was against the Husák regime and the Party's repressive "leading role," a detailed societal conversation was still necessary to determine what exactly it was *for*. As the constitutional negotiations show, fundamental concepts such as national sovereignty and legitimate authority needed to be defined. Given the distance between the Czech and Slovak experiences during the Communist state's final decades, as well as the history of conflict over these questions, both common ground and mutual trust were lacking at the outset of this process. Thus, as constitutional negotiations proceeded, a contentious broader conversation (to describe it politely) between members of the two nations accompanied them, extracting lessons from the past and attempting to interpret the nature and implications of the "other side's" perspective for continued common statehood.

The first notable volley came from the Czech side. In May 1990, shortly after the resolution of the "hyphen war," Ludvík Vaculík, who had become a Charter 77 dissident during Normalization, published an article in *Literárni noviny* titled "Our Slovak Question." He began by acknowledging that the Czechs had consistently failed to make an effort to understand Slovak concerns and perspectives. He then turned his attention to the Slovaks, arguing that they had behaved immaturely throughout the period of common statehood: they had never critically assessed their "fascist experience," they had expected the Czechs to oust the Communists during the Prague Spring without their help, and, though they had endured less repression than the Czechs under Normalization, they had continued to demand autonomy. Thus, "misled by their history, spoiled by Czech intervention in their behalf, the Slovaks do not know how an autonomous and proud nation should act. In the future they will continue to seek excuses for their own failures, blaming them on the Czechs."[18] All this prompted Vaculík to ask, "do we need such a coexistence?" Given the Slovaks' separatist tendencies, he concluded that it might be better for all concerned if they were allowed to go their own way.

The prominent Slovak writer Vladimír Mináč responded. His was a more complicated relationship with former regime than Vaculík's: having been a critic of the state in 1965, and the author of a reappraisal of Štúr that departed from the official line,[19] he led the official Slovak cultural organization Matica Slovenská from 1974 to 1990 and was allowed to publish. His response to Vaculík was an essay titled "Our Czecho-Slovak Problem," in which he argued that Vaculík's condescending attitude toward Slovak identity was reminiscent of Czechoslovakism, where the Slovak is seen as a needy younger sibling dependent on Czech assistance. "For more than 100 years," Mináč wrote, "Slovak politics has deserved to be reproached often. Slovakia was not free: it flattered Vienna, then Budapest, and repeatedly Prague. It was more rhapsodic than realistic; it was more tearful than energetic. More than once did the Slovaks demonstrate their determination to become autonomous, but they never could achieve their goal because of Prague's economic and administrative centralism, its armed and violent police. It was Prague's centralist thinking that would have made a 'social group' of our nation."[20] Mináč further argued that the Slovaks had dealt with their fascist experience at the time, having courageously challenged it through the Slovak National Uprising. This had not, however, signaled a desire to restore the Czechoslovak nation: "the Slovak does not want to be a Czechoslovak. He does not want to be forced to live behind an alien façade. He wants to be independent and sovereign." Although Mináč concluded that continued coexistence with the Czechs in some form could be "useful, advantageous, and reasonable," Slovaks would have "to debate issues freely . . . to agree or disagree on the basis of arguments rather than resentments."[21]

As Leff observes, "this exchange was but the opening round of a public and official debate that was often much more vituperative than the initial writers' dialogue."[22] While Vaculik and Mináč covered the span of common history, in the ensuing discussion, each twentieth-century regime was scrutinized. Thus, the First Republic and the agreements leading up to it once again became a matter of dispute. An example is a 1990 article in *Literárny týždenník* titled "What Nationalism Is and Is Not" by Štefan Polakovič, the wartime Slovak state's chief ideologist. He responded to Czech accusations that the Slovak position was nationalist, which he argued was a label that clearly connoted "all manifestations of haughtiness, disrespect, impatience, arrogance, force and cruelty toward other nations." They attached this disparaging term to the Slovak orientation for self-serving reasons:

> The central point is the effort to debase our growth into a mature nation and to discredit our natural desire for justice. Neither Štúr and his followers, nor the composers of the [1861] Memorandum, nor the post-Memorandum Slovak political leaders Paulini-Toth, Vajanský and others were nationalists—they worked for nothing other than the safeguarding of Slovak culture and the future of the nation.
>
> Neither the national leaders who continued the Memorandum's legacy, nor the Ľudaks [Hlinka's Slovak People's Party], who historically and ideologically stemmed from these national leaders, can be called nationalistic . . . they were only continuing the national and political movement and efforts to gain from the government control over their fate and the security of their inalienable rights, which the Masaryk-Beneš regime did not recognize.[23]

Thus, he argued, the Slovak national tradition involved none of the negative, destructive elements now associated with "nationalism." Polakovič further argued that the Czechs' behavior toward the Slovaks *was* nationalistic. In particular, he noted that "it is necessary to remember that Masaryk, who signed the Pittsburgh Agreement, pronounced it a scrap of paper and together with Beneš changed the term 'Czecho-Slovakia' of the peace agreement to the unitary 'Czechoslovakia.' Out of disrespect these Czech leaders testified to the doctrine that the Slovak nation does not exist."[24] Thus, he argued, from the very beginning of their union with the Slovaks, the Czechs had a history of duplicity and undermining Slovak national rights, while hypocritically asserting that the Slovak assertion of these rights constituted nationalist intolerance.

A typical Czech response to such arguments can be found in Ladislav Niklíček and Petr Nováček's essay, "Dynamite in the State's Foundations."[25] Adding the prefix "so-called" to the Pittsburgh Agreement's title, they argued (in Masaryk's tradition) that the "Czechoslovak Parliament never respected the agreement as a legally binding act." Moreover, they noted that Hlinka "made it continually more clear that he considered the unity of the Czechs and Slovaks in one state as conditional. Already in 1922 he wrote: 'The Polish are no less brothers to us than the Czechs. . . . Indeed, the Catholic and Christian mentality of the Poles is much closer to us than the Czech Hussitism, progressivism and erotic materialism.'" Drawing parallels to the present day, they continued: "If we take into consideration the recent statements of Ján Čarnogurský and F. Mikloško on the fallen, consumerist liberalism of the West, and consequently also their placing of Czech society on the one side, and the still pure, essentially more spiritual Slovak nation on the other, then it is surprising how long and continuously this ideology can complicate the Czech-Slovak relationship."[26] These authors thus not only identified continuities in the Slovak perspective, but also portrayed it as a divisive caricature of national differences.

Indeed, Čarnogurský did often highlight deep-seated differences between the Czechs and Slovaks,[27] which he put forward as defining elements of the relationship since the First Republic. For example, in a November 1991 speech, he observed that

> The second president of the Republic, E. Beneš, addressed the Slovaks in a speech about our national present and future in December 1933 thus: the Czechs must in this unifying process give the Slovaks their organizational fitness, their methodical work habits, their Western European ability to understand all of life rationally, their perseverance and reliability in daily activities, their activity and initiative in business. The Slovaks must give Czech life new contact with unspoiled folk culture in the biological-social sense, must give their emotional correction to Czech rationalism and humanize it, must carry to them a new supply of biological and emotional elements toward the creation of new cultural values, especially in the artistic and social areas . . . I am in favor of E. Beneš's words being fulfilled. And, at the same time, that both nations preserve and further their good qualities in order that the future republic achieves the conditions for their 'unfettered' development.[28]

As Nikliček and Nováček noted, Čarnogurský did emphasize the long-standing spiritual differences between the two nations. He also argued that the Catholic Church could "act as a bulwark against the moral crisis of Western secular liberalism,"[29] observing that "the church will never play such a role as in Israel or the Islamic countries, but it could be the base of basic solidarity of the people and certain political actions would not be possible." This position, articulated by a powerful and influential Slovak leader, indicates the continuing relevance of Catholicism for Slovak national identity, again, not only as a boundary marker but as a normative framework with profound implications for political life. While Čarnogurský's perspective (and that of the Christian Democratic Movement more broadly) was far more liberal than that of the clerical nationalists of pre-Communist times, it nevertheless highlights the impressive resilience of the religious element in Slovak political culture.

Unfortunately, tensions and misunderstandings between Czechs and Slovaks on this count proved resilient as well. Václav Malý, a former Czech religious dissident, observed that in contrast to Slovakia's deeply rooted religious traditions, Bohemia and Moravia comprised an "atheistic zone" that carried on the Czech anti-clerical tradition.[30] Noting an interesting parallel to the way tensions were stoked during the First Republic, Malý argued that in the post-Communist period the Czechs were often ignorant of the Slovaks' religious feelings and did not realize that replacing statues and images of Communist leaders with Masaryk's could offend Slovaks who saw the first president as anti-Catholic.[31]

Masaryk's image—along with Dubček's—was a frequent sight at demonstrations during the Velvet Revolution. Beyond the religious issue, the Czech celebration of First Republic symbols prompted Slovak suspicion of the Czechs' invocation of "civic" principles in constitutional negotiations. For example, at meetings between Pithart and Čarnogurský at Oxford, a reporter observed, "Mr. Pithart, the barrel-chested Czech, produced stern liberal rhetoric about the difference between the national and the civic impulses in nation-building, asking the Slovaks to weigh more carefully the importance of the civic, democratic impulse."[32] Ondrej Florek voiced the resulting Slovak frustration in a May 1992 *Nové slovo* article, asking, "How should we understand the continuous instruction from the Czech parties on constitutional questions, when they impose on us the construction of the state according to the civic principle and not the national? Are the Czech politicians aware that beneath the civic principle they pursue the outdated 'Czechoslovak' conception? We will submit to the civic principle in the construction of the state and will relocate the center of the federation from Prague to Brno, or Košice."[33] And in a much less civil expression of disapproval, in October 1990, protestors in Bratislava attacked President Havel and Finance Minister Václav Klaus, throwing eggs at them when they attempted to address a crowd on that state's 73rd anniversary.

The post-Communist controversy over the First Republic's legacy thus centered on long unresolved issues, whose interpretation in the post-Communist period shaped perspectives on both sides. That regime represented the only previous attempt to construct an overarching identity in a democratic context, and Slovaks could accurately argue that this project had strongly privileged Czech ethnocultural identity and denigrated Slovak identity (especially the religious aspects) and denied it distinct sovereignty. Recognizing this helps illuminate the nuances of a debate that was frequently characterized both by Czechs and international observers as a stark battle between neutral "civic" and particularistic "ethnic" ideas. As Kymlicka argues, identifying the cultural component of civic nationhood is key to understanding opposing movements: "The failure of liberalism to understand nationalism is directly related to its failure to acknowledge these unavoidable connections between state and culture. The myth that the state can simply be based on democratic principles, without supporting a particular national identity or culture, has made it impossible to see why national minorities are so keen on forming or maintaining political units in which they are the majority."[34] Indeed, as Vladimir Kusin argues, a "Czech takes his national identity for granted in the Czechoslovak context: a Slovak does not."[35] On the other side of the debate, to the Czechs Masaryk represented democracy and liberation, and they were irritated by the Slovak bitterness over his symbolic reemergence.[36] Moreover, they saw in many Slovak depictions of the Czech-Slovak relationship a sort of Hlinka-esque essentialization and exaggeration of national differences that needlessly undermined the development of common ground.

While the Czechs' embrace of First Republic symbols unsettled many Slovaks, Slovak celebrations of the wartime state, which began shortly after the Velvet Revolution, likewise unnerved the Czechs. On March 14, 1990, a demonstration in Bratislava marked the 51st anniversary of the Slovak state's founding. The crowd chanted such slogans as "Independent Slovakia!" "We've had enough of Prague!" "We've had enough of Havel!" "Hungarians across the Danube!" and "Jews to Palestine!"[37] The demonstration's extremist tenor was widely reported in the Czech media. A few months later, the alumni of the Teachers' Training College in Bánovce nad Bebravou, Slovakia, erected a plaque in honor of the school's founder, Jozef Tiso. Also participating in the ceremony were Catholic clergy, including a cardinal. There was such an outcry against the monument, however, that it was taken down.

Both Czech and international media coverage of such events tended to portray them as ominous signs concerning the nature of Slovak nationalism.

Many Slovak political leaders reacted with frustration to such appraisals of the Slovak post-Communist orientation, strongly disputing the Czech characterizations of Slovaks as "neofascists, neocommunists and anti-Semites."[38] As Čarnogurský explained, "some of us are afraid that we may be declared abroad as separatists, or even as clerical-fascists."[39] Indeed, the major parties did not join in the celebrations of the wartime state, and in December 1990 the Proclamation of the Slovak National Council and the Government of the Slovak Republic concerning the Deportation of the Jews from Slovakia, building on a 1987 document issued by dissidents (including Čarnogurský), expressed sorrow over the Slovaks' participation in the Holocaust.[40] In addition, Čarnogurský apologized for the Slovak state's misdeeds against the Czechs in a November 1991 speech, and in March 1992 several official events commemorated the fiftieth anniversary of the deportations.

Though the major parties were unsupportive, the spring of 1991 brought another round of anniversary celebrations for the wartime state. These included a rally of around 5,000 people in Bratislava, where loudspeakers played a recording of Tiso reading the Slovak state's Declaration of Independence. Unexpectedly, President Havel, on an unrelated trip to Slovakia, showed up with bodyguards and supporters. An angry crowd of around 200 set upon him, and although he escaped without injury, demonstrators kicked and spat on his car before it drove off.[41] Later that day, Havel addressed the Slovaks on television, asking them to participate in the building of a democratic federation and a civil society. He continued, "lately, however, you are being more and more frequently offered another alternative: to give national aspirations precedence over all other values."[42] That October (the same month as the egging incident described above), a new plaque dedicated to Tiso was unveiled in his birthplace, the town of Veľká Bytča, once again with clergy participation. Finally, the last round of anniversary celebrations during common statehood, in March 1992, lasted a week and were strongly pro-separatist and anti-Havel, anti-Czech, anti-liberal, and anti-Semitic.[43]

The Czechs reacted to these celebrations of the wartime state and its symbols with strong condemnation and increasing wariness. Havel admonished the celebrants by declaring, "World War II began on March 14," and Pithart noted that "in our historical calendar, this date is written in black."[44] From the first March rally in 1990, "Czechs saw the demonstration as a clear sign not only that the Slovaks were proudly celebrating their fascist past, of which they should be ashamed, but also that the political scene in Slovakia was again acquiring a distinctly fascist character."[45]

Although none of the major parties supported the separatist rallies or, aside from the Slovak National Party, expressed strong admiration for Tiso and the Slovak state, they nevertheless did seem somewhat ambivalent about its legacy. For example, Čarnogurský objected to the preamble of the Czechoslovak-German treaty, which affirmed Czechoslovakia's legal continuity after Munich, "on the ground that this continuity had been interrupted by international recognition of the independent Slovak state between 1939 and 1945."[46] More broadly, the state's leaders did not unequivocally condemn the state and its memory.

The Slovak population was also ambivalent about the Slovak state, which is unsurprising, given that this period of history was "virtually taboo" during the Communist regime.[47] An October 1990 poll showed that of the 69 percent of respondents in Slovakia who held a view of the Slovak state, half saw it positively and half negatively.[48] In addition, 47 percent felt that the state had "fulfilled Slovak desires for independence."[49] Only one-fifth of the Slovak population believed that the wartime leaders bore some responsibility for the state's participation in the Holocaust, with the rest placing all blame on Hitler.[50]

One factor shaping post-Communist Slovak attitudes toward the Slovak state was the return of a number of émigré nationalist activists to Slovakia soon after the Velvet Revolution. They came to rally the population to support an independent state, sometimes invoking self-serving portrayals of the Tiso regime.[51] For example, the Slovak National Party's journal, *Slovenský národ*, reprinted a letter to the editor of the *Chicago Tribune* in response to an article about Slovak celebrations of Tiso. Irena Uher, the letter's author, disputed the contentions that "Slovak nationalism is fraught with racism" and that "during the Second World War Slovaks helped to kill thousands of Jews." According to Uher, "From Slovakia were deported 60,000, from the Czech lands 200,000. The Slovak government was informed that the Jews were being sent for necessary labor in Germany (it was not only Jews who were deported to labor camps). The deportation of the Jews from Slovakia stopped in the year 1942, when they found out that they were being murdered in concentration camps. The current government has publicly apologized to the government of Israel. How long do you want to hold this over our heads?"[52] This letter reflected, in its every detail, the minimized and inaccurate portrayal of the state's role in the Holocaust that certain émigré nationalists had long cultivated in their publications abroad, and then personally brought to the post-Communist public.

While much condemnation of celebratory appraisals of the Slovak state came from Czech and international sources, some Slovaks sharply denounced them as well. For example, sociologist Vladimír Krivý warned in *Kultúrny život* that "authoritarian and even totalitarian perils and symbols are on the rise: the not uncommon uncritical appeals to the wartime Slovak state; the elevation of Tiso in one [political] current and the lack of distancing from this ascension on the part of parties in other currents; the revivification of the breeding grounds of anti-Semitism; declarations of 'national unity' from which may be excluded only 'national traitors' (those who think differently); intolerance, the breaking up the meetings of others, cases of physical intimidation of opponents of nationalism."[53] As a corrective, he called for greater respect for the ideals of "parliamentary democracy and tolerance," as well as "the civic principle, the legal state, a European orientation, greater individualism, and a liberal approach."[54]

While Krivý unpacked the implications of "uncritical appeals" to the wartime state, those who did celebrate it, or even saw its merits, tended to highlight its realization of Slovak sovereignty, rather than its illiberal governance. As Ladislav Holy observes, "for many Slovaks, the period of Slovak independence in 1939 represented a time when they were for the first and last time masters of their own destiny. In post-Communist Czechoslovakia the independent Slovak state became a powerful symbol invoked in demonstrations expressing a Slovak desire for sovereignty."[55] Like Krivý, however, the Czechs focused on the state's repressive behavior, and 66 percent of them categorized the state as definitely fascist. They were, therefore, disturbed by what they saw as "evidence that the Slovaks were unable to distance themselves from their fascist past."[56]

The Third Republic also played a small role in the debate over the future of Czech-Slovak relations. Some Slovaks pointed to this period to contradict the Czech accusation that the Slovaks were left-leaning and antidemocratic. For example, Florek argued that the period showed "that the [Slovak] nation did not want to be oriented toward totalitarianism, but democracy, which was confirmed by the delivery of 62 percent of the vote for the Democratic Party."[57] He compared this to the 40 percent of the Czech vote that went to the Communists.

On the Czech side, Pithart attempted to foster national reconciliation by revisiting the issue of Tiso's execution by the Third Republic. World War II, he argued, "injured both nations. The Czechs living in Slovakia were expelled from there in 1939. And in the year 1947 the president of the Slovak Republic was tried and condemned. And I assume that this was correct. Despite this, however, in Prague there was little heed for flexibility at least in that measure that was shown toward the fallen statesmen in postwar France."[58] This statement did little to improve national relations, however, and antagonized the Czechs. In attempting to bridge the national divide, then, Pithart became "vulnerable to attack as a betrayer of his own republic's interests."[59]

While the Third Republic was not central to the post-Communist discourse, the question of the Communist period's legacy, understandably, was. It was particularly important to the ascendance of two new parties, whose leaders would orchestrate the Velvet Divorce and then dominate Czech and Slovak politics for several years. On the Czech side, this leader was Václav Klaus, one of the Civic Forum's leading technocrats. He and his fellow monetarists had quickly gained positions of great influence in the post-Communist state, for two main reasons. First, they offered expertise necessary for the technical aspects of the transition, which most of the dissidents could not provide. And second, as Eyal argues, they had certain political-philosophical affinities with the dissidents. In part, this was based on liberalism, as both sought to empower individuals.[60] Equally important, they both saw Communism as utterly bankrupt, and reform Communists as not substantially different from Communists "without adjectives."[61] They thus agreed on the "rejection and condemnation of the past."[62] This agreement initially offered ground for a strong alliance, but over time, Klaus's desire for party leadership unhampered by continuous consultation with the dissidents—many of whom were not the fans of Milton Friedman and Margaret Thatcher that he was—prompted him to break away and found the center-right Civic Democratic Party (ODS) in 1991. The dissidents' idealistic conception of a new kind of moral civil society lost influence, and the transition began to move in a different normative direction, aptly described by Smolar: "the socialist ideology of equality yields to the liberal ideology of enrichment, and the idea of collective advancement to that of individual prosperity."[63]

On the Slovak side, the rising star was Vladimír Mečiar, who had been purged from the Party in 1968, but had not become a dissident and was allowed to practice law. As a member of the Public Against Violence (VPN), he served as Slovak minister of the interior after the Velvet Revolution, and then became prime minister in June 1990. During this period, Eyal argues, the now very familiar triadic configuration of elite orientations reemerged, with the Slovaks divided between deeply anti-Czech nationalists (represented by the Slovak National Party and the Matica Slovenská) and the pro-Czech federalists, represented by a minority of liberals in the VPN. Neither elite orientation, however, was strongly representative of the Slovak public, and Mečiar shrewdly positioned himself between them. He thus allied himself with the liberals against the nationalists' demands for a very restrictive language law. The liberals, however, also saw Mečiar as a threat, and had good reason to suspect him of antiliberal tendencies, especially as allegations grew that as interior minister he had used the secret police files to intimidate political rivals and to eliminate evidence of his own previous collaboration. The liberals thus ousted Mečiar in April 1991, replacing him as prime minister with Čarnogurský.

This move proved a terrible mistake for the VPN. Slovak popular opinion fell overwhelmingly in support of Mečiar, particularly as he and his supporters claimed that his opponents were stooges for the Czechs, doing their bidding.[64] Claiming to be the one who truly represented Slovak interests, he founded the Movement for a Democratic Slovakia (HZDS), whose ranks quickly filled with former state managers and Communist party cadres.[65] As the preceding chapter argued, these elites' relationship to the Normalization regime was very different from that of the Czech dissidents and monetarists, and as a result, in the post-Communist period, their relationship to the Communist past was different as well. In particular, they did not see the post-federalization Slovak reform Communist project, which focused on the development of authentic national autonomy and rational planning, as something to be "erased and purified; on the contrary, its remembrance was part of the work of imagining the nation."[66] These elites saw their current project as having significant lines of continuity with the best elements of reform Communism, and they made this argument in the discourse over the proper direction of future reform.[67]

The HZDS drew these ideological elements together under the rubric of national sovereignty. This is not to suggest that the HZDS ideology was philosophically sophisticated or that its members were especially principled. It does, however, contradict the contention made by Shari Cohen and others that the majority of Slovak elites who had been affiliated with Communist institutions (and especially those who joined the nationalist-populist HZDS thereafter) were entirely lacking in ideological commitment. In Cohen's formulation, this argument holds that during the late (certainly post-Soviet invasion) Communist period, the Party had "lost its ability to motivate, [and] all that was left were individuals and instrumental networks driven by egoism."[68] After the regime fell, they continued to be ideologically empty and "concerned solely with their reputations, power, and enrichment."[69] Of course, this is certainly an accurate description of *some* political elites, and Cohen may well be correct that there would be a higher proportion of such opportunistic elites in the post-Communist political landscape than in more established democracies.[70] Nevertheless, to argue that narrow self-interest was "pervasive and all-encompassing," with only a few elites not primarily so-motivated,[71] is to ignore the significant lines of continuity between pre-Communist, Communist and post-Communist projects and perspectives.

The HZDS electoral program in the run-up to the 1992 elections stated that it was the party's intention to follow the "democratic and legitimate path to complete the emancipatory development of Slovakia: to proclaim the sovereignty of the Slovak Republic, to pass a constitution of the Slovak Republic, to strive for the attainment of international-legal subjectivity, to call a referendum on independence and on a new arrangement of the relationship with the Czech Republic."[72] In a radio address, Mečiar explained that in negotiating the relationship with the Czech Republic, "that which was declared in the preamble of the present Constitution but has gone unfulfilled would have to be mutually understood. That is that [the Republics] are two sovereign wholes."[73] The electoral program also pledged to add the office of the presidency to the Republic's political institutions. On the economic front, the party promised "to continue with the economic transformation according to a new strategy, considering its social, ecological, and anti-monopolistic dimensions."[74] In essence, the HZDS promised national assertion and a "third way" for the economy.

The Czechs observed these developments with keen disapproval, and some suggested that the positive Slovak orientation toward the wartime state and the Communist regime were becoming mutually reinforcing within the HZDS. For example, when the Public Against Violence split in 1991, Havel's Press Secretary Michal Žantovský observed that "it looks as if a new coalition has been forming in Slovakia," consisting of "current Communists, reform Communists from 1968, and open separatists who remember the Slovak State as the golden age of the Slovak nation."[75] Many Czechs were further antagonized in the late fall of 1991, when Gustáv Husák died and Prime Minister Čarnogurský officially attended his funeral.[76] This symbolic act contributed to the growing sense among many Czechs that the Slovaks had either accepted as Communism as legitimate or, at a minimum, had not sufficiently recognized its evils. Thus, Pithart observed that

Since November 1989, it has become clear that Slovakia paid the most for the relatively peaceful repression, by the fact that it lacked the motivation for a more thorough self-examination. This sort of motivation is usually the experience of defeat. At the end of the twenty years of normalization, despite numerous signs of economic, environmental and moral crisis, despite the intensifying backwardness in terms of its civilization, technological decline and the growing political gap between it and the rest of Europe, there was in Slovakia little awareness of the fundamental political crisis and the unfeasibility or unreformability of the communist regime. After November 1989, there has been nothing so important as that awareness, the ability for sober-minded self-examination which asks: Who are we? Where did we come from? Where are we going? Not that there is a surplus of this sort of thinking in Czech society, but it was and is absent in Slovak society and will be for some time.[77]

Moreover, as the 1992 elections drew near, the HZDS's populist, at times bullying campaign tactics appeared to many Czechs as further evidence of the authoritarian nature of Slovak politics. Jiří Pejchl, a member of Klaus's ODS, observed in Český deník, "it is well known that there are verbal attacks on journalists in the context of pre-election campaigns, but what is unheard-of is the exclusion of foreign journalists and the majority of Czech journalists from recent HZDS press conferences. Such practices are inconsistent with democratic discussion and with the information methods of a democratic society. This strikingly recalls, above all, the history of Communist and fascist dictatorships."[78]

It was not only the Czech political leadership that expressed such views. According to Holy, the "prevailing Czech feelings were summed up in a reader's letter to the daily Český deník," which read: "I admire the Czech representation—Mr. Klaus and others. They have to deal with people who one day go to pay their respects to the memory of and to give homage to the fascist criminal Tiso and a few weeks later go to pay their respects to the memory of the Communist criminal Husák. Even the Slovak citizen can surely imagine the fate of an active politician in Germany who celebrated Hitler or some other Nazi criminal."[79] Opinion polls offer further evidence that the Czechs viewed the Communist regime more negatively than the Slovaks did. An autumn 1991 poll found that Slovaks were "significantly less critical of the old regime (though they were on balance negative)" and "whereas the support of the average Czech increased by 69 points from the old regime to the present, that of the average Slovakian respondent increased by only 11 points."[80] The following January, a study conducted by Comenius University in Bratislava showed that only 41 percent of Slovaks compared to 63 percent of Czechs felt that "the new government offered greater advantages than the communist government," and 37 percent of Slovaks compared to only 15 percent of Czechs said they were supporters of the Communist regime.[81] Two-thirds of Slovaks also said that the increase in unemployment was the fault of the post-Communist federal government, while the same proportion of Czechs "saw it as a consequence of the communists' policies."[82] Finally, a 1992 Central European University survey showed that Czechs expressed substantially greater agreement with the goal of "removing former communists from positions of influence" than Slovaks.[83] Clearly, then, Czechs and Slovaks tended to understand not only the more distant past, but also the regime they had overthrown together, quite differently.

By the time of the June elections in 1992, the two nations had aligned themselves decisively. In Slovakia, the HZDS won "handily,"[84] and a poll after the election found that 68 percent of Slovaks either agreed or agreed strongly with Mečiar's positions.[85] The Czech elections also produced an unambiguous winner in Klaus's ODS, which had campaigned on a platform of centrally directed free market reform that would be carried out throughout the state. The coordination necessary for such broad and consistent reform would require a tighter federation. After the elections 65 percent of Czechs either somewhat or strongly supported his vision.[86]

Thus, the 1992 elections produced clear but incompatible mandates for the Czech and Slovak leaders. When Mečiar pressed for a confederation, Klaus dismissed the idea, stating that "to speak about two states, each with its own international standing and a separate seat in the United Nations, but still maintaining it as a common state, is nothing but a joke. . . . No one can take it seriously." Moreover, he warned, "sustaining this strange phenomenon of a quiet dismantling of the federation, and still formally calling it a federation but with everything downgraded to an absolutely empty shell, is something we shall never accept."[87] Thus, he predicted that the federation was no longer viable.[88]

On June 19, an agreement between the ODS and HZDS set September 30, 1992, as the deadline for resolving future constitutional arrangements.[89] Developments moved rapidly thereafter. On July 3, Mečiar and the HZDS blocked Havel's reelection as president (his term was set to expire in October). Mečiar explained, "I see a solution for the Czech Republic in that it can have its own president, just like Slovakia will have its own president. If it is Havel, that is their business."[90] Žák argues that Mečiar's move against Havel hammered "the last nail in the coffin for the idea of possibly transforming the federation",[91] as the President had been the strongest advocate for a referendum on the division of the state.

The next step toward divorce came on July 17, when the Slovak National Council overwhelmingly passed a declaration of Slovak sovereignty. It stated:

> We, the democratically elected Slovak National Council, solemnly proclaim that the Slovak nation's 1000-year old drive for sovereignty has been completed. At this historic moment, we declare the natural right of the Slovak nation to self-determination, as allowed under all international accords and treaties on self-determination.
>
> Recognizing the right of nations to self-determination, we proclaim that we also want freely to choose the path and form of our national and state life, and that at the same time we respect the rights of all, of each citizen, nations, national minorities and ethnic groups as well as the democratic and humanistic heritage of Europe and the world.
>
> By this declaration, the Slovak National Council proclaims the sovereignty of the Slovak Republic as the foundation of the sovereign state of the Slovak nation.[92]

The only disapproval came from Čarnogurský's Christian Democratic Movement and members of the Hungarian coalition. In a speech before the vote, Čarnogurský called the declaration "a dangerous political game, cynically playing on the emotions of our nation, a game pointing toward political destabilization of this part of Europe."[93] After the vote, the opposition deputies requested police protection against a crowd of a few thousand celebrants chanting, "long live Slovakia" and "long live Mečiar."[94] The Prime Minister appeared on the balcony and told the crowds who were booing the deputies, "we know who voted against the declaration. Let them leave; they are walking into the past."[95]

The course was now clearly set for dissolution. Still, the Federal Assembly initially could not agree on the necessary constitutional revision (which required a three-fifths majority for passage), and in October, Mečiar and some Czech opposition members of parliament attempted to pass a nonbinding resolution to explore the possibility of "Czech-Slovak Union," essentially a confederation of the type always favored by the Slovak negotiators, to be employed until European integration. As Leff argues, this reflected "lingering interest in preserving some form of joint political destiny."[96] Unsurprisingly, given its form, Klaus rejected it. Finally, on November 25, the Federal Assembly agreed to dissolve the federation. At midnight on December 31, 1992, the Czech and Slovak Federative Republic ended.

Conclusion

Eyal has convincingly argued that the Czech and Slovak post-Communist elite perspectives on political community had very strong continuities with those they had developed during the Normalization period, when they were dissidents, internal exiles, and co-opted intellectuals, technocrats, and state-enterprise managers. Thus, although economic and power-political concerns specific to the post-Communist period clearly played a role in how these elites developed and articulated their positions on the proper foundations for the new state, their guiding normative orientations did not *originate* in the post-Communist period. Eyal further argues that these orientations had their genesis in the different Czech and Slovak elites' responses to the crisis brought on by the Prague Spring's crushing.

These arguments raise three key questions for this study. First, how do the post-Communist elites' orientations relate to the understandings of nationhood that I have traced in this study, and which appeared, in many ways, quite resilient up through the Prague Spring? Second, what is the relationship between the elite and broader populations' orientations? In other words, how widely were the elites' views shared? And third, what do the answers to these questions mean for how we understand the nature, and in particular the malleability, of norms that constitute understandings of nationhood?

Beginning on the Czech side, there are clearly important continuities and discontinuities between the post-Communist elites' orientations and those of earlier periods. The most important continuity here is the centrality of the idea of the rights-bearing individual who has the moral standing to govern significant aspects of his or her own life and to refuse to obey illegitimate authority. This idea clearly has roots in the Czech intellectual tradition reaching back at least to the National Awakening. Where the Czech post-Communist orientation diverges significantly from previous periods is in its insistence on the exclusive use of the "civic principle" in defining the sovereign community. This clearly shows the influence of the dissident understanding of civil society and monetarist liberalism; while Masaryk had emphasized its importance, no Czechoslovak state had ever been built on this principle of sovereignty before. At the same time, the principle is actually more consistent with the liberal-individualist currents in Czech political thought than the ethnic principle. The two had long existed in the Czech tradition in some tension with one another, as can be seen in the disagreements between Palacký and Havlíček over the relative priority of ethnonational and individual rights, as well as in Masaryk's philosophical attempts to bring universalist and particularlist/ethnonationalist principles into harmony. There is no doubt, however, that these leaders defined the nation in ethnic terms, as did those in the Third Republic who justified not only state sovereignty but also mass expulsions on ethnonational criteria. The Prague Spring reformers, by contrast, had strongly emphasized democracy and individual rights; ethnic sovereignty was not their concern, except as it related to the Slovak federalists' demands. Thus, the Czech tradition offers a supportive framework for the strict assertion of the civic principle, but no precedent, while at the same time offering a long history of the contrary ethnic definition, both constitutionally and within the broader political culture. Importantly, the post-Communist Czech Republic also offered an easier demographic framework for using the civic principle than in the past, as it was the first time that the Czechs had founded a democratic state without the potentially complicating factor of a substantial ethnic German minority present on the territory. The post-Communist response to Sudeten German (now mostly living in Germany) demands for a repeal of the Beneš Decrees that authorized deportation and property confiscation is notable in this context. As Leff reports,

> the issue has colored all aspects of Czech relations with Germany, complicating what has otherwise been a largely cooperative economic and political interaction. The treaty of German-Czechoslovak cooperation signed in 1992 (subsequently renegotiated after Czech independence) became a battleground, as the document was scrutinized paragraph by paragraph and word by word to assure that the Czechoslovak government was making no concessions on the Sudeten German issue. To Sudeten German demands for high-level official talks with the Czech government, Czech Foreign Minister Jozef Zieleniec sharply responded in 1994 that he had no intention of changing the results of World War II.[97]

Clearly, then, the Czechs also had no interest in retroactively applying the civic principle to past regimes.

On the Slovak side, there is far more continuity on the issue of sovereign community. Strongly in line with the Slovak intellectual tradition, most post-Communist elites defined the nation in ethnic, even organic, terms. This orientation, moreover, did not necessarily depend on a particular member of the elite's relationship with the Communist regime. For example, the philosopher Andrej Kopčok, who was purged in 1972 and excluded from publishing for the entirety of the Normalization period, returned to public life in the post-Communist period to write: "We witness a surprising resistance on the part of national identities which even the brutal oppression during Communist regimes could not liquidate. This is because nations are the optimal form of human existence at this stage of human development. The following view can be accepted in this context without the slightest reservation."[98] He then quoted Mináč, who, as a co-opted intellectual, had written in 1972:

A nation is human flesh; it is a natural organism, as self-evident as mountains and rivers, as people and life itself. No one had devised a more suitable environment for communication among people, for social coexistence and the rise of cultural values. These are the only imperishable values proper to civilization. The world of feeling and awareness of nationality are as unique and unrepealable as are one's identity and individuality. There always comes a time—usually one of anxiety—when subterranean rivers burst to surface, when a nation breathes in one breath and sounds in one sound, when the awareness of a common fate is so mighty that under it all barriers break down, when deposits of dogma and fabricated values are washed away and the depths are laid bare: there is something in these depths that unites all members of a nation.[99]

Kopčok concluded that the "present time of the collapse of totalitarian Communist regimes seems to be such a time."[100]

These authors' conception of nationhood (which has clear continuities with the thought of Štúr and Hlinka, among other past Slovak leaders) holds sovereignty and self-determination not only as rights, but in fact as *duties* in furtherance of the collective wellbeing and development. Moreover, the view that the "unique and unrepealable" national identity provides "the only imperishable values proper to civilization" implicitly rejects the idea that a community could be legitimately founded on universal principles unrelated to ethnonational identity.

Not only the definition of the sovereign community, but also its prioritization over other issues reflects continuity with earlier eras, including the Prague Spring. At the same time, this offers the starkest *dis*continuity with that period: except for a very small minority, the more liberal-democratic Slovaks no longer allied themselves with the Czechs, but instead pushed hard for national sovereignty. Eyal argues, persuasively, that this was critical to the polarization that led to the Velvet Divorce. The question that this raises in the broader context of this study is whether this means that the liberal Slovak elites had substantially reoriented their understanding of nationhood. The brief period between the Velvet Revolution and the Velvet Divorce does not give a conclusive answer on this because the *core* of the Slovak position in the constitutional debate concerned the issue of the source of sovereignty, not the nature of resulting authority as it would relate, for example, to government accountability and the scope of individual rights and freedoms. Of course, the two sets of questions are bound up together, but it was the former, not the latter, that Slovaks elites agreed upon.

That the question of legitimate authority was, in fact, contentious can be seen in the power struggles between Mečiar and his rivals in both the Public Against Violence and the Christian Democratic Movement. While such conflicts inevitably have many facets, there were principles at stake. Many of Mečiar's more liberal fellow elites found his leadership as prime minister to be autocratic, and the allegations that he and his underlings misused the secret police files, including as blackmail, "to manipulate Slovak politics to their advantage" were confirmed in a report presented to the Slovak National Council in March 1992.[101] Opposition to Mečiar drove more liberal Slovaks to oust him from the Public Against Violence (which ultimately served to his advantage).

Thus, the issue of national sovereignty was far more unifying for Slovak elites than that of legitimate authority. Moreover, the agreement on sovereignty's priority was based not simply on principle (leaving aside here the question of how principled certain leaders were personally), but also on an interpretation of the previous seventy-plus years of history that saw Slovak sovereignty repeatedly imperiled by union with the Czechs. And, on the other side, the Czechs articulated a mirror interpretation of this same history, in which the Slovaks repeatedly privileged national sovereignty to the detriment of democracy and individual rights (especially in 1938–39 and 1968). In the context of these views of the past (which, though often maximally uncharitable, were mostly accurate), differences over principle became extremely polarizing.

That the elites' understandings of nationhood had roots in both their particular experiences under Normalization and in the longer past raises the question of whether these understandings were broadly shared by the public. To begin, it is worth stressing that opinion polls showed substantial political *similarities* among Czechs and Slovaks. Still, the two nations threw their weight very strongly behind parties that stood in stark opposition to one another. To gauge the nature of this support, it is useful to again look separately at the two elements of understandings of nationhood. On the question of sovereignty (without equating this with full independence), it appears that the Slovak public generally agreed with its leadership's position. As Deegan-Krause has shown, national questions were highly relevant to the Slovaks' voting choices. Moreover, he argues that history was relevant as well, as "the intensity and range of attitudes about the split correspond well with recurring historical themes: Slovaks' ambivalence toward Czechoslovakia, and Czechs' puzzled disregard for Slovak national aspirations. Slovaks who perceived the first Czechoslovak republic as undemocratic and unfair to Slovaks were far more likely also to prefer more autonomy for Slovakia, if not outright independence (r = 0.253). The same is true for those who saw the wartime Slovak state as relatively positive (r = 0.316) and those who believed that Czechs prevented a fully developed federation from developing after 1968 (r = 0.427)."[102]

For the Czechs, however, history was not highly relevant for views on the future of Czechoslovakia. Altogether, ethnonational issues were far less important; economic issues (in particular, the direction of reform) were central to voting choices, and over time became closely related to voters' views on the future of the common state.[103] Thus, there is good reason to question whether support for Klaus and the ODS reflected popular endorsement of the "civic principle" as the constitutional cornerstone of sovereignty. Rather, it is fairly clear that the Czechs did not see *their* sovereignty as being at issue, or under threat, in the Czechoslovak state. It is also important to note that although Slovaks were less supportive of free market reform than Czechs,[104] Slovak views on the economic and nationality issues were *not* correlated.[105] To suggest that economic issues drove the Slovaks' desire for sovereignty, or were the primary factors making ethnic identity relevant, would be (to use Walker Connor's apt phrase) "an unwarranted exaggeration of the influence of materialism upon human affairs."[106] Thus, while the Slovaks were largely in principled agreement with their leaders' ethnic definition of the sovereign community, it is much less clear that the Czechs similarly endorsed a civic definition of nationhood.

There remains, then, the question of the level of congruence between elite and broader views on the nature of legitimate authority. Polling results, which generally did not focus on this question, give a hazy picture. A 1992 poll showed Slovaks to be significantly more likely to agree that it would "be better for our country to be ruled by a strong hand and someone who would clearly say what to do rather than lead discussions about different solutions to our problems."[107] Other surveys, however, showed much less difference with regard to the question of "firm hand" leadership.[108] The different attitudes about past regimes nevertheless lend insight into national views on authority, as Slovaks tended to regard the illiberal wartime and Communist states more positively than the Czechs. Though many Slovaks were deeply hostile to both regimes, the overall national difference is striking. Moreover, the Slovaks' support for Mečiar and the HZDS even after the report on his abuse of power was made public in 1992 indicates a certain tolerance of, if not support for, more authoritarian patterns of governance. Still, given the complicated meanings attached to the historical periods, the broad Czech compliance with the wartime and Communist regimes, and the easier economic impact of post-Communist reform on the Czech than Slovak Republic, it is important not to make too much of these differences.

What, then, does all this mean with regard to the nature of the norms that constitute understandings of nationhood? To begin, central elements of the Czech and Slovak understandings of nationhood that informed, and ultimately deadlocked, the constitutional negotiations over continued common statehood had roots in the Normalization era and in the preceding century, both in terms of political thought and, for most, lived experience of at least some periods. There certainly was no true ideological vacuum; the positions that garnered popular support drew substantially on existing normative frameworks. In the Czech case especially, their substance and popular legitimacy had survived the regime's intense hostility. This is strong evidence of the existence of a political culture distinguishable from the official regime norms, which strong-armed political leadership could not eradicate.

When set in this study's longer historical context, then, the last period of joint Czech-Slovak statehood offers evidence that, on a broad scale, understandings of nationhood and related national identities are not essentially, or even highly, situational. That said, many of the post-Communist elites had been active during the Prague Spring, and the perspectives they offered twenty-plus years later reflected reassessments and reprioritizations based on different views of Stalinism, the ultimately failed reform period, its aftermath, and historical patterns in the Czech-Slovak relationship. The norms that are linked to traditional understandings of nationhood are not static or abiding in a narrow sense; they were not preserved like an insect in amber. It is more accurate to think of them as frameworks for judgment that may support active reasoning; they often contribute to or inform decisions, positions, and behaviors, but do not determine them.

Clearly, then, post-Communist Czech and Slovak elites had engaged with understandings of nationhood, and were not passive recipients or unreflective purveyors of them. At the same time, the context and nature of the elite (and especially dissident) engagement with these norms during Normalization was not broadly representative of the experiences of the larger populations. This raises a final question of whether these elites were able to convince their post-Communist constituencies of the legitimacy of all key facets of their perspectives, including the new elements. If they did—and specifically, if post-Communist Czech leaders successfully reoriented the Czechs to see the sovereign community in civic rather than ethnic terms, and if Slovaks came to a consensus on the nature of legitimate authority—this would indicate quite substantial *malleability* of these norms. The period between Velvet Revolution and Divorce simply does not offer a clear answer to this question.

This leads me, in the following two chapters, to my second set of concerns: the implications of the Czech and Slovak constitutional definitions of sovereignty for individual rights and minority membership in the new, independent states. I draw on the evidence I have developed to assess whether elite interpretations of regime principles reflect any political-cultural patterns, and, further, whether there is any relationship between the level of consonance of these interpretations with previous political culture and how legitimate people found them to be. In this context, then, I examine the extent to which the Czechs actually accepted a civic definition of nationhood, and whether the cleavage between Slovaks' understandings of nationhood diminished in the post-Communist period. I begin with Slovakia.

CHAPTER EIGHT

The Implications of the Ethnic Model of Sovereignty in Slovakia

As THE PREVIOUS chapter showed, the disagreement between Czech and Slovak leaders that led to the Velvet Divorce centrally concerned sovereignty's source and constitutional implications. The issue proved not just contentious, but polarizing. This, in turn, supported a tendency among both the Czech media and international observers to portray the differences as reflecting the stark dichotomy between civic and ethnic orientations used in traditional scholarship on nations and nationalism. According to this portrait, the more liberal-democratic, universalistic Czechs founded their new state on the "free and equal citizen," while the nationalistic Slovaks used the exclusivist ethnic principle, long a source of trouble in the region. For several years thereafter, the two states also continued to diverge dramatically, with the Czech Republic apparently smoothly consolidating its market democracy, and Slovakia careening toward authoritarianism. Thus the unflattering comparisons continued, captured in the *Economist*'s 1994 description of Slovakia as the Czech Republic's "ugly sister."[1]

Recognizing that many factors shaped Czech and Slovak post-Communist politics, the question I pose in the final chapters of this study is: what, actually, have been the implications of the Czech "civic" and Slovak "ethnic" constitutional definitions of sovereignty for individual rights and minority membership? Are there discernable, practical differences between them, and if so, how significant are they? Exploring these questions, first with regard to the Slovaks, and then the Czechs, allows me to bring the substantial, comparative evidence from these two cases to bear on the debate over the civic/ethnic dichotomy that has intensified in recent years.

Let me begin, then, by briefly recalling the theoretical perspectives on ethnic sovereignty that I discussed in the introduction, with consideration of what they might expect in the Slovak context. Ghia Nodia had the least trepidation about founding a state on ethnic sovereignty, seeing some tensions with liberalism, at least at the level of principle, but no necessary connection with authoritarianism. He also sees a positive link between nationalism, democracy and liberalism, as the nation (even if ethnic) offers a definition of the "we, the people," who become self-determining. Based on this conceptualization, his theory would likely predict that if Slovak democracy (including here minority membership and individual rights) foundered, it was not due to some *necessary* implication of ethnic sovereignty, but rather to the profound pressures and strains of the transition, which may pervert and corrupt an otherwise sound political-philosophical understanding. According to Kymlicka's analytical framework, ethnic sovereignty would be one more illiberal element of a broader nation-building project. It would be particularly supportive of the promotion of a "thick" national identity, but it, in itself, would not be the *primary* factor undergirding illiberalism (Kymlicka does not identify any particular factor as primary, but rather looks at a constellation of factors). Hayden's theory predicts far more dire consequences, as this exclusive principle will necessarily marginalize and aggravate minorities, which in turn allows leaders to justify restricting broader civil liberties to protect the state-forming nation's sovereignty against the alien within. Finally, Greenfeld's theory would expect that if the ethnic principle supported a collectivistic ideology, it would logically demand authoritarian governance; someone needs to be the leader.

While these theories focus on the practical implications of nationalist principle, many authors who have specifically analyzed post-Communist Slovakia emphasize the role that elite power-political strategizing and competition, rather than principle, played in shaping how its governments exercised their authority. For example, though their analytical approaches are different, Deegan-Krause, Haughton, and Harris make a very convincing case that Slovakia's most authoritarian, illiberal period during the mid-1990s resulted from the attempts by the Mečiar government to undermine all limits on its power. In doing so, the government used nationalism instrumentally, not from primarily principled motives.

In setting up my investigation, I agree that this is true. My focus, however, is somewhat different from these analyses. I am looking at the role of a principle that is part of the constitutional regime, and therefore has a certain political status independent of whether particular leaders honestly believe in it. Moreover, I am not trying to explain the entirety of Slovak government behavior, but rather exploring what relationship (if any) exists between this particular principle and political practices affecting individual rights and minority membership. Again, principles do not "act" on their own; they need to be interpreted and applied by those with the authority to do so. I look, then, at how Slovak elites have done this. I am particularly interested in how much elasticity the principle appears to have across different governments, and what factors have enabled or limited particular interpretations, such as judicial oversight, executive vetoes, and the electoral process (the people's ability to choose their leaders). In addition, I look at the role that international bodies (such as the EU) have played in shaping the state's behavior with regard to these issues.

In drawing conclusions about what has constrained and/or enabled particular interpretations of ethnic sovereignty, I also attend to one factor that may underlie others: political culture. Many instrumentalist analyses of Slovakia either downplay or dismiss this, as their focus is, again, on the strategic motivations of elites within the particular institutional and power competitive post-Communist environment. Deegan-Krause, however, gives substantial weight to culture, arguing that opinion polls indicate that the orientation most supportive of Mečiar's governance was composed of elements that leaders shrewdly drew together: concern for national sovereignty with support for unaccountable authority. He also argues that these appear not to be otherwise stably linked either in the initial post-Communist period or in the post-Mečiar period. I engage with these findings by asking whether the contending post-Communist normative orientations show any continuities with the Slovak understandings of nationhood that I have traced throughout this study.

In this chapter, then, I look at how successive post-Communist Slovak governments related ethnic sovereignty to governance and at how this affected both the state's ethnic Hungarian minority, which comprises roughly 10 percent of Slovakia's population, and the scope of individual freedom more broadly. To measure these effects, I examine the extent to which the expectations of the theorists surveyed above are borne out. I also employ a model of minority membership in multiethnic societies developed by Ivan Gabal (which he applied to the Czech Republic's Roma minority) that both includes many of the theorists' concerns and goes somewhat beyond them by dividing the state's relationship to minority populations into four dimensions. The first encompasses "negative protections against violent discrimination and persecution,"[2] and the second, state "protection against non-violent discrimination" through "the guarantee and full enforcement of civil and human rights even for members of minorities" and the maintenance of equal opportunity for minorities to participate in the public, political, social, economic, and cultural areas of the society's life. The third dimension concerns the state's protection of the "right to self-fulfillment and development of one's own ethnic, national, or cultural identity," as it relates to the "internal life of the minority community." Finally, the fourth dimension points to "the full integration of the minority into the society" and the opportunity for mobility in "all positions and levels inside the majority society."[3]

As defined above, dimensions 2 and 3 are open to fairly wide interpretation as to what could constitute their fulfillment. With dimension 2, this would in part depend on the terms of inclusion for these various areas of a society's life, which could (drawing here on Kymlicka) fall on a spectrum ranging from liberal to illiberal. On the liberal end, knowledge of the majority or "state" language might be required for full participation in at least some aspects of the political and public spheres, but these would be fairly narrowly defined and allow for the unregulated use of other languages and expressions of minority culture in most areas of societal life. A more illiberal position might require the use of the state or majority language in most areas of life outside the home, and a highly illiberal position would allow participation in these areas only if individuals not only use the majority language, but also conform to many or all other aspects of majority culture (dress, religion, and so on). Another area open for interpretation would be whether the state's role in protecting equality of opportunity should involve the active promotion of minority inclusion, or should be more limited, and just prohibit exclusion based on ethnonational status. Similarly, on dimension 3, concerning the state's protection of the development of ethnonational or cultural identity as it relates to the minority's internal life, interpretations could range from a positive to a negative rights perspective. On the positive rights end, the state would actively promote and support the minority culture, and on the negative rights end, it would protect the right of minorities to sustain their culture, but privately and with the members' own means.

Clearly, these two dimensions are interrelated. If, for example, a state takes a liberal position on dimension 2, then minority cultural development may in fact take place broadly throughout the society, accomplishing the requirements of dimension 3. On the other hand, if a state takes an illiberal position on dimension 2, then the "internal life" will be pressed so far into the private sphere that it will be marginal to, if not entirely excluded from, the broader society's life, and dimension 3 will be difficult to fulfill.

I use the above measures, then, to assess the impact of the ethnic principle on minority membership. I begin by examining the debates over sovereignty during the constitution-drafting process. I then follow the zigzagging development of Slovak politics related to this principle from independence through the state's first decade-and-a-half.

Defining Slovak Sovereignty

The negotiations between Czech and Slovak leaders over a new federal constitution were so frustrating that Slovak leaders quickly began unilateral state-building. In 1991, they started drafting a new Slovak constitution, which was to be a " 'full constitution,' meaning a constitution independent of the contents of the federal one."[4] A central purpose was to establish ethnic Slovak sovereignty on the territory of the Slovak Republic, which touched off a heated debate between the ruling Slovak coalition and Hungarian minority leaders. These discussions particularly concerned the proper definition and use of the terms *národ* (nation) and *národnosť*. This second term is difficult to translate, as it lacks an exact English equivalent. The closest translation is "nationality," but this term does not share the important political connotations of the Slovak term, as the following discussion will show.

In a January 1992 interview, Ivan Čarnogurský made the Christian Democratic Party's (KDH) position on the terminological controversy clear. Noting the tensions arising between Slovak and Hungarian minority leaders in the constitution-drafting process, he observed that the Slovak parties understood "that the Hungarian language does not have an adequate term for 'nationality.' It does not distinguish between the concepts of 'nationality' and 'nation.' Because Hungarian uses the same word for both concepts, the [Hungarian minority coalition] Coexistence deputies requested that the above-mentioned 'nation' be used everywhere. We believe that a nation is an ethnic group that lives in one state and that a citizen may retain their nationality even when they are in a different state, or anywhere in the world."[5] The Hungarian minority in Slovakia thus has the status of a "nationality," but not a "nation." Čarnogurský observed that the minority leaders did not, however, appear to understand this, as they argued that "the Hungarian population is autochthonous, that is, original, and in that case state-forming [*štátotvorný*], that it is not a 'Slovak Republic' but at minimum a bi-national republic, that its founders are also of the Hungarian nationality." This claim is illegitimate, Čarnogurský continued, because the Trianon Agreement that led to the First Czechoslovak Republic's founding in 1918 "stated that it was formed by Czechs and Slovaks and it was asserted that it incorporated territory inhabited by Hungarians, because at that time there was an almost equal number of Slovaks living in Hungarian territory." Observing that "no one then claimed that the Hungarian Republic was not 'Hungarian,' that it should have been 'Hungary-Slovakia,' though half a million Slovaks lived there," he concluded, "the Slovak Republic secures the national sovereignty and self-determination of the Slovaks just as the other nationalities in the Slovak Republic secure human rights to the extent of every international freedom."

According to Čarnogurský's argument, then, status as either a "nation" or a "nationality" has profound political implications. As the state-forming community, the nation has an essential bond with the state through which it realizes its right to self-determination and exercises its sovereignty. A nationality, by contrast, is excluded from this relationship. Čarnogurský's interviewer therefore asked, "How are questions of minority nationalities resolved in mature democratic countries?" Given the Slovak leadership's insistence on ethnic sovereignty as the basis for state-building, Čarnogurský's answer is interesting: "Exclusively on the civic level. That means that a citizen of one nationality may not have more rights than a citizen of a second, different nationality. The areas of culture, education and so on are only secured as civil rights." Čarnogurský thus appears to employ both the ethnic principle to define sovereignty and the civic principle as the basis for civic equality. He does not address the tensions between these, and was not forced to; by early summer, the KDH had lost its leadership of the constitution-drafting process.

After the June 1992 elections swept Mečiar and the HZDS into power, efforts to complete a Slovak constitution rapidly accelerated, culminating in the document's approval on September 1. Its preamble begins: "We, the Slovak Nation, mindful of the political and cultural heritage of our forefathers and of hundreds of years' experience in the struggle for our national existence and our own statehood, in the spirit of the Cyrilo-Methodian tradition and the historical legacy of Great Moravia, based on the natural right of nations to self-determination, together with the members of minority nationalities and ethnic groups living on the territory of the Slovak Republic . . . therefore, we, the citizens of the Slovak Republic adopt through our representatives this Constitution."[6] The preamble thus distinguishes the self-determining ethnic Slovak nation from the state's other citizens, a distinction reinforced in the Constitution's body. In particular, Article 34(3) states that "the exercise of the rights of citizens belonging to minority nationalities and ethnic groups guaranteed in this Constitution must not lead to the endangerment of the sovereignty and territorial integrity of the Slovak Republic and to discrimination against the rest of the population." In seeking to protect the majority against the minority, the Constitution implies that non-Slovaks could be hostile to the sovereign community.

The Constitution also makes Slovak "the State language in the territory of the Slovak Republic." It is important to note that it thereby changed status, as it had been made the "official language" in the 1990 Language Law. Again, the implications are not obvious in English. Discussing the distinction, the Secretary of the Matica slovenská told *Práca*, "State and official language are not the same thing. The first belongs to the fundamental symbols of the state, and the second is only one of its components."[7] Miroslav Kusý explained that this is because the Slovak language's constitutional status as "state" language "issues from the dominant state-forming position of the Slovak nation."[8] The Constitution also addresses minority language rights, stating that, "respecting the conditions ordained by law," citizens belonging to minority nationalities and ethnic groups have the right "to education in their mother tongue" and "to use their language in administrative relations."[9] At the same time, it holds that "the use of languages other than the State language in administrative relations will be regulated by law."[10] There is therefore tremendous room for interpretation in implementing legislation.

Unsurprisingly, the Hungarian minority representatives opposed these aspects of the Constitution. When Parliament rejected a draft of the preamble beginning, "We, the citizens of Slovakia," the minority representatives walked out in protest and were absent during the vote on the Constitution. Miklós Duray, a Charter 77 signatory and chairman of Coexistence, subsequently told the Czech journal *Lidové noviny* that "the source of the Constitution, the methods of its negotiation and its contents alone do not comply with the civic principle or the full Slovak 'complexity.' This constitution establishes a national state and does not secure sufficient space for either civil society or the rights of minority nations and ethnic groups at today's levels."[11]

Reacting to such criticism, Milan Čič, one the Constitution's leading drafters and subsequently chief justice of the Slovak Constitutional Court, argued that the document provides for the "unity of civic and national interests."[12] In a television interview, Slovak National Party (SNS) leader Jozef Prokeš further articulated the government's response to critics, explaining that the preamble's use of the phrase " 'We, the Slovak nation' does not mean we would want to deny the rights of minority nationalities," which are "clearly defined."[13] Indeed, "the whole constitution shows unambiguously that it is oriented toward the civic principle." The main issue in the preamble, however, is the identity of "the state-forming element or founder," which, in Slovakia, is "we, the Slovak nation."

Early Attempts to Renegotiate the Regime

The Constitution's passage, followed three months later by the Slovak state's founding, did not reconcile the Hungarian minority's representatives to their place in the new regime. Through a series of statements, proposals, and memoranda, they set about challenging the constitutional distinction between "state-forming nation" and "minority nationality." In essence, they asserted that ethnic Hungarian citizens of Slovakia had the right to state-forming status alongside the majority and that they should have equal right to state protection of their ethnocultural identity.

These demands met a generally hostile response. A representative example is a *Literárny týždenník* article, whose authors argued that Hungarian minority proposals for collective minority rights were illegitimate because "the rights of members of minority nationalities and ethnic groups are everywhere specifically individual rights in conformity with the present international documents."[14] The authors moreover criticized the minority leaders' "terminological shortcomings," such as their use of the phrase "minority nation" instead of "minority nationality," and argued that they did not sufficiently differentiate between "the needs of nations, the needs of nationalities, and the needs of ethnic groups." Equating these categories "contradict[s] the endeavors of the national state by attempting to have minority nationalities develop the full diversity of life as would a nation having its own state." This is not a right belonging to minorities, as "minority nationalities and ethnic groups must be distinguished from the state-forming nation, insofar as they do not have the ambition to affiliate 'their' territory with their mother nation, which has its own state. National and state sovereignty must be realized only within the precisely defined borders of the state territory, which is indivisible from the whole, under which the national state exercises its sovereign state power directly or by means of elected organs, as is unequivocally declared in the Constitution of the Slovak Republic. Therefore it is not possible to speak of minority nationalities and ethnic groups as "state-forming components of the Slovak Republic."[15]

This analysis further explicates the minority's status; not only do they not belong to the sovereign community, but their essential communal ties actually lie with their "mother nation," beyond the borders of the state of which they are citizens. They are thus, in a fundamental way, *foreign* to the political community. Moreover, the fact that minorities may constitute majorities in certain areas within the state carries no moral weight: the authors were outraged by a February 1993 proposal in which the Hungarian parties "even speak of a 'Slovak minority' in mixed regions, even though the majority and state-forming nation on the territory of the Slovak Republic is indisputably the Slovak nation."[16] Because of their vital relationship to the state, members of the state-forming nation cannot share the diminished political stature of the minority.

Clearly, then, Slovakia's sovereign community is based on membership in a pre-political ethnic community. This creates different classes of citizenship, as those who belong to a minority ethnic community have, by definition, a lesser relationship to the state than those of the majority, as it is neither the minority's "sovereignty" nor its "self-determination" that the state secures and expresses. The question this raises, then, is whether this regime principle and the distinctions within the citizenry that it produces are merely symbolic, or whether they have actually affected minority membership and individual rights in the new state.

The Politics of Sovereignty in the Second Mečiar Government: June 1992–March 1994

The question of the practical implications of the constitutional distinction between "nation" and "nationality" was, in fact, raised shortly after the state's founding, when Slovakia sought to join the Council of Europe. Based on a rapporteur's report as well as communications from Slovakia's minority representatives, the Council admitted Slovakia on June 29 on the condition that it remedy several laws and policies restricting minority rights. This did not proceed smoothly. On July 4, Chairman of the Parliament Ivan Gašparovič reproached the Hungarian minority leaders for their role in the negotiations, stating that this "had led him to doubt the loyalty of these parties toward the

Slovak Republic."[17] Still, in the following days, the Parliament moved to fulfill its obligations. One of these was to amend a 1950 law that prevented minorities from registering their names in their own language and required that women add the Slovak feminine suffix "-ová" to their surnames. Parliament dutifully approved an amendment to rescind these requirements. However, Slovak nationalists, with the support of the head of the Institute of Linguistics of the Slovak Academy of Sciences, declared that the law contradicted both the rules of Slovak grammar and "the spirit of the Slovak Constitution."[18] Using a constitutional prerogative, Prime Minister Mečiar requested that President Michal Kováč return the law to Parliament, which he did.

The following day, the government ordered that signs bearing the Hungarian names of towns and cities be removed by the end of the month—a move that contradicted a second agreement with the Council of Europe.[19] Some communities initially refused to comply, prompting standoffs with authorities and worrisomely escalating ethnonational tensions. This, however, was not justified with reference to the Constitution: Ivan Václavík, the spokesman for the Ministry of Transportation and Communication, simply explained that it was "necessary to carry out the order so that all the road signs will be uniform."[20]

By the beginning of autumn, the government's relationship with the minority was seriously strained. In September, the Commission on Security and Cooperation in Europe (CSCE) issued a scathing report on developments in the new Slovak state, observing that the law on names remained in place, overseen by the Ministry of the Interior, and that a "state bureaucracy existed for the purpose of screening the names of newborns to ensure they were acceptable to the government."[21] As justification, the Slovak government had claimed that the Council's recommendations were not binding, and moreover that the Council "could not 'dictate grammar' to Slovakia." More broadly, the CSCE reported, the "government has given assurances to the international community that it is committed to protect human rights and fundamental freedoms. But at home, the message is often qualified: public leaders sometimes suggest that some rights, such as the right to a free press or the rights of persons belonging to minority groups, hold second place to advancing a Slovak state as conceived of by those leaders. . . . When reporting on the government is negative, it has been portrayed by some officials as 'anti-Slovak,' as though the current government may be equated with the Slovak state itself."[22] In addition, the CSCE noted "signs of chauvinism outside the halls of parliament," including anti-Roma, anti-Hungarian, anti-Czech, and anti-Semitic graffiti that "echo slogans of the Tiso era."[23] The report concluded: "although true extremists may be a minority in Slovakia, the silence of Slovak society in general and the Slovak government in particular in the face of acts and statements of intolerance has been deafening."[24]

In the face of growing international criticism (which was by no means confined to the CSCE), government representatives lashed out at the Hungarian minority representatives. On September 17, Mečiar told a Belgian newspaper that he was ready to conform to European minority rights standards, but that this entailed certain dangers: "The threat here is the temptation to return to a 'Great Hungary,' supported by Budapest as well as by the Hungarian parties in Slovakia. And for Europe, a Great Hungary is more dangerous than a Great Serbia."[25] Still, the Parliament did attempt, somewhat half-heartedly, to comply with the Council of Europe, and on September 24 passed a law on personal names that allowed their registration in minority languages. The procedure was, however, expensive and complicated, and the law continued to require the use of the "-ová" suffix on female names.[26] As HZDS Deputy Marcela Gbúrová argued during the debate, "in the end it is necessary to respect the opinions of experts—linguists and the rules of our standard language. This is in essence the minimum that is possible to require of the minority parties." Her comments were followed by applause.[27]

As the year drew to a close, new storm clouds appeared on the horizon. In early December, Hungarian minority leaders—including parliamentary representatives and a large number of mayors—held a meeting to discuss the government's plan to reorganize Slovakia's regional administration. According to this plan, the country would be divided from north to south rather than from east to west, thereby dividing the Hungarians concentrated in the south into five regions. At the meeting, the Hungarian leaders agreed to call a second meeting to discuss the possibility of establishing a province with significant autonomy.

Many Slovak leaders responded with outrage, arguing that these plans confirmed their suspicions about the minority's plans to separate from Slovakia, and that it could even lead to "ethnic cleansing" of Slovaks in the area.[28] Other leaders (particularly in the opposition) offered a more measured response. Ján Čarnogurský, in particular, blamed the government's failure to address minority issues for the increased tensions.[29] Ľubomír Fogaš of the (formerly Communist) Party of the Democratic Left (SDĽ) agreed, but also called the minority's initiative "irresponsible," admonishing, as Slovakia's political leaders regularly did, that "the protection of minority rights is guaranteed on the principle of the protection of individual, not collective, rights."[30]

Ultimately, the minority meeting went smoothly, producing a resolution that was much less inflammatory than many had feared. It refrained from using the terms "independence" and "autonomy" and called for increased language rights and a proportional share of representation in state and public institutions and in their budgets. In essence, according to the minority leaders, it called for the construction of a "community of equals."[31]

Though the furor over the minority's meeting died down relatively quickly, by the time the new state faced its second year, many of its leaders were convinced that it needed a new direction. The controversies over minority rights had been accompanied by a weakening economy with rising unemployment, government struggles to control the media, a worsening reputation abroad (making investment scarce), and increasing conflict among the ruling coalition partners. In February, the SNS split. Mečiar's self-serving handling of the privatization portfolio, combined with the generally unhappy state of political affairs, also led to heavy defections from the HZDS, and by mid-March the growing opposition was able to oust the government.

Though the second Mečiar government lasted only lasted fifteen months after the Velvet Divorce, developments actually bore out key elements of the expectations of all four of the theorists discussed above. To begin, the state did remain a democracy; as Deegan-Krause observes, "political institutions in Slovakia overstepped their institutional boundaries in their own interests, but the actual number and severity of their encroachments remained relatively minor."[32] On the question of liberalism's relationship to ethnic sovereignty, as raised by Nodia, we indeed see real tensions: the law on personal names, even as amended, would certainly qualify as illiberal nation-building according to Kymlicka's standards. It would also qualify for a somewhat illiberal position on my spectrum of possible interpretations of Gabal's dimension 2, and limit the realization of dimension 3, concerning the development of the minority community's internal life. As Edit Bauer, a member of the Hungarian coalition, argued during the September parliamentary debate, "this law is about one of the most fundamental human freedoms, about the protection of human identity."[33] Björn H. Jernudd, an expert on linguistic human rights, similarly argues that "names are intensely individual and mark identity both of the unique person and of the person as a member of the group."[34] Clearly, the Slovak government gave higher value to the state language's grammar (and its dominance) than to the individual autonomy necessary for minority self-identification. This prioritization palpably reinforced the distinction between the majority and minority: the Slovak nation is guaranteed state support for its ethnic identity by virtue of its sovereignty, whereas the minority is only offered recourse to individual rights, which may be overridden when they come in conflict with the sovereign nation's collective rights, suggesting that individual rights are of a lower order.

In choosing to defy the Council of Europe (and, indeed, the Slovak Parliament) on the highly charged, deeply symbolic issue of the right to choose and register minority-language personal names by pointing to its incompatibility with the spirit of the Constitution, the Slovak government sent a very strong message to the minority about its secondary status in the new state. The ensuing political conflict bore out Hayden's expectation that such diminishment and marginalization will prompt a hostile response, which allows the government to claim that the minority is disloyal. This positions the government well to define itself as the sovereign nation's protector, which in turn allows it to categorize all criticism as anti-Slovak. This claim is buttressed by the ethnic definition of the sovereign community, which is, of course, defined not by voluntary but rather by pre-political, organic bonds. It is thus possible to justify a conception of the relationship between the leadership and the community that follows the logic Greenfeld describes in her analysis of collectivistic ideologies. This is not to say that authoritarian governance automatically ensues, but rather that the authority *claimed* by the "father" of the nation (who secured the realization of it its sovereignty) fits quite rationally into that framework.

The state's first fifteen months also show that not all illiberal policies are justified according to the principle of ethnic sovereignty. The government explained its policy of taking down minority-language place name signs in practical, not principled, terms. Still, the very close proximity of the government actions on personal and place names, as well as their common status as Council of Europe requirements, links the two, and allows the justification for one (based on sovereignty) to color the other. Likewise, the proximity of the two issues allowed the government to condemn minority reactions with the same set of accusations concerning their loyalty.

The Moravčík Government: March–October 1994

Following Mečiar's ouster, a broad coalition led by Jozef Moravčik, who had left the HZDS and joined other defectors to form the Democratic Union (DU), took over the government. This coalition was "a rather artificial one, united primarily on the need to block Mečiar from retaining power but otherwise widely divergent in priorities and political orientation."[35] To both shore up vital Hungarian minority support (the coalition's numbers were not strong enough alone) and bring policy in line with European expectations, the government finally amended the law on personal names to allow fuller use of minority-language names and also passed a law allowing place name signs. This produced a level of good will between the government and minority leaders higher than any time since the state's founding. Moreover, the government improved relations with Hungary and began to turn the ailing economy around, winning international approval for its accomplishments.

Still, the Hungarian leaders did not see the alliance as stable; as Laslo Molnar, the spokesman for Coexistence observed, "if you play with the idea of more [deputies] defecting from Mečiar's party, then they wouldn't need the Hungarian vote."[36] Moreover, after the government scheduled early elections for the fall, Bélá Bugár, the leader of the Hungarian Christian Democratic Movement, expressed fear that the HZDS and SNS would "take advantage of nationality problems in the electoral campaign."[37] The governing coalition parties shared this worry. As David Lucas argues, "the fact that the Moravčík government attained parliamentary approval through the support of, and with concessions to, the Hungarian coalition had pronounced effects on Slovak parties, both in government and out. The governing parties clearly suffered losses in their popularity due to a generally perceived softness toward Hungarians. . . . In contrast, the MDS [Movement for a Democratic Slovakia] and SNP [Slovak National Party] found common cause in bashing the government, effectively capitalizing on the government's affiliation with the Hungarian parties."[38] Indeed, one of their favorite taunts was that "the Moravčík government hangs on the strings of [minority leader Miklós] Duray's underpants."[39]

Given the Moravčík government's more liberal-democratic orientation, Western observers looked on with dismay and alarm when Mečiar's HZDS won by far the strongest electoral support of any party in the autumn elections. The *New York Times* reported that this victory followed a campaign where "Mr. Mečiar revved up crowds with anti-Hungarian comments, saying that the coalition Government had sold Slovakia out to Hungary . . . Mr. Mečiar, who has cast himself as the 'father of the nation' and filled his campaign talk with phrases about being a 'good Slovak,' struck a chord with many. He promised to cut taxes by 25 percent, stop privatization and curb foreign investment."[40] For these efforts, the HZDS, running in coalition with the small Agricultural Party of Slovakia, was rewarded with 35 percent of the vote. In a three-way tie for second place with 10 percent each of the vote were the Common Choice (SDĽ in coalition with the Social Democratic Party, Peasants' Movement, and Green Party), the Hungarian Coalition, and the KDH. Moravčik's DU received 9 percent, the Association of Slovak Workers (ZRS) 7 percent, and the SNS 5 percent.

Sandwiched between Mečiar's second and third governments, the brief Moravčík period helps illuminate the complexity of Slovak politics. In particular, it makes clear that the ethnic principle did not *require* the illiberal interpretation of government authority that the Mečiar government gave it, at least with regard to personal names (and somewhat by extension, place names). That said, it is unclear the extent to which the Moravčík government's position on this was based on more liberal principles, as opposed to the strategic necessities of both the Hungarian minority's support and conforming state policy to European expectations, with the eventual goal of EU accession. Moreover, the government paid dearly for this alliance, given the effectiveness of the HZDS's rhetoric. While the HZDS also appealed to material interests, the centrality of the Hungarian issue in the opposition's electoral campaign suggests that a substantial portion of the Slovak electorate saw the Moravčík government as too liberal toward the minority. The HZDS got nowhere near an absolute majority of the vote, but a sufficient proportion of voters threw their support in more illiberal directions to effectively act as a constraint on more liberal interpretations of the ethnic principle. And, indeed, politics moved quickly in a more illiberal direction.

The Politics of Sovereignty in the Third Mečiar Government: 1994–1998

Mečiar's third government (a coalition of the HZDS, SNS, and ZRS) was so problematic from a liberal-democratic perspective that in 1998 U.S. Secretary of State Madeleine Albright called Slovakia "a hole in the map of Europe."[41] Comparing it to the Czech and other Slovak governments, Deegan-Krause offers an excellent, comprehensive overview of how it attempted to expand its authority beyond all accountability:

> Between 1994 and 1998 Slovakia's ruling coalition boldly attempted to unify legislative, executive, and oversight bodies within a single coali-

tion. The breadth and speed of these efforts dwarfed the tentative efforts in the same direction that were made by other governments in both countries. Whereas those other governments sometimes took the largely symbolic step of excluding opposition parties from committee chairs, the third Mečiar government excluded the opposition members from all parliamentary leadership and from key committees. Whereas other governments put occasional pressure on certain newspapers and television stations, the third Mečiar government incorporated public broadcasting into its own organizational structure and used it for political ends. Whereas the other governments accepted bribes worth hundreds of thousands of dollars in exchange for political influence in privatization projects, the third Mečiar government directly managed the privatization process and privatized property worth hundreds of millions of dollars directly to coalition party members and supporters. Whereas other governments may have used intelligence service agents to shadow political opponents, the third Mečiar government used the intelligence service to engage in political sabotage and the physical intimidation of its political rivals. Finally, when other governments faced sanction for their relatively moderate violations, the third Mečiar government was able in many cases to eliminate sanctioning bodies or pressure them into silence.[42]

This, then, was the context of the legal/political developments I consider here. As I noted at the outset of this chapter, I do not claim that the application of the principle of ethnic sovereignty explains these wider patterns. Indeed, there are only two major laws that were centrally justified according to this principle: the Law on the State Language and the Law on the Protection of the Republic. At the same time, the debates surrounding these laws produced conceptualizations of the nature and implications of, and threats to, national sovereignty that were important elements of the government's broader justification of its own authority.

Ironically, the laws that invoked ethnic sovereignty grew out of Mečiar's attempts to improve the country's chances of joining the European Union. To this end, shortly after returning to the office of prime minister, he began negotiating with Hungary toward a Hungarian-Slovak Basic Treaty. This included an agreement to protect minority rights according to the stipulations of certain international documents, including the Council of Europe's Recommendation 1201 on the rights of national minorities. This was a controversial aspect of the treaty, as some interpreted it as guaranteeing collective minority rights. Though all the opposition parties supported the treaty, the SNS objected to it strongly on these grounds. Slovakia and Hungary signed the treaty in March 1995, and the Hungarian Parliament passed it the following June. In Slovakia, however, the SNS took the opportunity to place conditions on its passage, demanding the passage of two pieces of legislation. The first was a new language law.

After much debate, the law came up for a vote in mid-November 1995. Though some members of the opposition had criticized the bill (especially concerning ambiguities in its wording), it passed with the overwhelming support of 108 (of 150) deputies, including a substantial portion of the opposition (the seventeen Hungarian coalition deputies voted against it, and the seventeen KDH deputies abstained, largely based on "church-related concerns"[43]). The law's preamble states: "The National Council of the Slovak Republic, following from the fact that the Slovak language is the most important feature of the individuality of the Slovak nation, the most precious value of its cultural heritage and the expression of sovereignty of the Slovak Republic and the universal communication mean [sic] of its citizens, that ensures their freedom and equality in dignity and rights on the territory of the Slovak Republic, has adopted the following law."[44]

The law then details the areas of life in which Slovak must be used, including official contacts with state organs (the law revoked the 1990 language law, thereby removing a provision for the use of minority languages in communities with a 20 percent minority population); official written records including material written by religious communities for the public;[45] community chronicles; all textbooks, except those used by minorities; periodicals and all other publications, except those regulated by a separate provision; radio and television programs, except those governed by other regulations (which initially caused concern over what would happen to the substantial amount of Czech-language television in Slovakia, some of which was very popular[46]; it has mostly stayed on the airwaves, though note the exception below); the statutes of associations and political parties; contacts between health workers and patients, provided the patient speaks Slovak; and signage, though a translation may follow. Section 5 applies the law to cultural and educational events, though paragraph 7 states that an exception may be made for "cultural events of national minorities, ethnic groups, foreign artists appearing as guests and music works with original texts. Accompanying presentation of programmes will first be expressed in the state language." (This was particularly ambiguous during the drafting, as some interpreted this to mean that the entire performance would first have to take place in the state language.) Section 5 (2) requires that "other language audiovisual works determined for children up to 12 years old must be dubbed into the state language" (which, for example, in 2005 led the Czech-language children's puppet show *Spejbl and Hurvinek* to be withdrawn from Slovak air after three days[47]). Finally, Section 3 (6 and 7) declares that "each citizen of the Slovak Republic has the right to free [of charge] adjustment of his name and surname into Slovak spelling form." The Culture Minister is given the power to monitor compliance with the law and levy substantial fines in the case of violations.

The law states that it "does not treat the usage of languages of national minorities and ethnic groups. The usage of these languages is treated by special laws." No separate bill on minority languages had been passed, however, leaving the legal status of Hungarian in question. President Kováč signed the law because Mečiar assured him that his cabinet would soon submit a bill on minority languages to Parliament.[48] This turned out to be an empty promise, and no such bill was submitted until after Mečiar left office.

The law's supporters used four lines of argument to justify it. The first centered squarely on the ethnic principle, holding that because the Slovak language is an expression of national sovereignty, it should have dominant status in the state. A corollary of this idea was that where Slovak was threatened by the use of Hungarian, the situation should be remedied. For example, Slovak commentator Dobroslava Krajačičová stated that, while "the state language belongs among the fundamental factors of national and state identity and pride . . . the neglect of the care and cultivation of the state language has caused the total decline of Slovak, especially in the southern mixed areas of Slovakia. It seems that some of our Hungarian fellow citizens have no interest at all in learning the language of the state-forming nation, and why should they?"[49] Along the same lines, HZDS deputy Ján Cuper observed that Slovak lawyers sometimes had to ask for interpreters during trials in southern Slovakia, "as though they were in a foreign country."[50] Another article pointed out disapprovingly that, in one town where Slovaks comprised 16 percent of the population, "the majority of jobs require knowledge of Hungarian."[51]

A second line of argument concerned the disintegrative potential of minority language rights. According to Cuper, "obvious irredentism and imperial great-Hungarianism is concealed within Duray's interpretation of the struggle against linguistic and cultural assimilation." He concluded, "linguistic diversity threatens the political cohesion and stability of the Slovak Republic and supports the pursuit of regionalism and irredentism at the expense of the interest of Slovakia as a whole."[52] In essence, the cultivation of a minority's language will lead it to strive to have or rejoin its "own" state.

A third line of argument centered on the need for a common language to ensure the society's smooth functioning. According to Minister of Culture Ivan Hudec, the unimpeded "flow of information," particularly in the army, police, and fire department, required a language law.[53] Likewise, Prokeš argued that the "task of the language law is nothing other than solely to secure intelligible communication between every citizen of the Slovak Republic. It is not an effort against anyone. It is actually a factor integrating the state."[54] (In another radio interview, however, Prokeš expressed a somewhat different view of the law's purpose: "we will reinforce the national identity, state sovereignty, and territorial integrity of the Slovak Republic."[55])

A final line of argument built further on the idea of the Slovak language's integrative potential. Adding another layer to his analysis, Cuper argued that "Slovak is not just a symbol of the Slovak nation, but also equally, and above this, a symbol of Slovak patriotism—a symbol of Slovakness [*slovenskost'*] from which members of the nationalities are not excluded."[56] This makes the boundaries of "Slovakness" penetrable, but at potential cost to minority linguistic identity.

Although the language law's supporters tended to use different combinations of these four lines of argument, the first two and the second two are based on understandings of the purposes of state language policy that are difficult to reconcile. The first two, concerning Slovak as a pillar and expression of national sovereignty and the divisiveness of minority language rights, are premised on the fundamentally different and unequal political status of ethnic Slovaks and ethnic Hungarians. The second set of arguments, concerning the state's interest in promoting a common language both as a practical necessity and toward the development of an inclusive civil society, is based on the notion of Slovak as a neutral, integrative tool. Clearly, there is a tension between these two visions, with the first undercutting the second's attractiveness or acceptability to minorities.

Though the need to get the SNS to support the Slovak-Hungarian Basic Treaty was a key impetus for the 1995 language law, it garnered much broader support. The final tally (noted above) included nearly all the opposition deputies from two of three ethnic Slovak opposition parties (most of the SDL' and Democratic Union voted for the law). This may have been partly out of fear of being labeled "anti-Slovak,"[57] but, according to Pieter van Duin and Zuzana

Poláčková, it may also be an "illustration of the strength of the ethno-national *Weltanschaung* and of the appeal for Slovak national identity at moments of crucial national decision-making."[58] Indeed, speaking broadly of his constituents' situation, Duray argued that "responsibility for this is not solely attributable to the Government of Vladimir Mečiar and the ruling governmental coalition, since the laws were also approved by a significant segment of the opposition in the Slovak parliament."[59] Poláčková and van Duin also point to a January 1997 poll showing that 54 percent of Slovaks approved of the Mečiar government's minority policies—"a decidedly higher percentage than the proportion of Slovaks who would have supported the Mečiar government parties at the time."[60]

There was, then, a fair amount of societal support for a law that was strongly illiberal according to both Kymlicka's criteria and Gabal's model. It produces a very wide scope for government control of societal communication, including spaces such as churches and cultural events where, from a liberal perspective, the means of expression should be open, and constricting possibilities for minority participation on Gabal's dimension 2. The law thereby also restricts the ability of individuals to preserve identities and communities of their heritage and choosing, central to dimension 3. This is an important restriction, as government leaders repeatedly admonished the minority that all rights relating to their culture and identity are individual rights. Clearly, however, this law secures the collective right of the sovereign community to wide-ranging linguistic dominance at the expense of minority individuals' sphere of autonomy. Moreover, the law's sponsors and supporters partially justified this restriction by arguing that the development of minority ethnic identity is likely to be subversive to the state. Because state protection and promotion of ethnonational identity flow from, and are symbolic of, the state-forming nation's sovereignty, the reasoning goes, a minority demanding equal protection indicates hostility to the state's purposes and a potentially separatist agenda, as such claims are only legitimate in relation to one's *own* sovereign community. Understood in these terms, demands for minority language rights indicate disloyalty to the state; this again highlights the fundamentally different relationship of minority citizens to the state. Clearly, then, the exclusive, ethnic definition of the sovereign community provides the basis for the law's justification.

While the Slovak language law placed particular burdens on the minority, the second piece of legislation that the SNS demanded in return for its support of the Slovak-Hungarian Treaty illustrates ethnic sovereignty's potentially wider-ranging implications. The law had been a long-standing nationalist demand, voiced already in 1993 as ethnic tensions mounted. They raised it again when, in April 1995, a month after the signing of the Hungarian-Slovak treaty, some 7,000 ethnic Hungarians held a mass rally in Komarno, southern Slovakia, and produced a resolution demanding an elected body composed of ethnic Hungarian representatives with decision-making power on minority policy, increased subsidies for Hungarian periodicals and cultural institutions, and a halt to plans to replace Hungarian-language education with bilingual schooling.[61] SNS leader Ján Slota responded to this rally in an interview with the Czech *Lidové noviny*, rejecting its demands and warning, "If anyone wants to question Slovak sovereignty, he must be punished accordingly. We want to pass the 'law on the protection of the republic.' In this we are supported by our coalition partners. And then we shall apply it."[62]

In January of the following year, Mečiar agreed to the SNS condition that a law on the protection of the republic be passed alongside the Treaty.[63] A few days before the SNS, in turn, agreed to these terms, Jerguš Ferko, editor of the HZDS-owned newspaper *Slovenská republika*, wrote: "The head of Coexistence repeatedly demanded the right to self-determination for the 'Hungarian national community' in Slovakia. That right is defined very precisely in political dictionaries—it is the right to sovereign decision-making, it is the right to one's own state. In Europe it is necessary to use a magnifying glass to look for another state, aside from Slovakia, where Members of Parliament along with chairmen of political entities are able to pronounce obviously anti-constitutional and treasonous demands and face no punishment whatsoever."[64].

On 27 March 1996, both the bill on the protection of the republic and the Treaty came up for a vote. The bill held that "individuals who organize public rallies 'with the intention of subverting the country's constitutional system, territorial integrity or defense capability'" would face imprisonment from six months to three years. Those who "spread false information" that could be damaging to Slovakia's interests could be jailed for up to two years.[65] The *Independent* of London reported that "opposition deputies banged their desks and jeered as news came through that the law had been approved by a margin of 77 to 57."[66]

Because the law's vague wording left ample room for interpretation by the authorities, many worried that it would be used to silence critics of the government, including minority representatives, opposition politicians, and journalists. The opposition thus condemned the law strongly before and after the vote. Christian Democrat Ivan Simko pronounced the law "the most fundamental turning point in Slovakia since 1989,"[67] and SDĽ Chairman Peter Weiss told Slovak radio that "the governing coalition has definitely started on the road to the construction of an authoritarian regime established on the provocation of fear and terror in the citizenry."[68] Radio news also reported former Prime Minister Moravčik's view that the law "may endanger the free competition for political power. It is a law for the protection of a totalitarian state, aimed against the foundations of the democratic republic."[69] The Slovak Helsinki Committee, the Association of Slovak Judges, and the Slovak Catholic Church opposed the bill as well. They were joined, internationally, by the European Union and the Organization for Security and Cooperation in Europe's (OSCE) High Commissioner for National Minorities, Max van der Stoel.[70]

Justice Minister Jozef Liščák dismissed such criticism, arguing that the law "will never harm anyone who has not acted with the intent of subverting the republic." He further noted that the law was "compatible" with the "legal arrangements" of EU members and that it was merely a "precaution, which will make recourse possible especially against new forms of criminal activity."[71]

Prime Minister Mečiar justified the law very differently. In a striking interview on Slovak radio, he essentially confirmed the opposition's allegations about the government's true motives. He began by stating that Slovakia needed a law to protect the state. In assessing this need, he continued,

We must start from the reality of who is in Slovakia. There is the Christian Democratic Movement, which for five years has openly propagated disintegration as its program's goal. . . . There are real, permanent and intensifying attacks against the state organs with the goal of dismantling them morally and politically and discrediting them before the public without regard for facts. . . . We see that there are likewise certain political groups who declare that it is necessary to call a referendum on the self-determining status of minorities in southern Slovakia, because they openly declare that it [the minority] is a nation . . . and that this nation has the right to self-determination. As all these merge at certain intervals, and are not diminishing but growing, it is necessary to put forward the question of whether the state has the legal instruments for its own protection and currently we do not have such instruments.[72]

The prime minister further argued that the law protected four interests: "territorial integrity," "dispersion of the constitutional system," "the internal and external security of the state," and "state sovereignty," meaning "the independence of state power from any other power outside the borders or within the state." He then turned to the issue of the opposition's hostility to the law, arguing that its allegations about the governing coalition's motives were "the beginning of fascism. Not this law. The law protects against just this, so that those forces in the state do not take the hill."

The EU responded to the March 27 votes by praising the Hungarian-Slovak Treaty, but criticizing the new law and calling on Slovakia to resolve its issues in a way that was consonant with EU membership accession criteria.[73] A few days later, President Kováč vetoed it.[74] The government coalition would not give up, however, and a similar, slightly watered down bill on the protection of the republic appeared before Parliament and passed again that December. This time, the Czech news service CTK reported, it "no longer makes it punishable to spread false information, harming Slovakia's interests in connection with a foreign country or a foreign official. However, the clauses on treason and calls for mass disturbances with the aim of overturning the constitutional setup, territorial integrity, Slovakia's sovereignty and the ability to defend itself remain."[75] Kováč vetoed this as well, and a third and final attempt in February 1997 to pass still another iteration failed.

Though ultimately squashed, the Law on the Protection of the Republic bears out Hayden's predictions concerning the kinds of broadly repressive measures that the principle of ethnic sovereignty may justify. Though the law was not ethnically specific the way the language law was, the context and discourse surrounding its passage made clear that it took as its impetus the presence of forces internal to the body politic deeply hostile to Slovak sovereignty. Indeed, some of the law's supporters quite freely identified these forces as members of the Hungarian coalition and their purported allies among the opposition parties. The ethnic principle was at the very core of this portrayal, as it supports the argument that a segment of the citizenry can be considered collectively alien and potentially hostile *by the nature of its constitutional status*. Moreover, by promoting this inherently oppositional relationship between sovereign community and the not-sovereign minority, the government was able again to portray itself as the protector of the Slovak nation and thereby to equate an attack on its policies with an attack on both state and nation. This, in turn, allowed the government to accuse minority leaders and all other critics of a level of hostility to the Slovak state and nation that bordered on—or even was—treason, and thereby to justify placing criticism of the government *legally* beyond the scope of legitimate political discourse. Thus, ethnic sovereignty's differentiation between "state-forming" and "non-state-forming" communities provided an avenue for restricting civil liberties. Every citizen's right to freedom of speech was threatened, but the minorities' all the more because they belong to this suspect category—thereby undermining the guarantee and equal enforcement of civil rights in Gabal's dimension 2. More broadly, this interpretation of ethnic sovereignty can also be implicated in the government's attempts to undermine constraints on its accountability, as it helped encourage the kind of voter that Deegan-Krause argues was crucial to Mečiar's support base: "one who would cede power to a strong, unaccountable leader if it would preserve the new country's sovereignty."[76]

That said, the law's repeated thwarting by the executive (backed by international organizations) is also very important. Clearly, many Slovaks (including one with the power to return legislation to Parliament) did not see ethnic sovereignty as justifying the kind of political authority that the law would have sanctioned. Indeed, the opposition was far more up-in-arms about this interpretation of sovereignty's implications than that which underlay the language law. Thus, the ethnic principle does not *necessarily* produce this kind of restriction of civil liberties, and in fact, in Slovakia, there were sufficient constraints on the principle's elasticity to prevent this. Moreover, the opposition that Mečiar feared soon did move to "take the hill."

The Dzurinda Coalition: 1998–2006

As the debate over the Law on the Protection of the Republic shows, by the mid-1990s Slovak politics had become extremely polarized. In the run-up to the 1998 elections, a diverse group of parties joined together with the primary common goal of ousting Mečiar's government. This included the new Slovak Democratic Coalition (SDK), comprised of the KDH and the DU, plus three small parties, and the new Party of the Hungarian Coalition (SMK), which brought together previously separate Hungarian parties.[77] This was the first time that the Hungarian and ethnic Slovak parties had decided to cooperate officially, made possible partly by the Hungarians' renunciation of any claims to territorial autonomy.[78] Still, during the campaign, the anti-Mečiar ethnic Slovak parties were largely silent on minority issues. The Social Democrats and the SDK did at times criticize the Mečiar government's nationalism, but, as Zsuzsa Csergo observes, very "few in the Slovak opposition openly expressed views on the nation-state and its Hungarian rejection."[79] Indeed, she identifies Miroslav Kusý as the only ethnic Slovak public intellectual to take up the issue of the relationship between Slovak ethnic sovereignty and the Hungarian minority's political demands.[80] Van Duin and Poláčková as well argue that "the democratic Slovak political parties obviously wanted to avoid the controversial Hungarian issue as much as possible, particularly during the election campaign. What is more, they did not seem to be willing to give the matter much thought, or public comment anyway, or, for instance, to prepare some serious proposals for a minority language law."[81]

In the end, the anti-Mečiar coalition was successful at the polls. Karen Henderson argues that there was a "very high turnout (84.2 percent) because of the deep polarization in society and the sense that the election would decide the future of the country."[82] The previous year, the EU had taken the dramatic step of downgrading the country's candidacy from first to second-tier status because of democratic deficits—a "damning indictment" of the Mečiar government.·Most importantly, according to Henderson, many Slovaks saw the lack of democratic political and economic reform as proof that "the country was headed in the wrong direction." Nevertheless, the HZDS did fairly well, winning 27 percent of the vote, to the SDK's 26.33 percent. The HZDS was not able to form a government, however, because only the SNS was willing to go into coalition with it. Instead, the new governing coalition included the SDK, SDĽ, the small Party of Civic Reconciliation, and, for the first time in the state's history, the Hungarian minority. The SDĽ initially resisted this but eventually agreed, and with the SMK the coalition reached the three-fifths majority necessary to pass changes to the Constitution.

Under the leadership of Prime Minister Mikuláš Dzurinda, one of the new government's priorities was getting Slovakia readmitted to the first tier of EU candidates. In March 1998, the EU Association Council decision on Slovak accession had called for minority language legislation and implementation.[83] Most analysts agree that this consideration, first and foremost, led the government to rapidly propose a minority language law. Drawing on recommendations from the OSCE, the Dzurinda government drew up a draft and rushed it to a shortened parliamentary session in June and July 1999.[84] They had to work quickly because EU officials were set to meet in July to consider the Slovak petition to be re-included in the first-round entry talks at the Helsinki summit that December.[85]

The government's draft placed the use of minority languages on an equal footing with Slovak in all official transactions and documents dealing with state and local government in towns and villages where the minority made up at least 20 percent of the population. The SMK was unhappy with this, arguing both that the population threshold was too high, and should be set at 10 percent, and that its scope was too limited, as it focused on official communications and did not deal with language use in education, culture and the media—key areas restricted by the 1995 law. Minority leaders thus called for a "'de-fragmented' codification of all minority language rights into one comprehensive law," including rights found in various other laws. In addition, they asked that the dubbing of videos available for rent in ethnically mixed areas and the still informal right to use their language in secondary school admission exams and in birth, marriage, and funeral ceremonies be included in the law.[86] The government did not, however, include their recommendations, prompting Hungarian minority leaders to charge that the government was more interested in pleasing the European Union than the minority to whom the law would apply.[87]

Introducing the bill to Parliament on June 30, 1999, Minister of Culture Milan Knažko stated, "The Slovak Republic, since its beginning, has signed onto all of the international political and legal documents concerning the observance of fundamental human rights, including the rights of individuals belonging to national minorities. In this connection, the Slovak Republic not only respects the linguistic, ethnic, and cultural identity of every individual belonging to a national minority, but at the same time develops the appropriate conditions for the full-fledged integration of such individuals into the life of the society. . . . [The bill is] in agreement with the Constitution and valid legal guidelines."[88]

The debate that followed was several days long and turbulent. The HZDS and SNS deputies offered the bulk of the arguments against the bill, and several themes emerged. First, they argued that a minority language law was unnecessary, as minority rights were "sufficiently embodied in existing legislation" and were actually "above-standard" internationally.[89] Second, some deputies questions the legitimacy of these standards, particularly as many Western countries do not uphold them; as Jozef Prokeš argued, if California does not provide a system of minority-language schools, it is questionable whether it is really a "fundamental human right."[90] Third, many critics argued that the law would undermine societal integration, as it would "further facilitate ignorance of the state language among the Hungarian minority" and produce a "linguistic Babylon."[91] The state's development and prosperity required a common means of communication, and expecting the minority to learn the majority language was entirely justified. Moreover, if not every minority member in an official capacity was bilingual (and this would be beyond the state's means), then the majority would be discriminated against. And fourth, many deputies argued that the law would fuel disintegration that could ultimately lead to the destruction of the state. They pointed to Kosovo and the Balkans more broadly, as well as to more distant history, to illustrate this argument. For example, Cuper argued that the idea that the Hungarian minority had rights equal to the Slovak majority reflected the same "perverse" philosophy used by the Sudeten Germans to demand self-determination in Czechoslovakia before World War II. Moreover, he argued, demands based on this principle are entirely precluded by the Constitution, which states clearly that the Slovaks' right to self-determination is exclusive.[92] Katarina Tóthová (HZDS) also warned that, "in 1997 the Vice Chaiman of the-then Hungarian government observed, 'Hungary is everywhere, where Hungarians live,'" prompting her to wonder about the possibility that the formulation could change to "Hungary is everywhere that Hungarian is spoken."[93]

Tóthová also raised a concern that seemed to be common among deputies when she asked the minister of culture why the bill was "so hurried? Do you not deem this law important for citizens, that they should become acquainted with it? Do you deem this law to be important only for the relationship with the European Union?"[94] Slavkovská as well argued that "it is absolutely improper, immoral and distressing that the European Union was already acquainted with this law long ago, even instigated it . . . but the citizens of Slovakia, whom this law concerns, do not know anything about it."[95] Marián Andel (SNS) also noted that not only the "HZDS and SNS, but also 80 percent of the citizens of the Slovak Republic are against the passage of this law."[96]

Members of the governing coalition responded to these criticisms in a number of ways. Some offered reassurances. Knažko, for example, stated that "this government is doing everything so that members of minority nationalities in Slovakia have the conditions to learn the language of the country in which they live well, or even excellently."[97] Many responses, however, accused the HZDS and SNS of overreacting and attempting to manipulate their compatriots. Ivan Simko (SDK) accused them of demagoguery,[98] and Lajos Mészáros (SMK) admonished Anna Maliková that she would be unsuccessful in using "half truths" and "ungrounded claims" to "sow hatred between minorities in the south of Slovakia and Slovaks in the north."[99] Milan Hort (SDKU) argued that the opposition party members portrayed those who disagreed with them as "the nation's worst enemies," and warned that it was this kind of politics that should raise fears about a domestic Sarajevo and Kosovo.[100] Peter Weiss (SDĽ) similarly argued that the SNS and HZDS were attempting to "stimulate collective hysteria and offer the Slovaks leadership that offers protection against the Hungarian danger. Where such application of cynical political techniques and promotion of false national mythology may lead, we have seen in the Balkans."[101]

While members of the government coalition often argued that the HZDS and SNS were taking an extremist position, they also sought to position themselves as moderates between *two* poles—the other being Hungarian minority. Ladislav Orosz (SDĽ), noting that he himself was bilingual, argued that language is an emotional subject that makes logical and rational arguments difficult, especially when one side attempts to make the minority into the image of the enemy of Slovak statehood, and the other regards the interests of the minority as paramount.[102] Ladislav Ballek (SDĽ) advised that "political wisdom" required compromise—"otherwise, everyone will be disappointed."[103]

The coalition members also emphasized the bill's importance to Slovakia's relationship with Europe. Knažko, for example, noted that the law sought "to partially mitigate the damages in the foreign-political context" caused by the preceding government,[104] and Ján Budaj (DU/SDKU) similarly argued that the HZDS had driven the country into international isolation, in part by causing discontent within the minority.[105] Ballek also reminded his colleagues that if they did not adjust to the times, they would "call the eyes of the world to attention on us."[106] More positively, a number of deputies argued that the law was central to Slovakia's relationship to a "flourishing Europe," as Jirko Malchárek (SOP) described it.[107] Stephan Slachta (SOP) expanded on this idea, arguing that the path to a "united Europe" was not to be taken in "the spirit of the 19th century, the spirit of hatred, chauvinism, and nationalism. Hence I beseech you, that you try to see the problem of the law on the language of minority nationalities from the bird's eye perspective of the European future . . . we are not only Slovak, we are European. . . . This is not about whether our fellow citizens can have the possibility of speaking Slovak, Russian, Polish, or Hungarian in city offices; it is about much more. It is about the future of our children in a common Europe, it is about the future of Slovakia."[108] Weiss put it more darkly, observing that the Parliament was deciding whether Slovakia's "strategic direction" would be toward Europe or toward the Balkans.[109]

Opposition members responded to these calls for compromise and a broader view by explaining why these would not be acceptable. Pavol Števček (HZDS), for example, paraphrased Štúr's view of linguistic conflict: "This is not about grammar, for us this is about life." He then addressed his friend and fellow writer, Ladislav Ballek, arguing, "compromise in politics, yes, only this is not about politics, but about the life of the Slovak nation . . . it is about the existence of the Slovak Republic and its borders and its perspective . . . compromise, yes, but compromise, as to the nature of the national culture and the type of democracy in the Slovak Republic, that compromise I would find inadvisable to call for or to honor."[110] Dušan Švantner also stated unequivocally: "As citizens of a free nation we refuse to be passive witnesses to the bargaining with the sovereignty of our state, as well as with the sovereignty of our own mother tongue on the territory of our Slovak Republic as an indivisible, state-forming whole. For such proceedings we know only one word: treason."[111]

The vote took place on July 10. Of 150 total deputies, only 89 were present for the vote; most of the others (particularly SNS and HZDS representatives) waited in the Parliament bar.[112] In the final vote, 70 deputies voted in favor, 18 against (including all the SMK members), and one abstained. Béla Bugár responded to the outcome by stating: "the approved law does not reduce the negative impact of the existing Law on State Language and does not respect the international standards that represent part of the Slovak legal order. According to the SMK, minorities on behalf of their own identity's protection will have to break the existing Law on State Language and the new law as well."[113] Nevertheless, Pavol Hamžík, the Slovak deputy prime minister for European integration, told the *Slovak Spectator*, "this law will still be respected by the European Commission and the EU."[114] And on this, he was correct. The state rejoined the first-tier category, and gained EU membership in 2004.

The debate over, and outcome of, the minority language law offers important insights into the elasticity of the principle of ethnic sovereignty. The opposition's arguments were based on essentially the same principled and practical reasoning that they used in favor of the state Language Law and the Law on the Protection of the Republic. Quite interesting, however, is the case the law's proponents made for it, as this appears to represent the liberal end of the ethnic principle's elasticity in Slovakia. Clearly, they were guided in part by important practical considerations. As van Duin and Poláčková argue, in preparing the law, the government parties "tended to act 'pragmatically' in a double sense: they felt that the law was necessary mainly in connection with EU demands and, at the same time, they wanted to ensure that it would be only a minimal law so as to prevent a populist backlash from both within and without their own ranks."[115] On the question of principle, they did criticize the opposition's "nationalism," "hysteria," and "demagoguery," but primarily

in relation to their bad effects, such as domestic divisiveness and diminishment of the state's reputation abroad, rather than on a principled counter-
argument concerning the proper foundations of the relationship between the
state and citizens of different ethnic backgrounds. The governing coalition
did not appear to have its own internal political-philosophical framework for
what the minority's political status should be, but depended instead on the
international norms put forward by the European Union as criteria for admission, which, in turn, lack a cohesive, clearly articulated political/philosophical
justification. Indeed, as Csergo argues, "no consistent Western standards exist on any of the minority-related strategies that European officials actively
advocated in CEE [Central and Eastern Europe], not even in the prevention
of violent ethnic conflict."[116] Broadly speaking, then, the government position
indicates that its members (except the SMK) held the ethnic principle as valid,
but saw it as allowing a *somewhat* more liberal exercise of the ensuing authority
regarding language use (constrained here, again, also by public opinion). In
fact, the legal situation remains quite illiberal on Gabal's dimension 2, which
again complicates the minority cultural development of dimension 3.

Thus, while the Dzurinda government certainly improved the majority's
relationship with the minority, it fell far short of the minority's hopes. From
the time the Constitution was passed, the minority had called for a redefinition of the state's founding principles. For example, in a 1996 document,
Coexistence warned of the rise of extremist nationalism, arguing that "in the
absence of a democratic counterweight, these forces could further destabilize
the region, balkanize Central Europe and endanger the entire European con-
tinent." Thus, it argued, "new means must be found which will create lasting legal guarantees for the equality of national and ethnic communities and
ensure that the respect of the rights of national minority communities does
not depend entirely on the mere goodwill of the majority."[117] Coexistence then
proposed a broad model that would recognize "the multi-national character
of states and the equal right of national minority communities to co-rule, as
a partner-nation, the state which they co-inhabit. In this sense the concept of
'minority' is a strictly quantitative category and does not signify lower status
or capability."

As the foregoing analysis makes clear, however, this met an intensely hostile response from Slovak leaders. Thus, in the run-up to the 1998 elections,
the Hungarian Coalition declared in its Program that Slovakia should "not
be built as a national state, but only based on the civic principle as a community of several cultures."[118] At its fourth congress, the Hungarian Coalition

leadership stated that "irrespective of what is laid down in the Constitution, we are a state-forming community in Slovakia."[119] The minority once again joined the ruling Dzurinda coalition thereafter, but in the ensuing years made no progress on this issue. Indeed, by that point, the EU was long convinced that minority issues were satisfactorily resolved in Slovakia, and in fact the European Commission never considered the issue of the Constitution's defini- tion of sovereignty in its preamble "as a source of potential friction."[120] Nev- ertheless, in its 2006–2010 electoral program, the Hungarian Coalition again argued in its list of objectives that "it is necessary to improve the constitu- tional status of minority nationalities. The SMK will strive for the modifica- tion of the Constitution's preamble from the national to the civic principle."[121] Clearly, the issue of how the sovereign community is defined has been an abiding source of deep frustration for the Hungarian minority, and has had real implications for its membership. The 2006 election, however, brought a dramatically different coalition to power, and the Hungarian Coalition moved into the opposition.

The Fico Government: The First Two Years (July 2006–July 2008)

In some ways, the Dzurinda government was quite successful. It secured both EU and NATO membership, rehabilitated the state's image abroad, and fos- tered economic growth of nearly 20 percent during its final term.[122] Still, the coalition, made up of Christian Democrats, former Communists, economic liberals, and the Hungarian minority, was fractious, and "broken promises, incessant infighting between the coalition partners, and more than a whiff of corruption" disappointed the electorate.[123] Unemployment was also quite high (15.5 percent) and many pensioners disgruntled. In February 2006, the KDH quit the government when Dzurinda refused to allow a treaty with the Vatican on objections of conscience to go up for a vote. This led to early elections in June, which had the following results: Smer, 29.14 percent and 50 seats; SDKU, 18.35 percent and 31 seats; SNS, 11.73 percent and 20 seats; SMK-MKP, 11.68 percent and 20 seats; HZDS, 8.79 percent and 15 seats; and KDH, 8.31 percent and 14 seats.

The most popular party by far, Smer ("Direction"), was relatively new, founded in 1999 by a young and charismatic former member of the post- Communist party, Robert Fico. Framed as a social-democratic party, it is nev- ertheless ideologically ambiguous, "not least," as Haughton observes, because

Fico "launched his party as a nonideological formation. . . . The party's political program describes the party's objectives pithily as 'poridok, spravodlivost, a
stabilitu.' The second and third of these are relatively easy to translate ('justice'
and 'stability' respectively). But the first, which can be simply translated as 'order,' carries both a meaning of organized according to the rules and has echoes
of the so-called 'normalization' period which followed the Prague Spring in
1968."[124] Economically, it called for something of a third way. The party's politics also incorporated an anti-Roma and anti-Hungarian sensibility. With regard to the latter, for example, Fico (before founding Smer) wrote an article in
Pravda about the minority language law, in which he argued that the Hungarian coalition's politics could "create excellent conditions for the development
of extremism. The increase in support for the SNS party, and to a certain
extent also the increased vitality of the opposition HZDS party, are clearly the
results of the SMK's performance to date in the government coalition."[125]

Interestingly, after their June 2006 victory and a period of negotiation
with various potential partners, Smer's top board unanimously decided to
go into coalition with these very parties. Speculation on the coalition possibilities had been intense, and Western and liberal Slovak sources frequently
called a Smer-SNS-HZDS government the "worst case scenario." When the
coalition was announced, internal response was mixed. Some analysts voiced
grave concern; Samuel Abrahám, for example, called it a "tragic start" to Fico's
leadership.[126] A poll conducted shortly after the announcement showed that
the broader population was divided, with 36 percent seeing it positively, 38
percent negatively, and 26 percent having no opinion or not answering.[127] The
Hungarian minority response was, however, unequivocally negative, and the
party issued a statement in which it "expresses profound concern with the
nationalistic orientation of the new government" and noted that it would
"inform the international community about [its] every negative step."[128]

The international response to the "red-brown" coalition was also very unwelcoming. In particular, the president of the Party of European Socialists,
the second-largest faction in the European Parliament, sent an open letter to
Fico warning that "the make-up of the ruling coalition raises a lot of concerns
regarding the protection for human rights, especially the rights of ethnic minorities, as well as commitments to democracy, the EU, and European values and policies."[129] The Party called for Smer's temporary suspension, which
was formalized in a "historical" resolution in October 2006.[130] This not only
rescinded Smer's voting powers in the pan-European Party, but also limited
Smer's (and thereby, Slovakia's) participation in EU gatherings before sum-

mits. In addition, the center-right European People's Party Chairman stated that he was "astonished that the most extreme xenophobic party should be part of the next Slovak government,"[131] and the United States sent word via Ambassador Rudolph Vallee that it would be carefully following Slovakia's observance of human and minority rights.[132]

In explaining why the SNS was unacceptable as a government partner, many critics pointed to the public comments of its chairman, Ján Slota. Like Mečiar, he was too controversial a figure to receive a ministerial post, but both party leaders became part of the coalition council, an important decision-making body. In mid-July, the *Slovak Spectator* reported that "information from the EU indicated that members of the European Parliament (MEPs) had received bulk compilations of Slota's past statements via e-mail. *Hospodárske noviny* reported that these statements have become a popular topic of discussion in Brussels."[133] Eleven pages long, the list quoted Slota's declaration that "Hungarians are a tumor on the Slovak nation that needs to be immediately removed."[134] Other notorious statements, repeated widely in the Western press, included his threat that Slovaks could "get in our tanks and go and flatten Budapest" and his view the best way to deal with the Roma is with "a long whip and a small courtyard."[135] Many also noted that Slota had called Tiso "one of the greatest sons of the Slovak nation," and as mayor of the town of Žilina, oversaw his honoring with a plaque.[136]

As international condemnation grew, Slovak Foreign Minister Ján Kubiš traveled to Hungary to smooth relations. After a July 11 meeting, Hungarian Foreign Affairs Minister Kinga Göncz told journalists, "I asked Mr. Kubiš to ensure that the Slovak PM Robert Fico clearly distance himself from Slota's numerous anti-Hungarian statements and to reassure us that such statements do not represent the government's point of view."[137] For his part, Kubiš stated that "we will respect not only our commitments but also contribute to the development of the human rights of minorities. We will push through the principle of tolerance."[138] In an interview, SNS MP Rafael Rafaj also rejected the idea that his was a nationalist party, stating that such parties "are based on an ethnic principle that is meant either to unsettle the post-war status quo or try to achieve ethnic separatism." He further stated that "the SNS appreciates the fact that other minorities [aside from the Hungarian minority leadership] are uncontentious and loyal towards Slovakia. The SNS respects the Slovak Constitution and international charters, but it also expects others to respect clause 34 of the Slovak Constitution, which states that the exercise of minority rights must not be to the detriment of the majority. It is a tragedy of Slovak politics that, in 1998, assuming power had to be done by joining with ethnic separatists. I can assure democratically-minded people that the SNS's third time in government since 1990 will be a contribution to Slovakia's civil, national and political cohesion."[139]

Less than two weeks after Kubiš's visit to Hungary, however, Slota added fresh and abundant fuel to the fire. In an interview with the Czech daily *Lidové noviny*, he stated that the SNS "struggles only against the representatives of the SMK, who as a minority oppress the majority nation on its sovereign territory, the territory of the Slovak Republic." He also noted that the Fico government is a "national government, because the party of the Hungarian coalition is not in the government and in the cabinet are only Slovak political subjects." Most inflammatory, however, was his statement that he "envies" the Czechs their mass expulsion of the Sudeten Germans after World War II, via the Beneš Decrees.[140]

Unsurprisingly, both Sudeten Germans and Hungarians expressed outrage at these statements.[141] Hungarian Foreign Minister Göncz first unofficially,[142] then via an official letter, called on the Slovak government to distance itself from Slota's statements. In response, Kubiš sent a letter to Göncz stating that the "government resolutely rejects any statements and steps that could damage bilateral relations with Hungary and the peaceful co-existence of people."[143] While the Hungarians accepted this statement, many observers also noted Fico's apparent reluctance to distance himself from Slota's remarks. When asked about this at a press briefing on July 26, Fico answered, "This coalition is stable and will be stable, and I have already said several times that I am responsible for the activities and matters that occur in the government of the Slovak Republic, I am responsible for the ministries, I am responsible for the work of this government, but I cannot be, and will not be, a glossator or commentator on political statements that someone else makes. That is all that I can say on that matter."[144] He also asserted that the relationship between Slovakia and Hungary was "completely normal." These comments were then widely quoted in the Slovak media.

As the summer went on, tensions between Hungarians and Slovaks rose, and several provocative and violent incidents occurred in August. These included the brief appearance of a video of a burning Hungarian flag on the "youtube" internet site, and the display of anti-Slovak banners at soccer matches in Budapest, followed by anti-Hungarian banners at matches in Slovakia (two men were arrested at a Banská Bystrica match for holding up an 11-meter banner calling for "Death to Hungarians"). More worryingly, in separate incidents, a woman and two men were reportedly attacked while speaking Hungarian in southern Slovakia.[145] The incident with the young woman, Hedviga Malinová, became especially high profile, as she alleged that her attackers had not only beaten her and torn the earrings form her ears, but also forced her to remove her shirt and written "Hungarians Back over the Danube" on it.

Following this wave of ethnic hostility, Hungarian Prime Minister Ferenc Gyurcsány called on the Slovak government to condemn the assaults and the growing anti-Hungarian sentiment in Slovakia. Fico responded, "I don't need any appeals to respond to what Mr. Bugár wants, or to what Mr. Gyurcsány wants. . . . We are a sovereign nation in a sovereign state. We know what we have to do to combat extremism and hate crimes." Kubiš, moreover, pointed his finger at the Hungarian coalition, accusing it of participating in a "campaign" to "discredit Slovakia, the government of Slovakia, and the political forces that support it."[146]

The next dramatic move came on September 12, when Fico, along with Interior Minister Robert Kaliňák, announced at a press conference that Slovak police had concluded that Malinová had fabricated the attack. Kaliňák pointed to several inconsistencies in her testimony, and reported that DNA matching Malinová's had been found on the stamp on the envelope in which her stolen identification had been returned to her.[147] When Fico took the stage, he argued that not only had the Malinová attack never happened, but that another reason for criticizing the government also had turned out to be invalid: Slota's interview in *Lidové noviny*. Fico said that the article's author had told him that the paper's editor, an ethnic Hungarian, had told him to change the title from his original "I Am Not an Extremist" to "I Envy You the Expulsion of the Germans" ("Vyhanie Nemcov vám závidím"). Thereafter, the "Slovak government [had been] attacked and criticized for a statement of one of the coalition partners, that was never said, never."[148] Indeed, Slota did not make the exact statement that became the title, but he did say that he envied the postwar Czechs—"I envy them" ("Já jim závadím")—for being able to expel the Germans.

As autumn turned to winter, the intensity of ethnonational tensions waned. In May 2007, however, the issue of Hedviga Malinová resurfaced when she was charged with filing a false report. In July, Hungarian MPs Csaba Tabjdi and Kinga Gal announced that they planned to bring the Slovak charges against Malinová to an international court (she eventually brought a complaint to the European Court of Human Rights that November), prompting an expression of concern from Slovak authorities over

Hungarian political interference in the work of domestic criminal justice bodies.[149]

Ethnic tensions within Slovakia rose further with the fifteenth anniversary of the Slovak Declaration of Sovereignty. For the occasion, Fico issued a proclamation stating that through the Declaration, "Slovaks as the state-forming nation manifested responsibility for themselves. . . . The Prime Minister of the government of the Slovak Republic Robert Fico dearly wishes that the Slovak Republic will, for the Slovak nation, as well as for loyal minorities, be built as a true and peaceful home."[150] Unsurprisingly, some took exception to the adjective qualifying the minorities. The government issued a clarification, stating that "members of minorities that honor the legal order and minority rights guaranteed in the Constitution and international agreements are loyal to the Slovak Republic."[151] The next day, *Sme* ran a critical article in which leaders of both the Hungarian and Roma minorities reacted with anger and perplexity. Alexander Patkoló of the Slovak Roma Initiative stated that "no representatives of the state may divide the citizens into loyal and disloyal."[152] SMK representative József Berényi also observed, "I do not know any disloyal minority representatives. I do not know who the Premier is thinking of." Miroslav Kusý and Grigorij Mesežnikov, head of the prominent Slovak nongovernmental think tank Institute for Public Affairs (IVO), also reacted negatively, though the latter noted that while the statement had clear nationalistic elements, the SNS did not need to worry about Fico's appeal to its voters, "because their voters are used to much harder notions." In addition, *Sme*'s chief political commentator, Marián Leško, wrote an editorial condemning the Prime Minister's use of the term "loyal" as "superfluous and harmful," and concluded that the categorization of minorities itself "would be disloyal toward citizens and the Constitution of the Slovak Republic."[153]

As 2007 wore on, official expressions and gestures of Slovak nationalism continued. In September, Parliament began debating an SNS-submitted bill that would have given Andrej Hlinka official status as the "Father of the Slovak Nation" and made "besmirching his name" prosecutable. The final version, passed in November, left these elements out, instead noting, in the *Slovak Spectator*'s words, "that Hlinka contributed more than anyone else to the emergence of the Slovak nation and the Slovak Republic in 1993."[154] Also in September, Parliament passed a resolution declaring the Beneš Decrees inalterable, further troubling relations with Hungary.

Tensions between Slovaks and Hungarians flared still higher the following month, as the ruling coalition and the SMK traded allegations that the other was undermining relations between Slovakia and Hungary.[155] In this soured atmosphere, both Hungarian President László Sólyom and Speaker of the Hungarian Parliament Katalin Szili made unofficial visits to Southern Slovakia, where they met with SMK representatives but no top Slovak government officials. This prompted an angry response from Fico, who said in a press conference, "The government of the Slovak Republic is a government of a sovereign country. We simply cannot allow top representatives of other countries, especially Hungary, to behave in the south of Slovakia as if they were in the north of Hungary." He further noted that protocol should be followed in the future, so that "the president of the Hungarian Republic can be ordered out to the place where he belongs, when it comes to private or official visits to Slovakia."[156] The following day, the Party of European Socialists (PES) decided to continue Smer's suspension. The reasoning included the tensions between Slovaks and Hungarians, as well as the continued coalition with the SNS. Slota had also recently brought censure from the PES with his late September remark about SMK leader Pál Csáky: "This type, he is vomit, a rotten excrement." PES Chair Poul Nyrup Rasmussen had thereafter noted that "Smer needs more time for pushing extremism out of its government."[157]

No such development was, however, forthcoming. On May 9, 2008, at a press conference with Fico, Slota held up and described the cover of a history textbook used by the Hungarian minority in Slovakia, which has a picture Saint Stephen, Hungary's patron saint, with the observation: "Hungarian flags on the front, and here is some Hungarian clown on a horse in Budapest."[158] Fico sat next to him and said nothing. In response, Hungarian Prime Minister Gyurcsány put on hold his long-planned visit with Fico, a reaction that the latter called "ridiculous."[159] The day after Slota's comments, Fico gave a speech commemorating the 160th anniversary of the 1848 "Demands of the Slovak Nation" for national equality in the Habsburg Empire in Liptovský Mikuláš, declaring, "Slovakia must now be united. If in Hungary the political party Fidesz wins, we can await manifestations of nationalism and extremism in the relationship to the Slovak Republic."[160] These comments prompted some observers to express concern about Fico's continuing appeals to Slovak nationalism and their effects on the SMK relationship to the political system. Mesežnikov, for example, noted that the SMK cooperates with Fidesz, and moreover that "this was not just a criticism of Fidesz, but also a signal of mistrust towards Hungary and Hungarians."[161]

Ultimately, Fico's first two years in power offer a mixed picture with regard to the implications of ethnic sovereignty. Though the "worst case scenario" coalition included parties with a proven track record of highly illiberal governance, in its first years it neither rolled back the Dzurinda government's more liberal reforms (such as the minority language law) nor introduced new, strongly illiberal laws and policies. At the same time, the *rhetoric* from the coalition parties concerning the state's relationship to its minority citizens was dramatically more illiberal than that of its predecessor, and directly invoked the constitutional distinction between the state-forming, sovereign majority and minorities, as well as the constitution's protection of the former against the latter. In particular, Slota's comments to *Lidové noviny* endorsed an interpretation of the ethnic principle as even justifying ethnic cleansing, and his repeated vicious and insulting anti-Hungarian (and anti-Roma) comments sink to the level of linguistic dehumanization. Fico has been less radical, but has often been loath to reject Slota's statements, and frequently has him as official company at high-profile events. Fico also clearly suggested that minority citizens may be disloyal to the state. This all has occurred, moreover, in a context of increasingly hostile relations with Hungary: Slovak leaders have suggested that the minority's "mother nation" is a potential threat to national sovereignty, and called for unity in response.

These developments raise the question of whether illiberal rhetoric has an impact on minority political membership, even if it is not basis for specific policies. I would argue that it does, as such rhetoric from the state's leaders offers an authoritative categorizing of minority citizenship into a lower, suspect class. Moreover, linguistic dehumanization has historically contributed to the "crystallization of difference" supportive of extreme illiberalism and the persecution of targeted ethnic groups. The governing coalition's rhetoric and orientation, and its potential to become the basis for policy, is therefore understandably unsettling to both minorities and liberals more broadly. In particular, as Mesežnikov and others have observed, the SNS inclusion in the government and its articulation of a nationalist agenda have both encouraged nationalist tendencies within Smer and, more broadly, affected the "atmosphere in society. Nationalism has simply asserted itself much easier, as it got a green light from the ruling coalition."[162] Indeed, the nature and orientation of this coalition is clearly beyond the boundaries of what mainstream European social democratic parties consider acceptable, as Smer's suspension from the international party shows.

A strong proportion of Slovak population, however, does not seem to have considered Smer's alliance with the SNS, Fico's unwillingness as head of government to explicitly disavow Slota's statements, or Fico's own statements on the minority's relationship to the state to be entirely illegitimate, at least to the extent that it would undermine their support for the party. A July 2007 poll showed that 43 percent of respondents would vote for Smer "if parliamentary elections were held today"; the SNS came in second, with 12.4 percent.[163] A year later, July 2008 polls gave Smer its highest numbers ever, with 48.5 percent of respondents saying they would vote for it if elections were held that month. It was followed, again, by the SNS, in second place with 11.4 percent.[164]

Conclusion

During the post-Communist Slovak state's first fifteen years, it oscillated widely between more and less liberal approaches to nation-building. This has interesting implications for both the broader theoretical perspectives and the more targeted analyses that I discussed at the chapter's outset. To begin, it is clear that how the principle of ethnic sovereignty is interpreted is crucial to its practical implications. Thus, Hayden's expectations concerning restrictions of civil liberties were only borne out under one administration, and even there, ran up against a counter-interpretation that allowed the President to prevent the law's enactment. Likewise, a strongly collectivist interpretation of the sovereign community and its leadership emerged under some governments, but not others. That said, the *range* of policy has also been limited: even the more liberal interpretations of its implications retain illiberal elements, restricting minority language use in many areas of life and thereby undermining the minority's ability to develop its own culture. It never fully supported full civic equality, regardless of ethnicity.

This brings me to the question of leadership, a factor often stressed in analyses of Slovak ethnic politics. While it is clear that intense competition for power has shaped political rhetoric and policy concerning minority issues, the evidence indicates that two further factors constrained the elasticity of the leaders' interpretations. The first is the constitutional principle of ethnic sovereignty itself, as it gives the Slovak ethnic nation special political status. This principle has been a critical enabling factor for illiberal policies and rhetoric; it is not just one element of illiberal nation-building (as Kymlicka suggests), but is in fact its very corner-stone. It has also served to constrain the possibility of strongly liberal nation-building by supporting criticisms (voiced most often by the HZDS and SNS) of any policies that undercut Slovak ethnocultural dominance. While these may be cynically or instrumentally deployed, they nevertheless can claim constitutional grounding. Indeed, this foundational position of the ethnic principle allowed more illiberal elites to repeatedly allege *treason* in response not only to demands for minority equality, but also to criticism of state policy that the leaders justified as protecting national sovereignty. To the extent that people accepted this argument, it placed political opposition that would be considered legitimate in a liberal democracy outside the boundary of acceptable political discourse.

Furthermore, the more liberal parties have not offered a coherent defense of how minority rights and civic equality relate to the principle of ethnic sovereignty, but have instead pointed to international agreements to justify more liberal policies. Such justification runs into legitimacy problems with citizens who value domestic constitutional principles over those of foreign/international provenance. It also suggests that it is impossible, both philosophically and practically, to fully reconcile the principles of ethnic sovereignty and civic equality.[165]

A second factor helping determine the boundaries of the governments' interpretations of ethnic sovereignty has been political culture, which appears to have influenced both elite and broader choices. When viewed in the longer historical context, the more and less liberal post-Communist orientations show strong continuities with two broad understandings of nationhood, whose roots stretch back to the nineteenth century. Both hold the ethnic nation as sovereign but have differing views of the resulting political authority, and in particular, of the relative priority of democracy and individual autonomy versus the sovereign authority of the ethnic collective (usually as exercised by an elite). This has prompted repeated conflict within the Slovak nation: during the mid-nineteenth century, between the Czechoslovaks and the Young Slovaks; during the late nineteenth and early twentieth centuries, between the Hodža/Hlasists and the clerical nationalists; during the First Republic, between Czechoslovaks and clerical-nationalists; during the wartime state, between Communist-democratic alliance and the clerical-nationalists; and during the Communist state, between the Prague Spring "democratization first" and "federalization first" camps, and then between those who cooperated with the federalized Normalization regime and those who resisted it. Finally, in the post-Communist period, as Deegan-Krause has noted, the Mečiar governments "challenged voters to weigh the relative importance of accountability against other ends, particularly national ones. Central to this effort was the emphasis on the continued threats to the new country's sovereignty."[166] Here,

I would add that more illiberal Slovak leaders have tended to invoke not just the country's, but the *nation's* sovereignty, and to identify tradeoffs between this and both minority language rights and the civil liberties necessary to freely criticize the government. The evidence indicates that Slovaks are far more inclined to sacrifice the former than the latter; nevertheless, there is clearly a divide between those who see strongly illiberal authority to be justified by ethnic sovereignty (or purported threats thereto) and those who do not. Again, this is a matter not of invoking static orientations, but of confronting Slovaks with the need to actively prioritize political values. When so confronted, their decisions—and the tensions between them—have shown marked continuities with past decisions, indicating that key elements of these frameworks of judgment have been resilient over the course of time and different regime types.

The evidence from the Slovak case indicates, then, that the practical implications of the use of the ethnic model can be fully assessed neither by narrow focus on power-political competition, nor by narrow focus on the constitutional principle (because so much is left to interpretation), but rather by looking at the interaction between the two *in the context of*, and *as they relate to*, the broader, and often long-standing, normative orientations of the population.

CHAPTER NINE

The Implications of the
Civic Model of Sovereignty in the Czech Republic

In post-Communist Slovakia, the ethnic definition of sovereignty had decidedly illiberal effects. This raises the question of whether a state that uses the "civic principle," defining the sovereign community as the entire citizenry, is better able to secure minority membership and individual rights. Recalling the theoretical debate I discussed in the Introduction, the concept of a community of citizens (sometimes called a "civic nation") has traditionally been portrayed as avoiding the stratification of citizenship based on ethnic criteria and, therefore, as far more supportive of civic equality in a diverse society. According to this theory, such a community's bonds are based principally on a set of constitutional principles and rights. In Habermas's conceptualization, these "form the fixed point of reference for any constitutional patriotism that situates the system of rights within the historical context of a legal community. They must be enduringly linked with the motivations and convictions of the citizens, for without such a motivational anchoring they could not become the driving force behind the dynamically conceived project of producing an association of individuals who are free and equal."[1] This produces a different kind of community from the ethnic nation, as "the republican strand of 'citizenship' completely parts company with the idea of belonging to a prepolitical community integrated on the basis of descent, a shared tradition and a common language."[2] Critics, however, have argued that states and their nation-building projects are in reality incapable of being culturally neutral in this way, by virtue of the very nature of the human communities that constitute them. Thus, Kymlicka argues that it is more useful to explore how liberal or illiberal a nation-building project is than to classify nations as either "ethnic" or "civic."

The Czech Republic offers an excellent case through which to explore the issues raised by this debate, as it was indeed founded on the "civic principle." Although the state's transition to democracy has been much smoother than Slovakia's, it has also been repeatedly criticized by international and domestic observers for widespread discrimination against the Roma minority by both state and private actors, as well as worrisome levels of racially motivated violence. At the very outset of this exploration, then, it is possible to conclude that the civic principle has fallen short of securing civic equality for all Czech citizens regardless of ethnicity. Even a superficial comparison of this case with the Slovak one supports the contention by critics of the civic/ethnic dichotomy that a polar opposition between the two models' practical implications for civic equality and the ethnic neutrality of the state—where the civic model guarantees both just as surely as the ethnic model denies them—is untenable. Still, that the two models do not produce "opposite" outcomes does not in itself prove the contention, made by stronger critics, that there are no significant differences between their consequences. Conclusions on this count require comparative study of cases based on each model, and it is with this goal that I now turn to the Czech case.

I begin this exploration as I did the Slovak one, by looking at the constitutional definition of the source of state sovereignty. I also look at the citizenship law, which further defined that community. After this, I chart a somewhat different course from that in the preceding chapter, because the principled (or ideal) relationship the civic and ethnic models set up between the state and the citizenry is sufficiently different that an investigation of their effects cannot go down exactly parallel tracks. Because the civic model defines the state as neutral in relation to its citizens' pre-political identities, the laws, policies, and practices that specifically invoke the civic principle will be ones that have the proclaimed intent to protect or foster civic equality (even if this is not always the outcome) and/or to assert government neutrality; there would be no true civic equivalent to the Slovak language law, which justified privileging the majority by pointing to the ethnic principle. It is therefore necessary to look at, but also beyond, the laws and policies invoking the civic principle to explore the realities of minority membership and individual rights, and thereby to gauge the extent to which the principle is borne out in practice.

In the following analysis, then, I use Gabal's measure of minority membership, which, again, assesses the state's relationship to minority citizens along four dimensions: the extent to which it protects them against violent discrimination and persecution;[3] the extent to which it protects them against nonviolent discrimination by enforcing civil and human rights and ensuring equal opportunity for minorities to participate in the broader society's public, political, social, economic, and cultural life; the extent to which the state protects the "right to self-fulfillment and development of one's own ethnic, national, or cultural identity"; and finally, whether it has secured the minority's full societal integration, including the opportunity for complete social mobility regardless of ethnonational identity.[4] In the preceding chapter, I argued that several aspects of the second and third dimensions are open to fairly wide interpretation. I would here further argue that the civic principle narrows the scope of valid interpretation in important ways. Because the source of state authority is not specific to any pre-political group (including ethnic ones), but flows equally from every citizen, the state is not empowered to privilege or diminish citizens' membership on this basis. It thus precludes strongly illiberal terms of inclusion, where a "thick" form of ethnocultural conformity is a prerequisite for participation in most areas of the society's life. This is not to say that the state must then be entirely culturally neutral; as Kymlicka argues, it is essentially a practical necessity to privilege some language(s) as means of societal communication, and difficult to avoid official accommodation of certain cultural concerns like widely celebrated holidays. It is nevertheless clear that the state may not discriminate against or purposefully disadvantage a segment of the citizenry based on ethnic identity through laws or policies, and that it has an obligation to protect civic equality. Determining where the boundaries of state authority here should lie is admittedly difficult, as strong competing interests sometimes exist (for example, when religious or private educational institutions want latitude to discriminate according to central norms or purposes). Another contentious issue is whether the state needs to promote equality through such means as affirmative action or "positive discrimination," or just prohibit discrimination. This positive versus negative rights debate is also relevant in dimension 3; some argue that the civic principle requires the state to stay as neutral as possible with regard to ethnocultural communities within the citizenry, while others hold that equality requires that minority communities enjoy the same cultural benefits as those flowing from majority status. There are, then, gray areas in the life of communities founded on the civic principle, contentious in many liberal democracies. That said, important normative consensus has emerged over recent decades that the notion of "separate but equal" violates the civic principle, and that the state must provide recourse for those prevented from participating in the broader community's life on the same terms as other citizens, solely on the basis of their ethnic membership.

Taking these additional considerations into account, then, I assess the Czech Roma's situation on each of these dimensions in turn, and where the state has fallen short, I look at the government's specific responses, with attention to the role played by the civic principle. Having thus developed a portrait of the Roma minority's experience in the post-Communist Czech Republic, I turn to the question of how successive Czech governments have broadly framed the state's relationship to the Roma, including how they see the relevant implications of the state's founding principles, through speeches, reports, laws, and policy statements. I analyze how this framing has changed over time (thus gauging its elasticity); the factors, both domestic and international, that have shaped this evolution; the relationship between these perspectives and the political-cultural values traced throughout this study; and their implications for Roma civic equality. I then look at broader public opinion on majority-Roma relations, as it has been voiced both through polls and debates in the media, with a view to assessing the level of consonance of these popular views with both post-Communist official views and longer-standing political cultural orientations. In my conclusion, I assess whether the Czech case bears out criticisms of the civic/ethnic dichotomy made in the theoretical literature. This sets the stage for the concluding chapter, where I compare the two models' implications.

Defining the Sovereign Community, Part I: The Czech Constitution

In contrast to the Slovak Constitution, the Czech Constitution's preamble reads,

> We, the citizens of the Czech Republic in Bohemia, Moravia, and Silesia, at the time of the renewal of an independent Czech state, loyal to all good traditions of the ancient statehood of the Lands of the Czech Crown and the Czechoslovak statehood, resolved to build, protect and develop the Czech Republic in the spirit of the inviolable values of human dignity and freedom, as the home of free and equal citizens who are

conscious of their duties toward others and their responsibility toward the whole, as a free and democratic state based on the respect for human rights and the principles of civic society, as part of the family of European and world democracies, resolved to jointly protect and develop the inherited natural and cultural, material and spiritual wealth, resolved to abide by all time-tried principles of a law-observing state, through our freely elected representatives adopt this Constitution of the Czech Republic.[5]

The debate leading up to this wording was not particularly contentious. Most Members of Parliament appeared to agree with Prime Minister Václav Klaus's statement that the "foundation of the state is the free citizen."[6] Pavel Peška, director of the Department of Constitutional Law at Charles University, did object that "it is absurd, even though the civic principle is rightly emphasized, that the existence of the Czech nation would not be mentioned in the entire constitution."[7] The main resistance to the strictly civic definition of sovereignty came, however, from Moravian representatives, who argued that their national identity was not properly recognized.[8] Thus, Movement for Self-Governing Democracy-Society for Moravia and Silesia (HSD-SMS) deputy Jiří Bílý proposed that the words "civic society" be followed by the phrase "proceeding from the principle of the equal rights of nations," because "states are established not by citizens, but by nations."[9] His fellow deputy from southern Moravia Jiří Drápela (Liberal Social Union) also asked that the Constitution open with the phrase, "We, citizens of the Czechomoravian [*českomoravské*] Republic in the Czech lands, in Moravia, and in Silesia." Vice-Premier Ján Kalvoda argued against the Moravians' proposals, declaring that the rights of nations "have no place at the head of the constitution." His position won out.

While ethnicity is not a defining element of the sovereign community, the existence of a majority identity is implied by the guarantee of minority rights. Three constitutional articles protect these, two of which incorporate rights and freedoms from other documents. Article 6 states that "minorities shall be protected by the majority in decision-making," which, as Matthew Rhodes notes, is a "vague protection."[10] More concretely, Article 10 declares that "ratified and promulgated international accords on human rights and freedoms, to which the Czech Republic has committed itself, are immediately binding and superior to law." Finally, Article 3 makes the Charter of Fundamental Rights and Freedoms, adopted by the Czech and Slovak Federal Assembly in 1991, "part of the constitutional order of the Czech Republic." This then guarantees the right to choose one's own nationality free from pressure and that this national or ethnic identity will not be used to the individual's detriment (Articles 3 and 24). Article 25 of the Charter also provides that

> 1) Citizens who constitute national or ethnic minorities are guaranteed all-round development, in particular the right to develop with other members of the minority their own culture, their right to disseminate and receive information in their language, and the right to associate in ethnic associations. Detailed provisions are set by law.
> 2) Citizens constituting national and ethnic minorities are also guaranteed under conditions set by law:
> a) the right to education in their language
> b) the right to use their language in official contact
> c) the right to participate in the settlement of matters concerning national and ethnic minorities

In a report on its compliance with the UN Convention on the Elimination of All Forms of Racial Discrimination, the Human Rights Office of the Ministry of Foreign Affairs of the Czech Republic summarized the state's approach to minority rights:

> The overriding principle of the Czech policy in respect of national minorities is that the holder of minority rights is an individual belonging to a particular national minority and that such individual is primarily [a] citizen of the Czech Republic. Since minority rights are safeguarded by law, they are "rights" in the legal sense and consequently are protected by law and may be asserted in court. The Czech Republic takes care to enforce the so-called collective rights exclusively on the basis of the claims of individuals, not by groups; enforcement of such rights would otherwise conflict with the citizenship [civic] principle. This approach is based on the assumption that collective rights safeguarded on a group basis do not have concrete implications for each individual belonging to a national minority, for his right to invoke them and assert them through procedures prescribed by law.[11]

Clearly, then, the Czech regime is based on the principle that the individual is the primary rights-bearing entity, and the initial ruling interpretation of this principle rejected group-differentiated rights.[12]

Defining the Sovereign Community, Part II:
The Czech Citizenship Law

Because the citizen was the building block of the new state, the question of who could gain this status was of defining importance. This was answered by the Law on the Acquisition and Loss of Czech Citizenship, passed 29 December 1992, which stated that only those who held "Czech citizenship" in the preceding Czechoslovak state were entitled to automatic citizenship in the new state. This previous citizenship was based on laws that accompanied the post-Prague Spring federalization of the communist state, giving all Czechoslovak citizens the designation of either "Czech" or "Slovak" according to their birthplace. Those born after the promulgation of these laws inherited their parents' status. These new designations were, however, only relevant within the country; "Czechoslovak" remained the internationally recognized citizenship. It was also a simple matter to change one's designation if one moved to the other republic.[13] Citizenship status was not printed on passports or similar identification documents and had "no relationship to any rights, privileges, or duties."[14] Its insignificance is reflected in a December 1992 article in Slovak *Pravda*, which asked readers, "Do you know whether you are a citizen of the Slovak Republic or the Czech Republic?"[15]

While the law gave automatic citizenship to Czech citizens, those the 1969 law deemed Slovaks were considered foreigners who had the right to apply for citizenship according to "marginally less restrictive conditions than those which apply to other potential immigrants."[16] These proved onerous for the Roma. Because nearly all the Czech Roma were murdered in the Holocaust (or, to use the Roma term, the Devouring), after World War II most Czechoslovak Roma were either born in Slovakia or had Slovak parents. Thus, even though only a third of the 200,000–300,000 Roma living in the Czech Republic at the post-Communist state's founding were born in Slovakia,[17] according to the 1969 law they were mostly Slovak.[18] For these, a complicated bureaucratic process followed, involving municipal, federal, and also Slovak authorities. As Human Rights Watch reported, "even for educated people, the process was obtuse and confusing. But for many Roma, who suffer disproportionately from low levels of education and literacy, it was at times incomprehensible. . . . For many, the very notion of citizenship was confusing."[19] Nongovernmental organizations stepped in to assist Roma applicants, but found that government authorities were often uncooperative and sometimes intentionally obstructive, misrepresenting rules or withholding details of appeal procedures.[20]

By far the most difficult obstacles, however, were the law's two main requirements of a clean criminal record for five years and proof of two years'
permanent residence—unofficially called the "Roma clause."[21] The clean
record requirement did not take into account of the severity of the crime,
and with Roma unemployment ranging from 70 to 90 percent,[22] convictions
for small-scale crimes of robbery and theft were common, especially among
young men.[23] Proving permanent residence also proved difficult for the Roma.
The processes of post-Communist privatization and restitution compounded
a housing shortage, and many Roma lived in apartments overflowing with
family members. Local authorities were often unwilling to register all the inhabitants of illegally overcrowded dwellings.

"As Czech officials admit," the CSCE reported in 1994, "virtually every
person excluded from Czech citizenship under the new law is a Roma."[24]
Prime Minister Klaus responded to concerns about this group-specific impact
by arguing that "the conditions for obtaining citizenship are binding for all
applicants who are citizens of other states, and do not apply to specifically
designated groups of persons."[25] While he acknowledged that the Roma were
more often affected than others by the clean criminal record requirement, he
held fast that "the government cannot change the accepted law for the sake of
one group of inhabitants."[26]

This claim of government neutrality was, however, seriously challenged.
While Human Rights Watch cautions that the charge is difficult to prove
conclusively, there is evidence indicating that the law was written "with the
specific intent of hindering citizenship for Roma and facilitating their removal
from the Czech lands."[27] Much of this evidence came from interviews Human
Rights Watch conducted with a large number of people who had fallen under
the law's scope or had kept track of its effects. There are also further reasons to
believe this allegation. One is an internal 1991 government document that addressed the possibility of the "catastrophic scenario" of a mass influx of Roma
into the Czech lands if the common state broke up. Portions were leaked to
the press in 1992, and two aspects were particularly scrutinized. The first was
the proposal that the government "take advantage of the departure of useless
individuals from enterprises, particularly for reasons of structural change, and
of the moving away of citizens of the Roma nationality to Slovakia."[28] The
second was the government's plan, if the state split, "to take measures toward
the prevention of the mass migration of Roma into the Czech Republic."

Still more supporting evidence comes from developments during the latter half of 1992. As the state moved toward dissolution, tension grew in the

economically depressed industrial areas of northern Bohemia between ethnic Czechs and Roma, whose numbers were growing as Slovak Roma migrated to the area to live with family and friends. Representatives of several of these towns responded by demanding that the Czech government "grant citizenship as well as permanent residence status only with the concurrence of the municipalities"[29] and "only to people without a criminal record."[30] It seems unlikely to be a coincidence that these became elements of the citizenship law.

The government's avowal of strict neutrality was also challenged when, in June 1995, Parliament amended the citizenship law to allow the Interior Ministry to waive the five-year residency requirement for foreigners who had been resettled in the Czech Republic by the government. The purpose was to grant citizenship to a group of 200–300 ethnic Czechs from Volnya, Ukraine. This action outraged such organizations as Human Rights Watch, which observed that "for many people, this illustrated the ethnic intentions of the citizenship law."[31]

Over time, the law continued to draw substantial criticism from both domestic and international sources, the latter including the Council of Europe, the Organization for Security and Cooperation in Europe, the United Nations Human Rights Commission for Refugees, and the Commission for Security and Cooperation in Europe of the U.S. Congress (the Helsinki Committee). After several smaller modifications, in 1999 Parliament passed a law allowing former citizens of Czechoslovakia who had lived in the Czech Republic since 1993 to gain citizenship through a simple declaration. The law thereby shed its most controversial aspects. As Rick Fawn argues, this was likely "the result of foreign pressure—the amendment originated in the parliamentary Foreign Affairs Committee and its chairman, Jiří Payne, explained that the change was intended to make the Czech citizenship application process more akin to that of Western Europe."[32] Clearly, then, for its first six years, the state effectively excluded many Roma from membership in the sovereign community. As Jan Rusenko, a member of the Roma Democratic Congress, put it, the law was "only an administrative way of separating the wheat from the chaff."[33] In this sense, the citizenship law appears to be an example of what Hayden calls "bureaucratic ethnic cleansing."[34]

Measuring Minority Membership

It is, then, certainly possible to seek to build a sovereign community that excludes a particular ethnicity while claiming the neutrality of the civic principle, especially if the targeted group has higher levels of some behavior falling outside the majority community's general normative boundaries (such as wide-scale petty criminality). If this is what the Czech government did, then its leaders were clearly not viewing the potential citizenry as free and equal individuals, but rather in the context of pre-political collective identities. This raises questions concerning the extent to which the state thereafter actually treated citizens equally, regardless of ethnicity, and in particular how law and political practice affected the Roma minority. Before proceeding, however, it is important to note that the post-Communist state inherited a situation where the Roma were already strongly socioeconomically disadvantaged in comparison with the majority community. My concern here, though, is how the state *actively treated* its Roma citizens, not the roots of long-standing socioeconomic inequalities. I begin, then, with Gabal's dimension 1, the level of protection from violence and persecution—one of the state's most fundamental duties to its citizens.

Protection from Violent Discrimination and Persecution

In 1996, Human Rights Watch observed that "racist attacks—and the government's lack of response—are the most serious concern of Roma in the country today."[35] This remained true for the entire decade of the 1990s, and Czech state authorities were particularly criticized for five tendencies: when gangs of skinheads attacked Roma, few individuals were prosecuted; crimes were infrequently prosecuted under the provisions for racial motivation; perpetrators were charged with lesser crimes than warranted; courts were biased against the Roma; and police abuse of Roma was punished insufficiently, if at all.[36] In addition, observers pointed out that, because of the Roma's low level of education, they often understood the legal system inadequately, which left them "open to abuse."[37]

Several of these tendencies are well illustrated by the tortuous governmental response to the 1993 murder of Tibor Danihel, a seventeen-year-old Rom who drowned after being chased into a river by a group of around 40 rock-throwing skinheads in the town of Písek. According to various reports, the head of the district prosecutor's office, the judge in charge of the case, and the deputy mayor all made light of the crime, suggesting it was a prank that had gotten out of hand.[38] When the case finally reached court (which was filled with skinhead observers), the charges were thrown out against most

of the accused and only two were convicted of "damaging the health resulting in death," for which they were given suspended sentences of one year.[39]
The verdict was annulled on appeal by the regional court and returned for
further investigation. The resulting new indictment again did not contain a
murder charge against any of the four defendants, accusing them instead of
a "violation of civic co-existence."[40] In March 1997, the district court handed
down sentences of 22–31 months for three of the defendants and a suspended
two-year sentence for the fourth, which were affirmed by the regional court in
June of that year. In February 1998, the Supreme Court ordered a retrial, stating that the light sentences constituted an "abuse of the law to the benefit of
the accused."[41] Finally, in June 1999, three skinheads were convicted of racially
motivated murder and attempted murder and sentenced to prison terms ranging from six-and-a-half to eight-and-a-half years.[42]

    According to Hana Fristenská, the Czech government's response to "in-
terethnic violence" developed in several stages. The first, from 1990–92, was
characterized by a "complete lack of reaction to the growing intensity of racist violence."[43] During the second stage, from 1993 through the first half of
1995, the government came to understand that conditions were worsening,
but failed to fully recognize the relationship between the Roma's situation and
the attitudes of the majority society.[44] The next turning point came in the second half of 1995, largely as a result of widespread outrage at the light sentences
handed down to a group of skinheads who beat a Rom named Tibor Berki
to death in front of his family. After the crime, Justice Minister Jiří Novak
wrote in *Mladá fronta dnes*, "The role of the state in solving this problem is
clearly important and cannot be replaced. This is a democratic state and its
institutions should assure citizens equal standing and protection against those
who challenge these institutions and, on the other hand, take action against
all those who do not respect this principle."[45] The state was thus prompted to
tighten its policies on racially motivated violence.

    Two years later, however, when around 1,200 Czech Roma left the coun-
try to apply for refugee status in Canada (after a television program incorrectly
suggested that the country had a "special asylum program for Roma"[46]), many
referred in their applications to the lack of police protection against skinhead
violence. Canada eventually imposed visa requirements for Czechs, prompting Czech consternation and also an increased flow of Czech Roma asylum-
seekers to Britain, as well as, in smaller numbers, to France and Belgium. In
the context of growing frustration in these receiving countries, in October
1997 the Czech government published a report on the Roma's situation (*Pro*

schůzi vlády české republiky: Zpráva o situaci romské komunity v české republice a opatření vlády napomáhající její integraci ve společnost, often referred to as the "Bratinka Report" after its sponsor, Pavel Bratinka, president of the Council for National Minorities and minister without portfolio in Prime Minister Klaus's government). It was written largely by the head of Bratinka's office, Viktor Dobal, who had long experience working with the Roma in Prague's fifth district. The report addressed issues that had been raised in the Council for National Minorities and critically assessed current policies.[47] The government initially returned the report, but ultimately adopted it with very few revisions, as the asylum issue began to damage the state's reputation abroad. The report offered a number of recommendations for better addressing violent persecution of the Roma, which included having the Minister of the Interior screen police force candidates for prejudice and racism, admitting as many Roma candidates as possible to police training schools, preventing the formation of groups based on racial or ethnic intolerance and fascism, and securing financial support for programs aimed at the prevention of criminality and drug dependency in the Roma community.[48] In addition, the report proposed that the Ministry of Justice closely follow racially motivated crime and inform the government regularly about the trends it observed.[49]

The central government's efforts did lead to some improvements. Even before the Bratinka Report, the European Commission against Racism and Intolerance (ECRI, a body of the Council of Europe) noted that the prosecution of racially motivated crime by the government had shown a "marked improvement over recent years."[50] At the same time, ECRI stated that neither police enforcement nor sentencing policy had been particularly vigorous or consistent. Moreover, observers reported that the denial of equal protection continued to occur primarily at the lower levels of the criminal justice system. As Roma activist Ondrej Gina told the Canadian Immigration and Refugee Board, while "Roma are equal to other citizens in the eyes of the country's constitution and laws . . . in practice it is difficult and sometimes impossible for Roma to obtain protection at the local or district level."[51] Human Rights Watch agreed, reporting that Roma's rights are often violated in local "police stations, courtrooms and administrative offices."[52] ECRI also expressed concerns about "the compatibility of local actions with national priorities."[53]

These patterns of state behavior thus constitute a very serious violation of the civic principle. Such wide-scale failure to protect and respect Roma individuals on an equal level with the majority suggests that many, especially at lower levels of government, do not see the civic principle as applying to or encompassing the Roma—a position that logically and philosophically violates that principle. Such state behavior is thus based not an *interpretation* of this principle, but *resistance* to it.

Protection for Minority Citizens Against Nonviolent Discrimination and the Provision of Equal Opportunity

During the 1990s, nonviolent discrimination against the Roma was far more prevalent than violent discrimination, and was also the subject of some debate in the Czech Republic. In particular, the specific targeting of local policies and decrees against Roma sparked confrontations between central and lower levels of government. The first occurred at around the time of the Velvet Divorce, when the Jirkov City Council passed decrees—which its members admitted were directed at the Roma—allowing authorities to evict people from apartments they deemed unsanitary or overcrowded.[54] The decrees also restricted visitors to the city, requiring the town hall to approve them and limiting their stay to one week. A family could only have visitors twice a year and the police were given authority to enter an apartment where they suspected that unregistered guests were staying. The General Prosecutor declared that the "Jirkov Decrees" violated the Charter on Fundamental Rights and Freedoms, but no action was taken against city authorities. Five other northern Bohemian towns quickly followed Jirkov's lead, adopting measures based on aspects of the decrees.

Since then, there have been a number of controversies over local government treatment of Roma. For example, in 1996, the mayor of Kladno was charged with inciting racial hatred after banning Roma children from a public swimming pool during a hepatitis outbreak.[55] His eventual conviction after one acquittal sparked a debate in the Czech press over the permissible scope of local policy. In 1999, still another scandal erupted when it was revealed that government employment offices had been marking Roma files with an "R" as a signal to potential employers,[56] and the policy was quickly prohibited.

Probably the most famous example of local government policy directed against Roma was the wall in the town of Ústí nad Labem, which became a topic of international scrutiny in May 1998. Reacting to complaints from ethnic Czechs living near two apartment complexes housing a large number of Roma families about the conditions around the buildings, a municipal council decided to build a four-meter-high wall (some called it a fence) around them.[57]

According to Mayor Ladislav Hruška, the wall was "not racially motivated," but rather intended to "separate the decent people from those who are not."[58] The central government responded by declaring the wall racist and discriminatory and ordering the council executive to reconsider the decision. The council reconsidered, but approved a resolution declaring that the decision did not violate Czech law. In October 1999, the Chamber of Deputies voted by a large majority to overturn the council's decision. That same day, the city preemptively completed the project.

This action provoked renewed internal and international criticism. While Klaus (now chairman of the Chamber of Deputies) "dismissed or ridiculed" much of it (commenting, for example, that he had seen "walls in Northern Ireland which are far greater in significance than that in Matiční Street and no one threatens to expel Britain from the EU"[59]), President Havel called on the city to tear it down immediately, noting that "not just the town of Ústí nad Labem but the whole of the Czech Republic is identified with this symbol of intolerance and discrimination. Above all, the wall has a symbolic importance."[60] After negotiating with central government leaders, the municipal council finally agreed to remove it in exchange for a 10 million crown (about U.S.$285,000) payment from the Czech government, part of which reportedly went to buy out ethnic Czech families from properties nearby.[61] While the wall's removal did allay tensions, the matter was not closed. The local authorities appealed to the Supreme Court concerning the Chamber of Deputies' power to overrule local decisions and, in April 2000, it ruled that the lower house of Parliament did *not* have this power.[62]

The conflict over the wall's legality again indicates tensions between central and local government perspectives on the principles that should govern the state's relationship with the minority. Moreover, the conflict's ambiguous resolution suggests both confusion over the balance of power between central and local government and the lack of a straightforward legal framework for challenging state-sponsored discrimination, and it left no clear precedent to guide state authorities through similar future controversies.

Another aspect of Gabal's second dimension of minority membership is the protection of equality of opportunity. One key way that this may be ensured is through public education, and there is a general consensus among Roma leaders, human rights activists, and Czech government representatives that the Roma continue to be marginalized in large part because of their very low levels of education. According to official estimates during the 1990s, less than 20 percent of Roma students finished the ninth grade and less than 5 percent graduated from high school.[63] University graduation was accordingly even lower. There was also a consensus on a critical reason for this situation: following a pattern of placement carried over from the Communist school system, Roma children were 15 times more likely than non-Roma children to be sent to "special schools" for those with serious learning disabilities.[64]

There is no evidence that this proportion of Roma children have such disabilities compared with the rest of the population.[65] Nevertheless, the funneling of Roma children into these schools was "often quasi-automatic."[66] There appear to be two main reasons for this. First, the children had trouble with the school placement tests. In particular, many had insufficient knowledge of the Czech language:[67] reflecting their Slovak origins, many speak a "hybrid Czech that includes elements of Slovak, Hungarian, and Romani and often uses Romani grammatical elements and cases."[68] Because the tests were language-oriented, children who were not fluent in Czech were seriously disadvantaged. Both the Bratinka Report and nongovernmental sources also condemned the tests as strongly culturally biased; in the ERRC's view, they were "dependent upon the projected cultural uniformity of the people tested."[69]

A second reason for the generally low level of Roma education is that many Roma families, uneducated themselves, place little value on formal education. Teachers often react by placing Roma children at the back of regular classrooms, where they are largely ignored by staff[70] and often abused by other children.[71] Moreover, as Roma activist Karel Holomek observes, "in school the children learn nothing of Roma history, let alone anything positive."[72] Many Roma children thus experience the curriculum as "white history," "white music," and "white customs."[73] Because of the pervasive sense of the classroom as a "hostile, foreign environment," Roma parents often preferred that their children attend schools where there were many other Roma children,[74] and normal intelligence test scores could be disregarded if the parents requested such a transfer.[75] A European Roma Rights Center (ERRC) report also cited many examples of parents being pressured to do so.[76]

Thus, although in "theory, the procedure which governs sending children to special schools is colour blind,"[77] it created a de facto segregated school system. As Fristenská argues, such discrimination is "systemic"[78] and has had devastating effects. Until a new measure was passed in late 1999, the law prohibited a person holding a degree from a special school from further study in a regular secondary school, and prospects for graduates of special schools were limited to unskilled and poorly paying jobs.[79] This situation in turn fostered such problems as "high unemployment, drug abuse, criminality, political marginalization dependency on the state."[80] As the ERRC succinctly observed, such "schools create what they are designed to treat."[81] Moreover, the situation made government-sponsored affirmative action difficult, as there are few suitable Roma candidates for promotion.[82] As government officials admitted in 1997, the education of Roma children was one of "the most fundamental problems" facing Czech society.[83]

One final indication during the 1990s that the state was not effectively protecting all of its minority citizens from nonviolent discrimination was the pervasive denial of Roma access to public spaces, including restaurants, discos, hotels, cafés and bars. Some spaces even displayed signs stating that Roma were unwelcome. Even when they did not, Roma were often denied service; for example, a 1996 study by the group HOST (Movement for Civic Solidarity and Tolerance) found that well-dressed Roma were refused service in 24 of 40 restaurants in five Bohemian towns.[84] Importantly, although such discrimination is unconstitutional, the government has not provided its citizens with effective legal means to protect themselves against it: no specific law against the denial of services based on race or ethnicity in public spaces exists. When such discrimination was prosecuted, it was usually dealt with according to statutes against inciting racial hatred. This tactic proved relatively unsuccessful, as two cases from the mid-1990s show. One was an incident in which Rudolf Baranek, a parliamentary candidate for the Free Democrats-Liberal National Social Party (SD-LSNS), posted a sign outside a hotel he operated in Břeclav, southern Moravia, stating: "Because of repeated stealing, access is forbidden to those of Romani origin."[85] Roma and national political leaders reacted with outrage, and President Havel called the sign "scandalous."[86] Nevertheless, the Břeclav District Attorney declared the action "improper, discriminatory, not, however, criminal."[87] Baranek took the sign down, and his party demoted him from second to fifth place on its list. Still, the party co-chairman, former Czechoslovak foreign minister and Charter 77 signatory Jiří Dienstbier, was unwilling to call the sign racist.[88] The party's failure to respond to the issue is significant: it had a liberal orientation and a noteworthy dissident membership, making it (seemingly) among the more likely candidates to take a stronger stand against such discrimination.

A second case that captured broad attention began in 1995, when Roma-rights activist Ondrej Gina filed a criminal complaint against Ivo Blahout, owner of the Na železne bar in Rokycany, for refusing to serve Roma. Gina had videotaped evidence of refusals, and police officers were willing to testify that Blahout had expressed racial grounds for his actions. He was charged with inciting national and racial hatred, but found not guilty by a Rokycany court. A state attorney appealed the verdict, and he was retried, and acquitted again. Another appeal, another trial, and another acquittal followed (three in all).[89] The media took significant interest in this litigation, which the U.S. State Department called "the country's first prominent antidiscrimination case."[90] Explaining his actions to *Práce*, Blahout stated, "I simply threw a group of Roma out of the bar who, not for the first time, were giving me problems. They take entirely the same measures when there are objectionable white customers in a restaurant."[91] Ultimately, after the third acquittal, the Plzeň regional court transferred the case to another court. While awaiting this decision, Blahout was elected to the Rokycany town council. Finally, in 2001, he was fined 8,000 crowns—about U.S.$200. He declared that he would not pay it, but rather take the case to the Human Rights Court in Strasbourg. (Radio Prague noted that a community worker in Rokycany advised against this, as the country was trying to enter the EU and needed to "prove that it respects its minorities."[92])

These cases prompted a fair amount of discussion of the legal framework available for dealing with discrimination. A spokesman for the Ministry of Justice defended the approach of using the statues against inciting racial hatred, stating, "I cannot think of any kind of discrimination that would not be covered by the law as it now exists."[93] Claude Cahn of the ERRC, however, argued that, "discrimination and racially motivated violence are not the same thing, and Czech law is equipped to handle the latter but not the former."[94] Václav Žák, vice-chairman of the SD-LSNS, elaborated on this point in a September 1996 article in *Právo*, quoting the criminal statute applied to private owners of public accommodations like Blahout, which states, "whoever publicly incites the hatred of any nation or race or the restriction of the rights and freedoms of their members, will be punished with imprisonment of up to two years."[95] According to Žák, however, "liberal democratic laws" in fact

carefully differentiate the criminal act of inciting racial hatred from discrimination. If someone in the USA operates an accommodation into which more than 25 people can enter, they may not place a notice above the door prohibiting entry of any group on the basis of race, religious affiliation or political membership. If he would, for example, write "Negroes' entry prohibited," he would await a civil action from the federal organs according to federal law, from state organs according to state law, and he might even have charges filed by individuals, civic associations. He might even have charges filed because of lost profits (for example, if he thwarted the realization of business engagements.) He would not, however, be criminally prosecuted for the incitement of racial hatred.[96]

Žák concluded that a specific law dealing with discrimination was needed—a conclusion reached by many analysts of the Czech Republic in the 1990s.[97] None, however, was forthcoming during that period.

These examples of discrimination by local governments, the educational system, and private owners of public spaces again indicate widespread and very serious violations of the civic principle. As with violent discrimination and persecution, this appears to be mostly based not on a particular interpretation of the civic principle, but rather on wide-scale resistance to its necessary implications with regard to the Roma by local officials and the broader population. In addition, it makes clear that instruments are lacking for interpreting and implementing the principle; without legislation that defines and prohibits discrimination, constitutional principles are often overridden in practice by antithetical popular norms.

Self-Fulfillment and Development of Minority Ethnic, National, or Cultural Identity

The question of cultural development is much less contentious than persecution and discrimination, and the Czech government has a long record of offering support in this realm. In 1994, it established the Council for National Minorities, which brought Magyar, Polish, Roma, Slovak, German, and Ukrainian minority leaders together with representatives from Parliament, the ministries, and the office of the president. Their main role was to consult with the government, and their main achievement (to the frustration of some, who hoped for more wide-ranging influence) was to "secure financial support for minority press and cultural activities."[98] For example, the government provides funding to several Roma publications and a museum of Romani culture in Brno.[99] Czech law also requires that public television and radio grant access to minorities, although the decisions about when and how often programs air have been made by the station management, and scheduling is not always ideal from the standpoint of the program producers. Jarmila Balážová, who worked in Roma-themed media, has also argued that programming during the 1990s offered a largely one-dimensional portrayal of the Roma.[100] More positively, since 1999, the government has supported the annual Khamoro festival, held in Prague, which celebrates Roma culture and addresses such issues as women's role in society, coexistence with the majority population, and the relationship between modern life and Roma traditions.[101]

The Roma have also been active in forming groups to promote their own interests. During the post-Communist period, a large number of Roma civic organizations sprang up, and several political parties have been founded as well.[102] A problem for these parties, however, is that the Roma population is too small to reach the 5 percent threshold for parliamentary representation. Roma politicians must therefore find room in other parties, and according to Holomek the dominant parties have been unwelcoming.[103] He also argues that Roma representatives, who "markedly differ and always will differ from the majority," face a difficult task in balancing the requirements of relating effectively to both their constituencies and to the larger society.[104] At the time of this writing (after the 2006 Parliamentary elections), there are no Roma representatives in the Czech Parliament and have not been any since Monika Horáková won a seat with the Freedom Union in 1998.[105]

Ultimately, while Roma culture does enjoy monetary support from the Czech government, this must be viewed in the context of the state's failure to secure the first two dimensions of Roma membership. Given the threat of violence and the pervasive nonviolent discrimination, assimilative pressures could be seen as extreme. At the same time, assimilation is potentially unfeasible because of the racist element of the exclusion (skin color is often mentioned in discussions about discrimination). Clearly, then, although state leaders have interpreted the civic principle as being compatible with such state support of ethnic culture, its benefits must be viewed in the context of more fundamental violations of this principle.

Models for Roma Integration and Civic Equality: Czech Government Perspectives

From the evidence offered above, it is clear that the Roma are extremely marginalized; their "full integration" (Gabal's fourth dimension) is hardly imaginable in the near term. Czech leaders appear well aware of this, and so I look here at the ways that that successive Czech governments have conceived of the proper relationship between the state and its Roma citizens, including potential pathways for their integration, as well as at how these conceptions relate to the civic principle.

One of the first post-Communist statements on the Roma came in July 1990 from President Václav Havel, who attended a Roma festival in Brno. There, the president gave a speech in which he acknowledged a history of terrible injustice against the Roma, including genocide during World War II and oppression under the Communism. Now, in the new state, he declared that

> Roma—just as everyone else—have the right to their national self-realization and to respect for their ethnic identity. They must have the same rights and the very same responsibilities as every citizen of our state, and they should enjoy—just as other national or cultural minorities—also specific collective rights, and it is not permissible on this basis to assert the principle of collective guilt or collective responsibility.
>
> The democratic state that we are building must be established on the idea of human rights. Only this way is it possible to join the family of civilized states. To human rights belong also the rights to equality before the law, to a dignified life and to their own national or ethnic existence.
>
> People are not good or bad because they belong to this race or to that nation. Whoever does not acknowledge this truth is a racist.[106]

Lauding the "joyful and dignified" festival as helpful to the entire society's progress toward building a state that is "humane, tolerant, just, cultured, and civilized," Havel's speech—and his very presence—strongly endorsed a vision of a political community that combined minority cultural rights with civic equality.

The following year, in 1991, state leaders produced a resolution titled Principles of the Government of the Czech and Slovak Federative Republic on a Policy Toward the Romany Minority. "Mainly symbolic," according to Peter Vermeersch, it "made clear that current policies differed from the communist way of dealing with the Roma in that assimilation was now no longer the ultimate goal. To the contrary, the resolution stated, the development of Romani identity—and not its destruction—was a crucial element in equalizing the position of the Roma with the rest of society."[107]

Despite the resolution, the Czech Republic did not devote significant attention to the Roma minority for several years thereafter. Prime Minister Klaus, the new state's most powerful leader from 1993 to 1997, was much less interested than President Havel in actively promoting goodwill and tolerance between the majority and the Roma. He did meet with Roma leaders, and strongly condemned the Tibor Berki murder, calling for stricter sentences for the perpetrators and thereafter for life sentences for racially motivated murder.[108] On the other hand, as his above-noted comments on the citizenship law and the Ústí nad Labem wall indicate, he was often hostile and dismissive of criticism of the state's treatment of the Roma minority. This was particularly the case when it came from international sources; for example, he stated that a letter from the U.S. Congress Helsinki Committee expressing concern about the citizenship law was unofficial and required no reply, and in any case "tens, if not hundreds, of letters come to my desk every day."[109]

The year 1997, with its exodus of Czech Roma to Western countries, was a turning point, as international scrutiny intensified and began to carry with it potentially serious repercussions. In particular, the EU, which during the first half of the decade had paid little attention to Roma issues in the post-Communist states, responded with increasing firmness, linking treatment of the minority to the states' conditions for accession. This was partly because member states were alarmed by the westward flow of Roma asylum-seekers and pushed the EU to pressure candidate countries to improve the situation of their Roma citizens (problematic throughout the region). The EU was also prompted to increased attention by NGOs like Amnesty International, Human Rights Watch, the European Roma Rights Centre, and the Project on Ethnic Relations, which all produced substantial research on the Roma situation and related it to measures of the states' progress toward democratization.[110] In addition, the Czech government felt direct pressure from the states most affected by the asylum claims to stem the flow.[111]

As noted above, these developments gave Pavel Bratinka the opportunity to press the Klaus government, which initially had shown little interest in his report, to adopt it. Clearly, then, while outside pressure influenced its acceptance, the report itself was not simply the *product* of this pressure. It is worth examining this document in more detail, as it represents the Czech government's first attempt to grapple substantively with the problem of how a state founded on the civic principle should deal with a particular group experiencing serious, wide-scale difficulties not substantially faced by other citizens.

The report begins with a definition of key concepts, and here explains three reasons why its authors used the "concept of 'Roma community' and not the concept of 'Roma minority nationality'" throughout their analysis. First, only a small proportion of "citizens of Roma descent" declared themselves as such in the last population count, and it was "necessary to respect this choice."[112] Second, they observed that what "we are dealing with is not problems of nationality politics (preservation of language, schools in the native language, etc.), but with social problems (low living standards, high unemployment levels, etc.)." And finally, it would be "discriminatory" to categorize an entire nationality as having a set of socioeconomic problems that are not, in fact, universally shared by citizens of Roma descent.[113]

The report then moves on to give a broad overview of the roots of the issues it dealt with, asserting that "the primary cause of the problems in the common life of the majority society and the Roma community is the inadequate adaptation of a substantial part of that community to the rules and values which the rest of society considers as a matter of course. The revolutionary changes in the past few years, which fundamentally increased the importance of education and qualifications, dramatically emphasized this deficit in these areas of adaptation."[114] While some members of the majority society also suffer from social problems and "high rates of criminality," the report argues that there are a number of contributing factors unique to the Roma community. These include the "historically originating handicaps" of "weak interest in education and qualification," "low levels of knowledge of the Czech language," "weak consciousness of the need to be concerned about the future," and "weak ability to act independently as an individual."[115] The Roma's problems are not, however, entirely due to internal weaknesses: "the majority society reacts to this deficit [in adaptation] with numerous demonstrations of distrust, hostility, and simplistic prejudice, which are often openly supported even by some members of parliamentary parties. The dominant social atmosphere then encourages racist elements toward violent criminal acts against citizens of Roma descent. Within the Roma community, these processes intensify the sense of alienation from the society and further weaken their will to integrate."[116] Ultimately, discrimination against the Roma reflects the fact that the rest of the citizens are "not respecting the civic principle."[117] Thus, the solution to the Roma's problems requires "not only steps aimed at the Roma community, but also measures aimed at the majority part of the society."[118]

Having outlined its perspective on Roma inequality, the report notes that "the promotion of some concrete programs aimed at the improvement of the situation of the members of the Roma community at times gets bogged down by the argument that any kind of specific approach to ethnically and nationally defined groups contradicts the civic principle."[119] This "interpretation," however, "in some cases may function as a buck-passing defense against demands for the solution of real problems." Arguing that the report's approach was, in fact, consistent with this regime principle, its authors wrote that the concept of this report and its recommendations start from the view that the civic principle is an instrument for the assertion of the equality of every citizen. This is in no way obstructed when the state attempts— precisely in the interest of ensuring this equality also for a disadvantaged group of inhabitants—to realize such measures that would help this group become involved in social processes, to make full use of the achievements of civil society and to fulfill the basic prerequisites that the other groups are, to a considerable degree, provided through their historical, social and cultural backgrounds. It is possible to understand this approach more as compensation for their initial disadvantages, which are in their consequences also a burden for the whole society. Analogously— and entirely naturally—the state applies such an approach particularly toward those with health problems.[120]

Thus, it is in the "framework of state assistance to socially weak groups" that the government's focus on the Roma's problems can best be understood.[121]

After the government approved the report as a resolution, it founded the Interdepartmental Commission for Romany Community Affairs, an advisory body drawing Roma activists together with representatives of government ministries. "From this time onwards," Vermeersch argues, "the Roma were clearly treated as a minority group in need of special support on top of the existing support as provided to minorities in general."[122] Shortly after the Commission's founding, however, the Klaus government fell because of a financial scandal involving the Civic Democratic Party (ODS). A period of some uncertainty about the Commission's role followed. In the meantime, President Havel continued to stress the issue's importance, stating in his December 1997 Address to Members of Parliament:

I regard culture as the most important thing of all, which therefore deserves to be mentioned in conclusion of my remarks. Of course, I do not limit the notion of culture only to human occupations, such as conservation of national heritage, making films or writing poetry. I speak of culture in the broadest sense of the word, that is, of the culture of human relations, human coexistence, human labour, human ventures; of the culture of public and political life; of the culture of our behaviour in general. I am afraid this is a sphere where we have most of our debts to pay, and most of our work to do. Culture in the broadest sense is not measured by the number of splendid rock stars who visit this country, or by the beauty of dresses by prominent designers presented here by world-class models. It is measured by something else—for example: by that which is chanted by skinheads in a pub; by the number of lynched or murdered Romanies; by the dreadful behaviour of some of our people toward their fellow humans simply because of the different colour of their skin.[123]

After the elections in 1998, Social Democrat (ČSSD) Miloš Zeman replaced Klaus as Prime Minister, and declared that "the government shall . . . devote attention to all ethnic groups living in the Czech Republic, although the most serious, and undoubtedly most complex, issue is, in the Government's view, the coexistence of a part of the majority society with the Romany minority. The Government considers the Romany community a natural component of Czech society. The civic principle, as the basis for the solution of this problem, will be complemented by specific programs designed for the Romany minority in those cases where the hitherto existing handicaps cannot be overcome by measures aimed at the society as a whole."[124]

Under Zeman, the Interdepartmental Commission continued its work, producing, most notably, a "policy concept" on Roma integration that was adopted by the government in April 1999. This came in the context of continued clear communication from the EU that an improvement in the state's relationship with the Roma was required for membership. The resulting Conception of Government Policy Towards Members of the Roma Community Designed to Facilitate Their Social Integration departed somewhat from the Bratinka Report's qualified emphasis on government neutrality in relation to the citizens' ethnocultural identity by defining its goal as the Roma's integration into a "multicultural society." The Conception sets twelve tasks for the government to undertake in the next two decades: the elimination of discrimination, affirmative action (or "positive discrimination"), guaranteed minority individual and group rights, incorporation of Roma culture and history into the general education of all children, education reform to allow Roma children full equality within the system, Roma participation in decision making on Roma community affairs, provision of free legal, social and psychological counseling, education at all schools in tolerance "aimed at building a multicultural society," instruction for judges and those working in the judicial system on issues regarding racism and Roma affairs, research on methods of ethnic coexistence, subsidy of nonprofit groups that offer social education programs to Roma youth, and an employment policy that decreases Roma unemployment while placing more emphasis on "people's positive motivation to work."[125]

While the Conception offered a vision of sweeping reform, the version that was ultimately enacted in June 2000 was "severely weakened."[126] The number of tasks for ministries was significantly reduced, the plan to assist Roma businesses was discarded, and a proposal to establish an Office of Ethnic and Racial Equality with the power to issue legally binding rulings on racial discrimination cases was rejected in favor of an advisory role for the Inter-Ministerial Commission for Romany Community Affairs.[127] A report by the Czech Commissioner on Human Rights indicates that government leaders nonetheless hoped that the new policy would ease tensions with the EU, stating: "It can be expected that the result of this social edification of the hitherto marginalized Romany community and the gradual formation of an emancipated Romany minority will lead to a perceptible fall in Romany migration to European Union countries."[128]

The Conception fell short very quickly in its application. Although it set a December 2000 deadline for a review by eight ministries on the question of how to develop stronger anti-discrimination law, this was missed. The ERRC reported to the UN in mid-2002 that it could not discern any progress in fulfilling this task, attributing this to "the Czech Government's lack of real will to make substantive improvements."[129]

Doubts about the government's "new approach" toward the Roma were enhanced by the December 2000 Conception of the Ministry of Foreign Affairs in Relation to the Romany Problematic, which set out several goals for the Ministry. The first was the "Europeanization" of the Roma "problematic," to be accomplished by promoting the idea that both the problems of the Roma and their solution should be explored in a multinational European context.[130] The second point suggests that the positive measures that the Czech Republic had already taken should be emphasized abroad. Third, criticisms of the country's treatment of the Roma should be rejected; this did not mean "that racism and cases of discrimination do not exist here, but only the rejection of interpretations suggesting that just these phenomena are the fundamental cause" of the problems of Roma coexistence with the "majority society." Fourth and finally, the document pointed to the "distorting description of the Roma problematic exclusively in terms of human rights," as this is only part of the problem, and "not at all a pivotal aspect. The Roma problematic is first and foremost a social problematic." The tone of this document thus clearly differs from that heralded by the government.

More in line with the Conception, however, was Act 273, "On the Rights of Members of National Minorities," passed in July 2001. Its preamble states that Parliament, in passing the act, was "considering the creation of a multicultural society and attempting to facilitate the harmonious coexistence of national minorities with the majority population."[131] In its "definition of basic concepts," it states that "a national minority is a community of citizens of the Czech Republic who live on the territory of the present Czech Republic and as a rule differ from other citizens by their common ethnic origin, language, culture and traditions; they represent a minority of citizens and at the same time they show their will to be considered a national minority for the purpose of common efforts to preserve and develop their own identity, language and culture and at the same time express and preserve interests of their community which has been formed during history."[132] As Vermeersch argues, this "was to some extent a further deviation from the earlier civic principle approach and the modest beginning of an approach of active protection of minority culture in public life, without, however, granting minorities self-government rights or far-reaching cultural autonomy."[133] In an interview, Petr Uhl, an ex-dissident who became chairman of the Interdepartmental Commission on Romany Affairs, told Vermeersch that this new multicultural approach reflected the state's efforts to comply with the Council of Europe's Framework Convention for the Protection of National Minorities.[134]

The state's adoption of the Framework at the end of 1997, in turn, was an implicit precondition for EU membership.[135] Clearly, then, the Czech government's response to the Roma's situation was at least partly driven by repeated expressions of concern from the European Commission.[136] Nevertheless, little progress was made in the years after the Conception's adoption. Human Rights Watch reported that "de facto discrimination against ethnic Roma in the country remained the most disturbing human rights problem in 2001," and was a "major stumbling block" in the state's progress toward EU accession.[137] It particularly noted that police and prosecutors often failed to investigate allegations of violence against the Roma, and also that both the United Nations Human Rights Committee and the U.S. government's Helsinki Commission considered the state's antidiscrimination legislation inadequate. In May 2002, the Czech Helsinki Committee published a report on human rights in the Czech Republic in 2001, in which it observed that between 70,000 and 100,000 Roma had by this point emigrated. It further noted that the reasons for this vast migration reflected the persistence of key problems: racist violence and widespread discrimination in the criminal justice system, public administration, the provision of services, education, employment, and housing. Moreover, the answer to the question of what the émigrés hoped for in their new homes abroad was almost always the same: "a dignified life."[138]

Although the EU noted all these issues, stating in its 2003 assessment that "the problem of discrimination and multifaceted social inclusion remains a source of concern," the Czech Republic met sufficient membership criteria to accede in May 2004.[139] It was nevertheless expected to bring its legislation into line with European antidiscrimination norms. To this end, late that year Parliament passed a new Employment Act (435/2004) that included antidiscrimination provisions, and these have been used to some effect by Roma since. In 2005, a new School Act was also passed, reorganizing most "special schools" into the mainstream education system as "basic practical schools" (though critics note that "as far as desegregation goes, the change has been mostly terminological").[140] A law dealing with discrimination in areas beyond employment, however, remained lacking, and to remedy this, in January 2006 the Czech government under Prime Minister Jiří Paroubek (ČSSD) submitted a comprehensive antidiscrimination bill to the Senate. Introducing it, Vice-Premier Pavel Němec stated, "The anti-discrimination bill reacts to the reality, that instruments for the protection against discrimination in the Czech Republic are not adequate," from "two standpoints." The first was the role of the Charter of Fundamental Rights and Freedoms, which "prohibits discrimination, but the object of discrimination does not have effective legal means of protection." The second centered on the state's commitments to the EU, as the law "averts the possible accusation in the European Court of Justice on the grounds of non-performance of these commitments."[141]

The debate that immediately followed helps illuminate the Czech political elites' perspectives on the state's proper relationship to differences within the citizenry. One of the first to speak was Senator Jaromír Volný (ODS), who reported on the Senate Constitutional Law Committee's reaction to the bill. The Committee found that it "ought to be rejected," for three sets of reasons that Volný described as "political-philosophical." The first had to do with "what the bill discreetly calls positive measures" but which are better known as "positive discrimination." Some on the Committee found that "it would be unacceptable or inappropriate if we were to introduce this into our legal order." Second, the Committee "pointed to badly written text. It gave us the impression that this concerned a slavish translation from a foreign language. . . . For example, it speaks about persons whose quality is superior. This is an entirely impermissible formulation, and is nearly reminiscent of Adolph

Hitler's terminology in his book *Mein Kampf,* where he speaks about inferior people and superior people . . . this simply does not belong in a legal text of this type. And there were more such things. The creation of an upsetting environment—what is an upsetting environment, and what will define it, who will decide, whether the environment is upsetting or not?" The third problem concerned the expansion of the scope of the powers of the Public Defender of Rights (which already existed as an ombudsman position). Volný noted that the "trend toward" expanding the role of "non-state legal and physical persons" in dealing with discrimination was "problematic."[142] He then reiterated the Committee's recommendation to reject the bill.

Volný was followed by Senator Miroslav Škaloud (ODS), who echoed Volný's concerns about "positive discrimination." He further argued that "in the private sphere it is appropriate to forbid those expressions of discrimination which are hateful and which have the appearance of appeals toward aggression against another person, which also is in substantial measure dealt with in the criminal law. All other discrimination in private contacts, in my view, are elements of freedom, that freedom that ensures for us high productivity, living standards and a secure, stable society. I think that the basis of the private sphere is precisely decision-making about with whom one associates and with whom one does not, with whom one has contact and with whom one does not, with whom one makes agreements and with whom one does not. This decision-making always introduces some kind of discrimination and is based on it." He continued, "Questions may arise, whether I would have the freedom to establish a club whose members would, for instance, be only men. Or would a private school have the freedom to decide that its pupils would only be girls. Or would purely Roma firms have the freedom not to employ people that are not Roma. Or would a private Jewish high school have the freedom to accept as its pupils only children of Jewish families. I could go on for ages." In addition, Škaloud argued that the bill did not make clear "what rights and obligations the citizen has and who and what methods are obliged to fulfill them." Altogether, he found that the bill was full of "indeterminate and unclear concepts" and "interpretational problems."[143]

Next to speak was Senator (and Professor of English and American Literature) Josef Jařab. In contrast to the preceding speakers, he described the bill as concerning not just the "approach of civilized Europe," but "the approach of the civilized world. This concerns the protection of individuals. I repeat, the protection of every individual, and not groups, and the possibility of a civil law route to find redress. And this is important and crucial. It is not true that this law would introduce some kind of positive discrimination." Moreover, he responded to those who considered the bill "another diktat from Europe" by pointing out that it drew most fundamentally from the Anglo-Saxon conception of rights, which first underlay the mid-1960s United States civil rights legislation, and then the British law on racial equality. This conception had then spread to Western Europe, and then to post-communist Europe.[144] Jařab thus called on the Senate to pass the bill.

Ultimately, the critical voices—who particularly stressed the issue of positive discrimination and argued that the law was unnecessary—won out,[145] and the bill was defeated by a vote of 39 to 27. In July 2007, the United Nations Human Rights Committee stated in its final conclusions and recommendations on the report from the Czech Republic that it "regretted that no anti-discrimination bill had been adopted and that discrimination against Roma continued to persist despite relevant programmes."[146] As Vermeersch argues, then, it is important not "to overestimate the impact of the pressure exerted by the EU" in shaping minority policy.[147]

The EU nevertheless continued to push the Czech Republic on the issue, and in late 2007, the government proposed a framework antidiscrimination law covering numerous categories (including race, nationality, gender, age, religion, sexual orientation, and disability) and areas of societal life (including education, employment, housing, and social services). As with the previous bill, it was contentious; this time, the Social Democrats criticized it for being too narrow and weak and the Communists called for it to include status in the former regime as a category protected against discrimination (which would, in turn, prohibit lustration).[148] After much debate, Parliament passed it.

President Klaus, however, vetoed it. In a letter to the chairman of the Chamber of Deputies explaining this decision, he wrote, "I consider the law to be useless, counterproductive and of poor quality and its repercussions to be very problematic."[149] Delving into his reasoning, he noted that the things covered in the law were mostly already covered by "existing legal norms," including the Charter of Fundamental Rights and Freedoms and other "concrete laws and special provisions." There was, therefore, no need for a "some kind of new 'umbrella' law" that would have a status similar to the Charter, in that it would stand as superior to other legal norms. He also argued that the "law's philosophy contradicts the fact that every person has a completely unique set of inborn and learned abilities, qualities, and qualifications. . . . It is not only bad, it is dangerous. The idea that any law will bring a socially engineered state of equality is—fortunately—false." In addition, Klaus criticized the law for placing the burden of proof on the accused. Particularly interestingly, Klaus closed the letter with this paragraph:

The extraordinariness and peculiarity of this law is also demonstrated in that the Senate, although it approved the law, accepted an unprecedented accompanying resolution with the following wording: "The Senate considers the anti-discrimination law as a tool for the implementation of requirements resulting from European law, whose nonimplementation threatens the Czech Republic with sanctions. It does not, however, identify with the character of the norms that in an artificial way encroach upon the natural development of society, do not respect the cultural differences of member states, and put the requirement of the equality of outcome above the principle of free choice. The Senate requests that the government would not consent to the adoption of further anti-discrimination regulations according to EU standards." These Senate arguments only strengthen my conviction that I cannot sign this law and must return it to the Chamber of Deputies. I believe that the Chamber of Deputies will deal seriously with these arguments and that it will prevent our legal order from being expanded by this inescapably bad law.

At the time of this writing (mid-2008), then, the Czech Republic remains the only EU state, of 27, that has not passed the required antidiscrimination legislation.

Since accession, some government leaders have also made public statements sharply rejecting the project of creating a multicultural society, which had become a refrain under the Zeman government (1998–2002). In July 2005, shortly after the London terrorist train and bus bombings, President Klaus stated in an interview to *Mladá fronta dnes*, "I am convinced that the common ideology of multiculturalism, which is an anti-liberal ideology, is extremely collectivistic and group-oriented, is profoundly mistaken. It is a tragic mistake of contemporary Western civilization," with a high cost: "In this I do not look for an explanation of the London killings. But who caused the inhumane monstrosities of the communist regime – the interrogator in a Stalinist jail in southern Moravia, or Karl Marx, who pushed that ideology on which everything was built? From Marx to the torturing interrogator is a seemingly long distance, but he was a forefather. From the same grounds the idea of multiculturalism and its various gurus are the origins of all such activity."[150] This interview caused a fair amount of controversy: Prime Minister Jiří Paroubek (ČSSD) expressed puzzlement, and Deputy Prime Minister Zdeněk Škromach (ČSSD) called Klaus's comments nonsense, especially as they regarded his wariness about large-scale immigration.[151] ODS Chairman Mirek Topolánek, however, voiced support for Klaus's view.

A little over a year later, in August 2006, Topolánek himself became prime minister, and in April 2007 made a speech on the Occasion of the Opening of the European Year of Equal Opportunities. This year, he said, concerned individuals, not groups, as "freedom is always based on individuals. You did not misunderstand what was said: I really said freedom, not equality. Because freedom is the basic value and all other values are derived from it." Equal opportunities, he declared, cannot be secured by positive discrimination, which he called a "contradiction in terms," observing that the phrase "sounds like a pleasant drubbing." Further, he argued that "it is important for the educational system to contribute to [the] cohesiveness of society and not to exclude different groups—ethnical and religious—into cultural ghettoes. On the contrary, the educational system must serve for assimilation, for [the] ability of minorities to fully integrate themselves into [the] majority society, into society of law and clear rules. Multiculturalism is a source of poignant inequalities and tension."[152] Toward the end of the speech he reemphasized this point, noting that regardless of whether the group is Roma, some other nationality, or Muslim, "inability to integrate any cultural minority causes problems and leads to the situation where these groups will never reach equal opportunities. Financial means that are spent by the state in this sphere must be spent for assimilation of individuals, not for a support of a chimera of multiculturalism."

Based on the above overview of government positions and perspectives, I find that the civic principle has been given four main, broad official interpretations in the post-communist Czech Republic. All hold the sovereign community as encompassing the entire citizenry but have different understandings of the resulting political authority. The first, espoused most prominently by Klaus, strongly emphasizes the centrality of the rights-bearing, abstract individual and the need for strict state neutrality in relation to pre-political identities in order to maximize individual autonomy. It allows for minority rights as included in the Charter of Fundamental Rights and Freedoms, but, again, emphasizes that these rights belong to individuals who freely choose to self-identify in particular ways. This political-philosophical orientation also clearly informed the Senate Constitutional Law Committee's 2006 rejection of the comprehensive anti-discrimination bill. It notably elevates the "free" in "free and equal," and in this sense, the society-wide scope of individual liberty is enhanced (though potentially to the detriment of equality, depending on how one conceptualizes it).

A second interpretation of the civic principle's implications can be found in the Bratinka Report, which while sharing with the first the view that the principle requires full autonomy for the individual to identify (or not) with any group, it does not see this as precluding group-specific measures where they respond to serious socioeconomic inequalities based on "initial disadvantages." This approach, then, puts more stress on state promotion of equality, and somewhat less on the circumscription of the state's authority in order to secure individual freedom.

The third interpretation is that of the Zeman government, as developed in the 2000 Conception on the Roma situation and the minority rights law, which holds the civic principle as compatible with a "multicultural" approach that actively encourages minority identity and uses "positive discrimination" to promote equality (and does not see this as a "privilege"). The stress on individual autonomy is much less pronounced.

The fourth interpretation, reflected in President Topolánek's 2007 speech on equal opportunities, has similar underpinnings to those of the first, in that it also places higher value on individual freedom than equality, arguing that the former is a precondition for the latter. This view does not however, make the same claim to strict state cultural neutrality, but instead straightforwardly demands that minorities assimilate into the majority culture. It also rejects "positive discrimination" that would in any sense favor or single out minority groups. Here, then, the sovereign community is not composed of abstract individuals, but is a culturally specific collectivity.

All four of these orientations have roots in Czech political culture. The emphasis on civic equality and individual rights can be traced back to such prominent political leaders as Havlíček, through Masaryk, to many Prague Spring reformers, and ultimately to the Normalization-era dissidents and internal exiles who went on to become key post-Communist elites. Likewise, the view that ethnocultural identity is politically relevant and deserving of state support can be traced back to Palacký, through Masaryk (who, again, sought to harmonize the universal and particular) and onward in each Czechoslovak state's embracing of the ethnic principle of sovereignty. There are also clear tensions between the four post-Communist interpretations, as they reflect different prioritizations of freedom and equality (both, of course, central to the civic principle).

These contemporary official interpretations of the civic principle have also been influenced by recent international developments. First and foremost, EU conditionality (along with numerous NGOs and the U.S. government) strongly pressured the Czech Republic to actively improve the Roma's situation. Thus, the shift (mostly after 1997) in Czech government policy toward a stronger engagement with problems facing the Roma, including "positive discrimination" and other measures designed to raise the Roma's position in society, quite clearly reflects this outside pressure, though it certainly had some domestic support as well. That said, that many Czech leaders found repeated EU demands (echoed by the U.S.) for stronger antidiscrimination legislation illegitimate (recall the senators' references to "diktats" from Europe and "slavish translations" of foreign documents) and ultimately *have not complied* with this accession requirement shows an important and rather striking limit on the elasticity of the governing Czech interpretation of the civic principle's requirements. A second international influence is the post-September 11 political climate, especially in Europe, as societies reassess their relationships with different cultural communities. In particular, in the Czech Republic (as in other European states), multiculturalism as a model has come under scrutiny in the context of the "war on terror" and increased tensions between the majority and the Czech Muslim population.

Interpretations of the civic principle have, then, proved to have some elasticity with regard to Gabal's first three dimensions. In particular, those that emphasize the importance of state neutrality and individual autonomy would seem to have the potential to undermine minority membership on dimension 3, having to do with the state support for the full development of minority culture. Some such support has, however, been forthcoming. Topolánek's assimilation approach is also in strong tension with the civic principle, as it appears to endorse an illiberal understanding of extent of ethnocultural conformity required for full participation in the society and a deep hostility to minority cultural development. The "thickness" of the societal culture he envisions is, however, unclear, and in any case the state has not pursued this type of policy. Rather, the most serious violations of civic equality have occurred within dimensions 1 and 2, and certain government perspectives have contributed to them. By rigidly emphasizing the need for state neutrality, the early Klausian approach allowed discriminatory and persecutory behavior fostered by widespread popular prejudices to be ignored or overlooked. This happened, for example, with the effects of the citizenship law, and thereafter with the general lack of focused concern on violence and discrimination against

Roma during the mid-1990s. Also deeply problematic is the view, shared by a significant number of Czech leaders, that the civic principle does not require more substantial implementing legislation than currently exists; they claim that discrimination is both legally well defined and sufficiently actionable to consistently and effectively address the issues discussed in this chapter. Leaving aside the question of the specific merits of the rejected framework laws (which do raise contentious "gray area" issues), this claim has been very strongly disputed by numerous domestic and international sources.

I would further argue that *none* of the above interpretations of the civic principle are *principally* responsible for the very serious violations of Roma civic equality surveyed here. The insufficient protection from violent persecution, the targeting of local government laws and policies against them, and the discrimination in employment, the judicial system, public education, and access to public spaces are not justified, and are incompatible, not only with the Constitution (and especially the Charter of Rights and Freedoms) but also with all of the above interpretations of the civic principle. The lack of comprehensive antidiscrimination legislation exacerbates this situation, but the argument against such legislation centers on an argument not that discrimination of the kind regularly directed against the Roma is permissible, but rather that sufficient protection against it already exists. Given, then, that widespread discrimination does not flow from any official interpretation of the civic principle, it is worth exploring broader societal attitudes concerning the Roma, to see whether norms or views contrary to the civic principle—which could fuel resistance to it—are widely shared.

Popular Views of the Roma Minority Relationship to the Majority Society

The Public Opinion Research Centre (Centrum pro výzkum veřejného mínění, CVVM), has done extensive polling on the Czech public's appraisal of the Roma situation and their relationship to the rest of society. The results tend to show high negatives on both counts. For example, one poll, conducted eight times between 1997 and 2008, asked Czech citizens to rate the "coexistence of Roma and non-Roma populations" on a scale from very bad to very good. The 1997 poll found 81 percent of respondents characterizing it as somewhat or very bad; in 2008, 79 percent characterized it the same way. Things seemed improved in 1999, 2001, and 2006 when negative appraisals went down to 66, 68, and 69 percent respectively, but most years they have been around 78 percent.[153] Interestingly, when respondents were asked about coexistence with Roma in the place where they live, views were less negative than those concerning the entire country, and more evenly divided: in 1998, 48 percent said good and 49 percent said bad; in 1999, the split was 52 percent good, 42 percent bad; in 2001, 43 percent fell on each side, and in 2003, 48 percent said good and 51 percent said bad.[154]

The CVVM has also conducted numerous polls asking for respondents' views on the majority society's relationships with various groups living in the Czech Republic, including the Roma. Polls conducted between 1991 and 2001 concerning relations with several nationalities found that respondents consistently rated the relationship with the Roma as the most negative, and usually substantially worse than that with other relatively unpopular groups—notably Vietnamese, citizens from the Balkans, and citizens from the former Soviet Union (this last was the only group to come close to rivaling the Roma, for a few years around the turn of the century).[155] In a 2006 version of the poll, only 9.4 percent rated the relationship with the Roma as good or very good.[156] (It is also worth noting in the larger context of this study that since 1991 respondents have consistently seen their most positive relationship in the country as being with the Slovaks!)

Roma scored similar rankings in polls asking respondents about who they would *not* want to have as a neighbor: in 1992, 90 percent placed Roma in this category,[157] and in 2003, 79 percent said the same, with only "heavy alcoholics" (86 percent) and drug users (85 percent) rated as less desirable. Slightly more welcome than Roma were "people with a criminal past" (78 percent undesirable), followed distantly by homosexuals (42 percent).[158] These findings paralleled answers to a survey question asked several times since 1995 about whether people in the Czech Republic are "tolerant" toward certain groups. Roma always ranked last, as the least tolerated group, until in 2003 the survey began to include drug users, alcoholics, and people with a criminal past; in 2003, the Roma came in second-to-last, tied with people with a criminal past, and in 2005, tied for the same position with drug users—though, notably, with their highest percentage ever of respondents (36 percent, up significantly from the lowest level, 13 percent, in 1995) seeing them as being viewed tolerantly.[159] In the 2007 and 2008 versions of this survey, Roma were no longer in the list of groups about whom respondents were asked.

Surveys conducted since 1997 also investigated whether respondents think that the Roma face "worse conditions" than other members of society. Well over 50 percent of respondents consistently stated that they thought Roma had worse chances for employment. Lower percentages (ranging from a third to about half) thought that Roma face worse conditions in public and civic life. Generally still fewer respondents stated that Roma had more problems than the rest of society with obtaining qualification (around a third), housing (a third to a quarter), and education (roughly a quarter). The respondents have also consistently identified the Roma's best prospects (or least inferior conditions) in the development of their own culture, followed by the safeguarding of their personal security.

The surveys on "coexistence" also asked respondents open questions about how relations can be improved, looking separately at what the non-Roma and Roma populations might do. The researchers then categorized the most frequently given answers. In 2007 and 2008, the category capturing the highest percentage of answers (22 and 27 percent respectively) concerning what the non-Roma could do stressed "tolerance" and a nonprejudiced approach.[160] The second most often given answer was "do not know" (16 percent and 14 percent). Third in 2007 came "nothing" (12 percent), followed by "equality of rights, non-discrimination, no favoritism, not making distinctions" (7 percent). In 2008, this latter answer concerning equality came third (9 percent), followed by "it depends on the Roma, we already do enough" (7 percent). With regard to respondents' views on "what the Roma population could do to contribute to improving mutual coexistence," the number one answer in 2007 was "adapt to the norms of the majority society" (21 percent). This was followed by "respectable behavior, order" (18 percent), "work" (17 percent), and "educate themselves" (9 percent). The following year, the most popular answer-categories were "bid for employment/work" (20 percent), "adapt to the norms of the majority society" (19 percent), "respectable behavior, improve morality" (13 percent), and "abide by the laws, decrease criminality" (11 percent). As a final note on poll results, the U.S. State Department *Report on Human Rights Practices in the Czech Republic: 2006* observed that in a STEM agency poll that May, over 75 percent of respondents thought that the government "should *not* give more attention to the rights of the Roma minority" (my emphasis).[161]

These opinion polls make several things clear: many people (indeed, a strong majority, if the samples accurately reflect the broader population) see the Roma's relationship with the rest of society as negative—indeed, worse than that with any other minority ethnic group as well as most groups regarded as somehow different from the majority—and would not like to have one as a neighbor; some (though far from all) see Roma as disadvantaged in at least some ways (especially in employment); and many think that certain shifts or changes in values and behavior on both sides would improve the relationship. While rich and in many ways illuminating, this polling evidence, even all taken together, clearly does not in itself constitute a full explanation for the widespread denial of Roma equality along Gabal's first two dimensions. They are pieces of orientations and perspectives, and the relationships between the various elements are not clear-cut; they are, in other words, not articulated political-philosophical positions. The polling data can contribute significantly to explaining Czech behavior toward the Roma, however, when examined in the context of the broader societal conversation on the principles that *do* and/or *should* govern the political community's relationship to Roma. This conversation (often a debate) helps flesh out some of the normative frameworks and reasoning in which the above opinions are situated and, in some case, activated. In turn, the polls also give some sense of how broadly shared particular views voiced in the popular discourse actually are.

During the first years after the Velvet Revolution, the media did not heavily cover issues concerning the Roma,[162] but there was some discussion in the lead-up to the Velvet Divorce as tensions between Roma and ethnic Czech communities rose. One article from this period was published by sociologists Kazimír Večerka and Markéta Štechová and titled "On our Racism." Taking a critical look at the relationship between the majority and the Roma, they observed, "we for the time being allow every sort of shabbiness towards one another reciprocally." They acknowledged that the Roma had higher rates of criminality and social pathology than the majority, but argued that the "aversion toward the Roma is not conditioned merely on their greater criminality. Along with this is the fact that people often do not like that they live differently, enjoy themselves differently, look different, talk differently. . . . Here exactly are the roots of our racism." This combined with the Roma's social problems to poison relations between the two groups. The authors also pointed to research showing that a portion of the citizenry "has the tendency to substitute individual responsibility of the citizen for their behavior with the collective responsibility of the Roma." The authors thus concluded by arguing that it would be necessary to teach the citizenry, and especially the young, to accept "the general democratic principle of the equality of *every* citizen before the law" (emphasis original). In addition, they noted that "criminal justice must acknowledge only the offender—the citizen, and must leave aside all of his further attributes which are not referred to in the criminal law (nationality, race, religion, wealth, etc.)."[163]

Not all analysts called for civic equality and state neutrality, however. In a 1994 *Mladá fronta dnes* article, titled "Roma and Czechs—the Clash of Two Levels of Civilization," Sora Šárovcová responded to a question in the magazine *Dnes*, which had asked readers whether they would want to live in a house with Roma. Referring to her own experiences, Šárovcová predicted that Czechs who did so "would be systematically stripped of their resistance to filth, vandals, hooligans, and so on, in order to manage to get to the level of irregular citizens."[164] As a better alternative, Šárovcová suggested that Roma be lifted to the "higher civilizational level of the Czechs" by being forced into orderliness and good hygiene. The idea of the "irregular citizen" contrasts rather starkly with Věrska and Štechová's emphasis on civic equality.

By December 1995, what had been a peripheral issue began to receive more attention, as Czech policies were subjected to increasing international scrutiny. Responding to the charge that "Czechs are the most racist nation in Europe," Michal Šestak wrote an article titled "The Negative Relationship with the Roma Has Objective Reasons." Here, he took issue with "pseudo-humanists," a term that would be invoked with increasing regularity to refer to those who, in the view of some, promoted an ideologically blinkered, overly tolerant view of the Roma and their rights. According to Šestak, "the laws of a democratic state apply in the same way to every citizen. If some group in the society (in this case the Roma) breaks the laws considerably more often than other groups, it must necessarily count on the displeasure of the rest. To the extent that Roma want to change their status, the change must first of all start among themselves."[165]

In 1996, the debate was further enlivened by an appearance by Miroslav Macek (ODS) on the Television Nova program *Sedmička*, in which he railed against "pseudo-humanism." In response, Ján Jařab, a member of the executive council of HOST, published an article in *Mladá fronta dnes* titled "Roma, Racists, and We Pseudo-Humanists," writing: "The claim that the same laws are valid for everyone is beyond dispute—and Miroslav Macek can be assured that it is just this that all defenders of civil rights push for in practice. Somewhat curious, however, is the view that 'under pressure of clear pseudo-humanism, fear is already rising of calling things by their true names, so as to avoid being accused of racism.'"[166] Jařab then related Macek's statement that he would be apprehensive about saying anything if a drunken Rom pushed into him on a bus, for fear of being called a racist. Jařab responded that he had never heard anyone claim that "to protest against hooligans could be a manifestation of racism." He continued: "If we had time to keep track of such banal demonstrations as common jostling and insults in buses, everything in our republic would be completely fine. Our daily bread is unfortunately the violent attacks by skinheads, which often have the character of organized pogroms, or attempts toward systematic discrimination against certain individuals only because of their membership in a certain ethnic group. In exactly this lies the root of the struggle for the law's validity for everyone equally." He also pointed out that, in keeping with Macek's desire to call things by their true name, most Roma criminality is petty and amounts to a great deal less thievery than that committed by the Czech Republic's corrupt bankers.

Responding to Jařab's critique of Macek, Martin Schmarcz published an essay titled "On the Heels of Pseudo-Humanism Marches Sládek" (referring to Miroslav Sládek, the leader of the virulently anti-Roma, extreme right-wing Republican Party; its biggest electoral success brought it 8 percent of the 1996 Chamber of Deputies vote; it has not since passed the 5 percent threshold). Schmarcz argued that the "overwhelming majority of people refuse to have Roma as neighbors (already far beyond Jews or blacks) not only because of the color of their skin, but more because of their entirely different cultural habits."[167] While their "bad reputation" cannot "in the sense of the presumption of guilt apply to every Rom," as long as the pseudo-humanists "hold the prejudice that observation of Roma criminality and pertinent analysis of the misuse of social welfare smacks of racism, a discriminating approach is not possible." Thus, Schmarcz argued, "this dangerous pseudo-humanism, about which Macek spoke, is rooted in a situation where otherwise logically behaving people who defend their lifestyle, possessions, or health may be, to the extent the consequences affect Roma, uncompromisingly and also fully insensitively criticized as racist." He continued,

> Let us look at a current popular problem. It frequently happens, is almost fashionable, to prosecute restaurants that prohibited entry into their establishments to Roma rowdies who had repeatedly "plundered" the bar, which police did not manage to prevent. It is difficult to reproach the bartenders that decided to defend themselves . . . of course, anyone can stand up to [the Roma] and still end up behind bars. The accusation threatens even mayors who, on the basis of noncompliance with basic hygienic regulations against hepatitis epidemics, prohibited entrance to the swimming pool to Roma children, who constituted

the overwhelming majority of those infected. (Strangely, no one laid blame on him when he prohibited the Roma children from entry into the school for the same reason.) The mayor's order had a definite racial impact—as did, for that matter, hepatitis on account of irresponsible Roma—hardly, however, a racial motivation.

He concluded by arguing that, "when people are not certain that they can, without fear of incarceration, come out against everyone who interferes with orderly life, and this without regard to skin color, racism definitely will not be eradicated. Rather the contrary. And to the extent that democratic parties would be afraid, in order that they would not be accused of racism, to call things by their rightful name, there could be no other outcome than the intensified preference for the Republicans."

Schmarcz's analysis in turn prompted a response from Marie Vodičková, the Chairwoman of the Fund for Children at Risk.[168] Titled "On Tolerance, Racism, and Pseudo-Humanism," Vodičková's piece pointed to evidence provided by film director Ljuba Václavová, who went to a number of nearly empty restaurants with her crew and five Roma "who definitely were not rowdy" and videotaped the repeated refusals of service.[169] According to Vodičková, this kind of "demonstration of racial intolerance" should be considered a "punishable act. Otherwise we could soon await the time when in stores, trams, at the doctor, and even at the office will hang the notice 'Roma prohibited to enter.'"

The specific controversy over "pseudo-humanism" eventually died down, but as the century turned and the state moved closer to EU membership, Czechs continued to struggle with the question of how the state should deal with group differences in what was increasingly termed a "multicultural" environment.[170] For example, in a piece titled, "The Civic Principle and Minorities," lawyer Petr Partyk argued that "every citizen has his individual rights, every citizen is equal. Apart from this the state must guarantee the protection of collective minority rights" by providing funds for culture and "other projects for minorities" which in a "completely liberal market setting" might be overrun by the mass culture of the majority, "and the minority would be condemned to assimilation."[171] As for the relationship between the Czechs and the Roma, he wrote, "I believe that the Roma are also Czechs, that they form an ethnic minority within the Czech nation. I would also say . . . that the Roma are a subset of the Czech set. From the standpoint of citizenship every citizen in the Czech republic is equal. Factually, individual and group differences exist. In particular, it perhaps depends first and foremost on the Roma themselves, who they wish to be. Whether completely Czech with all cultural and linguistic attributes, or members of the Czech nation as well as the Roma ethnic group at the same time, or citizens of the Czech Republic and Roma, who do not adopt Czech nationality. No one may pressure another to assimilate, but also no one may prevent someone from assimilating, as long as they decide to do it voluntarily."

Writing in 2003, Charles University Professor of legal philosophy and sociology Jiří Přibáň similarly stressed individual autonomy, but reached quite different conclusions about its implications for state policy: "Cultural identity in a democratic rule of law state may not be promoted by laws, because it is a very dynamic and fluid area of the life of modern society, in which the individual as a citizen has to have absolute freedom to make decisions. Various cultural identities may be developed freely within the institutional boundaries of civil society, and not through the coercive apparatus of the rule of law."[172] He further argued that "modern European democracy" had been shaped by both "nationalist culture and the civic principle. This polarity is also typical of Czech political history." Masaryk, in particular, had worked hard to elevate the civic element and diminish nationalism, as the "civic principle simultaneously conquers cultural collectivism and establishes its own liberal democratic political culture and tradition." It frees one from the strictures of "collective identity, because individual freedom and autonomy form its normative foundation." Přibáň thus called for an emphasis on the civic principle in the state's increasingly "multicultural situation."

This brief overview of the post-communist societal conversation on the Roma thus shows that it concerned all three of first three of Gabal's dimensions of minority membership—violent discrimination, nonviolent discrimination, and state support for equal cultural development. This last dimension was particularly relevant to the more recent discussion about multiculturalism. It is also less pressing than the first two, partly because the state has been relatively supportive of minority cultural development, and partly because such development's worth is diminished in an environment of pervasive discrimination in other crucial areas of life. It is, moreover, the issue of discrimination that has proved most contentious, and where the question of the civic principle's role in broader societal life is central. It is thus worth further unpacking the arguments in the two sides in this part of the debate.

To begin, neither side explicitly rejects the civic principle. One position (broadly construed) has, however, been quite critical of its invocation by the central government, human rights NGOs, and international sources in response to anti-Roma discrimination. Advocates of this perspective tend to focus on real problems faced by Czech communities: hepatitis outbreaks, squatting and overcrowding in apartments, rent and utility payment arrears, and noisy and disruptive behavior (by majority standards) in some neighborhoods. They argue that if many members of a particular group violate the majority society's norms in such ways, then that group will face repercussions—including the broader community looking at the group with "displeasure" (to use Šestak's term) and collective exclusion from certain public spaces.

These repercussions can be divided into two categories. The first involves a judgment about the group, whereby socially undesirable orientations and behaviors (at least in the majority view) of some members are seen as characteristic of all members. This is, in essence, the foundation of prejudice, and if the opinion polls are representative, it appears to be widespread against the Roma. Indeed, considering an entire ethnic group to be roughly as unwelcome as neighbors as hard alcoholics, drug users, and people with a criminal past certainly indicates hostility and judgment based on collective ethnic identity, rather than on an individual basis. Still, while ethnic prejudice clearly violates the spirit of the civic principle, it is an internal orientation—unfortunate, but beyond the scope of the liberal state's authority to control, even if it attempts to persuade people otherwise.

The second repercussion is the collective exclusion of Roma from public places and state measures directed at them. This, of course, constitutes discrimination. Discrimination may (and likely often does) stem from prejudice, but is also important to distinguish the two: it is one thing to find members of a certain group undesirable as neighbors, and another to prevent them from choosing where to live on the same terms as other members of society. As those who strongly defend Roma civic equality argue, the latter (and any other negative discrimination, violent or nonviolent, based on ethnonational identity) directly violates the civic principle and is entirely impermissible in a political community based on the "free and equal citizen." This, then, is the crux of the other side in the debate. Interestingly, however, the opinion polls showed little emphasis on equal rights and nondiscrimination as the preferred majority response to the Roma situation.

Both broad positions in the debate have strong roots in Czech political culture. Those who emphasize civic equality share in the long-standing traditions in which government leaders also based their views. The position critical of this view of civic equality is likewise of long standing, reflecting societal and governmental animosity toward the Roma and their culture that goes back centuries. (Within the recent past, the Communist government strongly pressured the Roma to assimilate and discriminated against them in education policy and other ways, including a campaign of forced sterilization of Roma women.) This position also employs an understanding of ethnic community as natural, unique, and playing a defining role in the identity of its members. Indeed, Havel expresses this view in his 1990 speech at the Roma festival (discussed above), when he observed that "in the world live a great many different races, nations, ethnic groups, tribes. The differ in their history, their beliefs, their traditions, their social habits, at times they differ even in their way of thinking, behavior, and temperament."[173] This view is characteristic of much Czech national thought from the nineteenth century onward and was an integral element in the definitions of national rights (for example, as a reason why nations have the right to sovereignty). Havel continued by stressing that "all are, however, people, are equal before God, and are not as individuals responsible for their [group's] good or bad deeds." This is a vital aspect of Havel's perspective, but it is also clear that one may agree with his description of group difference without accepting the accompanying moral caveat—as, for example, Third Republic leaders did when making deeply negative collective judgments about Sudeten Germans. The traditional view of ethnonational community can thus support both liberal and illiberal interpretations, and the tendency toward the latter was likely bolstered by the Communist regime's hostility to the notion of the individual as the primary rights-bearing entity.

The evidence is unambiguous, then, that the citizenry in the Czech Republic is not a community bonded exclusively by shared, rational political principles put forward in its constitution and laws. This then raises the question of whether the criticisms of the civic/ethnic dichotomy in the theoretical literature are borne out in the Czech case, and I turn to it now.

Conclusion

According to Kymlicka and Smith, in multiethnic states the societal dominance of some aspects of the majority's cultural identity is practically inevitable. In the Czech Republic, the Czech language and culture are clearly dominant, but broadly speaking, the violations of the Roma's civic equality do not stem from illiberal nation-building of the kind Kymlicka describes (such as strong restrictions on minority language usage) or broader limitations on cultural development central to Gabal's dimension 3. Bernard Yack offers a somewhat different critique of the dichotomy, emphasizing the extent to which norms and identities, regardless whether they stress political or ethnic values, are "culturally inherited" rather than rationally chosen by the citizens. The Czech case is perhaps not the best for testing this theory, as in the transitional post-Communist period the political community has engaged, precisely, in choosing its governing norms and defining its identity—which, of course, has also involved direct grappling with longer-standing norms and identities.

It is, however, this process in the Czech case that highlights one critical reason why a state based on the civic principle may fail to secure civic equality: there may be profound dissonance between official and dominant (or at least widely shared) political-cultural norms. When this is the case, then an element that Habermas argues is necessary for bonding the community of citizens is missing, that its core principles must be "enduringly linked with the motivations and convictions of the citizens" and thereby provide the crucial "motivational anchoring" for building and sustaining an association of free and equal individuals. In essence, the citizens must accept the principles as legitimate. If they do not, in the absence of strong state coercion, compliance becomes very problematic, since understandings of nationhood are not highly malleable (a conclusion here supported, again, not only by popular resistance to official norms, but also by government resistance to EU norms). Compliance is further complicated if some state authorities share the popular rejection or ambivalence, as well as if insufficient implementing legislation exists or leaders interpret the civic principle as requiring state neutrality such that discriminatory behavior in the citizenry is shielded from scrutiny or punishment.

Clearly, then, a civic definition of sovereignty in a state's constitution is far from sufficient to produce a community bonded by citizenship and committed to freedom and equality for all, regardless of pre-political identity. Indeed, it has not even secured the most basic protections of citizenship for an unpopular minority, resulting in the radical diminishment of its members' individual rights and membership. As in the Slovak case, the governmental and legal interpretations of the principle (the latter, here, notably lacking), international pressure, and the broader normative orientation of the population have all proven important in shaping how principle affects—or is violated by—practice. When the Czech and Slovak cases are placed side by side, then, they certainly contradict conceptualizations that hold the civic and ethnic principles as producing essentially opposite regimes, one ethnically neutral and the other ethnically exclusive. That said, the final question for this study remains: does the civic model's failure, in this case, to secure civic equality mean that its practical implications *do not differ significantly* from those of the ethnic model, as some stronger critics of the conceptual dichotomy hold? My concluding chapter explores this by comparing the two cases.

Conclusion

My findings have important implications for the theoretical debates over the nature of normative understandings of nationhood and the legitimacy of the civic/ethnic dichotomy. Beginning with the first, my examination of Czech and Slovak understandings of nationhood from the nineteenth century to the early twenty-first offers strong evidence that while they owed much to the individuals who defined their political-philosophical foundations, once broadly accepted, they were *not* particularly malleable. Rather, key elements proved resilient, contributing to frameworks for political judgment about the source and exercise of legitimate political authority. While authoritarian state leaders were able to secure compliance with official regime norms at odds with these understandings (and it is important not to minimize this), each period of freedom heralded an assertive return to orientations with long-standing political-cultural roots. The continuities over the course of dramatically different twentieth-century regimes thus challenge theories that see such norms as highly susceptible to elite manipulation. Likewise, socioeconomic development and equalization, which was substantial over the period covered here, did not markedly draw the Czech and Slovak understandings closer together. Indeed, at each historical stage in this investigation, I found no evidence that material interests were the *primary* factors driving Czechs and Slovaks to adopt or identify with particular understandings of nationhood, and the cumulative evidence of continuity further undermines materialist explanations. Rather, these norms are akin to the politics of citizenship that Rogers Brubaker describes: "The politics of citizenship is first and foremost a politics of nationhood. As such, it is a *politics of identity*, not a *politics of interests* (in the restricted, materialist sense). It pivots more on self-understanding than on self-interest. The 'interests' informing the politics of citizenship are 'ideal' rather than material. The central question is not 'who *gets* what?' but rather 'who *is* what?' "[1]

This study thus offers strong evidence of the need to view post-Communist understandings of nationhood in relation to their political-cultural and historical contexts. Analyses that ignore or undervalue this context will likely overemphasize the importance of situational factors, particularly having to do with the power-political ambitions of elites and material interests of the broader public, and thereby misunderstand the deeper roots of these norms' substance and enduring appeal. This can have very serious consequences, especially if such misunderstanding forms the basis for policy. As Kymlicka argued in 1998, "there are many people in ECE [East Central European] countries today who argue that ethnic conflicts are really just a substitute for, or displacement of, conflicts over incomplete democratization and inadequate economic development, and that we should therefore ignore the demands of ethnocultural groups and focus all our energies on the 'real' problem . . . since these demands will fade once real democracy, economic development and the rule of law are established. . . . This denial or denigration of the seriousness of ethnocultural identities is precisely the mistake which Western democracies have made again and again, often with terrible consequences. It is a mistake which I hope the ECE countries will not repeat."[2]

These issues have taken on a more strongly international dimension with the accession of the East-Central European states to EU membership. In particular, resilient understandings of nationhood have inhibited the smooth integration of the Czech and Slovak Republics into the legal frameworks the EU requires of its new members: many Czech leaders barely contained their contempt for EU-inspired antidiscrimination legislation, and the HZDS and SNS reacted even more hostilely to the minority language law in Slovakia. Fico also refused to let condemnation by the Party of European Socialists sway him from his strong relationship with the SNS or his increasingly nationalist orientation. While observers have noted that EU conditionality during the accession process made some difference for candidate countries' minority policies, now that they are members, there is no reason to assume that democratically accountable Czech and Slovak elites in Prague and Bratislava, let alone their constituencies, will prove more amenable to dictates from Brussels than, for example, Slovak autonomists were in response to those issued from

Prague, which had more coercive means at its disposal. Evidence of normative resilience also has implications beyond the immediate region, as it further substantiates arguments that outside states impose "regime change" on societies with inhospitable political cultures at their peril.

Turning to the second theoretical debate with which this study engages, concerning the specific implications of the civic and ethnic definitions of sovereignty for minority membership and individual rights, evidence offered in the preceding two chapters makes clear that ethnicity has remained relevant at the level of political practice in both the Czech and Slovak Republics, despite the Czech claim to neutrality. This has, moreover, been detrimental to minority membership and individual rights (at least of minority citizens) in both cases. These findings strongly support critiques pointing to exactly such problems.

Not yet addressed, however, is the question whether these findings support the argument that the civic/ethnic dichotomy is ultimately invalid because governance based on one does not differ significantly from the other. Here, my evidence shows that the actual treatment of minorities *has* differed in the two cases. In Slovakia, the state-sponsored "societal culture" has circumscribed the ethnic Hungarians' ability to sustain and express their distinct culture. The goal of more illiberal laws (such as the state language law) appears to be—and has sometimes been articulated as—the ethnolinguistic assimilation of the Hungarian minority, at least to the extent that they use the majority language in most areas of community life. Some more illiberal Slovak leaders (such as Slota, but also others) have even suggested that many ethnic Hungarians are actually Magyarized Slovaks. State energy is expended, then, to push minorities to conform to a thick, ethnically specific societal culture. In the Czech Republic, by contrast, the Roma's exclusion from the regular public school system, from housing (prompting increasing ghettoization), from employment, from community spaces such as swimming pools, from privately owned public spaces such as restaurants, and even from citizenship itself in the state's early years all served to *bar* Roma from membership in the societal culture. This is, of course, deeply inimical to civic equality—but it is a different kind of discrimination from that practiced against the Hungarians in Slovakia.

This difference between the practices of civic inequality in the two states is directly related to their definitions of state sovereignty. Helpful here again is Charles Taylor's distinction between regime types, one of which seeks to secure the individual's autonomy to choose her own "good life," and the other, which defines the "good life" in a way that must be sought in common. The civic principle supports the former, and produces much more limited exercise of government authority with regard to group identity and culture. The principle does *not* justify the anti-Roma measures described above. The risk to minorities comes, rather, from contrary norms, "unofficial" but widely shared among the majority population, holding that discrimination against a particular group is legitimate. Under such circumstances, an overemphasis on government neutrality may passively allow violations of the civic principle; the lower status of the Roma is de facto rather than de jure. Still, although it regularly falls short in practical application and requires better implementing legislation, the civic principle also serves as *recourse* for those who allege unjust treatment and as such has played a central, indispensable role in combating inequality.

The ethnic principle, by contrast, supports Taylor's second regime type, precisely because of the nature of several of the sovereign community's attributes: it is involuntary, it has a thick shared identity, it is exclusive, and its bonds may be interpreted as reflecting collectivistic unity. The state is constituted, in large part, to protect and foster the sovereign community; thus, when the state pursues these purposes according to an understanding of nationhood that emphasizes these particular qualities, circumscription of individual autonomy via illiberal laws and policies receives the sanction of regime principle. In Slovakia, such illiberal authority has largely targeted those seeking to express alternative ethnonational identities, but it also may support broader illiberalism by justifying the restriction of civil liberties to counteract the threat from the minority's disloyalty, (allegedly) flowing from its foreign relationship to the state (having a "mother nation" that realizes its sovereignty elsewhere). In addition, an ethnic definition of sovereignty supports an emphasis on the nation's organic unity, often illustrated as that of a collective individual or a family, with the implication that it requires authoritarian leadership (from its "head" or "father") that will protect it both from foreign elements ("cancers") and from unhealthy diversity within its own membership. Such an understanding strongly informed the wartime Slovak regime, and has also emerged prominently in the political rhetoric of both the HZDS and the SNS. That these are logical (if not necessary) interpretations of ethnic sovereignty with historical precedent forces minorities to rely on the majority's potentially precarious good will (and even the most liberal parties have never embraced the principle of *full* civic equality) and leaves the rights and liberties of all citizens insecure. The civic principle simply does not offer similar support for such far-reaching suppression of civil liberties; indeed, in the Czech Republic, although widespread discrimination and hostility are pernicious to the Roma, the rights of citizens belonging to both the Czech majority and other minorities are largely unaffected.

Ultimately, then, it matters whether the basis for the stratification of citizenship can be found at the level of regime principle. It is therefore not only possible but also necessary to differentiate between communities based on civic and ethnic constitutional definitions of sovereignty, as long as the conceptualization is amended to reflect the relevance of ethnocultural identity in the political practices of both. Moreover, from a liberal political/philosophical standpoint, the distinction is important as well. As Ronald Beiner argues, "what motivates some critics of nationalism to distinguish 'ethnic' and 'civic' conceptions of nationhood is not the absurd notion that language and cultural identity are politically irrelevant. Rather, what animates the 'civic' conception is the vision of a shared citizenship and civic identity that would be in principle capable of transcending these cultural preoccupations, however legitimate they may be, in a political community where linguistic and cultural identities are in potential conflict. . . . So I think that the ethnic nationalism/civic nationalism distinction, robustly criticized by some very acute theorists, or some version of that distinction, is still worthy of philosophical defense."[3] The evidence I have presented here reinforces such a defense, for when compared with a regime based on ethnic hierarchy, it is clear that the principle of equal citizenship offers stronger—albeit imperfect—support for substantial minority membership and individual rights.

NOTES

INTRODUCTION

1. Václav Havel, "Základ společného státu," *Národná obroda* (September 18, 1990), quoted in Stanislav Kirschbaum, *A History of Slovakia: The Struggle for Survival* (New York: St. Martin's-Griffin, 1995), 263.

2. Kevin Deegan-Krause, *Elected Affinities: Democracy and Party Competition in Slovakia and the Czech Republic* (Stanford, Calif.: Stanford University Press, 2006), 2.

3. I borrow this phrase from Rogers Brubaker, but define it more narrowly. See *Citizen and Nationhood in France and Germany* (Cambridge, Mass.: Harvard University Press, 1992).

4. On the concept of authentic authority, see Howard Adelman, "Quebec: The Morality of Secession," in *Is Quebec Nationalism Just? Perspectives from Anglophone Canada*, ed. Joseph H. Carens (Montreal: McGill-Queens University Press, 1995), 176–78.

5. Ibid.

6. Charles Taylor, "The Politics of Recognition," in *Multiculturalism: Examining the Politics of Recognition*, ed. Amy Gutmann (Princeton, N.J.: Princeton University Press, 1994), 57.

7. Ibid., 59.

8. Johann Gottfried von Herder, "Reflections on the Philosophy of the History of Mankind," in *The Nationalism Reader*, ed. Omar Dahbour and Micheline R. Ishay (Atlantic Highlands, N.J.: Humanities Press, 1995), 54.

9. Clifford Geertz, "Primordial and Civic Ties," in *Nationalism*, ed. John Hutchinson and Anthony D. Smith (Oxford: Oxford University Press, 1995), 31.

10. Jacques Rupnik, "The Reawakening of European Nationalisms," *Social Research* 63, no. 1 (1996): 41.

11. See, for example, Bill Clinton's "First Inaugural Address" (Washington, D.C., January 21, 1993), http://www.bartleby.com/124/pres64.html, and "The Struggle for the Soul of the 21st Century" (Richard Dimbleby Lecture, BBC Television, December 14, 2001), http://www.australianpolitics.com/news/2001/01-12-14.shtml.

12. Gil Eyal, *The Origins of Postcommunist Elites: From Prague Spring to the Breakup of Czechoslovakia* (Minneapolis: University of Minnesota Press, 2003), xv.

13. Sally Engle Merry, "Changing Rights, Changing Culture," in *Culture and Rights: Anthropological Perspectives*, ed. Jane K. Cowan, Marie-Bénédicte Dembour, and Richard A. Wilson (New York: Cambridge University Press, 2001), 42.

14. Jane K. Cowan, Marie-Bénédicte Dembour, and Richard A. Wilson, "Introduction," in *Culture and Rights*, ed. Cowan, Dembour, and Wilson, 10.

15. Ibid., 5.

16. Engle Merry, "Changing Rights, Changing Culture," 42.

17. Anthony Smith, *Nations and Nationalism in a Global Era* (Cambridge: Polity Press, 1995), 30.

18. Eric Hobsbawm, *Nations and Nationalism Since 1789: Programme, Myth, Reality*, 2nd ed. (Cambridge: Cambridge University Press, 1992), 9–10.

19. Milada Anna Vachudová and Tim Snyder, "Are Transitions Transitory? Two Types of Political Change in Eastern Europe Since 1989," *East European Politics and Societies* 11, no. 1 (1997): 6.

20. John Breuilly, for example, observes that "Bohemia tends to the western, marketization line and Slovakia, a less developed region, is more wary. It may be that it is this tension which gives significance to nationality difference, though recent polls indicate that this difference is more strongly represented in political parties than in the population as a whole." Breuilly also points out "that no 'nation' or 'ethnic group' in 1989–90 opted for separating from a clearly richer country from which they benefited or for joining a clearly poorer country populated by their 'own' nation. There are clear limits to the national commitment." Breuilly, *Nationalism and the State* (Chicago: University of Chicago Press, 1994), 353, 355.

21. Eyal, *Origins of Postcommunist Elites*," xiii–xiv.

22. Ibid., 136.

23. Ibid. xviii.

24. Ibid., xxv.

25. Deegan-Krause, *Elected Affinities*, 159.

26. Ibid., 157.

27. Smith, *Nations and Nationalism*, 33.

28. Ibid., 34.

29. Ibid.

30. Ibid., 34–35.

31. Ibid., viii.

32. Ibid., 158.

33. Ibid., 80–81.

34. David Paul, *The Cultural Limits of Revolutionary Politics: Change and Continuity in Socialist Czechoslovakia* (Boulder, Colo.: East European Quarterly, 1979), 3.

35. See Gabriel A. Almond and Sidney Verba, *The Civic Culture: Political Attitudes and Democracy in Five Nations* (Princeton, N.J.: Princeton University Press, 1963).

36. Robert C. Tucker, "Culture, Political Culture, and Communist Society," *Political Science Quarterly* 88, no. 2 (1973): 176.

37. H. Gordon Skilling, "Czechoslovak Political Culture: Pluralism in an Interna-

tional Context," in *Political Culture and Communist Studies*, ed. Archie Brown (Armonk, N.Y.: M.E. Sharpe, 1985), 118.

38. Ibid.

39. Carol Skalnik Leff, *National Conflict in Czechoslovakia: The Making and Remaking of a State, 1918–1987* (Princeton, N.J.: Princeton University Press, 1988).

40. Hans Kohn, "Western and Eastern Nationalisms," 1945, reprinted in *Nationalism*, ed. Hutchinson and Smith, 164.

41. Ibid., 165.

42. Michael Ignatieff, *Blood and Belonging: Journeys into the New Nationalism* (New York: Viking Penguin, 1993), 3–4.

43. Jürgen Habermas, "Citizenship and National Identity: Some Reflections on the Future of Europe," *Praxis International* 12, no. 1 (1992): 3.

44. Ibid., 17.

45. Jürgen Habermas, "Struggles for Recognition in the Democratic Constitutional State," in *Multiculturalism*, ed. Gutmann, 134–35.

46. Smith, *Nations and Nationalism*, 98.

47. Will Kymlicka, *Multicultural Citizenship* (Oxford: Clarendon Press, 1995), 200n15.

48. Ibid., 200.

49. Smith, *Nations and Nationalism*, 101.

50. Will Kymlicka, "Misunderstanding Nationalism," in *Theorizing Nationalism*, ed. Ronald Beiner (Albany: State University of New York Press, 1999), 132.

51. Smith, *Nations and Nationalism*, 97.

52. Bernard Yack, "The Myth of the Civic Nation," in *Theorizing Nationalism*, ed. Beiner, 105.

53. Ibid., 115.

54. Ibid., 106..

55. Kai Nielsen, "Cultural Nationalism, Neither Ethnic Nor Civic," in *Theorizing Nationalism*, ed. Beiner, 127.

56. Ghia Nodia, "Nationalism and Democracy," in *Nationalism, Ethnic Conflict and Democracy*, ed. Larry Diamond and Marc F. Plattner (Baltimore: Johns Hopkins University Press, 1994), 10.

57. This is Nodia's definition of a concept Francis Fukuyama uses to discuss nationalism.

58. Nodia, "Nationalism and Democracy," 17.

59. Will Kymlicka, "Nation-Building and Minority Rights: Comparing East and West," *Journal of Ethnic and Migration Studies* 26, no. 2 (2000): 178.

60. Robert M. Hayden, "Constitutional Nationalism in the Formerly Yugoslav Republics," *Slavic Review* 51, no. 4 (1992): 673.

61. Liah Greenfeld, *Nationalism: Five Roads to Modernity* (Cambridge, Mass.: Harvard University Press, 1992), 11.

62. Tim Haughton, *Constraints and Opportunities of Leadership in Post-Communist Europe* (Aldershot: Ashgate, 2005), 35.

63. Ibid., 37.

64. Erika Harris, *Nationalism and Democratisation: Politics of Slovakia and Slovenia* (Aldershot: Ashgate, 2002), 97.

65. Ibid., 20.

66. Ibid., 122.

67. Deegan- Krause, *Elected Affinities*, 174.

68. Ibid., 212.

69. Ibid., 224.

70. Eyal, *The Origins*, 88.

71. Deegan-Krause, *Elected Affinities*, 154–56.

72. Ibid, 161.

73. See for example Pavel Barša, "Ethnocultural Justice in East European States and the Case of the Czech Roma," in *Can Liberal Pluralism Be Exported? Western Political Theory and Ethnic Relations in Eastern Europe*, ed. Will Kymlicka and Magda Opalski (Oxford: Oxford University Press, 2001), and Peter Vermeersch, "Ethnic Minority Identity and Movement Politics: The Case of the Roma in the Czech Republic and Slovakia," *Ethnic and Racial Studies* 26, no. 5 (2003): 879–901.

74. Rick Fawn, "Czech Attitudes Towards the Roma: 'Expecting More of Havel's Country'?," *Europe-Asia Studies* 53, no. 8 (2001): 1193–1219.

75. See, for example, Peter Vermeersch, "EU Enlargement and Minority Rights Policies in Central Europe: Explaining Policy Shifts in the Czech Republic, Hungary and Poland," *Journal on Ethnopolitics and Minority Issues in Europe* 1 (2003), http://www.ecmi.de.

76. Miroslav Hroch, *Social Preconditions of National Revival in Europe: A Comparative Analysis of the Social Composition of Patriotic Groups Among the Smaller European Nations* (New York: Cambridge University Press, 1985).

77. I do not explore the Czechs' wartime experience as a Protectorate of the Third Reich.

CHAPTER 1. AWAKENINGS

1. John F. N. Bradley, *Czech Nationalism in the Nineteenth Century* (Boulder, Colo.: East European Monographs, 1984), 5–6.

2. George J. Svoboda, "The Odd Alliance: The Underprivileged Population of Bohemia and the Habsburg Court, 1765–1790," in *The Czech and Slovak Experience: Selected Papers from the Fourth World Congress for Soviet and Eastern European Studies, Harrogate, 1990*, ed. John Morison (New York: St. Martin's Press, 1992), 10, 15.

3. Bradley, *Czech Nationalism*, 6.

4. Ibid., 6–7.

5. Herman Freudenberger, "Progressive Bohemian and Moravian Aristocracy," in *Intellectual and Social Developments in the Hapsburg Empire from Maria Theresa to World War I: Essays Dedicated to Robert A. Kann*, ed. Stanley B. Winters and Joseph Held (Boulder, Colo.: East European Quarterly, 1975), 117.

6. Miroslav Hroch, *Social Preconditions of National Revival in Europe: A Comparative*

Analysis of the Social Composition of Patriotic Groups among the Smaller European Nations (New York: Cambridge University Press, 1985), 60.

7. Arnošt Klíma, "The Czechs," in *The National Question in Europe in Historical Context*, ed. Mikulas Teich and Roy Porter (Cambridge: Cambridge University Press, 1993), 234.

8. Joseph F. Zacek, "Metternich's Censors: The Case of Palacký," in *The Czech Renascence of the Nineteenth Century: Essays Presented to Otokar Odlozilik in Honour of His Seventieth Birthday*, ed. Peter Brock and H. Gordon Skilling (Toronto: University of Toronto Press, 1970), 98.

9. Hroch, *Social Preconditions*, 159.

10. Stanislav J. Kirschbaum, *A History of Slovakia: The Struggle for Survival* (New York: St. Martin's Griffin, 1995), 111.

11. See Ľudovit Holotik, "The Slovaks: An Integrating or Disintegrating Force?" *Austrian History Yearbook* 3, no. 2 (1967): 35–55.

12. Vaclav Beneš, "The Slovaks in the Hapsburg Empire: A Struggle for Existence," *Austrian History Yearbook* 3, no. 2 (1967): 335–64.

13. Ibid.

14. Kirschbaum, *A History of Slovakia*, 113.

15. Peter Brock, *The Slovak National Awakening: An Essay in the Intellectual History of East-Central Europe* (Toronto: University of Toronto Press, 1976), 18.

16. Ibid.

17. See Holotik, "The Slovaks."

18. R. W. Seton-Watson, *A History of the Czechs and Slovaks* (1943; Hamden, Conn: Archon Books, 1965), 260.

19. Ibid., 173.

20. Kirschbaum, *A History of Slovakia*, 96.

21. Brock, *The Slovak National Awakening*, 21–22.

22. Thomas G. Pešek, "The 'Czechoslovak' Question on the Eve of the 1848 Revolution," in *The Czech Renascence of the Nineteenth Century*, ed. Brock and Skilling, 132.

23. Ján Kollár, *Concerning Literary Reciprocity Between the Various Races and Dialects of the Slav Nation* (Pest, 1837), 2nd corrected ed., ed. Miloš Weingart (Leipzig, 1844) 119, quoted in Robert B. Pynsent, *Questions of Identity: Czech and Slovak Ideas of Nationality and Personality* (Budapest: Central European University Press, 1994), 54.

24. Brock, *The Slovak National Awakening*, 21.

25. Kollár, *Concerning Literary Reciprocity*, quoted in Pynsent, *Questions of Identity*, 56.

26. Ibid., 37, quoted in Pynsent, *Questions of Identity*, 50.

27. Ibid.

28. Ibid., 59.

29. Pynsent, *Questions of Identity*, 50–51.

30. Jan Kollár, *Cestopis obasahující cestu do Horní Itálie a Bavorsko se zvláštním ohledem na slavjanské živly roku 1841 konanou* (*A Travel Journal containing a journal made in 1841 to Upper Italy and thence through the Tyrol and Bavaria with special attention paid to Slavonic elements*), 133–34, quoted in Pynsent, *Questions of Identity*, 51.

31. Ibid.

32. Ján Kollár, *Básně* (Prague, 1952), 351, quoted by Pynsent, *Questions of Identity*, 55.

33. Ján Kollár, *Hlasové o potřebě spisovného jazyka pro Čechy, Moravany a Slováky* (*Voices or: Votes for the Need of a Unified Literary Language for Bohemians, Moravians and Slovaks*) (Prague, 1846), 108, quoted in Pynsent, *Questions of Identity*, 62.

34. Anthony Smith, *Nations and Nationalism in a Global Era* (Cambridge: Polity Press, 1995), 62.

35. Ibid., 63.

36. Ibid., 64.

37. Brock, *The Slovak National Awakening*, 27.

38. Hugh LeCaine Agnew, "Czechs, Slovaks and the Slovak Linguistic Separatism of the Mid-Nineteenth Century," in *The Czech and Slovak Experience*, ed. Morison, 23.

39. Manscript by Kollár dated 1826 and cited in Šafařík, *Listy*, 78–79; also Kollár's notes to his *Národnie spievanky*, vol. 2, 568, and Rosenbaum, *Poézia*, 202–4, quoted in Brock, *The Slovak National Awakening*, 26.

40. Kollár, *Myšlénky*, 47, quoted in Brock, *The Slovak National Awakening*, 23.

41. Kollár to Hanka, 9 April 1835, *Vzájemné dopisy*, 237, quoted in Brock, *The Slovak National Awakening*, 28.

42. Pynsent, *Questions of Identity*, 46.

43. Ibid., 47, and Kirschbaum, *A History of Slovakia*, 97.

44. Pavel Josef Šafařík, *Dejiny slovanského jazyka a literatury všetkých nárečí* (Bratislava: Vydavateľstvo Slovenskej Akadémie Vied, 1963), 86, quoted in Pynsent, *Questions of Identity*, 75.

45. Pynsent, *Questions of Identity*, 75.

46. Pavel Josef Šafařík, *Slovanské starožinosti Oddíl dějepisný Okres privní. Od 1. 456 před Kr. až do 469–76 po Kr.* (Prague, 1862), 84, quoted in Pynsent, *Questions of Identity*, 84.

47. Pynsent, *Questions of Identity*, 85.

48. Ibid., 52.

49. Ibid.

50. Šafařík, *Geschichte*, 34, cited in Brock, *The Slovak National Awakening*, 25.

51. Šafařík, "A Letter Dated 14 February 1821," *Dopisy* 47 (1873): 122, quoted in Brock, *The Slovak National Awakening*, 24.

52. "Šafařík to Kollár, 18 May 1827," *Dopisy* 48 (1874), 286, quoted in Brock, *The Slovak National Awakening*, 26.

53. Brock, *The Slovak National Awakening*, 26.

54. "Šafařík to Palacký, 11 October 1830," *Korespondence s Palackým*, 90–91, quoted in Brock, *The Slovak National Awakening*, 26.

55. Brock, *The Slovak National Awakening*, 27.

56. Pynsent, *Questions of Identity*, 53.

57. Šafařík, *Hlasové*, 124, quoted in Pynsent, *Questions of Identity*, 63.

58. Smith, *Nations and Nationalism*, 66.

59. Brock, *The Slovak National Awakening*, 45.

60. Kirschbaum, *A History of Slovakia*, 100.

61. Brock, *The Slovak National Awakening*, 49.

62. Ibid., 34.

63. Ibid., 32.

64. Pešek, "The 'Czechoslovak' Question," 141.

65. Ibid., 136.

66. Ľudovít Štúr, *Nárečie slovenské* (*Nárečja slovenskuo alebo potreba písanja v tomto nárečí* (old spelling), 15–20, quoted in Brock, *The Slovak National Awakening*, 48.

67. Pešek, "The 'Czechoslovak' Question," 137.

68. Ľudovít Štúr, *Die Beschwerden und Klagen der Slaven in Ungarn über die gesetzwidrigen Übergriffe der Magyaren* (Leipzig, 1843), in *Dielo*, II, *Slovania, bratia!*, ed. Jozef Abrus (Bratislava: Slovenské Vydavateľstvo Krásnej Literatúry, 1956), 116–17, quoted in Pynsent, *Questions of Identity*, 186–87.

69. Štúr, *Nárečie slovenské*, 54, quoted in LeCaine Agnew, "Slovak Linguistic Separatism," 31.

70. Ibid., 113, quoted in LeCaine Agnew, "Slovak Linguistic Separatism," 33.

71. Pynsent, *Questions of Identity*, 160.

72. Ľudovít Štúr, *Starý i nový věk Slováků*, 75 (manuscript from end of 1841, first published in book form, 1935), in *Dielo*, II, quoted in Pynsent, *Questions of Identity*, 161.

73. Ibid.

74. Ibid., 80, quoted in Pynsent, *Questions of Identity*, 153.

75. Ibid., 83–84, quoted in Pynsent, *Questions of Identity*, 164.

76. Ľudovít Štúr, *O poézii slovanskej* (a series of lectures given by Štur in his apartment after he lost his post at the Lutheran lyceum; they survive through notes taken by three of his students), ed. Pavel Vongrej (Martin, 1987), 23, quoted in Pynsent, *Questions of Identity*, 187.

77. Ibid., 45, quoted in Pynsent, *Questions of Identity*, 187.

78. Pynsent, *Questions of Identity*, 187.

79. Štúr, *O poézii slovanskej*, 69–70, quoted in Pynsent, *Questions of Identity*, 188–89.

80. Ibid., 93, quoted in Pynsent, *Questions of Identity*, 189.

81. Ibid., 86, quoted in Pynsent, *Questions of Identity*, 188.

82. Smith, *Nations and Nationalism*, 66.

83. Seton-Watson, *A History of the Czechs and Slovaks*, 176.

84. Frederick G. Heymann, "The Hussite Movement in the Historiography of the Czech Awakening," in *The Czech Renascence of the Nineteenth Century*, ed. Brock and Skilling, 230.

85. Joseph F. Zacek, "Metternich's Censors: The Case of Palacký," in *The Czech Renascence of the Nineteenth Century*, ed. Brock and Skilling, 95.

86. Ibid., 112.

87. Seton-Watson, *A History of the Czechs and Slovaks*, 177.

88. Ibid., 178.

89. Pynsent, *Questions of Identity*, 177.

90. Ibid.

91. Barbara K. Reinfeld, *Karel Havlíček 1821–1856* (Boulder, Colo.: East European Monographs, 1982), 4–5.

92. Ibid., 13.

93. Barbara Kohák Kimmel, "Karel Havlíček and the Czech Press," in *The Czech Renascence of the Nineteenth Century*, ed. Brock and Skilling, 116.

94. Reinfeld, *Karel Havlíček*, 17.

95. Ibid., 116.

96. Kimmel, "Karel Havlíček," 124.

97. Karel Havlíček, *Politické spisy*, 1, 137, quoted in Kimmel, "Karel Havlíček," 124.

98. Ibid., 142, quoted in Kimmel, "Karel Havlíček," 124.

99. Kimmel, "Karel Havlíček," 124.

100. Havlíček, *Politické spisy*, I, 70, quoted in Kimmel, "Karel Havlíček," 122–3.

101. Karel Havlíček, *Česká včela*, 1846, in Jan Jakubec, *Dějiny literatury české* II (Prague, 1934), 236, quoted in Pešek, "The 'Czechoslovak Question,'" 143.

102. František Palacký, "Letter to Frankfurt," in *We Were and We Shall Be: The Czechoslovak Spirit Through the Centuries*, ed. Zdenka and Jan Munzer (New York: Frederick Ungar, 1941), 76.

103. Seton-Watson, *A History of the Czechs and Slovaks*, 188. Kollár was detained in Hungary and could not attend.

104. Pešek, "The 'Czechoslovak' Question," 140.

105. Karel Havlíček, *Národní noviny*, 15 October 1848, quoted in Reinfeld, *Karel Havlíček*, 58.

106. Josef V. Polisensky, "America and Czech Political Thought," in *The Czech Renascence of the Nineteenth Century*, ed. Brock and Skilling, 221.

107. Reinfeld, *Karel Havlíček*, 68.

108. Stanley Kimball, "The Matice Česká, 1831–1861: The First Thirty Years of a Literary Foundation," in *The Czech Renascence of the Nineteenth Century*, ed. Brock and Skilling, 69.

109. Quoted in Mark Dimond, "The Czech Revolution of 1848: The Pivot of the Habsburg Revolutions," *History Compass* 2 (2004): 4.

110. Ibid., 3.

111. Kirschbaum, *A History of Slovakia*, 116.

112. Ibid., 117.

113. Ibid., 119.

114. Ibid.

115. Hroch, *Social Preconditions*, 187.

116. Seton-Watson, *A History of the Czechs and Slovaks*, 193.

117. Karel Havlíček, "The Slav Policy," 1850, in *We Were and We Shall Be*, ed. Zdenka and Jan Munzer, 62.

118. Reinfeld, *Karel Havlíček*, 92.

119. František Palacký, "Epilogue to 'Memorials,'" in *We Were and We Shall Be*, ed. Munzer and Munzer, 78.

120. František Palacký, "The Idea of the Austrian State," in *We Were and We Shall Be*, ed. Munzer and Munzer, 82.

CHAPTER 2. NATION-BUILDING IN THE EMPIRE'S WANING YEARS

1. Miroslav Hroch, *Social Preconditions of National Revival in Europe: A Comparative Analysis of the Social Composition of Patriotic Groups Among the Smaller European Nations* (New York: Cambridge University Press, 1985), 4.

2. Ibid.

3. Ibid., 179.

4. Ibid., 185.

5. Ibid.

6. Ibid., 186.

7. Miroslav Hroch, "National Self-Determination from a Historical Perspective," in *Notions of Nationalism*, ed. Sukumar Periwal (Budapest: Central University Press, 1995), 69.

8. Ibid., 71.

9. Ibid., 74–5.

10. Hroch, *Social Preconditions*, 153.

11. Frantisek Ladislav Rieger, *Program of the Prague Newspaper, Národni listy* (1861), in *We Were and We Shall Be: The Czechoslovak Spirit Through the Centuries*, ed Zdenka Munzer and Jan Munzer (New York: Frederick Ungar, 1941), 87–88.

12. R. W. Seton-Watson, *A History of the Czechs and Slovaks* (1943; Hamden, Conn: Archon Books, 1965), 200.

13. Ibid., 201.

14. Bruce M. Garver, *The Young Czech Party 1874–1901 and the Emergence of a Multi-Party System* (New Haven, Conn.: Yale University Press, 1978), 60.

15. Ibid., 50.

16. Ibid., 65.

17. Ibid., 63.

18. Ibid., 78–79.

19. Ibid., 69.

20. Ibid., 70.

21. Seton-Watson, *A History of the Czechs and Slovaks*, 213.

22. Ibid., 229.

23. Stanley B. Winters, "Kramar Kaizl, and the Hegemony of the Young Czech Party, 1891–1901," in *The Czech Renascence of the Nineteenth Century: Essays Presented to Otokar Odlozilik in Honour of His Seventieth Birthday*, ed. Peter Brock and H. Gordon Skilling (Toronto: University of Toronto Press, 1970), 302.

24. Karel Čapek, *Talks with T. G. Masaryk*, ed. Michael Henry Heim (North Haven, Conn.: Catbird Press, 1995), 166.

25. Tomáš Garrigue Masaryk, "Hus and Czech Destiny," in *The Spirit of Thomas G. Masaryk: 1850–1937: An Anthology*, ed. George J. Kovtun (New York: St. Martin's Press, 1990), 95.

26. Tomáš Garrigue Masaryk, "Our National Revival," in *The Lectures of Professor T. G. Masaryk at the University of Chicago, Summer 1902*, ed. Draga Shillinglaw (Lewisburg, Pa.: Bucknell University Press, 1978), 94.

27. Tomáš Garrigue Masaryk, "State Political Institutions in Austria," in *The Lectures of Professor T. G. Masaryk*, ed. Shilinglaw, 123.

28. Čapek, *Talks*, 166.

29. Roger Scruton, "Masaryk, Kant and the Czech Experience," in *T .G. Masaryk (1850–1937)*, vol. 1, *Thinker and Politician*, ed. Stanley B. Winters (London: Macmillan in Association with School of Slavonic and East European Studies, University of London, 1990), 49.

30. *Programme a organisační statut české strany pokrovké*, quoted in H. Gordon Skilling, *T. G. Masaryk: Against the Current, 1882–1914* (University Park: Pennsylvania State University Press, 1994), 69.

31. Roman Szporluk, *The Political Thought of Thomas G. Masaryk* (Boulder, Colo.: East European Monographs, 1981), 122.

32. Jan Herben, *T. G. Masaryk*, vol. 1 (Prague: Mánes, 1926), 275–83; Paul Selver, *Masaryk: A Biography* (Prague, 1940), 197–207, quoted in H. Gordon Skilling, "Masaryk: Religious Heretic," in *The Czech and Slovak Experience: Selected Papers from the Fourth World Congress for Soviet and East European Studies, Harrogate, 1990*, ed. John Morison (New York: Saint Martin's Press, 1992), 76.

33. Steven Beller, "The Hilsner Affair: Nationalism, Anti-Semitism and the Individual in the Habsburg Monarchy at the Turn of the Century," in *T. G. Masaryk (1850–1927)*, vol. 2, *Thinker and Critic*, ed. Robert B. Pynsent (London: Macmillan in Association with the School of Slavonic and East European Studies, University of London, 1989), 73.

34. Bruce M. Garver, "Masaryk and Czech Politics 1906–1914," in *T. G. Masaryk (1850–1937)*, vol. 1, *Thinker and Politician*, 249.

35. John F. N. Bradley, *Czech Nationalism in the Nineteenth Century* (Boulder, Colo.: East European Monographs, 1984), 62–63.

36. Carol Skalnik Leff, "Czech and Slovak Nationalism in the Twentieth Century," in *Eastern European Nationalism in the Twentieth Century*, ed. Peter F. Sugar (Washington, D.C.: American University Press, 1995), 116.

37. Hroch, "National Self-Determination," 80.

38. *Memorandum of the Slovaks to the Parliament of Hungary of 1861*, Appendix I in Joseph A. Mikus, *Slovakia: A Political History: 1918–1950* (Milwaukee, Wis.: Marquette University Press, 1963), 323.

39. Ibid.

40. Stanislav J. Kirschbaum, *A History of Slovakia: The Struggle for Survival* (New York: St. Martin's Griffin, 1995), 133–34.

41. Garver, *The Young Czech Party*, 208.

42. Seton-Watson, *A History of the Czechs and Slovaks*, 270.

43. Ibid.

44. Peter Brock, *The Slovak National Awakening: An Essay in the Intellectual History of East-Central Europe* (Toronto: University of Toronto Press, 1976), 83n82.

45. Hroch, *Social Preconditions*, 154.

46. Skilling, *T. G. Masaryk*, 66.

47. Kirschbaum, *A History of Slovakia*, 152.

48. Carol Skalnik Leff, *National Conflict in Czechoslovakia: The Making and Remaking of a State, 1918–1987* (Princeton, N.J.: Princeton University Press, 1988), 30.

49. Kirschbaum, *A History of Slovakia*, 153.

50. Leff, *National Conflict*, 15.

51. David Paul, "Slovak Nationalism and the Hungarian State, 1870–1910," in *Ethnic Groups and the State*, ed. Paul Brass (London: Croom Helm, 1985), 141.

52. Seton-Watson, *A History of the Czechs and Slovaks*, 273.

53. Paul, "Slovak Nationalism," 141.

54. Ibid., 142.

55. David Paul, *The Cultural Limits of Revolutionary Politics: Change and Continuity in Socialist Czechoslovakia* (Boulder, Colo.: East European Quarterly, 1979), 198–99.

56. Paul, "Slovak Nationalism," 140–41.

57. Skilling, *T. G. Masaryk*, 74.

58. Edita Bosák, "The Slovak National Movement, 1848–1918," in *Reflections on Slovak History*, ed. Stanislav Kirschbaum (Toronto: Slovak World Congress, 1987), 67.

59. Paul, "Slovak Nationalism," 123.

60. Bosák, "The Slovak National Movement," 67.

61. Susan Mikula, "Milan Hodza and the Politics of Power, 1907–1914," in *Slovak Politics: Essays on Slovak History in Honour of Joseph M. Kirschbaum*, ed. Stanislav Kirschbaum (Cleveland: Slovak Institute, 1983), 56.

62. Seton-Watson, *A History of the Czechs and Slovaks*, 279.

63. Paul, "Slovak Nationalism," 128.

64. James Mace Ward, "'Black Monks': Jozef Tiso and Anti-Semitism," *Kosmas: Czechoslovak and Central European Journal* 14, no. 1 (2000): 33.

65. Paul, "Slovak Nationalism," 128.

CHAPTER 3. THE FIRST REPUBLIC: CZECHOSLOVAKISM AND ITS DISCONTENTS

1. T. G. Masaryk, *The Making of a State: Memories and Observations, 1914–1918* (New York: Frederick Stokes, 1927), 390, quoted in Roman Szporluk, *The Political Thought of T. G. Masaryk* (Boulder, Colo.: East European Monographs, 1981), 139.

2. Štefan Osuský, "Slovakia's Place in the New Europe," in *Slovakia Then and Now: A Political Survey*, ed. R. W. Seton-Watson (London: Allen and Unwin; Prague: Orbis, 1931), 355.

3. William V. Wallace, "Masaryk and Benes and the Creation of Czechoslovakia: a Study in Mentalities," in *T. G. Masaryk (1850–1937)*, vol. 3, *Statesman and Cultural Force*, ed. Harry Hanak (London: Macmillan in Association with School of Slavonic and East European Studies, University of London, 1989), 79.

4. Carol Skalnik Leff, *National Conflict in Czechoslovakia: The Making and Remaking of a State, 1918–1987* (Princeton, N.J.: Princeton University Press, 1988), 35.

5. "Resolution Adopted at the Public Popular Meeting in Liptovsky Sv. Mikulas on

May 1, 1918," reprinted as Document 2 in Jozef Lettrich, *History of Modern Slovakia* (Toronto: Slovak Research and Studies Centre, 1955), 287.

6. Quoted in Jozef Butvin, "Slováci na ceste k Československej štátnosti,' *Nové slovo*, November 3, 1988, 24, quoted in Edita Bosák, "Slovaks and Czechs: An Uneasy Coexistence," in *Czechoslovakia 1918–1988: Seventy Years from Independence*, ed. H. Gordon Skilling (New York: St. Martin's Press, 1991), 65.

7. "Resolution of the Slovak National Party, May 24, 1918," reprinted as Document 3 in Lettrich, *History of Modern Slovakia*, 288.

8. On Slovak pronouncements during this period, see Peter A. Toma and Dušan Kováč, *Slovakia: From Samo to Dzurinda* (Stanford, Calif.: Hoover Institution Press, 2001), 60–61.

9. "Czecho-Slovak Agreement agreed on in Pittsburgh, Pa., May 30, 1918," reprinted as Document 5 in Lettrich, *History of Modern Slovakia*, 289–90.

10. "Declaration of the Slovak Nation," reprinted as Document 4 in Lettrich, *History of Modern Slovakia*, 288–89.

11. James Ramon Felak, *At the Price of the Republic: Hlinka's Slovak People's Party, 1929–1938* (Pittsburgh: University of Pittsburgh Press, 1994), 16.

12. Leff, *National Conflict*, 38.

13. Dorothea El Mallakh, *The Slovak Autonomy Movement 1935–1939: A Study in Unrelenting Nationalism* (Boulder, Colo.: East European Quarterly, 1979), 39.

14. Stanislav Kirschbaum, *A History of Slovakia: The Struggle for Survival* (New York: St. Martin's-Griffin, 1995), 161.

15. Lettrich, *History of Modern Slovakia*, 69.

16. Leff, *National Conflict*, 203.

17. Felak, *At the Price*, 23.

18. Quoted in Leff, *National Conflict*, 204.

19. R. W. Seton-Watson, *The New Slovakia* (Prague: Fr. Borový, 1924), 36.

20. Derek Sayer, *The Coasts of Bohemia: A Czech History* (Princeton, N.J.: Princeton University Press, 1998), 140.

21. Robert B. Pynsent, *Questions of Identity: Czech and Slovak Ideas of Nationality and Personality* (Budapest: Central European University Press, 1994), 201.

22. Seton-Watson, *The New Slovakia*, 39.

23. Ibid., 70.

24. Francis Hrusovsky, *This Is Slovakia: A Country You Do Not Know* (Scranton, Pa.: Obrana Press, 1953), 62.

25. "Memorandum of the Slovaks to the Peace Conference of 1919," reprinted in Appendix II in Joseph A. Mikus, *Slovakia: A Political History: 1918–1950* (Milwaukee: Marquette University Press, 1963), 331.

26. Ibid., 332.

27. Ibid., 335.

28. El Mallakh, *The Slovak Autonomy Movement*, 338.

29. *Die Verfassungsurkunde der Tschechoslowakishen Republik vom 29. Februar 1920*, in

Jorg K. Hoensch, *Dokumente zur Autonomiepolitik der Slowakischen Volkspartei Hlinkas* (Munich: R. Oldenburg, 1984), 131.

30. Fred Hahn, "The German Social Democratic Party of Czechoslovakia, 1918–1926," in *The Czech and Slovak Experience: Selected Papers from the Fourth World Congress for Soviet and East European Studies, Harrogate, 1990*, ed. John Morison (New York: St. Martin's Press, 1992), 213.

31. Carol Skalnik Leff and Susan B. Mikula, "Institutionalizing Party Systems in Multiethnic States: Integration and Ethnic Segmentation in Czechoslovakia, 1918–1992," *Slavic Review* 61, no. 2 (2002): 307.

32. Felak, *At the Price*, 18–19.

33. James Felak, "Slovak Considerations of the Slovak Question: The Ludak, Agrarian, Socialist and Communist Views in Interwar Czechoslovakia," in *The Czech and Slovak Experience*, ed. Morison, 141.

34. "'Die Erklarung der Sechs' (Abgeordneten der Slowakischen Volkspartei) im Verfassungausschuss der Provisorischen Nationalversammlung vom 19. Februar 1920," in Hoensch, *Dokumente*, 130.

35. T. G. Masaryk, interview with *Petit Parisien*, September 14, 1921, reprinted in T. G. Masaryk, *Spisy*, vol. 2 (Prague, 1934) 78, quoted in Leff, *National Conflict*, 138.

36. Vavro Šrobár, quoted in Zdenka Holotíková, "Marxistické a buržoázne koncepcie postavenia Slovenska po roku 1918," *Historický časopis* 22, no. 2 (1974): 199–200, quoted in Leff, *National Conflict*, 139.

37. *Ročenka československch profesorů* 1 (1921–22): 207, 217, quoted in Sayer, *The Coasts of Bohemia*, 174.

38. Pekař, *Dějiny československé* (1921) 19, quoted in Sayer, *The Coasts of Bohemia*, 171.

39. Seton-Watson, *The New Slovakia*, 35.

40. Sayer, *The Coasts of Bohemia*, 176–77, 356n89.

41. Antonín Štefánek, "Education in Pre-War Hungary and in Slovakia To-Day," in *Slovakia Then and Now*, ed. Seton-Watson, 116.

42. "Wahlprogramm der Slowakischen Volkspartei Hlinkas vom Oktober 1929," in Hoensch, *Dokumente*, 190.

43. Andrej Hlinka, "The Influence of Religion and Catholicism on States and Individuals," in *Slovakia Then and Now*, ed. Seton-Watson, 168.

44. Ibid., 171.

45. Ibid.

46. Ibid., 172.

47. Ibid., 173.

48. Ibid., 174.

49. Ibid.

50. Sayer, *The Coasts of Bohemia*, 175.

51. David Paul, *The Cultural Limits of Revolutionary Politics: Change and Continuity in Socialist Czechoslovakia* (Boulder, Colo.: East European Quarterly, 1979), 232.

52. Sayer, *The Coasts of Bohemia*, 171.

53. Ibid., 170.

54. Ibid., 168.

55. El Mallakh, *The Slovak Autonomy Movement*, 42.

56. Lettrich, *History of Modern Slovakia*, 62.

57. "Das Tyrnauer Manifest [Trnavský manifest] der Slowakischen Volkspartei Hlinkas vom 27./28. November 1925," in Hoensch, *Dokumente*, 175.

58. Václav Prucha, "Economic Development and Relations, 1918–89," in *The End of Czechoslovakia*, ed. Jiri Musil (New York: Central European University Press, 1995), 40.

59. Joseph A. Mikus, "Slovakia Between Two World Wars," *Slovak Studies* 1, no. 1 (1961): 99, and El Mallakh, *The Slovak Autonomy Movement*, 40.

60. Prucha, "Economic Development," 47–48.

61. Ibid., 52.

62. Ibid., 48–49.

63. Ibid., 51.

64. Paul, *The Cultural Limits*, 206.

65. Bosák, "Slovaks and Czechs," 74.

66. Paul, *The Cultural Limits*, 206.

67. El Mallakh, *The Slovak Autonomy Movement*, 42.

68. Leff, *National Conflict*, 140.

69. Ibid., 59.

70. Frederick M. Bernard, "Political Culture: Continuity and Discontinuity," in *Czechoslovakia 1918–1988*, ed. Skilling, 139.

71. Leff. *National Conflict*, 59.

72. Ibid., 74.

73. Ibid., 84.

74. El Mallakh, *The Slovak Autonomy Movement*, 65.

75. One interesting source on this is the 1931 volume *Slovakia Then and Now: A Political Survey*. It was compiled by R. W. Seton-Watson to show "not what the *Czechs* think of [the Slovak situation], but what *Slovaks themselves* think." The volume contains chapters by twenty-four Slovaks on the relationship of the Slovaks to the Czechoslovak state.

76. Osuský, "Slovakia's Place in the New Europe," 351–52.

77. Milan Hodža, *Federation in Central Europe: Reflections and Reminiscences* (London: Jarrods, 1942), 206–7.

78. Ivan Dérer, *The Unity of the Czechs and Slovaks: Has the Pittsburgh Declaration Been Carried Out?* (Prague: Orbis, 1938), 75–76.

79. Antonín Štefánek, *Kollárov nacionalizmus (homoetnologicka studia)* (Prague: Odtlacok zo Sbornika Jana Kollára, Slovansky ustav, 1937), 50.

80. Vavro Šrobár, *Osvobodené slovensko: pamäti z rokov 1918–1920* (Praha: Cin, 1928), 12.

81. Osuský, "Slovakia's Place in the New Europe," 351–52.

82. Felak, *At the Price*, 87.

83. Ibid., 89.

84. Ibid., 91.

85. *Slovák*, December 30, 1932, 1, quoted in ibid., 96.

86. Felak, *At the Price*, 96.

87. 225-1164-1, PPDK, 7582/38, May 2, 1938, quoted in El Mallakh, *The Slovak Autonomy Movement*, 101.

88. Felak, *At the Price*, 185.

89. James Mace Ward, "'Black Monks': Jozef Tiso and Anti-Semitism," *Kosmas: Czechoslovak and Central European Journal* 14, no. 1 (2000): 36–39.

90. Čerý mních, "Pieseň o čerých mníchoch," *Nitra*, March 9, 1919, 1, quoted in Ward, "Black Monks," 37.

91. "Chráňme si republiku," *Nitrianské noviny*, October 6, 1919, 1, quoted in Ward, "Black Monks," 33.

92. Rajecký (Andrej Škrábik), *Červené Slovensko*, 2nd ed. (Tvarna: Spolok Sv. Vojtecha, 1926), 19, quoted in Ward, "Black Monks," 33.

93. SSUA, PR, K. 228, F. 478–79, June 5, 1938, quoted in Felak, *At the Price*, 189.

94. El Mallakh, *The Slovak Autonomy Movement*, 108.

95. DGPF, D, IV, 210, quoted in El Mallakh, *The Slovak Autonomy Movement*, 107.

96. El Mallakh, *The Slovak Autonomy Movement*, 110.

97. Ibid.

98. Number 299 Constitutional Act of November 22, 1938 Concerning the Autonomy of Slovakia, Appendix O in El Mallakh, *The Slovak Autonomy Movement*, 234.

99. 2002/442276, quoted in El Mallakh, *The Slovak Autonomy Movement*, 135.

100. David Paul, "Slovak Nationalism and the Hungarian State, 1870–1910," in *Ethnic Groups and the State*, ed. Paul Brass (London: Croom Helm, 1985), 126.

101. Leff, *National Conflict*, 27.

102. Leff and Mikula, "Institutionalizing Party Systems," 304.

103. Ibid., 296.

104. Ibid., 307.

105. Ibid., 304–5.

106. Joseph M. Kirschbaum, *Slovakia: Nation at the Crossroads of Central Europe* (New York: Robert Speller, 1960), 96.

Chapter 4. The Second Republic and the Wartime Slovak State

1. I look only at the Slovak experience, not the Czech, during this period because while the Slovaks were able to experience "independent" statehood for the first time, and to some extent, shape their own destiny, the Czechs living in the Nazi Protectorate were an occupied, oppressed, and in many ways compliant nation. The contrast in the two nations' experience is important in itself, as it contributed to Czech resentment in the postwar period. Still, in terms of the impact of the period for the development of understandings of nationhood, the Slovak experience is more relevant to the purposes of this study.

2. Lisa Guarda Nardini, "The Political Programme of President Tiso," in *Slovak Politics: Essays on Slovak History in Honour of Joseph M. Kirschbaum*, ed. Stanislav Kirschbaum (Cleveland: Slovak Institute, 1983), 221.

3. Yeshayahu Jelinek, *The Parish Republic: Hlinka's Slovak People's Party, 1939–1945* (Boulder, Colo.: East European Quarterly, 1976), 53.

4. Quoted in Joseph M. Kirschbaum, *Slovakia: Nation at the Crossroads of Central Europe* (New York: Robert Speller, 1960),166.

5. The treason charge resulted from Tuka's claim in the HSPP journal *Slovák* that there was a secret clause in the Martin Declaration of 1918 holding that after ten years of joint statehood with the Czechs, the Slovaks would be free to reconsider the union. According to Tuka, this meant that on the ten-year anniversary of the Martin Declaration, the laws of the Czechoslovak Republic would no longer be valid in Slovakia and a *vacuum juris* would follow. The HSPP leadership, including Hlinka, stood behind him throughout the trial and even placed him on the ballot in Košice in the 1929 elections.

6. Jozef Lettrich, *History of Modern Slovakia* (Toronto: Slovak Research and Studies Centre, 1955), 121.

7. Jelinek, *The Parish Republic*, 20.

8. Lettrich, *History of Modern Slovakia*, 116.

9. "Manifesto of the Slovak People's Party," Appendix N in Dorothea El Mallakh, *The Slovak Autonomy Movement 1935–1939: A Study in Unrelenting Nationalism* (Boulder, Colo.: East European Quarterly, 1979), 233.

10. Quoted in Lettrich, *History of Modern Slovakia*, 176.

11. Guarda Nardini, "Political Programme of President Tiso," 233.

12. Ibid.

13. "Excerpts from a despatch of February 17, 1939, from George F. Kennan (as Secretary of Legation at Prague) to the Department of State, on the Jewish problem in the new Czechoslovakia," in George F. Kennan, *From Prague After Munich: Diplomatic Papers 1938–1940* (Princeton, N.J.: Princeton University Press, 1968), 51.

14. Ibid., 52.

15. Ivan Kamenec, *Slovenský štát (1939–1945)* (Prague: Anomal, 1992), 107.

16. Ibid., 7.

17. Jozef Tiso, in *Slovák* 189, 1940, quoted in Kirschbaum, *Slovakia: Nation at the Crossroads*, 170.

18. *Nástup* 19, 1939, quoted in Kirschbaum, *Slovakia: Nation at the Crossroads*, 171.

19. Jozef Tiso, "Ideológia slovenskej ľudovej strany," 1930, reprinted in *Slovenská otázka v 20. Storočí*, ed. Rudolf Chmel (Bratislava: Kalligram, 1997), 89.

20. Ibid.

21. Ibid., 90.

22. Quoted in Kirschbaum, *Slovakia: Nation at the Crossroads*, 150.

23. Jelinek, *The Parish Republic*, 48.

24. Kamenec, *Slovenský štát*, 63–64.

25. Tiso, "Ideológia slovenskej," 83.

26. Teodor Münz, "Catholic Theologians and the National Question (1939–1945)," in *Language, Values, and the Slovak Nation*, ed. Tibor Pichler and Jana Gasparikova (Washington, D.C.: Paideia Press and Council for Research in Values and Philosophy, 1994), 94.

27. Štefan Polakovič, "Slovenský národný socializmus, jeho nevyhnutnosť a ráz," 1940, reprinted in *Slovenská otázka v 20*, ed. Chmel, 290–91.

28. Ibid., 281.

29. Ibid., 283.

30. Jozef [Joseph] Kirschbaum, "Boj o autoritatívny system," 1940, reprinted in *Slovenská otázka v 20*, ed. Chmel, 275.

31. Ibid.

32. Quoted in Kirschbaum, *Slovakia: Nation at the Crossroads*, 176.

33. Quoted in Jelinek, *The Parish Republic*, 87.

34. Quoted in Kirschbaum, *Slovakia: Nation at the Crossroads*, 158.

35. Quoted in Lettrich, *History of Modern Slovakia*, 146–47.

36. James Mace Ward, "'People Who Deserve It': Jozef Tiso and the Presidential Exemption," *Nationalities Papers* 30, no. 4 (2002): 574.

37. Quoted in Kirschbaum *Slovakia: Nation at the Crossroads*, 158.

38. Kamenec, *Slovenský štát*, 59.

39. Ibid., 31.

40. Jelinek, *The Parish Republic*, 112.

41. Münz, "Catholic Theologians," 99.

42. Ibid.

43. Tiso, "Ideológia slovenskej," 93.

44. Ibid., 95.

45. Jozef Tiso, "Dedičstvo Andreja Hlinku," 1939, reprinted in *Slovenská otázka v 20*, ed. Chmel, 270.

46. Quoted in Jelinek, *The Parish Republic*, 87.

47. Quoted in Kamenec, *Slovenský štát*, 63.

48. Jelinek, *The Parish Republic*, 87.

49. Quoted in ibid., 88.

50. Kamenec, *Slovenský štát*, 109.

51. "Government Decree of April 18, 1939, Concerning the Definition of the Term 'Jew' and the Restriction of the Number of Jews in Certain Free Professions," Annex to Document 24, in Kennan, *From Prague After Munich*, 151–52.

52. Lettrich, *History of Modern Slovakia*, 177.

53. Kamenec, *Slovenský štát*, 108.

54. Ward, "People Who Deserve It," 573.

55. Jelinek, *The Parish Republic*, 155n55.

56. Ward, "'People Who Deserve It," 575.

57. Ibid.

58. For details on who could be exempted, see Ward, "People Who Deserve It," 577–79.

59. "Katolíckej verejnosti," *Katolícke noviny*, April 26, 1942, reprinted in *Vatikán a Slovenská republika (1939–1945): dokumenty*, ed. Ivan Kamenec, Vilém Prečan and Stanislav Škorvánek (Bratislava: Slovak Academic Press, 1992), 119, quoted in ibid, 575.

60. Ward, "People Who Deserve It," 575.

61. Jozef Tiso, "Čo nám patrí, z toho nikomu nič nedáme," *Slovák*, August 18, 1942, quoted in James Mace Ward, "'Black Monks': Jozef Tiso and Anti-Semitism," *Kosmas: Czechoslovak and Central European Journal* 14, no. 1 (2000): 31.

62. Ward, "People Who Deserve It," 589.

63. Ibid., 583–84.

64. SNA, KPR, Kancelária prezidenta republiky, č. 3827/1942, May 22, 1942, carton 146, folder 3827/42, quoted in ibid., 584–55.

65. SNA, NS, t. 6/46, Affidavit of Tiso, 8 March 1946, carton 51, folio 287a/43, quoted in ibid., 586.

66. Jelinek, *The Parish Republic*, 76.

67. Michael Marrus, *The Holocaust in History* (New York: Meridian, 1989), 77.

68. Jelinek, *The Parish Republic*, 97.

69. "Agreement on the Founding of an Underground Slovak National Council Announced at Christmas, 1943," Document 26, in Lettrich, *History of Modern Slovakia*, 303–4.

70. Ibid., 304–5.

71. "Declaration of the Slovak National Council in Banská Bystrica, September 1, 1944," Document 28 in Lettrich, *History of Modern Slovakia*, 306.

72. Yeshayahu Jelinek, *The Lust for Power: Nationalism, Slovakia, and the Communists, 1918–1948* (Boulder, Colo.: East European Monographs, 1983), 71.

73. Ibid., 67.

74. Ibid., 72.

75. Ward, "People Who Deserve It," 589.

76. Quoted in R. W. Seton-Watson, *A History of the Czechs and Slovaks* (1943; Hamden, Conn.: Archon, 1965), 174.

77. Jörg K. Hoensch, *Dokumente zur Autonomiepolitik der slowakischen Volkspartei Hlinkas* (Wien: Oldenbourg, 1984), 33 and Jelinek, *The Parish Republic*, 51.

78. Heinrich Pesch, "Christian Solidarism," in *Church and Society: Catholic Social and Political Thought and Movements, 1789–1950*, ed. Joseph N. Moody (New York: Arts, Inc., 1953), 546–47.

79. Jelinek, *The Parish Republic*, 85.

80. Edgar Alexander, "Church and Society in Germany: Social and Political Movements and Ideas in German and Austrian Catholicism, (1789–1950)," in *Church and Society*, ed. Moody, 506.

81. Ibid., 507.

82. Ibid., 489.

83. John Haag, "Marginal Men and the Dream of the Reich: Eight Austrian National-Catholic Intellectuals, 1918–1938," in *Who Were the Fascists? Social Roots of European Fascism*, ed. Stein Ugelvik Larsen, Bernt Hagtvet, and Jan Petter Myklebust (New York: Columbia University Press, 1980), 241.

84. Ibid., 242–23.

85. Ibid., 246.

86. Greenfeld, *Nationalism: Five Roads*, 11.

87. Quoted in Kamenec, *Slovenský stát*, 109.

88. "Katolíckej verejnosti," *Katolícke noviny,* April 26, 1942, reprinted in *Vatikán a Slovenská republika (1939–1945): Dokumenty,* ed. Ivan Kamenec, Vilém Prečan, and Stanislav Škorvánek (Bratislava: Slovak Academic Press, 1992), 119, quoted in Kamenec, *Slovenský stát,* 575.

89. James Waller, *Becoming Evil: How Ordinary People Commit Genocide and Mass Killing,* 2nd ed. (Oxford: Oxford University Press, 2007), 202.

90. Alexander Laban Hinton, *Why Did They Kill? Cambodia in the Shadow of Genocide* (Berkeley: University of California Press, 2005), 284.

91. Waller, *Becoming Evil,* 209.

92. Ibid., 203.

93. Hinton, *Why Did They Kill?* 285.

94. Carol Skalnik Leff, *National Conflict in Czechoslovakia: The Making and Remaking of a State, 1918–1987* (Princeton, N.J.: Princeton University Press, 1988), 90.

CHAPTER 5. PUTTING AN END TO ALL OLD DISPUTES":
THE THIRD REPUBLIC

1. Yeshayahu A. Jelinek, *The Lust for Power: Nationalism, Slovakia, and the Communists* (Boulder, Colo.: East European Monographs, 1983), 81.

2. "Program nové československé vlády Národní fronty čechů a Slováků, 1945, 5 Duben, Košice," in *Cestou kvetna: dokumenty k pocátkum naší národní a demokratické revoluce, duben 1945–kveten 1946* (Prague: Svoboda, 1975), 35–36.

3. "Prohlášení Slovenské národní rady o věrnosti slovenského národa jednotné lidově demokratické československé republice," in *Cestou kvetna,* 52–53.

4. Carol Skalnik Leff, *National Conflict in Czechoslovakia: The Making and Remaking of a State, 1918–1987* (Princeton, N.J.: Princeton University Press, 1988), 213.

5. Ibid., 215.

6. Ibid.

7. *Dokumenty z historie,* vol. 1. Doc. 21, 51–53, quoted in Leff, *National Conflict,* 89.

8. Leff, *National Conflict,* 214–15.

9. Josef Dvořák, *Slovenská politika včera a dnes* (Prague: Pokrok, 1947), 67; Hubert Ripka, *Czechoslovakia Enslaved* (London: Gollancz, 1950), 108–9, quoted in Leff, *National Conflict,* 216.

10. Hadley Cantril, ed., *Public Opinion 1935–1946* (Princeton, N.J.: Princeton University Press, 1951), 155, 499, quoted in Leff, *National Conflict,* 154.

11. *Dnešek,* November 7, 1946, 18.

12. Leff, *National Conflict,* 216.

13. Jelinek, *The Lust for Power,* 84.

14. Ibid., 85.

15. Ibid., 91.

16. Bradley Abrams, "The Politics of Retribution: The Trial of Jozef Tiso in the Czechoslovak Environment," in *The Politics of Retribution in Europe: World War II and*

Its Aftermath, ed. István Deák, Jan T. Gross, and Tony Judt (Princeton, N.J.: Princeton University Press, 2000), 256.

17. David Paul, *The Cultural Limits of Revolutionary Politics: Changes and Continuity in Socialist Czechoslovakia* (Boulder, Colo: East European Monographs, 1979), 103.

18. Ibid.

19. Eugene Steiner, *The Slovak Dilemma* (Cambridge: Cambridge University Press, 1973), 81.

20. Leff, *National Conflict*, 52.

21. Steiner, *The Slovak Dilemma*, 95.

22. Ibid., 96.

23. Ibid., 99.

24. Abrams, "The Politics of Retribution," 254–55.

25. Document 16 in *Dva retribuční procesy: Dokumenty a komentáře*, ed. Karel Kaplan (Praha: ÚSD, 1992), quoted in ibid., 264.

26. Abrams, "The Politics of Retribution," 264–65.

27. Ibid., 266.

28. Ibid., 268.

29. Document 30 in *Dva retribuční procesy*, quoted in ibid., 270.

30. Ibid., 275.

31. Ibid., 277.

32. Ibid., 253.

33. Jan Rychlík, "From Autonomy to Federation, 1938–1968," in *The End of Czechoslovakia*, ed. Jiří Musil (Budapest: Central European University Press, 1995) 192.

34. Jelinek, *The Lust for Power*, 102–3.

35. Stanislav Kirschbaum, *A History of Slovakia: The Struggle for Survival* (New York: St. Martin's-Griffin, 1995), 230

36. "Program nové československé vlády," 37.

37. The text of President Beneš's radio speech in *Čas*, May 12, 1945, quoted in Kálman Janics, *Czechoslovak Policy and the Hungarian Minority, 1945–1948* (New York: Social Science Monographs, 1976), 108–9.

38. Norman M. Naimark, *Fires of Hatred: Ethnic Cleansing in Twentieth-Century Europe* (Cambridge, Mass.: Harvard University Press, 2001), 116.

39. *Dokumente zur Sudetenfrage: Veröffentlichung des Sudetendeutschen Archivs* (Munich: Fritz Peter Habel, Langen Mueller, 1984), 71–22, quoted in ibid.

40. Naimark, *Fires of Hatred*, 111.

41. Archives of the Herder Institute (AHI), *Pravo Lidu*, June 12, 1945, quoted in ibid., 115.

42. In one morning, the SS massacred the entire male population and burned the town to the ground. Women and children who did meet certain "racial" criteria were deported to concentration camps. See Benjamin Frommer, *National Cleansing: Retribution Against Nazi Collaborators in Postwar Czechoslovakia* (Cambridge: Cambridge University Press, 2005), 19–20.

43. Ibid., 233.

44. Karl Hermann Frank, *Zpověd' K. H. Franka: Podle vlasních výpodvědí v době vazby u Krajského soudu trasntního na Pankráci* (Prague: Cíl, 1946), 3–5, quoted in ibid., 234.

45. "Konec paté kolony," *Obrana lidu*, February 16, 1947, SÚA, F. MZV-VA II (j8I), k. 212, quoted in Benjamin Frommer, *National Cleansing: Retribution Against Nazi Collaborators in Postwar Czechoslovakia* (Cambridge: Cambridge University Press, 2005), 238.

46. Derek Sayer, *The Coasts of Bohemia: A Czech History* (Princeton, N.J.: Princeton University Press, 1998), 240.

47. Naimark, *The Fires of Hatred*, 119.

48. Frommer, *National Cleansing*, 240.

49. Alois Harasko, "Die Vertrieberung der Sudetendeustchen: Sechs Erlebnisberichte," in Wolfgang Benz, *Die Vertreibung der Deutschen aus dem Osten: Ursachen, Ereignisse, Folgen* (Frankfurt: Deutschen Taschenbuch Verlag, 1985), 117, quoted in Naimark, *The Fires of Hatred*, 118–19.

50. *Konfliktní společenství, katastrofa, uvolnění: náčrt výkladu německo-českých dějin od 19. Století* (Prague: Vyd. Společná česko-německá komise historiků), 71, quoted in Naimark, *Fires of Hatred*, 120.

51. Kálman Janics, *Czechoslovak Policy and the Hungarian Minority, 1945–1948* (Boulder, Colo: East European Monographs, 1982), 120.

52. Václav Kopecký's article in the July 15, 1944, issue of *Ceskoslovenské Listy*, reprinted in *Tvorba*, April 16, 1947, quoted in Janics, *Czechoslovak Policy*, 68.

53. *Ozbory*, October 11, 1947, quoted in ibid., 188.

54. *Historický časopis* 13, no. 2 (1975): 194, quoted in Jelinek, *The Lust for Power*, 109.

55. Jelinek, *The Lust for Power*, 114.

56. *Čas*, December 22, 1946, quoted in Janics, *Czechoslovak Policy*, 194.

57. H. Gordon Skilling, "Stalinism and Czechoslovak Political Culture," in *Stalinism: Essays in Historical Interpretation*, ed. Robert C. Tucker (New York: Norton, 1977), 264.

CHAPTER 6. THE COMMUNIST PERIOD: NEW VOWS

1. As Leff argues, the "protests of dissidents reflect political tensions that may be important to an understanding of the veiled political agenda" of submerged elites. Further, "the relationships among dissidents may tell something about the political fault lines that would otherwise be invisible or speculative; and the regime response may reveal something about the sensitivities of those in power." Carol Skalnik Leff, *National Conflict in Czechoslovakia: The Making and Remaking of a State, 1918–1987* (Princeton, N.J.: Princeton University Press, 1988), 263.

2. *Ústava Československé republiky, Ústavní zákon ze dne 9. Května 1948 (150/1948 Sb.)*, Parlament České republiky Poslaecká sněmovna, http://www.psp.cz/docs/texts/constitution_1948.html.

3. *Ústava Československé socialistické republiky, Ústavní zákon ze dne 11. Července 1960 (100/1960 Sb.)*, Parlament České republiky Poslaecká sněmovna, http://www.psp.cz/cgi-bin/win/docs/texts/constitution_1960.html.

4. Národní shromáždění republiky Československé, Pátek 18. Června 1948, RČS 1948–1954—stenoprotokoly, 7. Schůze, část 4/8, Společná česko-slovenská digitální parlamentní knihovna, http://www.psp.cz/eknih/1948/stenprot/007schuz/s007003.htm.

5. Quoted in "The New Party Statutes in Czechoslovakia," *Radio Free Europe Research*, *Czechoslovakia/43*, September 12, 1968, Open Society Archives Box-Folder-Report 19–2–257, http://files.osa.ceu.hu/holdings/300/8/3/text/19–2–257.shtml.

6. Vladimir Kusin, *Intellectual Origins of the Prague Spring: The Development of Reformist Ideas in Czechoslovakia, 1956–1967* (Cambridge: Cambridge University Press, 1971), 35.

7. Vladimir Kusin, *From Dubcek to Charter 77: A Study of "Normalization" in Czechoslovakia, 1968–1978* (Edinburgh: Q Press, 1978), 288.

8. Ján Pašiak, *Reišenie slovenskej národnostnej otázky* (Bratislava: VPL, 1962), 8, quoted in Leff, *National Conflict*, 141.

9. Leff, *National Conflict*, 142.

10. Viliam Plevza, "Aktuálne teoretické riešenia národnostných vzťahov v sučastnosti," in *Národnostné vzťahy v socialistickom československu* (Bratislava: Pravda, 1976), 11, quoted in ibid., 143.

11. Leff, *National Conflict*, 143–46.

12. Ibid., 142.

13. Karel Kaplan, *Utváření generální linie socialismu v ČSSR* (Prague, 1966), 103, quoted in Steiner, *The Slovak Dilemma* (Cambridge: Cambridge University Press, 1973), 91.

14. Jiří Pelikán, *The Czechoslovak Political Trials, 1950–1954: The Suppressed Report of the Dubček Government's Commission of Inquiry* (Stanford, Calif.: Stanford University Press, 1971), 87.

15. Quoted in Pavel Korbel and V. Vagassky, *Purges in the Communist Party of Czechoslovakia* (New York: National Committee for a Free Europe, 1952), 21, quoted in Leff, *National Conflict*, 169.

16. Leff, *National Conflict*, 169.

17. Pelikán, *The Czechoslovak Political Trials*, 128.

18. Skilling, "Stalinism and Czechoslovak Political Culture," in *Stalinism: Essays in Historial Interpretation*, ed. Robert C. Tucker (New York: Norton, 1977), 278–79.

19. Leff, *National Conflict*, 169.

20. Robert W. Dean, *Nationalism and Political Change in Eastern Europe: The Slovak Question and the Czechoslovak Reform Movement* (Denver: University of Denver Press, 1973), 8.

21. Gustáv Husák, "A Discussion About Czechoslovak Relations," *Historický časopis* 4 (1967): 7, quoted in Dean, *Nationalism*, 10–11.

22. Dean, *Nationalism*, 11.

23. H. Gordon Skilling, *Czechoslovakia's Interrupted Revolution* (Princeton, N.J.: Princeton University Press, 1976), 53.

24. Ibid., 69.

25. Ibid.

26. Stanley Riveles, "Breaking the Truce: The Fourth Writers Congress," *Radio Free*

Europe Research, July 24, 1967, http://www.files.osa.ceu.hu/holdings/300/8/3/text/17–5-283. shtml.

27. Ludvík Vaculík, "Comrades!" speech to Fourth Congress of Czechoslovak Writers, June 1967, reprinted in *Literární listy*, March 28, 1968 and in *Czechoslovakia: The Party and the People*, ed. Andrew Oxley, Alex Pravda, and Andrew Ritchie (London: Allen Lane, Penguin, 1973), 39.

28. Ibid., 38.

29. Milan Kundera, "A Nation Which Cannot Take Itself for Granted," speech to Fourth Congress of Czechoslovak Writers, June 1967, reprinted in *Literární listy*, March 21, 1968, and in Oxley et al., eds., *Czechoslovakia: The Party and the People*, 42–43.

30. Ibid., 45.

31. Karel Kosík, "Reason and Conscience," speech to Fourth Congress of Czechoslovak Writers, June 1967, in Oxley et al., eds., *Czechoslovakia: The Party and the People*, 26.

32. Ibid., 29.

33. Steiner, *The Slovak Dilemma*, 165.

34. *Život strany* 19, May 7, 1969, quoted in Skilling, *Interrupted Revolution*, 455.

35. *The Action Program of the Communist Party of Czechoslovakia, April 5, 1968*, Document 16 in Robin Alison Remington, ed., *Winter in Prague: Documents on Czechoslovak Communism in Crisis* (Cambridge Mass.: MIT Press, 1969), 97.

36. Skilling, *Interrupted Revolution*, 220.

37. Václav Havel, "On the Subject of Opposition," *Literární listy*, April 4, 1968, reprinted as Document 12 in Remington, ed., *Winter in Prague*, 64.

38. Ibid., 68.

39. Ludvík Vaculík, "2,000 Words to Workers, Farmers, Scientists, Artists, and Everyone," *Literární listy*, June 27, 1968, reprinted in Remington, ed., *Winter in Prague*, 196.

40. Ibid., 198.

41. Ibid.

42. Ibid., 201.

43. Skilling, *Interrupted Revolution*, 275.

44. Kosík, "Reason and Conscience," 28.

45. H. Gordon Skilling, "Sixty-Eight in Historical Perspective," *International Journal* 33, no. 4 (1978): 697.

46. Gustáv Husák, "Dejinná príležitost," *Pravda*, Bratislava, May 9, 1968, quoted in Steiner, *The Slovak Dilemma*, 169.

47. Quoted in Viliam Plevsa, *Československá štátnosť a slovenská otázka v politike KSČ*, (Bratislava: Práca, 1971), 300.

48. *Stenografický záznam z rokovania mimoriadnej krajskej konferencie KSS v Banskej Bystrici 13.–14. Júla 1968*, quoted in Plevsa, *Československá štátnosť*, 240.

49. Julius Strinka, "Federalizácia a demokratizácia," *Kultúrny život* 23, no. 14 (April 5, 1968): 1.

50. Ibid., 6.

51. Anonymous, "Češi, Slováci, a federace," *Listy* 9, no. 3 (1979): 18.

52. Dean, *Nationalism*, 35.

53. *Rudé právo*, May 5, 1968, quoted in Skilling, *Czechoslovakia's Interrupted Revolution*, 243.

54. Jaroslaw Piekalkiewicz, *Public Opinion Polling in Czechoslovakia, 1968–1969: Results and Analysis of Surveys Conducted During the Dubček Era* (New York: Praeger, 1972), 84, cited in Leff, *National Conflict*, 171.

55. Skilling, *Interrupted Revolution*, 523.

56. Ibid., 522–23.

57. Poll of Party Delegates (1968), Appendix B in ibid., 857.

58. Dean, *Nationalism*, 31.

59. *Nové slovo*, July 11, 1968, quoted in Skilling, *Interrupted Revolution*, 481.

60. Leff, *National Conflict*, 127.

61. *Ústavní zákon ze dne 27. října 1968 o československé federaci, 143/1968 Sb.*, Parlament České republiky, Poslanecká sněmovna, http://www.psp.cz/cgi-bin/win/docs/texts/constitution_1968.html.

62. Skilling, *Interrupted Revolution*, 874.

63. Miroslav Kusý, "Slovenský fenomén," *Listy* 15, no. 5 (1985): 34.

64. See Leff, *National Conflict*, 173–5.

65. Kusý, "Slovenský fenomén," 33.

66. Leff, *National Conflict*, 173.

67. Gil Eyal, *The Origins of Postcommunist Elites: From Prague Spring to the Breakup of Czechoslovakia* (Minneapolis: University of Minnesota Press, 2003), 40.

68. Ibid., 41.

69. Ibid., 42–43.

70. Ibid., 48.

71. Ibid., 49.

72. Ibid., 47.

73. Václav Průcha, "Economic Development and Relations, 1918–1989," in *The End of Czechoslovakia*, ed. Jiří Musil (Budapest: Central European University Press, 1995), 72–55.

74. H. Gordon Skilling, *Charter 77 and Human Rights in Czechoslovakia* (London: Allen and Unwin, 1981), 14.

75. "Charter 77—Declaration," January 1, 1977, reprinted in ibid., 209.

76. Skilling, *Charter 77*, 181.

77. Kusin, *From Dubček*, 310.

78. Aleksander Smolar, "From Opposition to Atomization," *Journal of Democracy* 7, no. 1 (1996): 24–25.

79. Ibid., 26.

80. Ján Tesař, "Totalitarian Dictatorships as a Phenomenon of the Twentieth Century and the Possibilities of Overcoming Them," *International Journal of Politics* 1, no. 1 (1981): 100.

81. Václav Havel, "The Power of the Powerless," in *Living in Truth*, ed. Jan Vladislav (Boston: Faber and Faber, 1990), 98.

82. For example, Charter Document 9 argued, "The impact of any school of thought is weakened if it is enforced by administrative means or by the use of force. This has been eloquently proved beyond measure by our national history. It is for this reason that the ideal

of freedom of religious belief was proclaimed in our country as early as Hussite times—before other European countries." "Charter 77 Document No. 9, 22 April 1977," reprinted in Skilling, *Charter 77* (London: Allen and Unwin, 1981), 247.

83. See for example Václav Trojan, "In Defense of Politics," *International Journal of Politics* 11, no. 1 (1981).

84. Skilling, *Charter 77*, 181.

85. Ibid., 193.

86. Ibid., 278.

87. Václav Havel, "Dear Dr. Husák," in Havel, *Open Letters: Selected Writings, 1965–1990*, ed. Paul Wilson (New York: Vintage, 1992), 56–7.

88. Václav Havel, "The Power of the Powerless," in *Open Letters: Selected Writings*, 132.

89. Eyal, *Origins of Postcommunist Elites*, 28.

90. See Pithart, "Towards a Shared Freedom," 215 and Karol Zlobina, "Slovensko: impresie a depresie," *Listy* 8 (1978): 45.

91. David Doellinger, "Prayers, Pilgrimages and Petitions: The Secret Church and the Growth of Civil Society in Slovakia," *Nationalities Papers* 30, no. 2 (2002): 216.

92. Abrams, "The Politics of Retribution," 279.

93. Doellinger, "Prayers, Pilgrimages and Petitions," 221.

94. Ibid., 222.

95. Ibid., 224.

96. Ibid., 226.

97. Ibid.

98. Ibid., 227.

99. "Podněty katolíků k řešení situace veřících občanů ČSR," KI: CD ROM 11/3 Protests, 2, quoted in ibid.

100. Doellinger, "Prayers, Pilgrimages and Petitions," 228.

101. Letter from František Mikloško to local authorities, reprinted in *samizdat* "Verejne zhromaždenie," *Bratislavské listy* 1 (1988): 9, and "Výzva k verejemu zhromaždenia," *Rodinné spoločenstvo* 2 (1988): 42, quoted in Doellinger, "Prayers, Pilgrimages and Petitions," 229–30.

102. Doellinger, "Prayers, Pilgrimages and Petitions," 230.

103. Ibid., 229.

104. Leff, *National Conflict*, 264.

105. Ibid.

106. Pithart, "Towards a Shared Freedom," 214.

107. Leff, *National Conflict*, 265.

108. Karol Zlobina, "Slovensko: impresie a depresie," 45.

109. Ibid.

110. Pithart, "Towards a Shared Freedom," 214.

111. Skilling, *Charter 77*, 57.

112. Anonymous, "Češi, Slováci," 24.

113. Pithart, "Towards a Shared Freedom," 217. Zlobina points out that the homogenization of the nation was far from complete, as the nation continued to be "divided into two irreconcilable camps: the Catholic and the Lutheran . . . to this day, it is possible to hear

in overcrowded public transportation vehicles: why are you shoving like a Lutheran—or possibly a Jew." This divide was also reflected in the two literary institutes within the top scientific institute in Slovakia. "Slovensko: impresie a depresie," 45.

114. Kenneth Jowitt, "An Organizational Approach to the Study of Political Culture in Marxist-Leninist Systems," *American Political Science Review* 68 (1974): 1177.

115. Kusý, "Slovenský fenomén," 35.

116. Pithart, "Towards a Shared Freedom," 218.

117. *Ústavní zákon ze dne 27. října 1968*, Parlament České republiky, Poslanecká sněmovna, http://www.psp.cz/cgi-bin/win/docs/texts/constitution_1968.html.

118. As Robert Tucker argues, in "the communist *party-state* as a cultural or political-cultural formation, we are dealing with a phenomenon that shows in its self-conception, and even in its institutional configuration, a suggestive resemblance to the classic church-state." "Culture, Political Culture, and Communist Society," 181.

119. Kusý, "Slovenský fenomén," 33.

120. Anonymous, "Češi, Slováci," 18.

121. Ibid., 34.

122. Eyal, *Origins of Postcommunist Elites*, 28.

123. Ibid., 103.

124. Ibid., 100–131.

125. Pithart, "Towards a Shared Freedom," 212.

126. Průcha, "Economic Development and Relations," 75.

127. Richard Rose, *Czechs and Slovaks Compared: A Survey of Economic and Political Behavior* (Glasgow: Centre for the Study of Public Policy, University of Strathclyde, 1992), 26–27.

128. Walker Connor, *Ethnonationalism: The Quest for Understanding* (Princeton, N.J.: Princeton University Press, 1994), 149.

129. Leff, *National Conflict*, 295–96.

130. Havel, "The Power of the Powerless," 132.

CHAPTER 7. FROM VELVET REVOLUTION TO VELVET DIVORCE

1. Timothy Garton Ash, *The Magic Lantern: The Revolution of '89 Witnessed in Warsaw, Budapest, Berlin, and Prague* (New York: Vintage, 1990, 1993), 78.

2. Quoted in ibid., 15.

3. Ibid.

4. Dusan Hendrych, "Constitutionalism and Constitutional Change in Czechoslovakia," in *Constitutional Policy and Change in Europe*, ed. Joachim Jens Hesse and Nevil Johnson (Oxford: Oxford University Press, 1995), 288.

5. Quoted in Václav Žák, "The Velvet Divorce: Institutional Foundations," in *The End of Czechoslovakia*, ed. Jiří Musil (Budapest: Central European University Press, 1995), 247.

6. Ibid.

7. Petr Pithart, News conference, November 13, 1991, as reported in "Pithart Meets

Press on 11–12 Nov. Federation Talks," Foreign Broadcast Information Service—East European Report *FBOS-EEI-91–220* November 14, 1991, 10, quoted in Sharon Wolchik, "The Politics of Ethnicity in Post-Communist Czechoslovakia," *East European Politics and Societies* 8, no. 1 (1994): 157.

8. Žák, "The Velvet Divorce," 247.

9. Jiři Pehe, "Growing Slovak Demands Seen as Threat to Federation," *Report on Eastern Europe*, no. 12 (March 22, 1991): 6.

10. Prague Home Service, September 17, 1990, translated and reprinted in Speech by Havel on Roles of Republics and Federation, BBC, EE/0873, September 19, 1990, at C 1/2, quoted in Roberta Barbieri, "Czechoslovakia's Movement Toward a New Constitution: The Challenge of Establishing a Democratic, Multinational State," *New York Law School Journal of International and Comparative Law* 13 (1992): 116.

11. Ibid., n200.

12. Václav Havel, "Základ identity společného státu," *Národná obroda*, September 18, 1990, quoted in Stanislav Kirschbaum, *A History of Slovakia: The Struggle for Survival* (New York: St. Martin's-Griffin, 1995), 263.

13. Hendrych, "Constitutionalism," 289.

14. Carol Skalnik Leff, *The Czech and Slovak Republics: Nation Versus State* (Boulder, Colo.: Westview Press, 1998), 144.

15. Ibid., 138.

16. Ibid., 139.

17. Valerie Bunce, "Should Transitologists Be Grounded?" *Slavic Review* 54, no. 1 (1995): 121.

18. Ludvik Vaculík, "Our Slovak Question," *Literárni noviny* 5 (1990), quoted in Peter Martin, "Relations Between the Czechs and the Slovaks," *Report on Eastern Europe* 36 (September 7, 1990): 2.

19. S. Riveles, "Slovak Nationalism Revisited," *Radio Free Europe Research, Czechoslovakia*, November 11, 1965, www.osa.ceu.hu/holdings/300/8/3/texxt/17–2-71.shtml.

20. Vladimír Mináč, "Our Czecho-Slovak Question," *Nové slovo*, no. 21, May 24, 1990, 5, quoted in Martin, "Relations Between the Czechs and the Slovaks," 3.

21. Ibid.

22. Leff, *Czech and Slovak Republics*, 142.

23. Štefan Polakovič, "Čo je a čo nie je nacionalizmus," *Literárni týždenník* 24 (June 15, 1990): 12.

24. Ibid., 13.

25. Ladislav Nikliček and Petr Nováček, "Dynamit v základech státu," *Zemedelské noviny*, November 25, 1991.

26. Ibid.

27. Nick Thorpe, "Hopes for Slovak Independence Fall as Ukraine Rises," *The Observer*, January 26, 1992.

28. *Vystoupení J. Carnogurského, předseda Slovenské vlády*, November 16, 1991.

29. Mary Hockaday, "Gap Grows Between Czechs and Slovaks," *The Independent*, December 9, 1991.

30. Quoted in Martin, "Relations Between the Czechs and the Slovaks," 5.

31. Ibid.

32. W. L. Webb, "The Czechs and Slovaks Find Fellow Feeling," *The Guardian*, December 18, 1991.

33. Ondrej Florek, "Bratia česi–spamätajte sa!" *Nové slovo*, May 25, 1992, 24.

34. Will Kymlicka, "Misunderstanding Nationalism," in *Theorizing Nationalism*, ed. Ronald Beiner (Albany: State University of New York Press, 1999), 140.

35. Vladimir V. Kusin, "Czechs and Slovaks: The Road to the Current Debate," *Report on Eastern Europe* 40 (October 5, 1990): 5.

36. A 2006 survey showed Masaryk's continuing relevance in the Czech Republic, where he was rated the second most important Czech figure from the past or present. Charles IV came in first and Havel third. Centrum pro výzkum veřejného mínění (CVVM), *Osobnosti a události českých dějin očima veřejného mínění*, February 1, 2006, http://www.cvvm.cas.cz/index.php?lang=1&disp=zpravy&r=1&shw=100556.

37. Ladislav Holy, *The Little Czech and the Great Czech Nation: National Identity and the Post-Communist Social Transformation* (Cambridge: Cambridge University Press, 1996), 109.

38. "Tisíc slov o Slovensku a stanovisko OSN," *Slovenský denník*, December 4, 1991, quoted in Leff, *Czech and Slovak Republics*, 142.

39. Quoted in Rudolf Procházka, "Väčšia autonómia Slovensku," *Svou denník*, January 8, 1992.

40. "Proclamation of the Slovak National Council and the Government of the Slovak Republic concerning the Deportation of the Jews from Slovakia," Appendix in Yeshayahu Jelinek, "Slovaks and the Holocaust: An End to Reconciliation?" *East European Jewish Affairs* 22, no. 1 (Summer 1992): 21–22.

41. Ibid.

42. Quoted in ibid., 9.

43. Steve Kettle, "Slovak Nationalists to Stage Pro-Independence Rally," B-wire (Reuter) FF0077, March 13, 1992.

44. Quoted respectively in Adam B. Schiff, "Slovakia Declares Its—Identity?" *Christian Science Monitor*, July 21, 1992, http://www.csmonitor.com/1992/0721/21181.html and Chris Bowlby, "Nazi Anniversary Raises Czech-Slovak Tensions," *The Independent*, March 16, 1992.

45. Holy, *The Little Czech*, 109.

46. Ibid.

47. Jelinek, "Slovaks and the Holocaust," 8.

48. M. Timoracký, "Verejná mienka o česko-slovenských vzťahoch," in *Dnešni krize česko-slovenských vztahů*, ed. F. Gál et al. (Prague: Sociologické nakladatelství, 1992), 81–82, cited in Jelinek, "Slovaks and the Holocaust," 8.

49. Holy, *The Little Czech*, 109.

50. Leff, *Czech and Slovak Republics*, 173.

51. Jelinek, "Slovaks and the Holocaust," 8.

52. Irena Uher, "Nacionalizmus Napája Túžby Slovenska," *Slovenský národ*, February 11, 1992, 28.

53. Vladmír Krivý, "Na križovatke či na krížovej ceste?" *Kultúrny život*, November 5, 1991, 13.

54. Ibid., 16.

55. Holy, *The Little Czech*, 109.

56. Ibid.

57. Florek, "Bratia," 24.

58. Petr Pithart, "Posolstvo českého premiéra občanom Slovenskej republiky: Vzbura proti l'ahkomysel'nosti," *Verejnost'*, November 11, 1991, 7.

59. Leff, *Czech and Slovak Republics*, 134.

60. Gil Eyal, *The Origins of Postcommunist Elites: From Prague Spring to the Breakup of Czechoslovakia* (Minneapolis: University of Minnesota Press, 2003), 88.

61. Ibid., 175.

62. Ibid., 161.

63. Smolar, "From Opposition to Atomization," *Journal of Democracy* 7, no. 1 (January 1996): 32.

64. Shari Cohen, *Politics Without a Past: The Absence of History in Postcommunist Nationalism* (Durham, N.C.: Duke University Press, 1999), 149.

65. Eyal, *The Origins*, 143.

66. Ibid., 13.

67. Ibid., 169–83.

68. Cohen, *Politics Without a Past*, 16.

69. Ibid., 20.

70. Ibid., 6.

71. Ibid.

72. Movement for a Democratic Slovakia, *Desatoro volebného programu Hnutia za demokratické Slovensko* (Campaign Brochure, titled Ten Key Imperatives of the HZDS Electoral Agenda), 1992.

73. Vladimír Mečiar, Radio address on Československo Radioforum, 6.33 hod., June 2, 1992.

74. *Desatoro volebneho programu.*

75. Quoted in Pehe, "Growing Slovak Demands," 8.

76. Schiff, "Slovakia Declares Its—Identity?"

77. Pithart, "Towards a Shared Freedom, 1968–89," in *The End of Czechoslovakia*, ed. Jiří Musil (Budapest: Central European University Press, 1995), 212.

78. Jiří Pejchl, "Podíl psychických komplexů na emancipaci Slovenska," *Český deník*, June 30, 1992, 19.

79. Letter to the Editor, *Český deník*, September 8, 1992, quoted in Holy, *The Little Czech*, 110.

80. William Mishler and Richard Rose, *Trajectories of Fear and Hope: The Dynamics of Support for Democracy in Eastern Europe* (Glasgow: Centre for the Study of Public Policy, University of Strathclyde, 1993), 18.

81. Iveta Radicova, "The Velvet Divorce," *Uncaptive Minds* 6, no. 1 (Winter–Spring 1993): 51.

82. Ibid., 52.

83. Central European University, "Party Systems and Electoral Alignments in East Central Europe," 1992 (computer file); see Appendix A in Nadya Nedelsky, "Divergent Responses to a Common Past: Transitional Justice in the Czech and Slovak Republics," *Theory and Society* 33, no. 1 (February 2004): 114. "Lustration"—the legally mandated removal from office of former highly placed regime officials and former secret police officials and their informers from positions of public influence—proceeded very differently in the two republics. In the Czech Republic, lustration has been pursued from 1991 up through this writing, while it was never seriously undertaken in Slovakia, and the relevant law was allowed to expire in 1996. I have argued elsewhere that the two nations' different approaches to transitional justice reflected significantly different appraisals of the previous regime's legitimacy; see 65–115.

84. Leff, *Czech and Slovak Republics*, 131.

85. Wolchik, "The Politics of Ethnicity," 176.

86. Ibid.

87. "Klaus Say[s] Better to Split Czechoslovakia," B-wire (Reuter) FF0095, W/CN 46/49, June 20, 1992.

88. Leff, *Czech and Slovak Republics*, 131.

89. "The Events of the Last Week: June 18–24," *Carolina* 33, June 24, 1992, http://carolina.cuni.cz/archive-en/Carolina-E-No-033.txt.

90. "HZDS's Mečiar: Party Will Not Support Havel," B-Wire (NCA/B) FF0004, June 17, 1992.

91. Žák, "The Velvet Divorce," 263.

92. "Text of the Declaration of Slovak Sovereignty," B-wire (AFP) FF0062, July 17, 1992.

93. *The Wall Street Journal*, July 21, 1992, quoted in Jan Obrman, "Slovakia Declares Sovereignty; President Havel Resigns," *RFE/RL Research Report* 1, no. 31, July 31, 1992, 25.

94. Bernard Meixner, "Havel to Resign, Slovak Parliament Proclaims Slovakia's Sovereignty," B-wire (AFP) FF0079, July 17, 1992.

95. *The Guardian*, July 20, 1992, quoted in Obrman, "Slovakia Declares Sovereignty," 26.

96. Leff, *The Czech and Slovak Republics*, 132.

97. Ibid., 251.

98. Andrej Kopčok, "The Slovak Nation and Communist Totalitarianism (1945–1949)," in *Language, Values and the Slovak Nation*, ed. Tibor Pichler and Jana Gasparikova (Washington, D.C.: Paideia Press and Council for Research in Values and Philosophy, 1994), 119.

99. Vladimir Mináč, *Dúchanie do pahrieb* (Bratislava, 1972), 151–52, quoted in ibid.

100. Kopčok, "The Slovak Nation," 119.

101. Ján Obrman, "Slovak Politician Accused of Secret Police Ties," *RFE/RL Research Report* 1, no. 15, April 10, 1992, 15.

102. Kevin Deegan-Krause, *Elected Affinities: Democracy and Party Competition in Slovakia and the Czech Republic* (Stanford, Calif.: Stanford University Press, 2006), 200.

103. Ibid., 208.

104. Sharon Wolchik, "The Repluralization of Politics in Czechoslovakia," *Communist and Post-Communist Studies* 26, no. 4 (December 1993): 426–27.

105. Deegan-Krause, *Elected Affinities*, 208.

106. Walker Connor, *Ethnonationalism: The Quest for Understanding* (Princeton, N.J.: Princeton University Press, 1994), 46.

107. Deegan-Krause, *Elected Affinities*, 133.

108. Ibid.

Chapter 8. The Implications of the Ethnic Model of Sovereignty in Slovakia

1. "Not Cinderella," *The Economist*, September 10, 1994, 83, quoted in Kevin Deegan-Krause, *Elected Affinities: Democracy and Party Competition in Slovakia and the Czech Republic* (Stanford, Calif.: Stanford University Press, 2006), 22.

2. Ivan Gabal, "Zahraniční inspirace k integraci Romů," in *Romové v česke republice, 1945–1998*, ed. Helena Lisá (Prague: Socioklub, 1999), 74.

3. Ibid., 74–75.

4. Jiří Pehe, "Slovakia Adopts Constitution," *RFE/RL Program Brief*, September 2, 1992.

5. Ľubo Meštanek, "Národné, či národnesté," *Večerník*, January 24, 1992.

6. *Ústava Slovenskej republiky*, Slovak Government Website, http://www-8.vlada.gov.sk/index.php?ID=1013.

7. Stanislav Bajaník, "Štát a jeho jazyk," *Práca*, March 31, 1993.

8. Miroslav Kusý, "Maďarský nárvh plný rozporov," *Národná obroda*, May 7, 1993.

9. Constitution of the Slovak Republic in *The Constitutions of the New Democracies in Europe*, ed. Peter Raina (Cambridge: Merlin Books, 1996), 293.

10. Ibid., 287.

11. Interview with Miklós Duray, "Slovensko o ústavě," *Lidové noviny*, September 5, 1992.

12. Milan Čič, "Spojenie princípu národného, občianského i medzinárodného," *Národná obroda*, August 3, 1992.

13. Television interview with Jozef Prokeš, *Co Tyden Dal*, Československá televise, 10.55 hod. (transcribed in original language by *Slovakia Today Monitoring*), August 2, 1992.

14. Jaroslav Chovanec, Peter Mozolík and Michal Gašpar, "Politici v ofenszife," *Literárný Tyždenník*, May 21, 1993.

15. Ibid.

16. Ibid.

17. "Gašparovič Questions Hungarian Parties' Loyalty to Slovakia," CTK (Czech News Agency), Bratislava, July 4, 1993.

18. Quoted in Alfred Reisch, "Slovakia's Minority Policy Under International Scrutiny," *RFE/RL Research Report* 2, no. 49, December 10, 1993, 41. In an interview with a German newspaper, Deputy Prime Minister Roman Kováč offered a slightly different

explanation. Responding to the interviewer's skeptical question, he asked, "Can you for example pronounce the name Gyröygyny? And you demand that a Slovak in southern Slovakia must pronounce this!" Sabine Herre, "daß ein Slowake dies aussprechen muß!" *Die Tageszeitung*, January 10, 1994.

19. Some 435 towns and municipalities with large Hungarian majorities had sanctioned such signs, and they stood set back from the official Slovak signs.

20. Quoted in "Road Blocked in Hungarian-Slovak Sign Dispute," Reuter: B-Wire (FF0107), August 12, 1993.

21. Commission on Security and Cooperation in Europe (CSCE), *Human Rights and Democratization in Slovakia* (Washington, D.C.: CSCE, September 1993), 12–13.

22. Ibid., 1–2.

23. Ibid., 12.

24. Ibid., 14–15.

25. Quoted in "Slovak Premier Warns against Hungarian Expansionism," Reuter: B-wire (FF0125), September 17, 1993.

26. Reisch, "Slovakia's Minority Policy," 42.

27. *Stenografická správa o 22. schôdzi Národnej rady Slovenskej republiky konanej 24. Septembra 1993* [September 23 stenographic transcript], Společná Česko-Slovenská digitálna parlamentná knižnica, http://www.nrsr.sk/dk/Documents.aspx?MasterID=75882.

28. Sharon Fisher, "Meeting of Slovakia's Hungarians Causes Stir," *RFE/RL Research Report* 3, no. 4, January 28, 1994, 42.

29. Bill Reynolds, "Ethnic Hungarians to Convene Assembly in Slovakia," *Prague Post*, December 30, 1993.

30. Fisher, "Meeting of Slovakia's Hungarians," 43.

31. Sharon Fisher, "Slovakia's Ethnic Hungarians Gather in Komarno," *RFE/RL Research Institute Program Brief*, January 10, 1994, 2.

32. Deegan-Krause, *Elected Affinities*, 24.

33. *Stenografická správa o 22. schôdzi Národnej rady Slovenskej republiky konanej 24. Septembra 1993*, Společná Česko-Slovenská digitálna parlamentná knižnica, http://www.nrsr.sk/dk/Documents.aspx?MasterID=75882.

34. Bjorn H. Jernudd, "Personal Names and Human Rights," in *Linguistic Human Rights: Overcoming Linguistic Discrimination*, ed. Tove Skutnabb-Kangas and Robert Phillipson (Berlin: Mouton de Gruyter, 1995), 121.

35. Carol Skalnik Leff, *The Czech and Slovak Republics: Nation Versus State* (Boulder, Colo: Westview Press, 1996), 151.

36. Quoted in Bill Reynolds, "Slovakia, Hungary Take First Steps Toward Reconciliation," *Prague Post*, May 11–17, 1994.

37. Quoted in Ondrej Dostál, "Pozitívne prvé kroky," *Sme*, April 5, 1994.

38. David Lucas, "Ethnic Bipolarism in Slovakia, 1989–1995," *Donald W. Treadgold Papers* (Henry M. Jackson School of International Studies at the University of Washington) 11 (November 1996): 14.

39. Ondrej Dostál, "Od konfrontácie k rezervanosti: Pokrok v slovensko-mad'arských

vzťahoch za roky 1992–1994," in *Quo Vadis Slovensko? Revue o človeku, spoločnosti and politike*, 1/85, (Bratislava: RaPaMan, 1995), 118, quoted in Lucas, "Ethnic Bipolarism," 80.

40. Jane Perlez, "Voters Back Ex-Premier in Slovakia," *New York Times*, October 3, 1994.

41. "Albright, Kováč Remarks at Washington Lunch," *TASR*, Bratislava, January 29, 1998, quoted in Deegan-Krause, *Elected Affinities*, 22.

42. Ibid., 73.

43. Farimah Daftary and Kinga Gál, "The New Slovak Language Law: Internal or External Politics?" ECMI Working Paper 8, European Centre for Minority Issues, September 2000, 25, http://www.ecmi.de/download/working_paper_8.pdf.

44. This is the official English translation of Law 270/1995 (On the State Language of the Slovak Republic) provided on the Slovak Ministry of Culture website, www.culture.gov.sk/english/legislation.html.

45. In an earlier draft of the law, all weddings were to be done in Slovak, but church protests led to a change in the final draft. The law does not govern liturgical language.

46. Vera Rich, "Slovakians Watch Their Language," *Times Higher Education*, January 19, 1996, http://www.timeshighereducation.co.uk/story.asp?storyCode=92111&sectioncode=26.

47. Pavla Horáková, "Slovak TV Withdraws Czech Children's Series in Breach of Slovak Language Law," *Czech Radio 7, Radio Prague*, September 7, 2005, http://www.radio.cz/en/article/70396.

48. Sharon Fisher, "Slovak President Signs Language Law," *OMRI Daily Digest*, Part II, no. 231, November 29, 1995.

49. Dobroslava Krajačičová, radio commentary on *Na Margo Dna*, Slovensko, 117.05 hod. (transcribed in original language by *Slovakia Today Monitoring*), August 30, 1995.

50. Ján Cuper, "Slovenčina bez výminky," *Koridor*, August 18, 1992.

51. Jerguš Ferko, "Politika odtrhnutých vagónov (I)," *Smena*, June 30, 1993.

52. Cuper, "Slovenčina."

53. Radio interview with Ivan Hudec, *Radiožurnál*, Slovensko 1, 12.00 hod. (transcribed in original language by *Slovakia Today Monitoring*), October 24, 1995.

54. Radio interview with Jozef Prokeš, *Radiožurnál*, Slovensko 1, 12.00 hod. (transcribed in original language by *Slovakia Today Monitoring*), November 24, 1995.

55. Radio interview with Jozef Prokeš, *Radiožurnál*, Slovensko 1, 7.00 hod. (transcribed in original language by Slovakia Today Monitoring), November 16, 1995.

56. Cuper, "Slovenčina."

57. Sharon Fisher, "Slovak Parliament Approves Language Law," *OMRI Analytical Brief*, no. 32, November 16, 1995.

58. Pieter van Duin and Zuzana Poláčková, "Democratic Renewal and the Hungarian Minority Question in Slovakia: From Populism to Ethnic Democracy?" *European Societies* 2, no. 3 (2000): 347.

59. Miklos Duray, "Hungarian Nation in Slovakia," http://slovakia.org/society-hungary.htm.

60. Van Duin and Poláčková, "Democratic Renewal," 344. The poll they cite is by Zora Bútorová, "Public Opinion," in *Slovakia 1996–1997: A Global Report on the State of Society*, ed. Martin Bútora and Thomas W. Skladony (Bratislava: Institute for Public Affairs, 1998), 72.

61. "SDĽ Will Not Support Creation of 'Minority Parliament,'" *CTK National Newswire*, April 24, 1995.

62. "Ethnic Hungarians on the Brink of High Treason—Slota," *CTK National Newswire*, April 27, 1995.

63. Judith Kelley, "International Actors on the Domestic Scene: Membership Conditionality and Socialization by International Institutions," *International Organizations* 58, no. 3 (Summer 2004), 447.

64. Jerguš Ferko, "Všubne si Vysoky komisár OBSE ako Vysoko rúbu Mad'arskí extrémisti?" *Slovenská republika*, January 9, 1996.

65. Sharon Fisher, "Slovak Parliament Approves Law on the Protection of the Republic and Ratifies Treaty with Hungary," *OMRI Analytical Brief* 1, no. 42, March 27, 1996.

66. Adrian Bridge, "Slovak Uproar over Free Speech," *The Independent*, March 27, 1996.

67. Sharon Fisher, "Slovak Opposition Criticizes Penal Code," *OMRI Daily Digest*, Part II, no. 54, March 15, 1996.

68. Peter Dúbrava, Slovak radio report, *Radiožurnál*, Slovensko 1, 18.00 hod. (transcribed in original language by *Slovakia Today Monitoring*), March 27, 1996.

69. Bernard Hornák, Slovak radio report, *Radiožurnál*, Slovensko 1, 12.00 hod. (transcribed in original language by *Slovakia Today Monitoring*), March 21, 1996.

70. Kelley, "International Actors," 448.

71. Radio interviews with Jozef Liščak, respectively *Popoludnie s rozhlasom*, Slovensko 1 (transcribed in original language by *Slovakia Today Monitoring*), April 15, 1996, and *Radiožurnál*, Slovensko 1,18.00 hod. (transcribed in original language by *Slovakia Today Monitoring*), March 27, 1996.

72. Radio interview with Vladimír Mečiar, *Rozhovor s premiérom*, Slovensko 1, 18.30 hod. (transcribed in original language by *Slovakia Today Monitoring*), March 29, 1996.

73. Kelley, "International Actors," 448.

74. Ibid.

75. "Slovak Parliament Passes Protection of Republic Amendment," *CTK National Newswire*, December 17, 1996.

76. Deegan-Krause, *Elected Affinities*, 221.

77. All this coalition-forming was necessary because of new electoral rules put in place by the Mečiar government, to the detriment of competing political forces. See Deegan-Krause, *Elected Affinities*, 56–57.

78. Van Duin and Poláčková, "Democratic Renewal," 348.

79. Zsuzsa Csergo, "Beyond Ethnic Division: Majority-Minority Debate About the Postcommunist State in Romania and Slovakia," *East European Politics and Societies* 16, no. 1 (2002): 18.

80. Ibid., n53.

81. Van Duin and Poláčková, "Democratic Renewal and the Hungarian Minority," 349.

82. Karen Henderson, "EU Influence on Party Politics in Slovakia," paper presented at European Union Studies Association Conference, Austin, Texas, March 31–2 April 2, 2005), http://aei.pitt.edu/3201/01/Austin,Henderson.txt.

83. Kyriaki Topidi, "The Limits of EU Conditionality: Minority Rights in Slovakia," *Journal of Ethnopolitics and Minority Issues in Europe* 1 (2003): 6.

84. Michael J. Kopanic, "The New Minority Language Law in Slovakia," *Central Europe Review* 1, no. 2 (July 5, 1999), http://www.ce-review.org/99/2/kopanic2.html.

85. Ibid.

86. "Cabinet Passes EU-Friendly Minority Language Law Despite Objections of Hungarian Party," *Slovak Spectator*, July 12–18, 1999, http://www.spectator.sk/articles/view/4171//.

87. Kopanic, "The New Minority Language Law."

88. Milan Knažko, in *Druhý deň rokovania, 17. schôdze Národnej rady Slovenskej republiky, 30 júna 1999* [June 30 stenographic transcript] Spoločná Česko-slovenská digitálna parlamentná knižnica, www.nrsr.sk/dk/.

89. Ján Cuper (HZDS), in *Druhý deň rokovania, 17. schôdze Národnej rady Slovenskej republiky, 30 júna 1999*. In particular, Anna Maliková and Marián Andel of the SNS argued that 36 legal norms already dealt with minority language in education, culture, medicine, and official contacts.

90. Jozef Prokeš, in *Druhý deň rokovania, 17. schôdze Národnej rady Slovenskej republiky, 30 júna 1999*.

91. Eva Slavkovská (SNS), in *Druhý deň rokovania, 17. schôdze Národnej rady Slovenskej republiky, 30 júna 1999*; Cuper, in *Druhý deň rokovania, 17. schôdze Národnej rady Slovenskej republiky, 30 júna 1999*.

92. Cuper, ibid.

93. Katarina Tóthová, in *Druhý deň rokovania, 17. schôdze Národnej rady Slovenskej republiky, 30 júna 1999*.

94. Ibid.

95. Slavkovská, in *Druhý deň rokovania, 17. schôdze Národnej rady Slovenskej republiky, 30 júna 1999*.

96. Marián Andel, in *Druhý deň rokovania, 17. schôdze Národnej rady Slovenskej republiky, 30 júna 1999*.

97. Milan Knažko, in *Druhý deň rokovania, 17. schôdze Národnej rady Slovenskej republiky, 30 júna 1999*.

98. Ivan Simko, in *Tretí deň rokovania, 17. schôdze Národnej rady Slovenskej republiky, 1 júla 1999* [July 1 stenographic transcript].

99. Lajoš Meszároš, in *Štvrtý deň rokovania, 17. schôdze Národnej rady Slovenskej republiky, 2 júla 1999* [July 2 stenographic transcript].

100. Milan Hort, in *Štvrtý deň rokovania, 17. schôdze Národnej rady Slovenskej republiky, 2 júla 1999*.

101. Peter Weiss, in *Tretí deň rokovania, 17. schôdze Národnej rady Slovenskej republiky, 1 júla 1999*.

102. Ladislav Orosz, in *Tretí deň rokovania, 17. schôdze Národnej rady Slovenskej republiky, 1 júla 1999*.

103. Ladislav Ballek, in *Tretí deň rokovania, 17. schôdze Národnej rady Slovenskej republiky, 1 júla 1999*.

104. Knažko, in *Tretí deň rokovania, 17. schôdze Národnej rady Slovenskej republiky, 1 júla 1999*.

105. Ján Budaj, in *Štvrtý deň rokovania, 17. schôdze Národnej rady Slovenskej republiky, 2 júla 1999*.

106. Ballek, in *Tretí deň rokovania, 17. schôdze Národnej rady Slovenskej republiky, 1 júla 1999*.

107. Jirko Malchárek, in *Tretí deň rokovania, 17. schôdze Národnej rady Slovenskej republiky, 1 júla 1999*.

108. Stephan Slachta, in *Tretí deň rokovania, 17. schôdze Národnej rady Slovenskej republiky, 1 júla 1999*.

109. Weiss, in *Tretí deň rokovania, 17. schôdze Národnej rady Slovenskej republiky, 1 júla 1999*.

110. Pavol Števček, in *Tretí deň rokovania, 17. schôdze Národnej rady Slovenskej republiky, 1 júla 1999*.

111. Dušan Švantner, in *Druhý deň rokovania, 17. schôdze Národnej rady Slovenskej republiky, 30 júna 1999*.

112. Van Duin and Poláčková, "Democratic Renewal," 353.

113. "Hungarians in the Slovak Government," UN Online Network in Public Administration and Finance, http://unpan1.un.org/intradoc/groups/public/documents/nispacee/unpan005083.pdf- 187.4KB - UNPAN Documents.

114. Lucia Nicholsonová, "Hungarian Language Bill Defeated," *Slovak Spectator*, July 26, 1999, http://www.spectator.sk/articles/view/4080//.

115. Van Duin and Poláčková, "Domestic Renewal," 349.

116. Zsuzsa Csergo, *Talk of the Nation: Language and Conflict in Romania and Slovakia* (Ithaca, N.Y.: Cornell University Press, 2007), 81.

117. Coexistence, *From Minority Status to Partnership: Hungarians in Czechoslovakia/Slovakia*, 1996, www://hhrf.org/egyutt/AD-PARTN.HTM.

118. Strana maďarskej koalície, *Volebný program 1998 (Úvod)*, http://www.mkp.sk/old/index.php?t=&p=&xp=&MId=1&Lev1=&Ind1=60&MId=1&P=index,sl,&Ind1=61.

119. Strana maďarskej koalície, *Speech to be delivered at the IVth SMK Congress*, http://www.mkp.sk/old/index.php?t=&p=&xp=&MId=1&Lev1=&Ind1=1&P=index,en,&Ind=52.

120. Topidi, "The Limits of EU Conditionality," 16.

121. Strana maďarskej koalície, *Volebný program 2006–2010*, June 17, 2006, http://www.smk.sk/index.php?option=com_content&task=view&id=28&Itemid=46&limit=1&limitstart=2.

122. "Trouble in New Europe," *Wall Street Journal*, July 20, 2006.

123. Tim Haughton, "Slovakia's Robert Fico: A Man to be Trusted or Feared?" *RFE/RL East European Perspectives*, May 29, 2002, http://www.rferl.org/reports/eepreport/2002/05/11-290502.asp.

124. Ibid.

125. Robert Fico, "Hungarians Brought Own Agenda to Coalition," reprinted from *Práca*, May 26, 1999 in *Slovak Spectator*, May 31, 1999, http://www.spectator.sk/articles/view/4432//.

126. Quoted in Martina Jurinová, "Fico Extends Hand to Mečiar, Slota," *Slovak Spectator*, July 3, 2006, http://www.spectator.sk/articles/view/23921/2/.

127. TASR, "Survey Shows Slovak Citizens Divided in Opinion on Current Coalition," July 21, 2006, www.tasr.sk.

128. Strana mad'arskej koalície, "Vyhlásenie Republikovej rady Strany mad'arskej koalície o situácii po parlamentných vol'bach v roku 2006," July 8, 2006, http://www.mkp.sk/index.php?P=index,sl.

129. Quoted in Martina Jurinová, "Cabinet Stung by Brussels Rejection," *Slovak Spectator*, July 10–16, 2006.

130. Lucia Kobosova, "EU Socialists Kick Out Slovaks in 'Historic' Move," *EU Observer*, October 13, 2006, www.europeanforum.net/news/274.

131. Quoted in Jurinová, "Cabinet Stung by Brussels Rejection."

132. "USA budú u nás sledovat' oblast' l'udských práv," *Sme*, July 14, 2006, http://www.sme.sk/c/2805371/usa-budu-u-nas-sledovat-oblast-ludskych-prav.html.

133. Martina Jurinová, "Kubiš Tries to Calm Hungarian Worries," *Slovak Spectator*, July 17, 2006, http://www.spectator.sk/articles/view/24161/2/.

134. Quoted in ibid.

135. Quoted in Jurinová, "Fico Extends Hand."

136. See, for example, Robin Shepherd, "Slovakia sets extremist challenge for Europe," *Financial Times*, July 6, 2006, http://us.ft.com/ftgateway/superpage.ft?news_id=ft007062 0061546465471.

137. Quoted in Jurinová, "Kubiš Tries to Calm Hungarian Worries."

138. Ibid.

139. Quoted in Martin Jurinová, "SNS: It Is All Biased Vilification," *Slovak Spectator*, July 13, 2006, http://www.spectator.sk/articles/view/24163/2/.

140. Ján Slota, interview with Samuel Kubáni, "Vyhnání Němců vám závidím," *Lidové noviny*, July 22, 2006, http://www.lidovky.cz/ln_rozhovory.asp?c=A060722_105415_ln_rozhovory_hlm. Though it caused much less of a stir, a few days later Slota gave another highly provocative interview, this time to the Austrian *Die Presse*. Asked about his role in the "new nationalism in Eastern Europe," he responded that it was "Absolute nonsense. We want to assert the rights of all minorities, not just for Hungarians. From the original 600,000 members of the Slovak minority in Hungary there are only 44,000 left. To where did the others disappear? Were they shot, or what? On the territory of Slovakia, by comparison, there used to be 250,000 members of the Hungarian minority, now there are 450,000. Did they fall from the moon? This is clear evidence of brutal Magyarization. In southern Slovakia the Hungarians occupy thousands of firms. Whoever wants work there has no chance if he does not speak Hungarian." Quoted in "Slota: 'Vom Pharisäertum wird mir schlecht," *Die Presse*, July 29, 2006, http://diepresse.com/home/politik/aussenpolitik/66914/index.do?from=suche.intern.portal.

141. "Sudeten Germans Outraged by Slota Comments in Lidove Noviny Daily," *TASR*, July 25, 2006, www.tasr.sk.

142. "Hungary Appalled at Slota's Anti-Hungarian Statements," *CTK*, July 24, 2006, www.ctk.cz.

143. Quoted in Martina Jurinová, "Foreign Minister Irons Wrinkles," *Slovak Spectator*, August 7, 2006, http://www.spectator.sk/articles/view/24296/2/.

144. Urad vlády Slovenskej republiky, *Prepis brífingu predsedu vlády SR Roberta Fica po skončení vlády SR*, July 26, 2006, http://www.government.gov.sk/aktuality_start.php3?id_ele=6683.

145. Martina Jurinová, "Kubiš Accuses SMK of Waging Campaign," *Slovak Spectator*, September 4, 2006, http://www.spectator.sk/articles/view/24518/2/.

146. Both quoted in ibid.

147. Martina Jurinová, "Police: Hedviga Lied," *Slovak Spectator*, September 18, 2006, http://www.spectator.sk/articles/view/24629/2/.

148. Úrad vlády Slovenskej republiky, *Prepis spoločnej tlačovej konferencie predsedu vlády SR Roberta Fica a podpredsedu vlády a ministra vnútra Roberta Kaliňáka k objasneniu prípadu údajného napadnutia študentky maďarskej národnosti v Nitre*, September 12, 2006, http://www.government.gov.sk/aktuality_start.php3?id_ele=6741.

149. Zuzana Vilikovská, "Slovakia Concerned About Hungarian Rhetoric," *Slovak Spectator*, July 10, 2007, http://www.spectator.sk/articles/view/28385/10/.

150. Úrad vlády Slovenskej republiky, *Vylásenie predsedu vlády Slovenskej republiky Roberta Fica pri príležitosti 15. Výročia prijatia Deklarácie of zvrchovanosti Slovenskej republiky*, July 17, 2007, http://www.government.gov.sk/aktuality_start.php3?id_ele=7265.

151. Quoted in Marián Leško, "Lojálne menšiny," *Sme*, July 18, 2007, http://www.sme.sk/c/3399449/premier-rozdeluje-mensiny.html.

152. Quoted in "Premiér rozdeľuje menšiny," *Sme*, July 18, 2007, http://www.sme.sk/c/3399449/premier-rozdeluje-mensiny.html.

153. Leško, "Lojálne menšiny."

154. "Hlinka Is Honoured But Not Nation's Father: Bill," *Slovak Spectator*, November 5, 2007, http://www.spectator.sk/articles/view/29713/2/.

155 Beata Balogová, "2007 Was Turbulent for the Ruling Coalition," *Slovak Spectator*, December 17, 2007, http://www.spectator.sk/articles/view/30240/14/2007_was_turbulent_for_the_ruling_coalition.html.

156. Quoted in Ľuba Lesna, "PES Says No to Smer," *Slovak Spectator*, October 8, 2007, http://www.spectator.sk/articles/view/29385/2/.

157. Both quoted in ibid.

158. Quoted in Ľuba Lesná, "Slota jibe Nixes PMs' Meeting," *Slovak Spectator*, May 26, 2008, http://www.spectator.sk/articles/view/31847/2/slota_jibe_nixes_pms_meeting.html.

159. Quoted in Lesná, "Slota jibe." The opposition SDKÚ-DS also expressed outrage. Party Chairman Dzurinda stated, "We consider the behavior of the SNS MPs, and the way the Speaker of the Parliament and Prime Minister reacted to this behavior, incompatible with the values of democracy and rules of parliamentary democracy." "SDKÚ-DS Criti-

cises Fico for Not Reacting to Slota," *Slovak Spectator*, May 21, 2008, http://www.spectator. sk/articles/view/31821/10/sdku_ds_criticises_fico_for_not_reacting_to_slota.html.

160. Quoted in Marián Leško, "Stále 'iba' politik," *Sme*, May 12, 2008, http://www. sme.sk/c/3871263/stale-iba-politik.html.

161. Ľuba Lesná, "Fico's Hungarian Warning," May 19, 2008, http://www.spectator. sk/articles/view/31762/2/ficos_hungarian_warning.html.

162. Ľuba Lesná, "Nationalism Has Simply Asserted Itself Much Easier: Analyst Says Ruling Coalition Will Survive 2008, And It Will Keep Letting Nationalism Grow," *Slovak Spectator*, January 7, 2008, http://www.spectator.sk/articles/view/30331/2/nationalism_has_ simply_asserted_itself_much_easier.html.

163. Statistical Office of the Slovak Republic, *Political Approval and Preferences in 2007*, http://portal.statistics.sk/showdoc.do?docid=5401.

164. Štatistický úrad Slovenskej republiky, *Volebné preferencie v júli 2008*, July 15, 2008, http://portal.statistics.sk/showdoc.do?docid=4.

165. Indeed, the most liberal critics of Slovak ethnic politics, such as Miroslav Kusý and Vladimír Krivy, have both called for the use of the civic principle. Their perspective is not widely shared among the political elite.

166. Deegan-Krause, *Elected Affinities*, 220.

CHAPTER 9. THE IMPLICATIONS OF THE
CIVIC MODEL OF SOVEREIGNTY IN THE CZECH REPUBLIC

1. Jürgen Habermas, "Struggles for Recognition in the Democratic Constitutional State," in *Multiculturalism: Examining the Politics of Recognition*, ed. Amy Gutmann (Princeton, N.J.: Princeton University Press, 1994), 134.

2. Jürgen Habermas, "Citizenship and National Identity: Some Reflections on the Future of Europe," *Praxis International* 12, no. 1 (April 1992): 3.

3. Ivan Gabal, "Zahraniční inspirace k integraci Romů," in *Romové v česke republice, 1945–1998*, ed. Helena Lisá (Prague: Socioklub, 1999), 74.

4. Ibid., 74–75.

5. The Constitution of the Czech Republic, in *The Constitutions of New Democracies in Europe*, ed. Peter Raina (Cambridge, Mass.: Merlin Books, 1996), 30.

6. Václav Klaus, "Ideovy nárvh Ústavy české republiky," *Svobodné slovo*, July 31, 1992.

7. Pavel Peška, "Nedůstojná preambule," *Lidové noviny*, November 24, 1992.

8. See, for example, "Komise ČNR o návrh Ústavy," *Mladá fronta dnes*, August 1, 1992.

9. Parliament of the Czech Republic, Chamber of Deputies, *Začátek schůze české národní rady 17. prosince v 10.30 hodin* (December 17, 1992, stenographic transcript), http:// www.psp.sc/eknih/1992cnr/stenprot/010schuz/s010001.htm#r2.

10. Matthew Rhodes, "National Identity and Minority Rights in the Constitutions of the Czech Republic and Slovakia," *East European Quarterly* 29, no. 3 (September 1995): 355.

11. Human Rights Office, Ministry of Foreign Affairs of the Czech Republic, *The UN Convention on the Elimination of All Forms of Racial Discrimination: Initial and Second Periodic Report of the Czech Republic (1993–1996)*, 11.

12. See also Peter Vermeersch, *The Romani Movement: Minority Politics & Ethnic Mobilization in Contemporary Central Europe* (New York: Berghan, 2006), 80.

13. This remained the case until the end of 1992, which caused a rush of applications for Czech citizenship before the state's dissolution. See "Thousands of Slovaks Seek Czech Citizenship," *B-Wire* (AP: FF0093), 28 December 1992.

14. Commission on Security and Cooperation in Europe (CSCE), *Ex Post Facto Problems of the Czech Citizenship Law*, Washington D.C., September 1, 1996, http://csce.gov/index.cfm?FuseAction=ContentRecords.ViewDetail&ContentRecord_id=162&ContentType=R&CFID=16795256&CFTOKEN=98170339.

15. "Narodili ste sa na Slovensku?" *Pravda*, December 30, 1992.

16. CSCE, *Implementation of the Helsinki Accords: Human Rights and Democratization in the Czech Republic* (Washington, D.C.: CSEE, 1994), http://csce.gov/index.cfm?FuseAction=ContentRecords.ViewDetail&ContentRecord_id=178&Region_id=77&Issue_id=0&ContentType=R,G&ContentRecordType=R&CFID=16795799&CFTOKEN=92802741.

17. The number of Roma in the Czech Republic is disputed, as only slightly under 33,000 people declared Roma ethnicity in the 1991 census (out of a total population of 10 million). It is clear, however, that their numbers are much higher. See *CSCE Digest* 22, no. 7 (1999): 53.

18. Marta Miklušáková, "Stručny nástin důsledků zákona č. 40/1993 Sb., o nabývání a pozbývání státního občanství ČR," in *Romové v české republice*, ed. Lisá, 267.

19. Human Rights Watch, *Roma in the Czech Republic: Foreigners in Their Own Land* 8, no. 11, (June 1996), http:www.hrw.org/hrw/reports/1996/Czech.htm.

20. Ibid., and CSCE, *Implementation of the Helsinki Accords*.

21. See, for example, Council of Europe, *Czech Republic Legal Measures, Situation As of December 2002*, http://www.coe.int/t/e/human_rights/ecri/1 percent2Decri/3 percent2D general_themes/3 percent2Dlegal_research/1 percent2Dnational_legal_measures/czech_ republic/czerch_republic percent2osr.asp#P164_12100.

22. Office of the Government of the Czech Republic, Kancelař ministra vlády Ing. Pavla Bratinky, *Pro schůzi vlády české republiky: Zpráva o situaci romské komunity v české republice a opatření vlády napomáhající její integraci ve společnost*, Prague, October 29, 1997, 24.

23. "How Many Forms Must a Czech Gypsy Fill In?" *The Guardian*, September 23, 1994.

24. CSCE, *Implementation of the Helsinki Accords*.

25. Quoted in "V. Klaus píše Romům," *Telegraf*, February 24, 1993.

26. Viktor Krejčí, "Neviditelné v pozadí skinů?" *Telegraf*, February 9, 1993.

27. Human Rights Watch, *Roma in the Czech Republic*.

28. "Romská hrozba?" *Telegraf*, July 22, 1992.

29. Roman Krasnický, "Romové jdou na sever," *Lidové noviny*, December 10, 1992.

30. Jiří Pehe, "Law on Romanies Causes Uproar in Czech Republic," *RFE/RL Research Report* 2, no. 7 (February 12, 1993): 20.

31. Human Rights Watch, *Roma in the Czech Republic*.

32. Fawn, "Czech Attitudes Towards the Roma: 'Expecting More of Havel's Country'?," 1202.

33. Jindřich Šidlo, "Romům dôsla trpělivost'," *Respekt*, February 15–21, 1993.

34. Hayden, "Constitutional Nationalism," 668.

35. Human Rights Watch, *Roma in the Czech Republic*.

36. Office of the Government of the Czech Republic, *Information About Compliance with Principles Set Forth in the Framework Convention for the Protection of National Minorities According to Article 25, Paragraph 1 of this Convention*, www.vlada.cz.eng/vrk/rady/rnr/dokumenty/plneni.eng.htm.

37. Human Rights Watch, *Roma in the Czech Republic*.

38. European Roma Rights Center (ERRC), *Písek: Description of the Facts* (Budapest: ERRC, August 1997, and ERRC, *Written Comments of the European Roma Rights Center Concerning the Czech Republic, for Consideration by the United Nations Committee on the Elimination of Racial Discrimination at its 52nd Session, 6–9 March, 1998*, http://errc.org/publications/legal/index.shtml.

39. Human Rights Watch, *Roma in the Czech Republic*.

40. ERRC, *Pisek: Description*.

41. "Czech Supreme Court Wants Stiffer Sentences for Skinheads," *RFE/RL Newsline* 2, no. 40, February 27, 1998, http://archive.rferl.org/newsline/1998/02/3-CEE/cee-270298.asp#archive.

42. "Czech Court Sends Skinheads to Prison," *RFE/RL Newsline* 3, no. 128, July 1, 1999, http://archive.rferl.org/newsline/1999/07/3-CEE/cee-010799.asp#archive.

43. Hana Fristenská, "Interetnický konflikt po roce 1989 s ohledem na soužití s Romy," in *Romové v české republice, 1945–1998*, ed. Helena Lisá (Prague: Socioklub, 1999), 249.

44. Ibid., 251.

45. Quoted in Human Rights Watch, *Roma in the Czech Republic*.

46. Fawn, "Czech Attitudes," 1205.

47. Vermeersch, *The Romani Movement*, 83.

48. Office of the Government of the Czech Republic, Kancelař ministra vlády Ing. Pavla Bratinky, "Návrh usnesení," 2–3 (pagination starts anew in different sections), in *Pro schůzi vlády české republiky: Zpráva o situaci romské komunity v české republice a opatření vlády napomáhající její integraci ve společnost*, Prague, October 29, 1997.

49. Ibid., 4.

50. European Commission Against Racism and Intolerance, *ECRI's Country-by-Country Approach: Report on the Czech Republic*, Strasbourg, September 1997, 9, PDF available at http://www.coe.int/T/E/human_rights/Ecri/5-Archives/1-ECRI's_work/1-country_by_country/.

51. Canadian Research Directorate (CRD), Immigration and Refugee Board, *Roma in the Czech Republic: State Protection*, Ottawa, November 1997, http://www.cisr-irb.gc.ca/en/research/publications/index_e.htm?docid=132&cid=64.

52. Human Rights Watch, *Roma in the Czech Republic*.

53. European Commission on Racism and Intolerance (ECRI), *Second Report on the*

Czech Republic, Strasbourg, March 21, 2000, 11, PDF available at http://www.coe.int/t/ e/human percent5Frights/ecri/5 percent2Darchives/1 percent2Decri percent27s percent-5Fwork/5 percent2DCBC percent5FSecond percent5Freports/.

54. Human Rights Watch, *Roma in the Czech Republic.*

55. Alaina Lemon, "Deputy Mayor Charged over Swimming Pool Ban in Czech Town," *OMRI Daily Digest* 2, no. 118, June 18, 1996, http://archive.tol.cz/omri/restricted/ article.php3?id=9943.

56. "Czech Unemployment Offices Mark Roma with 'R'," *RFE/RL Newsline* 3, no. 210, October 27, 1999, http://archive.rferl.org/newsline/1999/10/3-CEE/cee-271099.asp# archive.

57. Vermeersch, *The Romani Movement*, 141.

58. Quoted in "Czech Roma Protest Plan to Wall Them In," *RFE/RL Newsline* 2, no. 105, June 3, 1998, http://archive.rferl.org/newsline/1998/06/3-CEE/cee-030698. asp#archive.

59. Kate Connolly, "Concrete and Steel to Wall in Gypsies," *The Guardian*, October 16, 1999, quoted in Fawn, "Czech Attitudes," 1209.

60. Michael Thurston, "Unblushing Locals Want Czech 'Wall of Shame' Strengthened," *Agence Press France*, October 18, 1999, quoted in Fawn, "Czech Attitudes," 1207. See also "Czech President Calls for Wall to Be Knocked Down," *RFE/RL Newsline* 3, no. 203, October 18, 1999, http://archive.rferl.org/newsline/1999/10/3-CEE/cee-181099. asp#archive.

61. "Czech City Gets Money to Tear Down Wall," *RFE/RL Newsline* 3, no. 229 November 24, 1999, http://archive.rferl.org/newsline/1999/11/3-CEE/cee-241199.asp#archive.

62. "Czech Court Scraps Parliament's Right to Overrule Municipalities," *RFE/RL Newsline* 4, no. 69, April 6, 2000, http://archive.rferl.org/newsline/2000/04/3-CEE/cee-060400.asp#archive.

63. U.S. Department of State, *Country Reports on Human Rights Practices: Czech Republic, 2000*, released by Bureau of Democracy, Human Rights, and Labor, February 23, 2001, http://www.state.gov/g/drl/rls/hrrpt/2000/eur/733.htm.

64. ERRC, *A Special Remedy: Roma Schools for the Mentally Handicapped in the Czech Republic*, Budapest, June 15, 1999, http://eric.ed.gov/ERICWebPortal/custom/ portlets/recordDetails/detailmini.jsp?_nfpb=true&_&ERICExtSearch_SearchValue_ 0=ED459273&ERICExtSearch_SearchType_0=no&accno=ED459273.

65. Tom Gross, "Improving Romany Life Helps All," *Prague Post*, August 25, 1993, http://www.praguepost.com/P02/pp.php/?id=12534&a=3.

66. ECRI, *Second Report.*

67. As a recognized minority nationality, the Roma are entitled to education in their own language. However, most Roma leaders have not pursued this. As Jan Rusenko of the Roma Democratic Congress explained, "We do not have an interest in purely Roma schools. If children leave the eighth grade speaking only Romani, it would be like graduating from a special school." Jindřich Šidlo, "Romům dôsla trpělivost'," *Respekt*, 15–21 February, 1993.

68. CRD, Immigration and Refugee Board, *Roma in the Czech Republic: Identity and Culture,* November 1997.

69. ERRC, *A Special Remedy,* 33.

70. Gross, "Improving Romany Life."

71. ERRC, *A Special Remedy,* 50–51.

72. Quoted in Tomas Horejší and Alena Slezáková, "Zabraňme etnické válce," *Týden,* November 20, 1995.

73. New School Foundation, *The Romani Education Program of the New School Foundation* (Prague: New School Foundation, September 15, 1997), 1.

74. Ibid.

75. CRD, Immigration and Refugee Board, *Roma in the Czech Republic: Education,* December 1997

76. ERRC, *A Special Remedy,* 27–28.

77. CRD, *Roma in the Czech Republic: Education.*

78. Fristenská, "Interetnický konflikt po roce 1989," 258.

79. CRD, *Roma in the Czech Republic: Education.*

80. New School Foundation, *The Romani Education,* 1.

81. ERRC, *A Special Remedy,* 21.

82. Petr Uhl, "Společnost bílých mužů," *Právo,* September 5, 1996.

83. Office of the Government of the Czech Republic, Kancelař ministra vlády Ing. Pavla Bratinky, "Předkládací zpráva," 3, in *Pro schůzi vlády české republiky: Zpráva o situaci romské komunity v české republice a opatření vlády napomáhající její integraci ve společnost,* Prague, October 29, 1997.

84. ERRC, *Written Comments.*

85. Human Rights Watch, *Roma in the Czech Republic.*

86. Quoted in Alaina Lemon, "Czech Candidate Demoted for 'No-Roma' Sign," *OMRI Daily Digest* 60, March 25, 1996, http://archive.tol.cz/omri/restricted/article. php3?id=6181.

87. Quoted in "Do Johannahofu Romové nesmějí," *Lidové noviny,* November 12, 1996.

88. Alaina Lemon, "Czech Politician's Anti-Roma Sign to Be Removed," *OMRI Daily Digest* 57, March 20, 1996, http://archive.tol.cz/omri/restricted/article.php3?id=6068.

89. European Roma Rights Centre (ERRC), "Prosecuting Discrimination and Hate Crime in the Czech Republic," http://www.errc.org/cikk.php?cikk=881.

90. U.S. Department of State, *Czech Republic Country Report on Human Rights Practices for 1998,* released by Bureau of Democracy, Human Rights, and Labor, February 26, 1999, http://www.state.gov/www/global/human_rights/1998_hrp_report/czechrep.html.

91. Quoted in "Vyhazov z rokycanské hospody," *Práce,* July 13, 1996.

92. Alena Skodová, "Pub Owner Fined 200 Dollars for Barring Roma Guest," *Radio Prague,* January 10, 2001, http://www.radio.cz/en/article/11036.

93. Quoted in Greg Nieuwsma, "A Depressing Decade: Czech-Roma Relations After the Velvet Revolution," *Central Europe Review* 1, no. 18 (October 25, 1999), http://www. ce-review.org/99/18/nieuwsma18.html.

94. Quoted in ibid.

95. Václav Žák, "Romové, restaurace a rasová nenávist," *Právo*, September 4, 1996.

96. Ibid.

97. For example, ECRI, *Second Report*, 4.

98. Peter Vermeersch, *The Romani Movement*, 81–82.

99. CRD, *Identity and Culture*.

100. Jarmila Balážová, "Role Romských novinářů a funkce Romsky orientovaných médii ve společnosti," in *Romové v české republice*, ed. Lisá, 332.

101. See for example, "International Romany Festival Begins in Prague," *RFE/RL Newsline* 6, no. 95, May 22, 2002, http://archive.rferl.org/newsline/2002/05/3-CEE/cee-220502.asp#archive.

102. Peter Vermeersch, "Roma Identity and Ethnic Mobilisation in Central European Politics," (paper prepared for the Workshop on Identity Politics ECPR Joint Sessions, Grenoble, 6–11 April 2001), http://www.essex.ac.uk/ecpr/jointsessions/grenoble/papers/ws19/vermeersch.pdf.

103. Karel Holomek, "Vývoj Romských representací po roce 1989 a minoritní mocenská politika ve vztahu k Romům," in *Romové v české republice,* ed. Lisá, 305.

104. Ibid., 309.

105. See Vermeersch, *The Romani Movement*, 108.

106. "Projev prezidenta ČSFR Václava Havla na 1. Světovém romském festivalu," Brno, July 27, 1990, http://www.vaclavhavel.cz/index.php?sec=7&id=4&kat=2&from=60.

107. Vermeersch, *The Romani Movement*, 81.

108. Fawn, "Czech Attitudes," 1209.

109. Quoted in Connolly, "Concrete and Steel to Wall in Gypsies."

110. Vermeersch, "Minority Policy," 8.

111. Fawn, "Czech Attitudes," 1206–7.

112. Office of the Government of the Czech Republic, Kancelař ministra vlády Ing. Pavla Bratinky, "Proč 'romská komunita'?" 1, in *Pro schůzi vlády české republiky: Zpráva o situaci romské komunity v české republice a opatření vlády napomáhající její integraci ve společnost,* Kancelař ministra vlády Ing. Pavla Bratinky, Prague, October 29, 1997. This "respect" is somewhat disingenuous, since there were of course serious disadvantages to self-identification as Roma.

113. Ibid.

114. "Usnesení vlády jako sourhn opatření směřují ke zplešení postavení romské komunity ve společnosti," 1–2, in *Pro schůzi vlády české republiky.*

115. "Obecné zdůvodnění požadavku vytvářet programy určené jmenovitě přislušníkům romské komunity," 2, in *Pro schůzi vlády české republiky.*

116. "Usnesení vlády," 2.

117. "Obecné zdůvodnění požadavku," 2.

118. "Usnesení vlády," 2.

119. "Vymezení a charakteristika problému," 2, in *Pro schůzi vlády české republiky.*

120. Ibid.

121. Ibid.

122. Vermeersch, *The Romani Movement*, 84.

123. "Address by Václav Havel, President of the Czech Republic, before the Members of Parliament Prague," Prague, December 9, 1997, http://www.vaclavhavel.cz/index.php?sec=3&id=1&kat=1&from=81.

124. Government of the Czech Republic, 1998, quoted in Vermeersch, *The Romani Movement*, 86.

125. Government of the Czech Republic, "Decision No. 279 of April 7, 1999 Concerning the Conception of the Government Policy towards Members of the Roma Community Designed to Facilitate Their Social Integration," www.vlada.cz/1250/eng/vrk/komise/krp/dokumenty/navrhk.eng.htm.

126. European Roma Rights Center (ERRC), "Written Comments of the European Roma Rights Center Concerning the Czech Republic for Consideration by the United Nations Committee on Economic, Social and Cultural Rights at its 28th Session, 29 April–17 May, 2002," http://errc.org/publications/legal/index.shtml.

127. Eva Sobotka, "Crusts from the Table: Policy Formation Towards Roma in the Czech Republic and Slovakia," *Roma Rights* 6, nos. 2–3, http://www.errc.org/cikk.php?cikk=1698&archiv=1.

128. Czech Government Commissioner, "A Report of the Government Commissioner for Human Rights on the Current Situation of the Romany Communities," 2000, quoted in Vermeersch, "Minority Policy," 15.

129. ERRC, "Written Comments, 2002."

130. Eva Sobotka offers a photocopy of the Ministry of Foreign Affairs document in her online article, "Crusts from the Table."

131. Government of the Czech Republic, *Act 273 On Rights of Members of National Minorities and Amendment of Some Acts*, Collection of Laws of the Czech Republic, Chapter 104, August 2, 2001, PDF available at: http://vlada.cz/assets/cs/rvk/rnm/dokumenty/vladni/menszakon_en_1.pdf.

132. Ibid.

133. Vermeersch, *The Romani Movement*, 87.

134. Ibid.

135. Ibid., 199.

136. See, for example, European Union, *Czech Republic: Adoption of the Community Acquis: Employment and Social Policy: International Dimension and Enlargement*, http://europa.eu/scadplus/leg/en/lvb/e02107.htm.

137. Human Rights Watch, *World Report 2002: Czech Republic*, http://hrw.org/wr2k2/europe8.html.

138. Petra Tomašková aand Laura Laubeová, *K situaci Romů a jiných národnostních menšin*, Czech Helsinki Committee, Prague, 2001, http://www.helcom.cz/view.php?cislo clanku=2003061826.

139. European Union, *Czech Republic: Adoption of the Community Acquis*.

140. Decade Watch, *Decadewatch: Roma Activists Assess the Progress of the Decade of Roma Inclusion, 2005–2006; Country Reports: The Czech Republic*, June 11, 2007, 81, PDF available at: http://www.romadecade.org/index.php?content=6.

141. Senát Parlamentu České republiky, *Těsnopisecká zpráva z 9. Schůze Senátu Parlamentu České republiky (1. Den schůze – 26. Ledna 2006*), [stenographic transcript, January 26, 2006] www.senat.cz.

142. Ibid.

143. Ibid.

144. Ibid.

145. Pavla Boucková, "Executive Summary Czech Republic Country Report on Measures to Combat Discrimination," Human European Consultancy (European network of legal experts in the anti-discrimination field), 2, PDF available at: http://ec.europa.eu/ employment_social/fundamental_rights/pdf/legnet/cssum07_en.pdf.

146. United Nations, Geneva, "Human Rights Committee Concludes Ninetieth Session," July 27, 2007, http://www.unog.ch/unog/website/news_media. nsf/(httpNewsByYear_en)/B67ED46A31093493C12573250040D176?OpenDocument&cnt xt=93CC7&cookielang=fr.

147. Vermeersch, "Minority Policy," 17.

148. "Czech Lower House Passes Anti-Discrimination Bill," *Romea/CTK*, March 19, 2008, http://www.romea.cz/english/index.php?id=detail&detail=2007_811.

149. Václav Klaus, "Prezident republiky vetoval antidiskriminační zákon," May 16, 2008, http://www.klaus.cz/klaus2/asp/clanek.asp?id=aHWarGTNbDC7.

150. Petr Šimůnek and Robert Čásenský, "Klaus: Paroubek ukazuje, že myslí jen na sebe a ne na stát," *Mladá fronta dnes*, July 16, 2005, http://mfdnes.newtonit.cz/default. asp?cache=988765.

151. Rob Cameron, "Klaus causes controversy with comments about multiculturalism, terror," *Radio Prague*, July 18, 2005, http://www.radio.cz/print/en/68640.

152. Vláda České republiky, Speech of the Prime Minister Mirek Topolánek on the Occasion of Opening of the European Year of Equal Opportunities at the Arch Theatre on 2.4.2007, Official English translation, http://www.vlada.cz/scripts/detail.php?id=22047.

153. Centrum pro výzkum veřejného mínění, *Občané o soužití a o jejich možnostech ve společnosti*, May 29, 2008, 2, PDF available at: http://www.cvvm.cas.cz/index.php?lang=0 &disp=kdojsme.

154. Centrum pro výzkum veřejného mínění, *Občané o soužití s Romy a o jejich možnostech ve společnosti*, March 11, 2003, 2, PDF available at: http://www.cvvm.cas.cz/ index.php?lang=0&disp=kdojsme.

155. Centrum pro výzkum veřejného mínění, *Náš vztah k jiným národnostem*, March 3, 2003, 1 and 3, PDF available at: http://www.cvvm.cas.cz/index. php?lang=0&disp=kdojsme.

156. Centrum pro výzkum veřejného mínění, *Vztah k jiným národnostem I*, January 8, 2007, 1–2, PDF available at: http://www.cvvm.cas.cz/index.php?lang=0&disp=kdojsme.

157. Petr Janyška, "Menšina a Většina," *Respekt*, January 6, 1992, cited in Fawn, "Czech Attitudes," 1196.

158. Centrum pro výzkum veřejného mínění, *Jak jsme tolerantní*, March 24, 2003, 2, PDF available at: http://www.cvvm.cas.cz/index.php?lang=0&disp=kdojsme.

159. Centrum pro výzkum veřejného mínění, *Jak jsou na tom Češi s tolerancí?*, April

13, 2007, 4, PDF available at: http://www.cvvm.cas.cz/index.php?lang=0&disp=kdojsme. The groups the surveys asked about (in order of strength of intolerance on the 2003 survey) were heavy alcoholics, people who use drugs, Roma, people with a criminal past, homosexuals, emotionally unbalanced people, foreigners living in the Czech Republic, people with different colored skin, wealthy people, politicians, Jews, young people, people with different religious beliefs, poor people, old people, people with different political views, and invalids.

160. Centrum pro výzkum veřejného mínění (CVVM), *Občané o soužití s Romy a o jejich možnostech ve společnosti,* June 15, 2007, 5, and CVVM, *Občané o soužití s Romy a o jejich možnostech ve společnosti,* May 29, 2008, 4, PDFs available at: http://www.cvvm.cas. cz/index.php?lang=0&disp=kdojsme.

161. U.S. Department of State, *Czech Republic: Country Reports on Human Rights Practices 2006,* released by Bureau of Democracy, Human Rights, and Labor, March 6, 2007, http://www.state.gov/g/drl/rls/hrrpt/2006/78808.htm.

162. An attachment to the 1997 Bratinka Report, titled "Roma and the Media," observed: "The fragmentation of the themes of individual commentators and their small numbers make evident that the media do not perceive the Roma question as especially relevant and the search for the cause of the conflict generated by the coexistence of the majority nation with the Roma minority is not, in their view, interesting." Úřad vlády České republiky, *Romové a média (obraz romské menšiny prezenovaný českými médii),* Přiloha č. 6, in *Zpráva o situaci romské komunity,* 9.

163. Kazimír Věrska and Markéta Štechová, "O našem rasismu," *Listy,* no. 1, 1992.

164. Sora Šárovcová, "Romové a Češi—střet dvou civilizačních rovin," *Mladá fronta dnes,* February 21, 1994.

165. Michal Šesták, "Negativní vztah k Romů má objektivní přičiny," *Telegraf,* December 12, 1995.

166. Jan Jařab, "Romové, rasisté, a my pseudohumanisté," *Mladá fronta dnes,* August 24, 1996.

167. Martin Schmarcz, "V patách pseudohumanismu kráči Sládek," *Mladá fronta dnes,* August 28, 1996.

168. The "Roma and the Media" attachment to the Bratinka Report also criticized Schmarcz's article, stating that "It is possible without great exaggeration to call the opinion contained in Schmarcz's commentary racist." *Romové a media,* 7.

169. Marie Vodičková, "O snášenlivost, rasismu a pseudohumanismu," *Mladá fronta dnes,* September 3, 1996.

170. For example, see Jiří Pehe, "Evropská unie stojí na občanském principu," *Svobodné slovo,* March 17, 1998, http://www.pehe.cz/clanky/1998/1998-EUstojinaobcanskem. html?p=2.

171. Petr Partyk, "Občanský princip a menšiny," *Britské listy,* June 7, 2000, http:// blisty.cz/files/isarc/0006/20000607j.html.

172. Jiří Přibaň, "Pochod plebejů v multikultuní situaci," *Listy,* no. 6, 2003, http:// www.listy.cz/archiv.php?cislo=036&clanek=060304.

173. Havel, *Projev prezidenta ČSFR Václava Havla na I. Světovem romském festivalu.*

CONCLUSION

1. Rogers Brubaker, *Citizenship and Nationhood in France and Germany* (Cambridge, Mass.: Harvard University Press, 1992), 182.

2. Will Kymlicka, "Ethnic Relations and Western Political Theory," in *Managing Diversity in Plural Societies: Minorities, Migration and Nation-Building in Post-Communist Europe*, ed. Magda Opalski (Nepean, Ontario: Forum Eastern Europe, 1998), 322.

3. Ronald Beiner, "Nationalism's Challenge to Political Philosophy," in *Theorizing Nationalism*, ed. Ronald Beiner (Albany: State University of New York Press, 1999), 14.

INDEX

ACKNOWLEDGMENTS

THIS BOOK GREW and developed alongside the then newly independent Czech and Slovak states that it studies. Many people have helped and inspired me over these years, beginning with Donald Schwartz, who offered superb, gracious, and tireless guidance, as did H. Gordon Skilling, whose legacy I hope here to honor. I am tremendously grateful to Liesbet Hooghe, Peter Solomon, Carol Skalnik Leff, Barbara Falk, Kevin Deegan-Krause, Megan Metzger, Paul Wilson, and Elizabeth Bakke and Soňa Muzikarová for their insights, advice, suggestions, and encouragement. I also thank Peter Schotten and Joseph Carens, each for providing a model of scholarly excellence and generosity. The Rudolf and Viera Frastacky Graduate Fellowship, Associates of the University of Toronto Travel Grant, and Open Society Archives at Central European University Research Fellowship funded crucial travel, and the OSA also provided an ideal research experience. Special thanks as well go to my exceptionally able research assistant Nishad Avari. This book's anonymous reviewer offered advice that greatly improved it, and I am grateful to Penn Press and series editors Peter Agree and Rogers Smith for believing in it. Finally, thanks to my family, for their love, support, warmth, and fun: Jennifer Nedelsky, Joe Carens, Michael and Daniel Carens-Nedelsky, Erika Lehmann, Marilyn and Gerhard Schmatterer, and Merle Pflueger. Thanks especially to Natalia for being the kind friend only a sister can be, my parents, Michael and Barbara, for unending support and providing a family home that feels like a sanctuary for everything best, my son Thomas for putting things in perspective, and, most of all, my husband Martin, who made this, as so much that is good in my life, possible.

Earlier version of parts of this book appeared previously in print, and I wish to thank the publishers for permission to use them here.

Parts of Chapters 1 and 9 first appeared in "Constitutional Nationalism's Implications for Minority Rights and Democratization: The Case of Slovakia," *Ethnic and Racial Studies* 26, no. 1 (2003): 102-28, reprinted by permission of Taylor & Francis Ltd., http://www.tandf.co.uk/journals.

Parts of Chapters 1 and 10 first appeared in "Civic Nationhood and the Challenges of Minority Inclusion: The Case of the Post-Communist Czech Republic," *Ethnicities* 3/1(2003), reprinted by permission of SAGE Publications Ltd.

Parts of Chapter 5 first appeared in "The Wartime Slovak State: A Case Study in the Relationship Between Ethnic Nationalism and Authoritarian Patterns of Governance," *Nations and Nationalism* 7, no. 2 (2001): 215-34, reprinted by permission of Blackwell Publishing.

Parts of Chapter 7 first appeared in "Divergent Responses to a Common Past: Transitional Justice in the Czech Republic and Slovakia," *Theory and Society* 33 (2004): 115, reprinted by permission of Spring Science+business Media.